CW01262115

EMPIRE OF CHAOS

THE ROVING EYE COLLECTION_VOL.1

PEPE ESCOBAR

NIMBLE BOOKS LLC

NIMBLE BOOKS LLC

Nimble Books LLC

1521 Martha Avenue

Ann Arbor, MI, USA 48103

http://www.NimbleBooks.com

wfz@nimblebooks.com

+1.734-330-2593

Copyright 2014 by Pepe Escobar

Special acknowledgment: This book would not have been possible without the sterling work of *Asia Times Online's* late editor Tony Allison as well as Thailand-based editors James Unwin and Chris Stewart, who kept bringing The Roving Eye to life in the internet.

All copy, unless from sources indicated otherwise, is copyright 2009-2014 Asia Times Online (Holdings) Ltd. All rights reserved. Reprinted in book form by Nimble Books LLC courtesy Asia Times Online.

Printed in the United States of America

ISBN-13: 978-1-60888-164-2

∞ The paper used in this publication meets the minimum requirements of the American National Standard for Information Sciences—Permanence of Paper for Printed Library Materials, ANSI Z39.48-1992. The paper is acid-free and lignin-free.

CONTENTS

Table of Abbreviations vii
Introduction: Roving in Chaos-istan 1
Obama, Osama and Medvedev 7
Liquid War: Welcome to Pipelineistan 13
Obama's Afghan Spaghetti Western 23
Globocop versus the TermiNATO 30
The myth of Talibanistan 38
Balochistan is the ultimate prize 43
Blue Gold, Turkmen Bashes, and Asian Grids 48
Slouching towards balkanization 62
Pipelineistan goes Iran-Pak 70
Iran and Russia, scorpions in a bottle 76
Iran, China and the New Silk Road 84
Jihad bling bling 91
The glitzy face of Eurabia 97
Enduring Freedom until 2050 103
Jumpin' Jack Verdi, It's a Gas, Gas, Gas 106
Iraq's oil auction hits the jackpot 116
Welcome, comrade Maobama 120
China plays Pipelineistan 128
Staring at the abyss 136
Happy birthday, Comrade Kim 142
The BRIC post-Washington consensus 152
Iran, Sun Tzu and the dominatrix 157

Mistah McChrystal—he dead 163

On the road in Patagonia 167

China's Pipelineistan "War" 186

Have (infinite) war, will travel 196

US a kid in a NATO candy store 201

The Odyssey Dawn top 10 206

There's no business like war business 213

Exposed: The US-Saudi Libya deal 221

Obama/Osama rock the casbah 227

The counter-revolution club 235

Disaster capitalism swoops over Libya 241

How al-Qaeda got to rule in Tripoli 246

The Decline and Fall of Just About Everyone 251

The US power grab in Africa 262

The Dead Drone sketch 269

The Myth of "Isolated" Iran 274

War, Pipelineistan-style 285

War porn: The new safe sex 288

A History of the World, BRIC by BRIC 302

Drone me down on the killing floor 314

Let's party like it's ... 1997 319

The myth of a free Hong Kong economy 327

Ground Zero redux 344

Visions make it all seem so cruel 348

Syria: A jihadi paradise 354

War on terror forever 359

All that pivots is gold 368

The Fall of the House of Europe 373

Search and Destroy: The rape of Iraq 382

The South also rises 388

The Islamic Emirate of Syriastan 396

How Bowiemania buries Thatcherism 400

Post-History Strip Tease 408

Catfight—and it's US vs EU 418

Pipelineistan and the New Silk Road(s) 423

See you on the dark side 432

The Chimerica Dream 436

Magic carpet ride 448

China: The Bo factor 452

Bandar Bush, "liberator" of Syria 459

Operation Tomahawk with cheese 463

US: The indispensable (bombing) nation 467

Dogs of war versus the emerging caravan 473

Al-Qaeda's air force still on stand-by 479

China stitches up (SCO) Silk Rd 484

Breaking American exceptionalism 491

Fear and loathing in House of Saud 496

The birth of the "de-Americanized" world 501

Turkey pushes crossroads politics 505

China vs US "sea-to-shining-sea" 512

All in play in the New Great Game 516

Reliving Machiavelli in Florence 523

We are all living Pasolini's Theorem 530

Asia will not "isolate" Russia 536

Breaking bad in southern NATOstan 540

Ukraine and the grand chessboard 546

The Birth of a Eurasian Century 551

The future visible in St. Petersburg 562

Return of the living (neocon) dead 568

Burn, Men in Black, burn 574

BRICS against Washington consensus 580

A chessboard drenched in blood 585

Operation Tomahawk The Caliph 590

Will NATO liberate Jihadistan? 594

Can China and Russia Squeeze Washington Out of Eurasia? 599

Pure War in Tehran 609

TABLE OF ABBREVIATIONS

ADB	Asian Development Bank
ADIZ	Air defense identification zone
AFRICOM	Africa Command
AIPAC	American Israel Public Affairs Committee
AP	Associated Press
AQAP	Al-Qaeda in the Arabian Peninsula
AQI	Al-Qaeda in Iraq
AQIM	Al-Qaeda in the Maghreb
ASEAN	Association of Southeast Asian Nations
AU	African Union
BLA	Balochistan Liberation Army
BP	British Petroleum
BRICS	Brazil, Russia, India, China
BTC	Baku-Tblisi-Ceyhan
BTS	Baku-Tblisi-Supsa
CCP	Chinese Communist Party
CIA	Central Intelligence Agency
CNOOC	China National Offshore Oil Corp
CNPC	China National Petroleum Corp
CPA	Coalition Provisional Authority
CPC	Caspian Pipeline Consortium

CRA	Contingent Reserve Arrangement
CTSA	Compania de Tierras Sud Argentino
CWC	Chemical Weapon Convention
DARPA	Defense Advanced Research Projects Agency
DNI	Director of National Intelligence
DPRK	Democratic People's Republic of Korea
EADS	European Aeronautic Defence and Space
EC	European Commission
ECB	European Central Bank
ECOWAS	Economic Community of West African States
ESPO	Eastern Siberia-Pacific Ocean
EU	European Union
FATA	Federally Administered Tribal Areas
FBI	Federal Bureau of Investigation
FSA	Free Syrian Army
GCC	Gulf Cooperation Council
GDP	Gross domestic product
GMMRP	Great Man-Made River Project
GMO	Genetically modified organisms
GWOT	Global war on terror
ICC	International Commerce Center
IEA	International Energy Agency
IFC	International Finance Center

IMF	International Monetary Fund
IMU	Islamic Movement of Uzbekistan
IP	Iran-Pakistan
IPI	Iran-Pakistan-India
IS	Islamic State
ISAF	International Security Assistant Force
ISI	Inter-Services Intelligence
ISIL	Islamic State of Iraq and the Levant
ISIS	Islamic State of Iraq and al-Sham
JSOC	Joint Special Operations Command
KBR	Kellogg Brown & Root
KRG	Kurdistan Regional Government
LIFG	Libyan Islamic Fighting Group
LNG	Liquefied natural gas
LRA	Lord's Resistance Army
MB	Muslim Brotherhood
MENA	Middle East-Northern Africa
MIST	Mexico, Indonesia, South Korea and Turkey
NAM	Non-Aligned Movement
NATO	North Atlantic Treaty Organization
NBC	National Broadcasting Corporation
NGS	Navajo Generation Station
NIOC	National Iranian Oil Company

NRF	NATO Response Force
NSA	National Security Agency
NWFP	North-West Frontier Province
OCO	Overseas contingency operation
OMB	Office of Management and Budget
OPCW	Organization for the Prohibition of Chemical Weapons
OPEC	Organization of Petroleum Exporting Countries
PLA	People's Liberation Army
PNAC	Project for a New American Century
POTUS	President of the United States
QDR	Quadrennial Defense Review
QIA	Qatar Investment Authority
SAR	Special Administrative Region
SAS	Special Air Service
SCO	Shanghai Cooperation Organization
SEZ	Special economic zones
SSR	Soviet Socialist Republics
SWIFT	Society for Worldwide Interbank Financial Telecommunication
TAP	Trans-Afghan Pipeline
TAPI	Turkmenistan-Afghanistan-Pakistan-India
TIA	Total Information Awareness

TNC	Transitional National Council
TPP	Trans-Pacific Partnership
TTIP	Transatlantic Trade and Investment Partnership
TTP	Tehrik-e Taliban-e Pakistan
UAE	United Arab Emirates
UFIO	Unidentified flying intellectual object
UNESCO	United Nations Economic and Social Organisation
WMD	Weapons of mass destruction
WTC	World Trade Center

NIMBLE BOOKS LLC

ABOUT THE AUTHOR

Pepe Escobar, born in Brazil, is the roving correspondent for A*sia Times Online*/Hong Kong - where he's published The Roving Eye column since the early 2000s. He's also a political analyst for RT/Moscow and TomDispatch.com. He has worked as a foreign correspondent since 1985, in Western Europe, North America and all across Asia, and is the author of *Globalistan: How the Globalized World is Turning into Liquid War; Red Zone Blues*; and *Obama does Globalistan*, all published by Nimble Books LLC.

ABOUT THE COVER

The cover typeface is modernist, democratic (slightly left of center) and created with a clear purpose of ordering and explaining. It's the most influential typeface of the early 20th century - originally commissioned in 1916 by Frank Pick of London Underground Railways to be used in signs on the railway system. Originally called "Underground", it became known as "Johnston's Railway Type", and later simply "Johnston".

For the Nimble Books logo, "the font is Zapf Chancery, based on the N of Nimble. The image is of a a guy practicing *parkour*, hanging in the air, in a position that evokes the Greek *triskeles*; three running legs spinning around a center."

INTRODUCTION: ROVING IN CHAOS-ISTAN

I met a traveller from an antique land
Who said—"Two vast and trunkless legs of stone
Stand in the desert. Near them, on the sand,
Half-sunk, a shattered visage lies, whose frown,
And wrinkled lip, and sneer of cold command,
Tell that its sculptor well those passions read
Which yet survive (stamped on these lifeless things)
The hand that mocked them, and the heart that fed:
And on the pedestal these words appear:
'My name is Ozymandias, King of Kings:
Look on my Works, ye Mighty, and despair!'
Nothing beside remains. Round the decay
Of that colossal wreck, boundless and bare
The lone and level sands stretch far away."

—P.B.Shelley, Ozymandias

We had the experience and missed the meaning
And approach to the meaning restores the experience

—T.S. Eliot, The Dry Salvages

The Roving Eye came to light in early 2001; a long, winding and fascinating road after the first time I actually saw the physical *Asia Times*—the day it was launched, in December 1995. I was in Singapore; had already moved to Asia from Paris, technically leaving the West behind in the Spring of 1994 to plunge head down in the East. I picked up a copy at the Raffles bar. What a gorgeous newspaper, a stunning black and white pic splashed in the front page. After reading it, a mental note hit the hard drive. These guys have guts. They are taking on no less than the solemn heavyweights of Western corporate media. One day I'd be pleased to be associated with them.

I kept plunging deeper into Asia and the lands of Islam, commuting with Paris. In 1997 I published a book in Brazil titled *21st: The Asian Century*. By a simple twist of (Buddhist) fate, the book came out only a few days before the Asian financial crisis. I was covering the Hong Kong handover. The day after, I boarded a plane to Xian—then further on down the Chinese stretch of the Silk Road. That's when the Thai baht plunged—unleashing the Asian crisis. Yet I still thought the next century would be Asian. Actually, Eurasian.

I kept roving deeper into the myriad Silk Road(s), Central Asia and Southwest Asia—what the West calls the Middle East, across a large stretch of what the Pentagon would later describe as "the arc of instability." *Asia Times*—the newspaper—was forced to close down because of the financial crisis and later reopened, timidly, as a website. Then one day, waiting for a flight at Kuala Lumpur's airport, I learned that *Asia Times Online* was looking for correspondents.

When I was back from a long stretch on the road in Western Africa, we had a dinner by the river at the Oriental Hotel in Bangkok. The deal was closed on the spot. "How do you want to name your column?" "The Roving Eye", I snapped back. The name popped up as I was riding a jeep in Bali with my wife. I was already a rover—a foreign correspondent since 1985, across Europe, the US and then Asia. In the summer of 2001 I was writing for *Asia Times Online* from Pakistan, the tribal areas and Afghanistan. Then 9/11 happened. And the rest is 21st century history.

The columns selected for this volume follow the period 2009-2014—the Obama years so far. A continuum with previous volumes published by Nimble Books does apply. *Globalistan,* from 2007, was an extended reportage/warped travel book across the Bush years, where I argued the world was being plunged into Liquid War—alluding to energy flows but also to the liquid modernity character of post-modern war. *Red Zone Blues,* also from 2007, was a vignette—an extended reportage centering on the Baghdad surge. And *Obama does Globalistan,* from 2009, examined how the hyperpower could embark on a "change we can believe in". The outcome, as these columns arguably reflect, is Empire of Chaos—where a plutocracy progressively projects its own internal disintegration upon the whole world.

You will find some key overlapping nations/themes/expressions/acronyms in these columns; Iran, Iraq, Syria, Afghanistan, Pakistan, Central Asia, China, Russia, Ukraine, Pipelineistan, BRICS, EU, NATO, GCC, the Global South, GWOT (the global war on terror), The New Great Game, Full Spectrum Dominance. You will also find a progressive drift towards not conventional war, but above all economic war—manifestations of Liquid War.

Incrementally, I have been arguing that Washington's number one objective now is to prevent an economic integration of Eurasia that would leave the US as a non-hegemon, or worse still, an outsider. Thus the three-pronged "strategy" of "pivoting to Asia" (containment of China); Ukraine (containment of Russia); and beefing up NATO (subjugation of Europe, and NATO as global Robocop).

We are slouching towards Cold War 2.0, which Professor Stephen Cohen at Princeton argues will be even more dangerous, because it will be unopposed—by the US government, Congress, the media, university circles and think tanks.

And that brings us to the concept of Empire of Chaos.

"Empire of Chaos" is a tribute to French political strategist Alain Joxe, and his landmark 2002 book *L'Empire du Chaos*—whose analysis remains extraordinarily prescient. I first read it when I was deep into following the run-up towards Shock and Awe and the invasion, occupation and destruction of Iraq. Ten years later, Joxe would refine his analysis in *Les Guerres de L'Empire Global*.

Over the years, The Roving Eye found readers and interlocutors all over the world, especially in North America, and is now routinely translated into at least six languages (*L'Oeil Itinerant, Der Wandernde Auge…*) and republished by countless blogs and websites.

If you are not familiar with The Roving Eye, I should say that I never cease to be amused at being "defined"; everything from Taliban agent to al-Qaeda mole, CIA asset, communist, Putinista and sometimes, simultaneously, all of the above.

As I was born in multicultural Brazil, issuing from two European families—Dutch and Spanish; grew up drenched in American pop culture, film and music as well as the best of European-wide philosophy, the classics, and aesthetics; and lived and worked in virtually everywhere that matters in the Americas, Europe and Asia, I am indeed a nomad, a rootless cosmopolitan. As in "the road goes on forever"—both in a Buddhist and Allman Brothers sense.

I see ideologies—as much as fashion—as systems of signs. Signs are always simulacra. In our uber-capitalist system, these signs are in perennial circulation. So we are condemned to be oblivious to the ultimate essence of reality. Reality is virtual. All the world is a (bloody) stage. Virtually everything over which we could build a new politics or a new social theory seems to be an illusion.

So yes—I'm very close to the situationism of Guy Debord. But a radical nihilist? Not really. There's always humor to soothe our pain. Call me a pre-Socratic nostalgic, with Nietzschean overtones marinated in Epicurean fun, a Keatsian romantic clashing with his anarchist streak, everything tempered by waves and waves of percussive rhythm.

Since the 1980s, when I was deep into covering the excesses of pop culture and post-modernism, I used to get a great deal of my intellectual kicks from an interplay between Baudrillard and Cioran.

Cioran was a failed mystic—an angel devastated by a sense of humor. Baudrillard was the master of deconstructing hyper-reality. He argued—expanding on Guy Debord—that the way we see the world is all conditioned by Spectacle; nothing really happens if it is not seen. All the world is a stage, again. Thus the frantic spinning and spinning of relentless simulacra, fatal strategies, viruses, contagions—a "wilderness of mirrors", to quote Eliot.

I was also deeply influenced by Paul Virilio—who first theorized the notion of a planetary civil war; I call it Liquid War—drawing from Bauman and from my personal experience in following what I chose to describe as Pipelineistan.

I was too young for the Summer of Love, or to cover the Vietnam War as a journalist. Yet I still vividly remember my teenage years in the late 60s, early 70s fascinated by the American Dream—and its progressive demise—while recreating it with very few close friends. Little did I know that later in life I would be following, on a daily basis, the machinery of the Empire of Chaos; total power founded on dissuasion, security obsession, absolute control—and the odd "humanitarian" bombing.

And yet, symbolically, this power is vulnerable and in the end turns against itself. To quote Dylan, it's darkness at the break of noon—over and over again.

So even as we dwell among symbols, full of sound and fury, that mostly signify nothing, in parallel flows the inescapable, practical reality of horror—as in tectonic geopolitical shifts and the "banality of evil" reflected in war after war after war (Gaza, Iraq, Libya, Syria, Ukraine). Not much we can do, faced with the impossibility of living a "normal" life. I chose to keep roving against the dying of the light, attempting first drafts of History.

As I write, the future of *Asia Times Online* is uncertain—a long, painful death by a thousand cuts, not dissimilar to many players committed to independent information on the internet. Still, The Roving Eye, the column, will survive. Somewhere.

Now allow me to take you on a tour of Chaos-istan.

Paris, September 2014

OBAMA, OSAMA AND MEDVEDEV

For those who harbored any doubts about the Barack Obama administration's adoption of the George W Bush framework of the "war on terror"—it does feel like a back-to-the-future "continuity"—here are two key facts on the ground.

Obama has officially started his much-touted Afghanistan surge, authorizing the deployment of 17,000 US troops (8,000 marines, 4,000 army and 5,000 support) mostly to the Pashtun-dominated, southern Helmand province. Justification: "The situation in Afghanistan and Pakistan demands urgent attention." The marines start arriving in Afghanistan in May. Their mission is as hazy as it is hazardous: eradication of the poppy culture, the source of heroin (which accounts for almost 40% of Afghanistan's gross domestic product).

There are already 38,000 US troops in Afghanistan, plus 18,000 as part of the North Atlantic Treaty Organization (NATO)'s 50,000 contingent. Obama administration nominees, in confirmation testimony that seemed to have disappeared in a black hole, stressed they are in favor of continuing the Central Intelligence Agency (CIA)'s extraordinary rendition practices and detaining—ad infinitum—"terror" suspects without trial, even if they were captured far, far away from a war zone. (Considering the Pentagon's elastic definition of an "arc of instability," this means anywhere from Somalia to Xinjiang.) That has prompted *New York Times* writers to come up with a delightful headline: "Obama's War on Terror may resemble Bush's in some areas."

When in doubt, bomb 'em

Basically, the Obama administration's strategy—for now—boils down to turbo-charging a war against Pashtun farmers and peasants. Poppy cultivation has been part of Afghan culture for centuries. A high-tech aerial war on destitute peasants will have only one certified result: more of them increasing their support for, or outright migration to, the multifaceted fight against foreign occupation which the Pentagon insists on defining as an "insurgency."

Throughout his presidential campaign, Obama defined the key goal of the "mission" in Afghanistan (promoted to "the central front in the war on terror") as capturing Osama bin Laden and the al-Qaeda leadership. There's no evidence whatsoever that Osama is involved in the heroin trade. There's also scant evidence the sprawling, sophisticated US surveillance system is interested in actually finding Osama. After all, that would remove the only "war on terror" rationale for the US to be semi-occupying Afghanistan.

Plus there's no evidence these extra 17,000 troops are going after Osama in Helmand province. Assuming he has not gone to meet his 72 virgins in eternal bliss, Osama is supposed to be holed up in Parachinar, in Kurram province, at least according to the latest guess circulating among the vast legion of Osama watchers; this one is by University of California Los Angeles' Thomas Gillespie in the magazine *Foreign Policy*.

Before the legion starts swamping Google Earth with frantic searches, it's worth noting that by a quirky twist of history, Parachinar happens to be the same dusty village Osama and a few al-Qaeda operatives escaped to from a B-52-bombed Tora Bora in early December 2001—when the neo-cons were already salivating with the prospect of bombing not empty mountains but "target-rich" Iraq.

In fact, since the fabled escape to Parachinar in late 2001 there has been absolutely no credible intelligence on Osama. Obama's new poppy gambit does bypass Osama. So it's fair to assume Obama has not been presented by the US national security apparatus with any new intelligence breakthrough—not to mention pure and simple on-the-ground basic intelligence, as bombing peasants and farmers to oblivion with Predator drones in Helmand is not exactly the best strategy to seduce them into collaborating with the US in finding those al-Qaeda ghosts, as it has been amply demonstrated in the Pakistani tribal areas.

Of course, in all this charade there's never a slight mention in the US—even in passing—of why Afghanistan matters: as a transit node of Pipelineistan—that is, the key Caspian oil and gas branch of the New Great Game in Eurasia. Compared to the real game, the monochromatic Washington rhetoric of "winning Afghanistan for democracy" does not even qualify as a joke.

Moscow to the rescue

The 1,600-kilometer Karachi-Khyber-Kabul supply line envisioned by the US and NATO is for all practical purposes dead—thanks to the hit-and-run guerrilla tactics of neo-Taliban in the Pakistani tribal areas, and not Osama and his al-Qaeda ghosts.

Last week, Obama's Afghanistan/Pakistan envoy Richard Holbrooke was duly welcomed in Kabul—the day before he arrived—with a group of suicide bombers and gunmen raising hell in the Justice and Education ministries, killing 26 and wounding 57 and paralyzing the capital. This came after Kyrgyzstan had given Washington a six-month notice to pack up and leave the Manas air base contiguous to Bishkek's civilian airport. Yet more evidence that Central Asia now listens primarily to Moscow, not Washington.

What was not reported was how General David "Iraq surge" Petraeus—a man who calculates his each and every move in terms of ideal positioning for a 2012 presidential run—had rings run around him by those wily Russians. Petraeus told Obama in person on January 21, the day after the inauguration, that the US supply lines in Central Asia were totally secure. Obviously, he forgot to factor in a subsequent regional charm offensive by Russian President Dmitri Medvedev, which established exactly the opposite.

In the end, transit salvation for the US and NATO is indeed coming from no one else but Russia—but on Moscow's terms: this means Russia possibly using its own military planes to airlift the supplies. A deceptively charming Medvedev has been on the record identifying "very positive signs— in the new US-Russia chess match. Foreign Minister Sergei Lavrov has been on the record saying transit of US and NATO non-military supplies through Russia begins in effect only a few days after the 20th anniversary of the Soviets leaving Kabul.

Obama for his part would have little to lose by listening to the man who was in command at the time—retired Lieutenant General Boris Gromov. Gromov—speaking from personal experience—has said Obama's surge is doomed to fail: "One can increase the forces or not—it won't lead to anything but a negative result.—

The price for the US and NATO to have their Afghan supplies arrive via Russia is clear: no more encirclement, no more NATO extension, no more anti-missile shield in the Czech Republic and Poland for protection against non-existent Iranian missiles. All this has to be negotiated in detail.

Russian media have reported Medvedev wants a summit with Obama in Moscow—with Prime Minister Vladimir Putin obviously at the table.

But that still seems far-fetched; what will happen in Geneva in March is a meeting between Lavrov and US Secretary of State Hillary Clinton.

Assuming Medvedev has indeed given Obama a tremendous success story—in terms of a new transit route to Afghanistan—a pesky question remains; what is, after all, the US mission? It can't be nation-building; successive US administrations never cared about Afghanistan except as a sideshow. It can't be to "secure" the country and prevent it from becoming a base for attacks on the US because—as much as Russia, alongside the US, doesn't want a Talibanized Afghanistan—if there ever was a "base" it's now in the Pakistani tribal areas.

The best of it all—as usual—is left unsaid. Washington cannot admit that its only real interest in Afghanistan is as a transit corridor for a gas pipeline from Turkmenistan to Pakistan and India (the TAPI pipeline). Moscow cannot admit that the opportunity of helping the US to be bogged down in Afghanistan for a few more years is too good to pass.

And it gets better.

In the unlikely event Obama and Medvedev decide not to tango, the only other realistic possibility for the US/NATO to have a new supply route would be by courting Iran. Practically, that would mean a very long route from Turkey through Turkish/Iranian Kurdistan, Iran and then Kabul. A very convenient, shorter route would be from an Iranian port, say Bandar Abbas, and then into Afghanistan.

It's obvious that to play chess with Russia is much easier for the Obama administration than to play with Iran. In this case, to get what it needs, the US would have to forcefully end once and for all the three-decades-long "wall of mistrust" between Washington and Tehran; it would have to terminate the sanctions and the embargo; it would have to renounce regime change in Tehran; and it would even have to allow Iran to develop its civilian nuclear program, to which it has a right under the nuclear Non-Proliferation Treaty to which it is a signatory.

The Obama administration also would have to face unimaginable pressure from the Israeli hard right—from Likud supremo Bibi Netanyahu to the hardline, former Moldova bouncer Avigdor Lieberman—and their minions operating in the Israel lobby in Washington.

Iran is getting closer and closer to Russia. Russia currently holds the presidency of the Shanghai Cooperation Organization (SCO)—the Eurasian answer to NATO not only in terms of security but also in the economic and energy spheres. The SCO unites Russia, China, Kazakhstan, Tajikistan, Kyrgyzstan and Uzbekistan, with Iran and Pakistan as observers. In an interview with RIA Novosti, Iranian Foreign Minister Manouchehr Mottaki said, "Iran has officially addressed SCO members and expects its observer status to be finally upgraded to full membership during Russia's chairmanship period."

This is what it's all about in Eurasia—the inexorable march of Asian integration, via the Asian Energy Security Grid and, in security terms, via the SCO. Both China and Russia are deeply connected with Iran. China has signed mega-multibillion dollar deals to be supplied by Iranian oil and gas while selling weapons and myriad goods; and Russia is bound to sell more weapons and is already selling nuclear energy technology. All this while Washington is focused on bombing Pashtun peasants and chasing the ghost of Osama bin Laden.

February 2009

LIQUID WAR: WELCOME TO PIPELINEISTAN

What happens on the immense battlefield for the control of Eurasia will provide the ultimate plot line in the tumultuous rush towards a new, polycentric world order, also known as the New Great Game.

Our good ol' friend the nonsensical "Global War on Terror," which the Pentagon has slyly rebranded "the Long War," sports a far more important, if half-hidden, twin—a global energy war. I like to think of it as the Liquid War, because its bloodstream is the pipelines that crisscross the potential imperial battlefields of the planet. Put another way, if its crucial embattled frontier these days is the Caspian Basin, the whole of Eurasia is its chessboard. Think of it, geographically, as Pipelineistan.

All geopolitical junkies need a fix. Since the second half of the 1990s, I've been hooked on pipelines. I've crossed the Caspian in an Azeri cargo ship just to follow the $4 billion Baku-Tblisi-Ceyhan pipeline, better known in this chess game by its acronym, BTC, through the Caucasus. (Oh, by the way, the map of Pipelineistan is chicken-scratched with acronyms, so get used to them!)

I've also trekked various of the overlapping modern Silk Roads, or perhaps Silk Pipelines, of possible future energy flows from Shanghai to Istanbul, annotating my own DIY routes for LNG (liquefied natural gas). I used to avidly follow the adventures of that once-but-not-future Sun-King of Central Asia, the now deceased Turkmenbashi or "leader of the Turkmen," Saparmurat Niyazov, head of the immensely gas-rich Republic of Turkmenistan, as if he were a Conradian hero.

In Almaty, the former capital of Kazakhstan (before it was moved to Astana, in the middle of the middle of nowhere) the locals were puzzled when I expressed an overwhelming urge to drive to that country's oil boomtown Aktau. ("Why? There's nothing there.") Entering the Space Odyssey-style map room at the Russian energy giant Gazprom's headquarters in Moscow—which digitally details every single pipeline in Eurasia—or the National Iranian Oil Company (NIOC)'s corporate HQ in Tehran, with its neat rows of female experts in full *chador*, was my equivalent of entering Aladdin's cave. And never reading the words "Afghanistan" and "oil" in the same sentence is still a source of endless amusement for me.

Last year, oil cost a king's ransom. This year, it's relatively cheap. But don't be fooled. Price isn't the point here. Like it or not, energy is still what everyone who's anyone wants to get their hands on. So consider this dispatch just the first installment in a long, long tale of some of the moves that have been, or will be, made in the maddeningly complex New Great Game, which goes on unceasingly, no matter what else muscles into the headlines this week.

Forget the mainstream media's obsession with al-Qaeda, Osama "dead or alive" bin Laden, the Taliban—neo, light or classic—or that "war on terror," whatever name it goes by. These are diversions compared to the high-stakes, hardcore geopolitical game that follows what flows along the pipelines of the planet.

Who said Pipelineistan couldn't be fun?

Calling Dr. Zbig

In his 1997 magnum opus *The Grand Chessboard*, Zbigniew Brzezinski—realpolitik practitioner extraordinaire and former national security advisor to Jimmy Carter, the president who launched the US on its modern energy wars—laid out in some detail just how to hang on to American "global primacy." Later, his master plan would be duly copied by that lethal bunch of Dr. No's congregated at Bill Kristol's Project for a New American Century (PNAC, in case you'd forgotten the acronym since its website and its followers went down).

For Dr. Zbig, who, like me, gets his fix from Eurasia—from, that is, thinking big—it all boils down to fostering the emergence of just the right set of "strategically compatible partners" for Washington in places where energy flows are strongest. This, as he so politely put it back then, should be done to shape "a more cooperative trans-Eurasian security system."

By now, Dr. Zbig—among whose fans is evidently President Barack Obama—must have noticed that the Eurasian train which was to deliver the energy goods has been slightly derailed. The Asian part of Eurasia, it seems, begs to differ.

Global financial crisis or not, oil and natural gas are the long-term keys to an inexorable transfer of economic power from the West to Asia. Those who control Pipelineistan—and despite all the dreaming and planning that's gone on there, it's unlikely to be Washington—will have the upper hand in whatever's to come, and there's not a terrorist in the world, or even a long war, that can change that.

Energy expert Michael Klare has been instrumental in identifying the key vectors in the wild, ongoing global scramble for power over Pipelineistan. These range from the increasing scarcity (and difficulty of reaching) primary energy supplies to "the painfully slow development of energy alternatives." Though you may not have noticed, the first skirmishes in Pipelineistan's Liquid War are already on, and even in the worst of economic times, the risk mounts constantly, given the relentless competition between the West and Asia, be it in the Middle East, in the

Caspian theater, or in African oil-rich states like Angola, Nigeria and Sudan.

In these early skirmishes of the twenty-first century, China reacted swiftly indeed. Even before the attacks of 9/11, its leaders were formulating a response to what they saw as the reptilian encroachment of the West on the oil and gas lands of Central Asia, especially in the Caspian Sea region. To be specific, in June 2001, its leaders joined with Russia's to form the Shanghai Cooperation Organization. It's known as the SCO and that's an acronym you should memorize. It's going to be around for a while.

Back then, the SCO's junior members were, tellingly enough, the Stans, the energy-rich former Soviet Socialist Republics (SSRs) of the Soviet Union—Kyrgyzstan, Uzbekistan, Kazakhstan, and Tajikistan—which the Clinton administration and then the new Bush administration, run by those former energy men, had been eyeing covetously. The organization was to be a multi-layered economic and military regional cooperation society that, as both the Chinese and the Russians saw it, would function as a kind of security blanket around the upper rim of Afghanistan.

Iran is, of course, a crucial energy node of West Asia and that country's leaders, too, would prove no slouches when it came to the New Great Game. It needs at least $200 billion in foreign investment to truly modernize its fabulous oil and gas reserves—and thus sell much more to the West than U.S.-imposed sanctions now allow. No wonder Iran soon became a target in Washington. No wonder an air assault on that country remains the ultimate wet dream of assorted Likudniks as well as Dick ("Angler") Cheney and his neocon chamberlains and comrades-in-arms. As seen by the elite from Tehran and Delhi to Beijing and Moscow, such a US attack, now likely off the radar screen until at least 2012, would be a war not only against Russia and China, but against the whole project of Asian integration that the SCO is coming to represent.

Global BRIC-a-brac

Meanwhile, as the Obama administration tries to sort out its Iranian, Afghan, and Central Asian policies, Beijing continues to dream of a secure, fast-flowing, energy version of the old Silk Road, extending from the Caspian Basin (the energy-rich Stans plus Iran and Russia) to Xinjiang Province, its Far West.

The SCO has expanded its aims and scope since 2001. Today, Iran, India, and Pakistan enjoy "observer status" in an organization that increasingly aims to control and protect not just regional energy supplies, but Pipelineistan in every direction. This is, of course, the role the Washington ruling elite would like NATO to play across Eurasia. Given that Russia and China expect the SCO to play a similar role across Asia, clashes of various sorts are inevitable.

Ask any relevant expert at the Chinese Academy of Social Sciences in Beijing and he will tell you that the SCO should be understood as a historically unique alliance of five non-Western civilizations—Russian, Chinese, Muslim, Hindu, and Buddhist—and, because of that, capable of evolving into the basis for a collective security system in Eurasia. That's a thought sure to discomfort classic inside-the-Beltway global strategists like Dr. Zbig and President George H. W. Bush's national security advisor Brent Scowcroft.

According to the view from Beijing, the rising world order of the twenty-first century will be significantly determined by a quadrangle of BRIC countries—for those of you by now collecting Great Game acronyms, that stands for Brazil, Russia, India, and China—plus the future Islamic triangle of Iran, Saudi Arabia, and Turkey. Add in a unified

South America, no longer in thrall to Washington, and you have a global SCO-plus. On the drawing boards, at least, it's a high octane dream.

The key to any of this is a continuing Sino-Russian *entente cordiale*.

Already in 1999, watching NATO and the United States aggressively expand into the distant Balkans, Beijing identified this new game for what it was: a developing energy war. And at stake were the oil and natural gas reserves of what Americans would soon be calling the "arc of instability," a vast span of lands extending from North Africa to the Chinese border. No less important would be the routes pipelines would take in bringing the energy buried in those lands to the West. Where they would be built, the countries they would cross, would determine much in the world to come. And this was where the empire of US military bases (think, for instance, Camp Bondsteel in Kosovo) met Pipelineistan (represented, way back in 1999, by the AMBO pipeline).

AMBO, short for Albanian Macedonian Bulgarian Oil Corporation, an entity registered in the U.S., is building a $1.1 billion pipeline, aka "the Trans-Balkan," slated to be finished by 2011. It will bring Caspian oil to the West without taking it through either Russia or Iran. As a pipeline, AMBO fit well into a geopolitical strategy of creating a U.S.-controlled energy security grid that was first developed by President Bill Clinton's Energy Secretary Bill Richardson and later by Vice President Dick Cheney.

Behind the idea of that "grid" lay a go-for-broke militarization of an energy corridor that would stretch from the Caspian Sea in Central Asia through a series of now independent former SSRs of the Soviet Union to Turkey, and from there into the Balkans (thence on to Europe). It was meant to sabotage the larger energy plans of both Russia and Iran. AMBO itself would bring oil from the Caspian Basin to a terminal in the former SSR of Georgia in the Caucasus, and then transport it by tanker through the Black Sea to the Bulgarian port of Burgas, where another pipeline would connect to Macedonia and then to the Albanian port of Vlora.

As for Camp Bondsteel, it was the "enduring" military base that Washington gained from the wars for the remains of Yugoslavia. It would be the largest overseas base the US had built since the Vietnam War. Halliburton's subsidiary Kellogg Brown & Root (KBR) would, with the Army Corps of Engineers, put it up on 400 hectares of farmland near the Macedonian border in southern Kosovo. Think of it as a user-friendly, five-star version of Guantanamo with perks for those stationed there that included Thai massage and loads of junk food. Bondsteel is the Balkan equivalent of a giant immobile aircraft carrier, capable of exercising surveillance not only over the Balkans but also over Turkey and the Black Sea region (considered in the neocon-speak of the Bush years "the new interface" between the "Euro-Atlantic community" and the "Greater Middle East").

How could Russia, China, and Iran *not* interpret the war in Kosovo, then the invasion of Afghanistan (where Washington had previously tried to pair with the Taliban and encourage the building of another of those avoid-Iran, avoid-Russia pipelines), followed by the invasion of Iraq (that country of vast oil reserves), and finally the recent clash in Georgia (that crucial energy transportation junction) as straightforward wars for Pipelineistan? Though seldom imagined this way in our mainstream media, the Russian and Chinese leaderships saw a stark "continuity" of policy stretching from Bill Clinton's humanitarian imperialism to Bush's Global War on Terror. Blowback, as then Russian President Vladimir Putin himself warned publicly, was inevitable—but that's another magic-carpet story, another cave to enter another time.

Rainy Night in Georgia

If you want to understand Washington's version of Pipelineistan, you have to start with Mafia-ridden Georgia. Though its army was crushed in its recent war with Russia, Georgia remains crucial to Washington's energy policy in what, by now, has become a genuine arc of instability—in part because of a continuing obsession with cutting Iran out of the energy flow.

It was around the Baku-Tblisi-Ceyhan (BTC) pipeline, as I pointed out in my book *Globalistan* in 2007, that American policy congealed. Zbig Brzezinski himself flew into Baku in 1995 as an "energy consultant," less than four years after Azerbaijan became independent, and sold the idea to the Azerbaijani elite. The BTC was to run from the Sangachal Terminal, half-an-hour south of Baku, across neighboring Georgia to the Marine Terminal in the Turkish port of Ceyhan on the Mediterranean. Now operational, that 1,767-kilometer-long, 44-meter-wide steel serpent straddles no less than six war zones, ongoing or potential: Nagorno-Karabakh (an Armenian enclave in Azerbaijan), Chechnya and Dagestan (both embattled regions of Russia), South Ossetia and Abkhazia (on which the 2008 Russia-Georgia war pivoted), and Turkish Kurdistan.

From a purely economic point of view, the BTC made no sense. A "BTK" pipeline, running from Baku through Tehran to Iran's Kharg Island, could have been built for, relatively speaking, next to nothing—and it would have had the added advantage of bypassing both mafia-corroded Georgia and wobbly Kurdish-populated Eastern Anatolia. That would have been the really cheap way to bring Caspian oil and gas to Europe.

The New Great Game ensured that that was not to be, and much followed from that decision. Even though Moscow never planned to occupy Georgia long-term in its 2008 war, or take over the BTC pipeline that now runs through its territory, Alfa Bank oil and gas analyst Konstantin Batunin pointed out the obvious: by briefly cutting off the BTC oil flow, Russian troops made it all too clear to global investors that Georgia wasn't a reliable energy transit country. In other words, the Russians made a mockery of Zbig's world.

For its part, Azerbaijan was, until recently, the real success story in the US version of Pipelineistan. Advised by Zbig, Bill Clinton literally "stole" Baku from Russia's "near abroad" by promoting the BTC and the wealth that would flow from it. Now, however, with the message of the Russia-Georgia War sinking in, Baku is again allowing itself to be seduced by Russia. To top it off, Azerbaijan President Ilham Aliyev can't stand Georgia's brash President Mikhail Saakashvili. That's hardly surprising. After all, Saakashvili's rash military moves caused Azerbaijan to lose at least $500 million when the BTC was shut down during the war.

Russia's energy seduction blitzkrieg is focused like a laser on Central Asia as well. (We'll talk about it more in the next Pipelineistan installment.) It revolves around offering to buy Kazakh, Uzbek, and Turkmen gas at European prices instead of previous, much lower Russian prices. The Russians, in fact, have offered the same deal to the Azeris: so now, Baku is negotiating a deal involving more capacity for the Baku-Novorossiysk pipeline, which makes its way to the Russian borders of the Black Sea, while considering pumping less oil for the BTC.

President Obama needs to understand the dire implications of this. Less Azeri oil on the BTC—its full capacity is 1 million barrels a day, mostly shipped to Europe—means the pipeline may go broke, which is exactly what Russia wants.

In Central Asia, some of the biggest stakes revolve around the monster Kashagan oil field in "snow leopard" Kazakhstan, the absolute jewel in the Caspian crown with reserves of as many as 9 billion barrels. As usual in Pipelineistan, it all comes down to which routes will deliver Kashagan's oil to the world after production starts in 2013. This spells, of course, Liquid War. Wily Kazakh President Nursultan Nazarbayev would like to use the Russian-controlled Caspian Pipeline Consortium (CPC) to pump Kashagan crude to the Black Sea.

In this case, the Kazakhs hold all the cards. How oil will flow from Kashagan will decide whether the BTC—once hyped by Washington as the ultimate Western escape route from dependence on Persian Gulf oil—lives or dies.

Welcome, then, to Pipelineistan! Whether we like it or not, in good times and bad, it's a reasonable bet that we're all going to be Pipeline tourists. So, go with the flow. Learn the crucial acronyms, keep an eye out for what happens to all those US bases across the oil heartlands of the planet, watch where the pipelines are being built, and do your best to keep tabs on the next set of monster Chinese energy deals and fabulous coups by Russia's Gazprom.

And, while you're at it, consider this just the first postcard sent off from our tour of Pipelineistan. We'll be back (to slightly adapt a quote from the Terminator). Think of this as a door opening onto a future in which what flows where and to whom may turn out to be the most important question on the planet.

March 2009, originally at TomDispatch.com

Obama's Afghan Spaghetti Western

As the Barack Obama administration releases the details of its strategic review of Afghanistan's "good war," an acronym-plagued global public opinion is confronted with a semantic dilemma: what in the world is happening to George W Bush's "global war on terror" (GWOT), then slyly rebranded by the Pentagon as "The Long War" (TLW)?

It all started when a mid-level bureaucrat in the Obama administration's Office of Management and Budget (OMB) sent an e-mail to the Pentagon stressing the White House was finally axing GWOT and giving birth to the delightfully Orwellian Overseas Contingency Operations (OCO).

As it happens, no Taliban will be OCOed—at least for the moment. The White House and the Pentagon still rely on GWOT. Pentagon press secretary Geoff Morrell was adamant: "I've never received such a directive." Asked by a reporter what nomenclature he would prefer, Morrell took no prisoners: "Another way to refer to it would be, you know, a campaign against extremists who wish to do us harm." So exit GWOT, enter CAEWWTDUH.

What's in a name?

There's still no evidence that the Obama administration's new strategy will be all-out CAEWWTDUH. Or that the US-backed international conference on Afghanistan in The Hague next Tuesday—which Iran has confirmed it will attend—will go CAEWWTDUH. Or that the NATO summit in Brussels next Friday will re-evaluate all its CAEWWTDUH options.

It's widely accepted in acronym-infested US foreign policy circles that what's happening in the Afghanistan-Pakistani theater are in fact three overlapping wars. But the Shakespearean doubt remains: are they CT or COIN?

Afghanistan itself is certainly privileged COIN (counter-insurgency) territory—as per Bush's "main man," Central Command supremo General David "I'm always positioning myself to 2012" Petraeus strategy. And so are the tribal areas, the Pakistani North-West Frontier Province and now parts of the Punjab as far as the offensive against the neo-Taliban Baitullah Mehsud and Mullah Fazlullah are concerned. But there's also CT (counter-terrorism) going on in the tribal areas focusing on a few dozen "historic" al-Qaeda, including lecturer-in-chief Ayman al-Zawahiri and elusive icon Osama "dead or alive" bin Laden.

Strategically reviewed or not, what is de facto happening in the Afghan theater of CAEWWTDUH during the Obama administration—courtesy of Petraeus, a "The Long War" (TLW) General if there ever was one—is nothing but a remix of a British Raj policy of buying off peace with Afghan tribes as a means to bide time until a way is found to smash them to pieces. It didn't work for the Brits and there's no evidence it will work for the Americans and NATO.

As for Taliban and neo-Taliban commanders and foot soldiers, it's irrelevant if from now on they are designated as Overseas Contingency Operations (OCO) targets or the principals in CAEWWTDUH. They don't fight acronyms; they fight "Western invaders." So in the interests of neo-realism, let's examine how CAEWWTDUH—or OCO, or plain old COIN—are faring when applied to a crucial microcosm of the vast Afghanistan-Pakistan theater, the western Afghanistan region around Herat.

Calling Sergio Leone

To sum it all up, the whole picture looks like nothing less than an Afghan version of the Sergio Leone-directed, Ennio Morricone-scored *The Good, the Bad and the Ugly*. Move over, Spaghetti Western, and call it a deadly Spaghetti Eastern.

There are three military bases ("camps" in Pentagon terminology) in western Afghanistan. One is American. The other one is Afghan (these two are basically forts in the middle of nowhere, manned by no more than 100 soldiers). And the most important—the regional command of NATO/International Security Assistant Force (ISAF) troops—is Italian.

Only in the first two months of 2009, "hostile acts" against Westerners—chiefly car bombs and improvised explosive devices—in this "Italian" zone around Herat were up by 50%. General Paolo Serra commands a multinational force of only 3,000 men (half of them Italian) who are charged to control an area the size of northern Italy.

Only 600 of these—Italian and Spanish—are actually soldiers. Total forces in the area number 10,000 men—including American and Afghan soldiers and 1,000 Afghan policemen. Everyone familiar with the war theater remembers that during the 1980s anti-Soviet jihad the Soviets had ten times more men—with subsequent well-known results.

The best roads in Afghanistan are in the Herat region—because of Iranian investment; after all this used to be a very important satrapy of the Persian empire. The border at Eslam Qal'eh is only a 40-minute drive from Herat. The whole region is absolutely strategic for Iran. It straddles a New Silk Road. Iran wants Central Asian trade and commerce—from

Tajikistan, Uzbekistan and Turkmenistan—flowing to Iranian ports instead of Pakistani ports.

And then there's the all-encompassing Pipelineistan angle. Iran—as well as Russia—has no interest whatsoever in seeing the construction of the perennially troubled, US-backed, $7.6 billion Turkmenistan-Afghanistan-Pakistan-India (TAPI) pipeline that would cross western Afghanistan east of Herat and advance south through Taliban-controlled territory towards Pakistani Balochistan province.

So no wonder the Iranian secret service is absolutely ubiquitous. And its best ally in the region is none other than legendary anti-Soviet mujahid warlord Ishmail Khan—with whom President Hamid Karzai in Kabul has been clashing virtually non-stop since 2002.

For the Italians, the black—not olive—oil in the pizza is not Iran, but the "Taliban," a true portmanteau word. In an ultra-remote base in Bala Murghah, a village very close to the Turkmenistan border in what is now Taliban-controlled territory, the Italians' security perimeter varies from a mere 500 meters to 1.5 kilometers. If they stay inside, they are protected by the village, controlled by—who else—a former mujahid. If they venture outside, they are at the mercy of the "lions"—a joke referring to the Colosseum days of the Roman Empire.

Any "Taliban" foot soldier is worth $5 a day. Anybody can assemble a private army. Anybody with good tribal connections can make the very profitable career move from tribal chief to drug warlord.

And that brings us to Qulum Yahya Sia Shoon.

The Italians are virtually encircled. There's a very small base in Farah, in the homonymous province, south of Herat. South of Farah, Taliban groups fleeing American air power are encroaching. North of Herat the region is infested with pro-Taliban smugglers. And in Guzara—halfway between Herat and the Iranian border—is a new Western public enemy number one, the flamboyant Qulum Yahya Sia Shoon, the former, anti-inflation mayor of Herat who, after losing a political battle, did an about-face and became—what else?—a crime boss.

He's not with the Taliban—whom he used to fight—but he's not with the doomed Karzai's people in Kabul either. He used to be an Ishmail Khan faithful—until he turned against his master. So this means he's his own man, with his own private agenda (and militia), who wants no interference from foreigners. Virtually everyone in the region knows where he's hiding. But he always eludes capture—a source of endless puzzlement for General Paolo Serra.

So in this enormous expanse, Westerners are confronted with vast no-government zones; villages totally controlled by tribal clans; the web of the tribes themselves; the various *shura* (tribal councils) composed by a web of cross-marriages; a web of enemies; and chiefly local warlords enjoying very good relations with the Taliban. This Mafia-style controlled territory with Godfathers aplenty is not too dissimilar from Sicily or the region around Naples controlled by the Camorra.

"Local economy" means opium and heroin produced in Helmand and Nimruz provinces that have to go through Herat before crossing to Iran and Turkmenistan and then to Europe. Hence a phenomenal cast of local characters including opium smugglers, human traffickers, kidnappers, mercenaries working for the Taliban and even a few, very fanatic, hardcore Sunni Islamists. Being "for" or "against" Kabul under these circumstances is a mere detail. Pragmatism trumps ideology. After all, the Afghan war in its various incarnations has been raging for 30 years virtually non-stop.

The pizza surge

What the Pentagon, with General David McKiernan, the overall commander of NATO, ISAF and US troops on top, wants from NATO troops such as the Italians is less prudence and more manly, gung-ho, trigger-happy action. This is the kind of stuff from which people recoil in horror in European capitals—and even classic Obama in next week's turbo-charm offensive in Europe won't be able to change the parameters.

The debate in Italy, for instance, centers on a minimum of extra troops to be sent to Afghanistan so the Pentagon shuts up. This "pizza surge" would mean a maximum of 200 troops. It's also a matter of constrained budget. Rome spends something like 1,000 euros (US$1,357) a minute for its 2,800 troops in Afghanistan. The idea is to get maximum bang for the euro.

For starters, this means more "coaches." In NATO's world, one coach is worth ten regular soldiers. So if you deploy 50 coaches (equipped with radios accessing air strikes by four Tornado jet fighters and 13 Mangosta attack helicopters), they count for 500 people in Brussels. And in a much more efficient set up—with the Tornados based in Herat (and not in distant Mazar-i-Sharif), more airpower (16 helicopters instead of 13) but with less flight hours each, spending the same amount, and four advance bases instead of the current three.

It's painfully, obviously impossible to win local hearts and minds, curb drug smuggling, invest in nation-building and fight a CAEW-WTDUH or OCO under these circumstances with such a set up. NATO is on a losing war—and the best political minds in Brussels know it.

But the crucial problem remains; the Obama administration is just remixing the Pentagon's operational priorities—same as with the acronym fiasco. For all practical purposes, strategically reviewed or not, GWOT,

TLW, CAEWWTDUH or OCO goes on, with no end in sight, with the Persian Gulf as a secondary theater, Afghanistan-Pakistan and Central Asia as the primary theater, and ideology poisoning strategic vision.

This framework, inherited from Bush and his former vice president Dick Cheney, is incompatible with what can be glimpsed from some of Obama's speeches and actions, the lineaments of maybe a new, more equitable, American project. Yes we can? Not yet. There will be blood—a lot more blood—in this Afghan Spaghetti Western.

March 2009

GLOBOCOP VERSUS THE TERMINATO

The people of Strasbourg have voted in their apartment balconies for the French-German co-production of NATO's birthday this Saturday. Thousands of "No to NATO" banners, alongside "Peace" banners, sprung up all around town until forcibly removed by French police.

Prime "liberal democracy" repression tactics were inevitably on show—just as in the much-hyped "we had 275 minutes to save the world and all we could come up with was half-a-trillion dollars for the IMF" Group of 20 summit in London. Protesters were tear-gassed as terrorists. Downtown was cordoned off. Residents were forced to wear badges. Demonstrations got banished to the suburbs.

Then there's the musical metaphor. When NATO was created in Washington on April 4, 1949, the soundtrack was Gershwin's *It Ain't Necessarily So*. When seven countries from the former Warsaw Pact were admitted in 2004, the soundtrack came from the ghastly *Titanic* blockbuster. For the 60th birthday bash in Baden-Baden—with the Barack Obama, Nicolas Sarkozy, Angela Merkel trio attending—it's Georges Bizet's *Carmen*.

As much as *Carmen* is a gypsy who believes a fortune-teller and ends up dead, NATO is a global traveler who may end up dead by believing fortune-teller Washington.

Sultans of swing

NATO certainly has plenty to celebrate. France, under adrenalin junkie Sarkozy—known in NATOland as the "Sultan of Bruni," in reference to his smashing wife Carla—is back to NATO. Obama is presenting his new, comprehensive Afghanistan-Pakistan strategy to NATO. NATO "secures the peace" in Mafia-ridden Kosovo (an entity not recognized even by NATO members such as Spain and Greece). NATO, in full "war on terror" mode, acts like a supercop in the Mediterranean. NATO patrols the Horn of Africa looking for pirates. NATO trains Iraqi security forces. For a body of 60, NATO is fully fit.

Physically, NATO is a bureaucratic nightmare occupying a huge, horrid building on Blvd Leopold III in Mons, outside of Brussels, employing 5,200 civilians divided into 320 committees sharing an annual budget of $2.7 billion. These committees manage 60,000 combat troops scattered all around the world.

NATO should have been dead immediately after the fall of the enemy it was created to fight—the Soviet Union. Instead, NATO had a ball during the 1990s, when Russia was down and out and Russian president Boris Yeltsin spent more time filling up his vodka glass than worrying about geopolitics.

In 1999—to the delight of weapons makers in the US industrial-military complex—NATO expanded to the Balkans via its devastating air war on Russian ally Serbia, sold to world public opinion by then US President Bill Clinton on humanitarian grounds when it was, in fact, humanitarian imperialism.

To say that NATO—a North Atlantic body—is overextended is an understatement. Members Romania and Bulgaria are nowhere near the Atlantic Ocean. Hungary, the Czech Republic and Slovakia are landlocked. In Central Asia, Afghanistan (or at least the non-Taliban-controlled parts of it) is de facto occupied by NATO. Mega-bases such as Ramstein (Germany), Aviano (Italy) and Incirlik (Turkey) now have a counterpart halfway around the world in Bagram (Afghanistan).

Decades after the British Empire, "Europe" tries to (re)occupy the Hindu Kush. Afghanistan is NATO's first war outside Europe and first ground war ever. It involves all 26 members (now 28; Albania and Croatia were finally admitted) plus 12 "partners," including five European nations that used to be neutral: Austria, Finland, Ireland, Sweden and Switzerland. All of them are bound by NATO's first-ever invocation of Article 5 of its charter, which determines mutual military assistance.

In a mix of reading the writing on the wall (this is an unwinnable war) and appeasing the fury of their pacifist public opinions, most European governments will never relent to Obama's appeal—as charm offensive-laden as it may be—for more troops in Afghanistan. Opposition to the Afghan war in Germany, for instance, is around 70% (humanitarian aid is a different story).

Many countries, including the most powerful, will shun Obama's demands based on secret "national provisos." As lawyers in Berlin told NATO, for example, German soldiers are prohibited from launching a pre-emptive, on-the-ground attack on the Taliban.

That utterly misleading acronym, ISAF (International Security Assistance Force) used to be in charge of the Western occupation of Afghanistan starting in December 2001—until, Transformer-style, it became a huge counter-insurgency (COIN) drive expanding all over the country all the way to western Pakistan. The management of this COIN is obviously American—first and foremost because it totally bypasses NATO's very complex political voting mechanisms.

There's nothing "international" about ISAF. ISAF is NATO. And with swarms of combat troops and air strikes there's nothing "assistance" about it either.

ISAF/NATO is headquartered in Kabul, in a former riding club on renamed Great Masoud Road which was rebuilt into a veritable fortress. The buck stops with—what else is new—not an European, but an American, four-star General David McKiernan. As much as his personal mission in the 1970s was to prevent the Warsaw Pact from infiltrating West Germany, his mission nowadays is to prevent al-Qaeda from, in his words, "infiltrating Europe or the United States."

By the way, if anybody had any doubts, this whole thing still falls under ongoing "Operation Enduring Freedom," according to the Pentagon. This really "enduring" freedom applies to no less than Afghanistan, Pakistan, Cuba (because of Guantanamo), Djibouti, Eritrea, Ethiopia, Jordan, Kenya, Kyrgyzstan, the Philippines, Seychelles, Sudan, Tajikistan, Turkey, Uzbekistan and Yemen.

McKiernan's big thing had to be the upcoming Obama Afghan surge—which will be executed by American, not NATO soldiers. After all, hardcore combat has nothing to do with ISAF's original mandate. But the problem is the fog of war and ISAF/NATO has become a TermiNATO—ensnared as much as the Americans in a peace-by-Predator logic. Call it the coalition of the unwilling. No wonder European public opinion is horrified.

And that leads to the breakdown of Obama lecturing NATO on his "AfPak" war, which needed, according to him, a "more comprehensive strategy, a more focused strategy, a more disciplined strategy." In the end, Obama is reduced to hitting up the Europeans for more money.

The ISAF/NATO commander for all of southern Afghanistan, Dutch Major-General Mart de Kruif, believes the surge is the right thing—as US troops will go to "where they are most needed: to Kandahar and Helmand provinces," where Taliban commanders "are capable of launching major operations." As he told Dutch daily NRC Handelsblad, "we need more boots on the ground" and "we will also be able to transport more men and material via air transport."

But when De Kruif talked about Petraeus' Iraq-surge-replay plan of arming local militias, he at least let it be known how hard it will be. "If you're going to arm local militia you need to make sure that they mirror the local power structure," he said. "Also, the local police has to be effective enough to guide and control the militia. You don't want some vague commander running the militia. You need to give the militia members the prospect of a job in the police force. And you need to have an exit strategy, a way to disband the militia again without having all those weapons disappear."

Another Dutchman, pro-Iraq war Bush "poodle" Jaap de Hoop Scheffer, has been NATO's secretary general since January 2004 (he leaves next July). At least he's now admitting—to German weekly Der Spiegel—that the Afghan war "can't be won militarily." Instead, he believes success lies in capturing the "hearts and minds of the people." Certainly not by accumulating bomb-a-wedding "collateral damage." ("We must be careful to avoid civilian casualties while battling the insurgents," he says.) Scheffer is also forced to admit that "cooperation with Iran" in Afghanistan is essential.

Time for PATO?

Key NATO powers France and Germany simply can't afford to antagonize Russia. Germany is a virtual energy hostage of Gazprom. Unlike irresponsible Eastern Europeans, no French or German government would even contemplate being a hostage of a New Cold War between Russia and the US (one of the key reasons why NATO membership for Georgia and the Ukraine is now virtually dead in the water). Paris and

Berlin know Moscow could easily station missiles in Kaliningrad or in Russian-friendly Belarus pointed towards them.

Russia's colorful ambassador to NATO Dmitry Rogozin has the definitive take on NATO's spy-versus-spy obsession of encircling Russia. As he told Der Spiegel, "The closer their bases get to us, the easier it is for us to strike them. We would have needed missiles in the past. Today, machine guns are sufficient." As for Georgia and Ukraine as NATO members, Rogozin adds, why not invite "Hitler, Saddam Hussein and [Georgian president Mikhail] Saakashvili."

Russia, Rogozin told French daily Le Monde, expects NATO to become "a modern political and military alliance," not a "globocop" (as Der Spiegel dubs it). Russia expects a partnership—not encirclement. Rogozin could not be more explicit on the Russian position regarding Afghanistan: "We want to prevent the virus of extremism from crossing the borders of Afghanistan and take over other states in the region such as Pakistan. If NATO failed, it would be Russia and her partners that would have to fight against the extremists in Afghanistan."

The NATO-Russia Council is bound to meet again. Moscow's official view is of a security order stretching "from Vancouver to Vladivostok." Something even more ambitious than NATO: "Perhaps NATO could develop into PATO, a Pacific-Atlantic alliance. We just cannot allow troublemakers to deter us."

Messing with Russia, anyway, was never a good idea—except for history and geography deprived neo-conservatives. In 2008 alone, no less than 120,000 US and NATO troops transited through Manas airbase in Kyrgyzstan (the base will be closed this year). This, along with the neo-Taliban bombing of NATO's supply routes in the Khyber Pass, has forced Petraeus to turn to the Caucasus (Georgia and Azerbaijan) as alternative military transit routes, and beg Kazakhstan and Tajikistan in Central

Asia for help; this will only materialize if Russia says "yes." Magnanimously, meanwhile, Russia has opened its territory for the transit of NATO supply convoys.

What is NATO for?

As much as Palestine is an invaluable test lab for the Israeli Defense Forces, Afghanistan, and now AfPak, is a lab for both the US and NATO for test driving weapons systems and variations of Petraeus' COIN.

On the other hand, NATO incompetence has been more than evident in the drug front. Afghanistan under NATO occupation was back to being the world's number one producer and exporter of opium. And that, in turn, led to the current US/NATO drug war.

So AfPak has really been a true Transformer war—from the hunt for Osama bin Laden to war against that portmanteau word "the Taliban" and to a Colombia-on-steroids drug war. And all this leaves aside the eternally invisible Pipelineistan angle—centered on the $7.6 billion TAPI pipeline which the Bill Clinton administration wanted to go ahead with via an (aborted) deal with... the Taliban, who were in power in the second half of the 1990s.

Watching Obama's actions so far, and considering the Pentagon mindset, there's no evidence to support the possibility that Washington and NATO would abandon crucially strategic Afghanistan, which happens to be a stone's throw from the heart of Eurasia.

Just ask China, Russia and observer member Iran of the Shanghai Cooperation Organization (SCO). The SCO was founded in June 2001, at first to fight transnational drug smuggling and Islamic fundamentalists and then started to promote all sorts of cooperation on energy, transportation, trade and infrastructure.

Both the US and NATO have totally ignored one of the SCO's aims: to find a regional, non-weaponized solution for the enduring Afghan tragedy. The US and NATO's intransigence during the Bush era is much to blame for the process of the SCO turning into Asia's NATO. In Asian and Russian eyes, NATO has nothing to do with "nation-building," peacekeeping or "humanitarian assistance." And Afghanistan proves it. Asians don't need a globocop—much less a TermiNATO.

Obama, McKiernan, Scheffer, no one will admit it—but many in Washington and Brussels would actually love NATO to really be a borderless TermiNATO, bypassing the UN to perform humanitarian imperialism all over the globe, taking out "al-Qaeda" and "terrorists" anywhere, protecting Pipelineistan and pipeline lands for Western interests in all directions.

The US, supported by NATO, was the midwife of a new incarnation of "Islamic fundamentalism" which should, as it did, get rid of the Soviets in Afghanistan and in the former, energy-rich Soviet republics. The fact that, millions of dead and millions of displaced people later, NATO is now asking for Russian help so as not be stranded in Afghanistan is just another bitter irony of AfPak history, and certainly not the last.

April 2009

THE MYTH OF TALIBANISTAN

Apocalypse Now. Run for cover. The turbans are coming. This is the state of Pakistan today, according to the current hysteria disseminated by the Barack Obama administration and United States corporate media—from Secretary of State Hillary Clinton to the *New York Times*. Even British Prime Minister Gordon Brown has said on the record that Pakistani Talibanistan is a threat to the security of Britain.

But unlike St. Petersburg in 1917 or Tehran in late 1978, Islamabad won't fall tomorrow to a turban revolution.

Pakistan is not an ungovernable Somalia. The numbers tell the story. At least 55% of Pakistan's 170 million-strong population are Punjabis. There's no evidence they are about to embrace Talibanistan; they are essentially Shi'ites, Sufis or a mix of both. Around 50 million are Sindhis—faithful followers of the late Benazir Bhutto and her husband, now President Asif Ali Zardari's centrist and overwhelmingly secular Pakistan People's Party. Talibanistan fanatics in these two provinces—amounting to 85% of Pakistan's population, with a heavy concentration of the urban middle class—are an infinitesimal minority.

The Pakistan-based Taliban—subdivided in roughly three major groups, amounting to less than 10,000 fighters with no air force, no Predator drones, no tanks and no heavily weaponized vehicles—are concentrated in the Pashtun tribal areas, in some districts of North-West Frontier Province (NWFP), and some very localized, small parts of Punjab.

To believe this rag-tag band could rout the well-equipped, very professional 550,000-strong Pakistani army, the sixth-largest military in the world, which has already met the Indian colossus in battle, is a ludicrous proposition.

Moreover, there's no evidence the Taliban, in Afghanistan or in Pakistan, have any capability to hit a target outside of "Afpak"(Afghanistan and Pakistan). That's mythical al-Qaeda's privileged territory. As for the nuclear hysteria of the Taliban being able to crack the Pakistani army codes for the country's nuclear arsenal (most of the Taliban, by the way, are semi-literate), even Obama, at his 100-day news conference, stressed the nuclear arsenal was safe.

Of course, there's a smatter of junior Pashtun army officers who sympathize with the Taliban—as well as significant sections of the powerful Inter-Services Intelligence (ISI) agency. But the military institution itself is backed by none other than the American army—with which it has been closely intertwined since the 1970s. Zardari would be a fool to unleash a mass killing of Pakistani Pashtuns; on the contrary, Pashtuns can be very useful for Islamabad's own designs.

Zardari's government this week had to send in troops and the air force to deal with the Buner problem, in the Malakand district of NWFP, which shares a border with Kunar province in Afghanistan and thus is relatively close to US and NATO troops. They are fighting less than 500 members of the Tehrik-e Taliban-e Pakistan (TTP). But for the Pakistani army, the possibility of the area joining Talibanistan is a great asset—because this skyrockets Pakistani control of Pashtun southern Afghanistan, ever in accordance to the eternal "strategic depth" doctrine prevailing in Islamabad.

Bring me the head of Baitullah Mehsud

So if Islamabad is not burning tomorrow, why the hysteria? There are several reasons. To start with, what Washington—now under Obama's "Afpak" strategy—simply cannot stomach is real democracy and a true civilian government in Islamabad; these would be much more than a threat to "US interests" than the Taliban, whom the Bill Clinton administration was happily wining and dining in the late 1990s.

What Washington may certainly relish is yet another military coup—and sources tell *Asia Times Online* that former dictator General Pervez Musharraf (Busharraf as he was derisively referred to) is active behind the hysteria scene.

It's crucial to remember that every military coup in Pakistan has been conducted by the army chief of staff. So the man of the hour—and the next few hours, days and months—is discreet General Ashfaq Kiani, Benazir's former army secretary. He is very cozy with US military chief Admiral Mike Mullen, and definitely not a Taliban-hugger.

Moreover, there are canyons of the Pakistani military/security bureaucracy who would love nothing better than to extract even more US dollars from Washington to fight the Pashtun neo-Taliban that they are simultaneously arming to fight the Americans and NATO. It works. Washington is now under a counter-insurgency craze, with the Pentagon eager to teach such tactics to every Pakistani officer in sight.

What is never mentioned by US corporate media is the tremendous social problems Pakistan has to deal with because of the mess in the tribal areas. Islamabad believes that between the Federally Administered Tribal Areas (FATA) and NWFP, at least 1 million people are now displaced (not to mention badly in need of food aid). FATA's population is around 3.5 million—overwhelmingly poor Pashtun peasants. And obviously war in FATA translates into insecurity and paranoia in the fabled capital of NWFP, Peshawar.

The myth of Talibanistan anyway is just a diversion, a cog in the slow-moving regional big wheel—which in itself is part of the New Great Game in Eurasia.

During a first stage—let's call it the branding of evil—Washington think-tanks and corporate media hammered non-stop on the "threat of al-Qaeda" to Pakistan and the US. FATA was branded as terrorist central—the most dangerous place in the world where "the terrorists" and an army of suicide bombers were trained and unleashed into Afghanistan to kill the "liberators" of US/NATO.

In the second stage, the new Obama administration accelerated the Predator "hell from above" drone war over Pashtun peasants. Now comes the stage where the soon over 100,000-strong US/NATO troops are depicted as the true liberators of the poor in AfPak (and not the "evil" Taliban)—an essential ploy in the new narrative to legitimize Obama's AfPak surge.

For all pieces to fall into place, a new uber-bogeyman is needed. And he is TTP leader Baitullah Mehsud, who, curiously, had never been hit by even a fake US drone until, in early March, he made official his allegiance to historic Taliban leader Mullah Omar, "The Shadow" himself, who is said to live undisturbed somewhere around Quetta, in Pakistani Balochistan.

Now there's a US$5 million price on Baitullah's head. The Predators have duly hit the Mehsud family's South Waziristan bases. But—curioser and curioser—not once but twice, the ISI forwarded a detailed dossier of Baitullah's location directly to its cousin, the CIA. But there was no drone hit.

And maybe there won't be—especially now that a bewildered Zardari government is starting to consider that the previous uber-bogeyman, a certain Osama bin Laden, is no more than a ghost. Drones can incinerate any single Pashtun wedding in sight. But international bogeymen of mystery—Osama, Baitullah, Mullah Omar—star players in the new OCO (overseas contingency operations), formerly GWOT ("global war on terror"), of course deserve star treatment.

May 2009

Balochistan is the ultimate prize

It's a classic case of calm before the storm. The AfPak chapter of Obama's brand new OCO ("Overseas Contingency Operations"), formerly GWOT ("global war on terror") does not imply only a surge in the Pashtun Federally Administered Tribal Areas (FATA). A surge in Balochistan as well may be virtually inevitable.

Balochistan is totally under the radar of Western corporate media. But not the Pentagon's. An immense desert comprising almost 48% of Pakistan's area, rich in uranium and copper, potentially very rich in oil, and producing more than one-third of Pakistan's natural gas, it accounts for less than 4% of Pakistan's 173 million citizens. Balochs are the majority, followed by Pashtuns. Quetta, the provincial capital, is considered Taliban Central by the Pentagon, which for all its high-tech wizardry mysteriously has not been able to locate Quetta resident "The Shadow," historic Taliban emir Mullah Omar himself.

Strategically, Balochistan is mouth-watering: east of Iran, south of Afghanistan, and boasting three Arabian Sea ports, including Gwadar, practically at the mouth of the Strait of Hormuz.

Gwadar—a port built by China—is the absolute key. It is the essential node in the crucial, ongoing, and still virtual Pipelineistan war between IPI and TAPI. IPI is the Iran-Pakistan-India pipeline, also known as the "peace pipeline," which is planned to cross from Iranian to Pakistani Balochistan—an anathema to Washington. TAPI is the perennially troubled, US-backed Turkmenistan-Afghanistan-Pakistan-India pipeline, which is planned to cross western Afghanistan via Herat and branch out to Kandahar and Gwadar.

Washington's dream scenario is Gwadar as the new Dubai—while China would need Gwadar as a port and also as a base for pumping gas via a long pipeline to China. One way or another, it will all depend on local grievances being taken very seriously. Islamabad pays a pittance in royalties for the Balochis, and development aid is negligible; Balochistan is treated as a backwater. Gwadar as the new Dubai would not necessarily mean local Balochis benefiting from the boom; in many cases they could even be stripped of their local land.

To top it all, there's the New Great Game in Eurasia fact that Pakistan is a key pivot to both NATO and the Shanghai Cooperation Organization (SCO), of which Pakistan is an observer. So whoever "wins" Balochistan incorporates Pakistan as a key transit corridor to either Iranian gas from the monster South Pars field or a great deal of the Caspian wealth of "gas republic" Turkmenistan.

The cavalry to the rescue

Now imagine thousands of mobile US troops—backed by supreme air power and hardcore artillery—pouring into this desert across the immense, 800-kilometer-long, empty southern Afghanistan-Balochistan border. These are Obama's surge troops who will be in theory destroying opium crops in Helmand province in Afghanistan. They will also try to establish a meaningful presence in the ultra-remote, southwest Afghanistan, Baloch-majority province of Nimruz. It would take nothing for them to hit Pakistani Balochistan in hot pursuit of Taliban bands. And this would certainly be a prelude for a de facto US invasion of Balochistan.

What would the Balochis do? That's a very complex question.

Balochistan is of course tribal—just as the FATA. Local tribal chiefs can be as backward as Islamabad is neglectful (and they are not exactly paragons of human rights either). A parallel could be made with the Swat valley.

Most Baloch tribes bow to Islamabad's authority—except, first and foremost, the Bugti. And then there's the Balochistan Liberation Army (BLA)—which both Washington and London brand as a terrorist group. Its leader is Brahamdagh Bugti, operating out of Kandahar (only two hours away from Quetta). In a recent Pakistani TV interview he could not be more sectarian, stressing the BLA is getting ready to attack non-Balochis. The Balochis are inclined to consider the BLA as a resistance group. But Islamabad denies it, saying their support is not beyond 10% of the provincial population.

It does not help that Islamabad tends to be not only neglectful but heavy-handed; in August 2006, Musharraf's troops killed ultra-respected local leader Nawab Akbar Bugti, a former provincial governor.

There's ample controversy on whether the BLA is being hijacked by foreign intelligence agencies—everyone from the CIA and the British MI6 to the Israeli Mossad. In a 2006 visit to Iran, I was prevented from going to Sistan-Balochistan in southeast Iran because, according to Tehran's version, infiltrated CIA from Pakistani Balochistan were involved in covert, cross-border attacks. And it's no secret to anyone in the region that since 9/11 the US virtually controls the Baloch air bases in Dalbandin and Panjgur.

In October 2001, while I was waiting for an opening to cross to Kandahar from Quetta, and apart from tracking the whereabouts of President Hamid Karzai and his brother, I spent quite some time with a number of BLA associates and sympathizers. They described themselves as "progressive, nationalist, anti-imperialist" (and that makes them difficult to be co-opted by the US). They were heavily critical of "Punjabi chauvinism," and always insisted the region's resources belong to Balochis first; that was the rationale for attacks on gas pipelines.

Stressing an atrocious, provincial literacy rate of only 16% ("It's government policy to keep Balochistan backward"), they resented the fact that most people still lacked drinking water. They claimed support from at least 70% of the Baloch population ("Whenever the BLA fires a rocket, it's the talk of the bazaars"). They also claimed to be united, and in coordination with Iranian Balochis. And they insisted that "Pakistan had turned Balochistan into a US cantonment, which affected a lot the relationship between the Afghan and Baloch peoples."

As a whole, not only BLA sympathizers but the Balochis in general are adamant: although prepared to remain within a Pakistani confederation, they want infinitely more autonomy.

Game on

How crucial Balochistan is to Washington can be assessed by the study "Baloch Nationalism and the Politics of Energy Resources: the Changing Context of Separatism in Pakistan" by Robert Wirsing of the US Army think-tank Strategic Studies Institute. Predictably, it all revolves around Pipelineistan.

China—which built Gwadar and needs gas from Iran—must be sidelined by all means necessary. The added paranoid Pentagon component is that China could turn Gwadar into a naval base and thus "threaten" the Arabian Sea and the Indian Ocean.

The only acceptable scenario for the Pentagon would be for the US to take over Gwadar. Once again, that would be a prime confluence of Pipelineistan and the US Empire of Bases.

Not only in terms of blocking the IPI pipeline and using Gwadar for TAPI, control of Gwadar would open the mouth-watering opportunity of a long land route across Balochistan into Helmand, Nimruz, Kandahar or, better yet, all of these three provinces in southwest Afghanistan. From a Pentagon/NATO perspective, after the "loss" of the Khyber Pass, that would be the ideal supply route for Western troops in the perennial, now rebranded, GWOT ("global war on terror").

During the Asif Ali Zardari administration in Islamabad the BLA, though still a fringe group with a political wing and a military wing, has been regrouping and rearming, while the current chief minister of Balochistan, Nawab Raisani, is suspected of being a CIA asset (there's no conclusive proof). There's fear in Islamabad that the government has taken its eye off the Balochistan ball—and that the BLA may be effectively used by the US for balkanization purposes. But Islamabad still seems not to have listened to the key Baloch grievance: we want to profit from our natural wealth, and we want autonomy.

So what's gonna be the future of "Dubai" Gwadar? IPI or TAPI? The die is cast. Under the radar of the Obama/Karzai/Zardari photo-op in Washington, all's still to play in this crucial front in the New Great Game in Eurasia.

May 2009

Blue Gold, Turkmen Bashes, and Asian Grids

As Barack Obama heads into his second hundred days in office, let's head for the big picture ourselves, the ultimate global plot line, the tumultuous rush towards a new, polycentric world order. In its first hundred days, the Obama presidency introduced us to a brand new acronym, OCO for Overseas Contingency Operations, formerly known as GWOT (as in Global War on Terror). Use either name, or anything else you want, and what you're really talking about is what's happening on the immense energy battlefield that extends from Iran to the Pacific Ocean. It's there that the Liquid War for the control of Eurasia takes place.

Yep, it all comes down to black gold and "blue gold" (natural gas), hydrocarbon wealth beyond compare, and so it's time to trek back to that ever-flowing wonderland—Pipelineistan. It's time to dust off the acronyms, especially the SCO or Shanghai Cooperative Organization, the Asian response to NATO, and learn a few new ones like IPI and TAPI. Above all, it's time to check out the most recent moves on the giant chessboard of Eurasia, where Washington wants to be a crucial, if not dominant, player.

We've already seen Pipelineistan wars in Kosovo and Georgia, and we've followed Washington's favorite pipeline, the BTC, which was supposed to tilt the flow of energy westward, sending oil coursing past both Iran and Russia. Things didn't quite turn out that way, but we've got to move on, the New Great Game never stops. Now, it's time to grasp just what the Asian Energy Security Grid is all about, visit a surreal natural gas republic, and understand why that Grid is so deeply implicated in the AfPak war.

Every time I've visited Iran, energy analysts stress the total "interdependence of Asia and Persian Gulf geo-ecopolitics." What they mean is the ultimate importance to various great and regional powers of Asian integration via a sprawling mass of energy pipelines that will someday, somehow, link the Persian Gulf, Central Asia, South Asia, Russia, and China. The major Iranian card in the Asian integration game is the gigantic South Pars natural gas field (which Iran shares with Qatar). It is estimated to hold at least 9% of the world's proven natural gas reserves.

As much as Washington may live in perpetual denial, Russia and Iran together control roughly 20% of the world's oil reserves and nearly 50% of its gas reserves. Think about that for a moment. It's little wonder that, for the leadership of both countries as well as China's, the idea of Asian integration, of the Grid, is sacrosanct.

If it ever gets built, a major node on that Grid will surely be the prospective $7.6 billion Iran-Pakistan-India (IPI) pipeline, also known as the "peace pipeline." After years of wrangling, a nearly miraculous agreement for its construction was initialed in 2008. At least in this rare case, both Pakistan and India stood shoulder to shoulder in rejecting relentless pressure from the Bush administration to scotch the deal.

It couldn't be otherwise. Pakistan, after all, is an energy-poor, desperate customer of the Grid. One year ago, in a speech at Beijing's Tsinghua University, then-President Pervez Musharraf did everything but drop to his knees and beg China to dump money into pipelines linking the Persian Gulf and Pakistan with China's Far West. If this were to happen, it might help transform Pakistan from a near-failed state into a mighty "energy corridor" to the Middle East. If you think of a pipeline as an umbilical cord, it goes without saying that IPI, far more than any form of US aid (or outright interference), would go the extra mile in stabilizing the Pak half of Obama's AfPak theater of operations, and even possibly relieve it of its India obsession.

If Pakistan's fate is in question, Iran's is another matter. Though currently only holding "observer" status in the Shanghai Cooperation Organization (SCO), sooner or later it will inevitably become a full member and so enjoy NATO-style, an-attack-on-one-of-us-is-an-attack-on-all-of-us protection. Imagine, then, the cataclysmic consequences of an Israeli pre-emptive strike (backed by Washington or not) on Iran's nuclear facilities. The SCO will tackle this knotty issue at its next summit in June, in Yekaterinburg, Russia.

Iran's relations with both Russia and China are swell—and will remain so no matter who is elected the new Iranian president next month. China desperately needs Iranian oil and gas, has already clinched a $100 billion gas "deal of the century" with the Iranians, and has loads of weapons and cheap consumer goods to sell. No less close to Iran, Russia wants to sell them even more weapons, as well as nuclear energy technology.

And then, moving ever eastward on the great Grid, there's Turkmenistan, lodged deep in Central Asia, which, unlike Iran, you may never have heard a thing about. Let's correct that now.

Gurbanguly is The Man

Alas, the sun-king of Turkmenistan, the wily, wacky Saparmurat "Turkmenbashi" Nyazov, "the father of all Turkmen" (descendants of a formidable race of nomadic horseback warriors who used to attack Silk Road caravans) is now dead. But far from forgotten.

The Chinese were huge fans of the Turkmenbashi. And the joy was mutual. One key reason the Central Asians love to do business with China is that the Middle Kingdom, unlike both Russia and the United States, carries little modern imperial baggage. And of course, China will never carp about human rights or foment a color-coded revolution of any sort.

The Chinese are already moving to successfully lobby the new Turkmen president, the spectacularly named Gurbanguly Berdymukhamedov, to speed up the construction of the Mother of All Pipelines. This Turkmen-Kazakh-China Pipelineistan corridor from eastern Turkmenistan to China's Guangdong province will be the longest and most expensive pipeline in the world, 7,000 kilometers of steel pipe at a staggering cost of $26 billion. When China signed the agreement to build it in 2007, they made sure to add a clever little geopolitical kicker. The agreement explicitly states that "Chinese interests" will not be "threatened from [Turkmenistan's] territory by third parties." In translation: no Pentagon bases allowed in that country.

China's deft energy diplomacy game plan in the former Soviet republics of Central Asia is a pure winner. In the case of Turkmenistan, lucrative deals are offered and partnerships with Russia are encouraged to boost Turkmen gas production. There are to be no Russian-Chinese antagonisms, as befits the main partners in the SCO, because the Asian Energy Security Grid story is really and truly about them.

By the way, elsewhere on the Grid, those two countries recently agreed to extend the East Siberian-Pacific Ocean oil pipeline to China by the end of 2010. After all, energy-ravenous China badly needs not just Turkmen gas, but Russia's LNG.

With energy prices low and the global economy melting down, times are sure to be tough for the Kremlin through at least 2010, but this won't derail its push to forge a Central Asian energy club within the SCO. Think of all this as essentially an energy *entente cordiale* with China. Russian Deputy Industry and Energy Minister Ivan Materov has been among those insistently swearing that this will *not* someday lead to a "gas OPEC" within the SCO. It remains to be seen how the Obama national security team decides to counteract the successful Russian strategy of undermining by all possible means a U.S.-promoted East-West Caspian Sea energy corridor, while solidifying a Russian-controlled Pipelineistan stretching from Kazakhstan to Greece that will monopolize the flow of energy to Western Europe.

The Real Afghan War

In the ever-shifting New Great Game in Eurasia, a key question—why Afghanistan matters—is simply not part of the discussion in the United States. (Hint: It has nothing to do with the liberation of Afghan women.) In part, this is because the idea that energy and Afghanistan might have anything in common is *verboten*.

And yet, rest assured, nothing of significance takes place in Eurasia without an energy angle. In the case of Afghanistan, keep in mind that Central and South Asia have been considered by American strategists crucial places to plant the flag; and once the Soviet Union collapsed, control of the energy-rich former Soviet republics in the region was quickly seen as essential to future US global power. It would be there, as they imagined it, that the US Empire of Bases would intersect crucially with Pipelineistan in a way that would leave both Russia and China on the defensive.

Think of Afghanistan, then, as an overlooked subplot in the ongoing Liquid War. After all, an overarching goal of US foreign policy since President Richard Nixon's era in the early 1970s has been to split Russia and China. The leadership of the SCO has been focused on this since the US Congress passed the Silk Road Strategy Act five days before beginning the bombing of Serbia in March 1999. That act clearly identified American geostrategic interests from the Black Sea to western China with building a mosaic of American protectorates in Central Asia and militarizing the Eurasian energy corridor.

Afghanistan, as it happens, sits conveniently at the crossroads of any new Silk Road linking the Caucasus to western China, and four nuclear powers (China, Russia, Pakistan, and India) lurk in the vicinity. "Losing" Afghanistan and its key network of US military bases would, from the Pentagon's point of view, be a disaster, and though it may be a secondary matter in the New Great Game of the moment, it's worth remembering that the country itself is a lot more than the towering mountains of the Hindu Kush and immense deserts: it's believed to be rich in unexplored deposits of natural gas, petroleum, coal, copper, chrome, talc, barites, sulfur, lead, zinc, and iron ore, as well as precious and semiprecious stones.

And there's something highly toxic to be added to this already lethal mix: don't forget the narco-dollar angle—the fact that the global heroin cartels that feast on Afghanistan only work with US dollars, not euros. For the SCO, the top security threat in Afghanistan isn't the Taliban, but the drug business. Russia's anti-drug czar Viktor Ivanov routinely blasts the disaster that passes for a U.S./NATO anti-drug war there, stressing that Afghan heroin now kills 30,000 Russians annually, twice as many as were killed during the decade-long U.S.-supported anti-Soviet Afghan *jihad* of the 1980s.

And then, of course, there are those competing pipelines that, if ever built, either would or wouldn't exclude Iran and Russia from the action to their south. In April 2008, Turkmenistan, Afghanistan, Pakistan, and India actually signed an agreement to build a long-dreamt-about $7.6 billion (and counting) pipeline, whose acronym TAPI combines the first letters of their names and would also someday deliver natural gas from

Turkmenistan to Pakistan and India without the involvement of either Iran or Russia. It would cut right through the heart of Western Afghanistan, in Herat, and head south across lightly populated Nimruz and Helmand provinces, where the Taliban, various Pashtun guerrillas and assorted highway robbers now merrily run rings around US and NATO forces and where—surprise!—the US is now building in Dasht-e-Margo ("the Desert of Death") a new mega-base to host President Obama's surge troops.

TAPI's rival is the already mentioned IPI, also theoretically underway and widely derided by Heritage Foundation types in the U.S., who regularly launch blasts of angry prose at the nefarious idea of India and Pakistan importing gas from "evil" Iran. Theoretically, TAPI's construction will start in 2010 and the gas would begin flowing by 2015. (Don't hold your breath.) Embattled Afghan President Hamid Karzai, who can hardly secure a few square blocks of central Kabul, even with the help of international forces, nonetheless offered assurances last year that he would not only rid his country of millions of land mines along TAPI's route, but somehow get rid of the Taliban in the bargain.

Should there be investors (nursed by Afghan opium dreams) delirious enough to sink their money into such a pipeline—and that's a monumental *if*—Afghanistan would collect only $160 million a year in transit fees, a mere bagatelle even if it does represent a big chunk of the embattled Karzai's current annual revenue. Count on one thing though, if it ever happened, the Taliban and assorted warlords/highway robbers would be sure to get a cut of the action.

A Clinton-Bush-Obama Great Game

TAPI's roller-coaster history actually begins in the mid-1990s, the Clinton era, when the Taliban were dined (but not wined) by the California-based energy company Unocal and the Clinton machine. In 1995, Unocal first came up with the pipeline idea, even then a product of Washington's fatal urge to bypass both Iran and Russia. Next, Unocal talked to the Turkmenbashi, then to the Taliban, and so launched a classic New Great Game gambit that has yet to end and without which you can't understand the Afghan war Obama has inherited.

A Taliban delegation, thanks to Unocal, enjoyed Houston's hospitality in early 1997 and then Washington's in December of that year. When it came to energy negotiations, the Taliban's leadership was anything but medieval. They were tough bargainers, also cannily courting the Argentinean private oil company Bridas, which had secured the right to explore and exploit oil reserves in eastern Turkmenistan.

In August 1997, financially unstable Bridas sold 60% of its stock to Amoco, which merged the next year with British Petroleum. A key Amoco consultant happened to be that ubiquitous Eurasian player, former national security advisor Zbig Brzezinski, while another such luminary, Henry Kissinger, just happened to be a consultant for Unocal. BP-Amoco, already developing the Baku-Tblisi-Ceyhan (BTC) pipeline, now became the major player in what had already been dubbed the Trans-Afghan Pipeline or TAP. Inevitably, Unocal and BP-Amoco went to war and let the lawyers settle things in a Texas court, where, in October 1998 as the Clinton years drew to an end, BP-Amoco seemed to emerge with the upper hand.

Under newly elected president George W. Bush, however, Unocal snuck back into the game and, as early as January 2001, was cozying up to the Taliban yet again, this time supported by a star-studded governmental cast of characters, including Undersecretary of State Richard Armitage, himself a former Unocal lobbyist. The Taliban were duly invited back to Washington in March 2001 via Rahmatullah Hashimi, a top aide to "The Shadow," the movement's leader Mullah Omar.

Negotiations eventually broke down because of those pesky transit fees the Taliban demanded. Beware the Empire's fury. At a Group of Eight summit meeting in Genoa in July 2001, Western diplomats indicated that the Bush administration had decided to take the Taliban down before year's end. (Pakistani diplomats in Islamabad would later confirm this to me.) The attacks of September 11, 2001 just slightly accelerated the schedule. Nicknamed "the kebab seller" in Kabul, Hamid Karzai, a former CIA asset and Unocal representative, who had entertained visiting Taliban members at barbecues in Houston, was soon forced down Afghan throats as the country's new leader.

Among the first fruits of Donald Rumsfeld's bombing and invasion of Afghanistan in the fall of 2001 was the signing by Karzai, Pakistani President Musharraf and Turkmenistan's Nyazov of an agreement committing themselves to build TAP, and so was formally launched a Pipelineistan extension from Central to South Asia with brand USA stamped all over it.

Russian President Vladimir Putin did nothing—until September 2006, that is, when he delivered his counterpunch with panache. That's when Russian energy behemoth Gazprom agreed to buy Nyazov's natural gas at the 40% mark-up the dictator demanded. In return, the Russians received priceless gifts (and the Bush administration a pricey kick in the face). Nyazov turned over control of Turkmenistan's entire gas surplus to the Russian company through 2009, indicated a preference for letting Russia explore the country's new gas fields, and stated that Turkmenistan was bowing out of any U.S.-backed Trans-Caspian pipeline project. (And while he was at it, Putin also cornered much of the gas exports of Kazakhstan and Uzbekistan as well.)

Thus, almost five years later, with occupied Afghanistan in increasingly deadly chaos, TAP seemed dead on arrival. The (invisible) star of what would later turn into Obama's "good" war was already a corpse.

But here's the beauty of Pipelineistan: like zombies, dead deals always seem to return and so the game goes on forever.

A Turkmen bash

They don't call Turkmenistan a "gas republic" for nothing. I've crossed it from the Uzbek border to a Caspian Sea port named—what else—Turkmenbashi where you can purchase one kilo of fresh Beluga for $100 and a camel for $200. That's where the gigantic gas fields are, and it's obvious that most have not been fully explored. When, in October 2008, the British consultancy firm GCA confirmed that the Yolotan-Osman gas fields in southwest Turkmenistan were among the world's four largest, holding up to a staggering 14 trillion cubic meters of natural gas, Turkmenistan promptly grabbed second place in the global gas reserves sweepstakes, way ahead of Iran and only 20% below Russia. With that news, the earth shook seismically across Pipelineistan.

Just before he died in December 2006, the flamboyant Turkmenbashi boasted that his country held enough reserves to export 150 billion cubic meters of gas annually for the next 250 years. Given his notorious megalomania, nobody took him seriously. So in March 2008, our man Gurbanguly ordered a GCA audit to dispel any doubts. After all, in pure Asian Energy Security Grid mode, Turkmenistan had already signed contracts to supply Russia with about 50 billion cubic meters annually, China with 40 billion cubic meters, and Iran with 8 billion cubic meters.

And yet, none of this turns out to be quite as monumental or settled as it may look. In fact, Turkmenistan and Russia may be playing the energy equivalent of Russian roulette. After all, virtually all of Turkmenistani gas exports flow north through an old, crumbling Soviet system of pipelines, largely built in the 1960s. Add to this a Turkmeni knack for raising the stakes non-stop at a time when Gazprom has little choice but to put up with it: without Turkmen gas, it simply can't export all it needs to Europe, the source of 70% of Gazprom's profits.

Worse yet, according to a Gazprom source quoted in the Russian business daily *Kommersant*, the stark fact is that the company only thought it controlled all of Turkmenistan's gas exports; the newly discovered gas mega-fields turn out not to be part of the deal. As my *Asia Times* colleague, former ambassador M.K. Bhadrakumar put the matter, Gazprom's mistake "is proving to be a misconception of Himalayan proportions."

In fact, it's as if the New Great Gamesters had just discovered another Everest. This year, Obama's national security strategists lost no time unleashing a no-holds-barred diplomatic campaign to court Turkmenistan. The goal? To accelerate possible ways for all that new Turkmeni gas to flow through the *right* pipes, and create quite a different energy map and future. Apart from TAPI, another key objective is to make the prospective $5.8 billion Turkey-to-Austria Nabucco pipeline become viable and thus, of course, trump the Russians. In that way, a key long-term US strategic objective would be fulfilled: Austria, Italy, and Greece, as well as the Balkan and various Central European countries, would be at least partially pulled from Gazprom's orbit. (Await my next "postcard" from Pipelineistan for more on this.)

IPI or TAPI?

Gurbanguly is proving an even more riotous player than the Turkmenbashi. A year ago he said he was going to hedge his bets, that he was willing to export the bulk of the eight trillion cubic meters of gas reserves he now claims for his country to virtually anyone. Washington was—and remains—ecstatic. At an international conference last month in Ashgabat ("the city of love"), the Las Vegas of Central Asia, Gurbanguly told a hall packed with Americans, Europeans, and Russians that "diversification of energy flows and inclusion of new countries into the geography of export routes can help the global economy gain stability."

Inevitably, behind closed doors, the TAPI maze came up and TAPI executives once again began discussing pricing and transit fees. Of course, hard as that may be to settle, it's the easy part of the deal. After all, there's that Everest of Afghan security to climb, and someone still has to confirm that Turkmenistan's gas reserves are really as fabulous as claimed.

Imperceptible jiggles in Pipelineistan's tectonic plates can shake half the world. Take, for example, an obscure March report in the *Balochistan Times*: a little noticed pipeline supplying gas to parts of Sindh province in Pakistan, including Karachi, was blown up. It got next to no media attention, but all across Eurasia and in Washington, those analyzing the comparative advantages of TAPI vs. IPI had to wonder just how risky it might be for India to buy future Iranian gas via increasingly volatile Balochistan.

And then in early April came another mysterious pipeline explosion, this one in Turkmenistan, compromising exports to Russia. The Turkmenis promptly blamed the Russians (and TAPI advocates cheered), but nothing in Afghanistan itself could have left them cheering very loudly. Right now, Dick Cheney's master plan to get those blue rivers of Turkmeni gas flowing southwards via a future TAPI as part of a US grand strategy for a "Greater Central Asia" lies in tatters.

Still, Zbig Brzezinski might disagree, and as he commands Obama's attention, he may try to convince the new president that the world needs a $7.6-plus billion, 1,600-km steel serpent winding through a horribly dangerous war zone. That's certainly the gist of what Brzezinski said immediately after the 2008 Russia-Georgia war, stressing once again that "the construction of a pipeline from Central Asia via Afghanistan to the south... will maximally expand world society's access to the Central Asian energy market."

Washington or Beijing?

Still, give credit where it's due. For the time being, our man Gurbanguly may have snatched the leading role in the New Great Game in this part of Eurasia. He's already signed a groundbreaking gas agreement with RWE from Germany and sent the Russians scrambling.

If, one of these days, the Turkmenistani leader opts for TAPI as well, it will open Washington to an ultimate historical irony. After so much death and destruction, Washington would undoubtedly have to sit down once again with—yes—the Taliban! And we'd be back to July 2001 and those pesky pipeline transit fees.

As it stands at the moment, however, Russia still dominates Pipelineistan, ensuring Central Asian gas flows across Russia's network and not through the Trans-Caspian networks privileged by the US and the European Union. This virtually guarantees Russia's crucial geopolitical status as the top gas supplier to Europe and a crucial supplier to Asia as well.

Meanwhile, in "transit corridor" Pakistan, where Predator drones soaring over Pashtun tribal villages monopolize the headlines, the shady New Great Game slouches in under-the-radar mode towards the immense, under-populated southern Pakistani province of Balochistan. The future of the epic IPI vs. TAPI battle may hinge on a single, magic word: Gwadar.

Essentially a fishing village, Gwadar is an Arabian Sea port in that province. The port was built by China. In Washington's dream scenario, Gwadar becomes the new Dubai of South Asia. This implies the success of TAPI. For its part, China badly needs Gwadar as a node for yet another long pipeline to be built to western China. And where would the gas flowing in that line come from? Iran, of course.

Whoever "wins," if Gwadar really becomes part of the Liquid War, Pakistan will finally become a key transit corridor for either Iranian gas from the monster South Pars field heading for China, or a great deal of the Caspian gas from Turkmenistan heading Europe-wards. To make the scenario even more locally mouth-watering, Pakistan would then be a pivotal place for both NATO and the SCO (in which it is already an official "observer").

Now that's as classic as the New Great Game in Eurasia can get. There's NATO vs. the SCO. With either IPI or TAPI, Turkmenistan wins. With either IPI or TAPI, Russia loses. With either IPI or TAPI, Pakistan wins. With TAPI, Iran loses. With IPI, Afghanistan loses. In the end, however, as in any game of high-stakes Pipelineistan poker, it all comes down to the top two global players. Ladies and gentlemen, place your bets: will the winner be Washington or Beijing?

May 2009. Originally at TomDispatch.com

SLOUCHING TOWARDS BALKANIZATION

Happy Days are here again. It's as if the George W Bush years in Afghanistan had never left, with Washington still wallowing in an intelligence-free environment. A surge is coming to town—just like the one General David Petraeus engineered in Iraq. A Bush proconsul (Zalmay Khalilzad) wants to run the show—again. A hardliner (General Stanley McChrystal) is getting ready to terrorize any Pashtun in sight. A new mega-base is sprouting in the "desert of death" in the southern Afghan province of Helmand. And as in Bush time, no one's talking pipeline, or the (invisible) greatest regional prize: Pakistani Balochistan.

Bush's "global war on terror" (GWOT) may have been rebranded, under new management, "overseas contingency operation" (OCO). But history in Afghanistan continues to repeat itself as farce—or as an opium bad trip.

Zalmay does Pipelineistan

It was hardly stunning that Bush's pet Afghan hound Zalmay Khalilzad, a US citizen born in Afghanistan and former envoy to both Afghanistan and Iraq, would now be angling—via his pal President Hamid Karzai, who tried to get President Barack Obama on board—to become the unelected CEO of Afghanistan, or a sort of "unofficial" prime minister. Any Afghan that believes the West is not behind this racket must be a stone statue in the Hindu Kush.

United States Secretary of State Hillary Clinton and Obama's AfPak envoy Richard Holbrooke are supposed to be very excited about the scheme. Karzai and Khalilzad have had what the *New York Times* quaintly described as "a long and sometimes bumpy relationship." Khalilzad certainly has CEO experience—acquired as US ambassador to Afghanistan (2003-2005), when he was the real power behind Karzai's shaky throne (as much as he was totally blind to anything happening outside of Kabul).

Karzai has always denied—including to this correspondent—he was a minor Unocal employee plus entertainer of Taliban delegations visiting Houston and Washington in 1997. Khalilzad's relationship is less murky: he was a certified Unocal advisor. The "prize"—from President Bill Clinton to Bush and now Obama—is still the Turkmenistan-Afghanistan-Pakistan pipeline, then known as TAP and now known as TAPI, with the inclusion of India (See Pipelineistan goes Af-Pak *Asia Times Online*, May 14, 2009).

Khalilzad was a key player in setting up the Afghanistan-America Foundation in the mid-1990s, a lobby that during the Clinton administration became very influential because of its spinning of TAP, hyped as a key pipeline to bypass both Iran and Russia.

Karzai's brother Qayum was on the advisory board, along with Khalilzad and Ishaq Nadiri, who later conveniently became "economic advisor" to Karzai. Qayum and another Karzai brother—Mahmoud—owned a Baltimore-based restaurant chain in the US (that's why people in Kabul and western Pakistan call Karzai "the kebab seller"). Hamid got a lot of kebab money during his exile in Quetta right up until the end of 2001, when he was miraculously parachuted into Kabul by US Special Forces.

Khalilzad, as Bush's Afghan pet, was absolutely key in convincing suspicious former mujahideen, many of them Tajiks, to have Hamid (from a minor Pashtun tribe) installed as "interim" leader of Afghanistan after the Taliban fell in December 2001. The mujahideen wanted King Zahir

Shah. With the puppet guaranteed in power, Karzai, Pakistan's president General Pervez Musharraf and Turkmenistan's Saparmurat "Turkmenbashi" Nyazov signed an agreement to build TAP in December 2001. The pipeline, now TAPI, is an absolutely key plank of Washington's Central Asia strategy. Khalilzad as CEO will move mountains to make sure that TAPI defeats its much more sound rival, IPI, the Iran-Pakistan-India pipeline, also known as the "peace pipeline."

It will be a bumpy ride. And—tragedy of tragedies—it will eventually lead to Khalilzad having to talk pipelines with the Taliban all over again. Karzai does not even control Kabul, not to mention the rest of a ravaged country ranked as the fifth-most corrupt in the world by Transparency International. The more Karzai's local governors get corrupted, the more the Taliban advance village by village and tribal clan by tribal clan, propelled by their nasty mix of outright threats and hardcore punishment. The Taliban, on top of it, have struck alliances with myriad criminal groups, and are supported by their Pashtun cousins in the Pakistani tribal areas.

The helpless Karzai, profiting from the good services of Islamabad and Riyadh, is trying to talk to everybody—from the neo-Taliban to the historic Mullah Omar-commanded Taliban and also old Saudi/Pakistan favorite Gulbuddin Hekmatyar. And this while Obama's strategic advisors spin that the war is "winnable" if Washington captures—with a lot of cash—the hearts and minds of tribal Pashtuns.

Some of this new US cash flowing into Afghanistan has been diverted to the Orwellian Afghan Social Outreach Program, which builds anti-Taliban local councils, while the no less Orwellian Afghan Public Protection Force has started to build Sunni Awakening-style militias. Arming Pashtun militias who will inevitably turn against the Western occupiers does not exactly qualify as brilliant counter-insurgency.

Balochistan revisited

Meanwhile, Balochistan, the biggest prize in the region (see Balochistan is the ultimate prize *Asia Times Online*, May 9, 2009) remains totally under the radar of the frenetic US news cycle. Numerous Balochi readers pointed out to this correspondent that it is now in fact a 50% Balochi/Pashtun province. Most Pashtuns live near the Afghan border. And many happen to be neighbors of Afghanistan's Helmand province—the key site of the upcoming Obama surge.

In case of a hypothetical balkanization of Pakistan, Balochis and Pashtuns would go separate ways. Quetta, the provincial capital, in terms of population and business activity, is already dominated by Pashtuns.

Balochistan's internal politics are complex. Balochis and Brahvies are separate nationalities—with different spoken languages and culture. Quite a few Balochis do not accept Brahvies as Balochis. What all Balochi tribal leaders agree on is to demand maximum autonomy and control over their natural resources. Islamabad always responds with firepower.

What is now Balochistan and Sind in Pakistan was conquered centuries ago by the Balochi Rind tribe. They never submitted to the British. During the Ronald Reagan 1980s, Balochis tried—in secret—to strike a deal with the US for an independent Balochistan in return for the US controlling regional Pipelineistan. Washington procrastinated. Balochis took it very badly. Some decided to go underground or go for armed struggle. Islamabad still doesn't get it. Washington may.

If the Pashtunwali—the ancestral Pashtun code—is still king (don't threaten them, don't attack them, don't mislead them, don't dishonor them, or revenge is inevitable), Balochis can be even more fearsome. Balochis as a whole have never been conquered. These are warriors of ancestral fame. If you think Pashtuns are tough, better not pick a fight with a Balochi. Even Pashtuns are terrified of them.

The geopolitical secret is not to antagonize but to court them, and offer them total autonomy. In an evolving strategy of balkanization of Pakistan—increasingly popular in quite a few Washington foreign policy circles—Balochistan has very attractive assets: natural wealth, scarce population, and a port, Gwadar, which is key for Washington's New Great Game in Eurasia Pipelineistan plans.

And it's not only oil and gas. Reko Diq (literally "sandy peak") is a small town in the deserted Chaghi district, 70 kilometers northwest of already remote Nok Kundi, near the Iran and Afghanistan borders. Reko Diq is the home of the world's largest gold and copper reserves, reportedly worth more than US$65 billion. According to the Pakistani daily *Dawn*, these reserves are believed to be even bigger than similar ones in Iran and Chile.

Reko Diq is being explored by the Australian Tethyan Copper Company (75%), which sold 19.95% of its stake to Chile's Antofagasta Minerals. Only 25% is allocated to the Balochistan Development Authority. Tethyan is jointly controlled by Barrick Gold and Antofagasta Minerals. The Balochis had to have a serious beef about that: they denounce that their natural wealth has been sold by Islamabad to "Zionist-controlled regimes."

Washington is focused on Balochistan like a laser. One of high summer's blockbusters will be the inauguration of Camp Leatherneck, a vast, brand new US air base in Dasht-e-Margo, the "desert of death" in Helmand province in Afghanistan. Quite a few of Obama's surge soldiers will be based in Camp Leatherneck—a cross-border, covert ops stone's throw from southeast Iran and Pakistani Balochistan.

Under McChrystal, the new US and NATO top commander in Afghanistan, one should expect a continuous summer blockbuster of death squads, search-and-destroy missions, targeted assassinations, bombing of civilians and all-out paramilitary terrorization of tribal Pashtun villages, community leaders, social networks or any social movement for that matter that dares to defy Washington and provide support for the Afghan resistance.

"Black Ops" McChrystal is supposed to turn former Chinese leader Mao Zedong upside down—he should "empty the sea" (kill and/or displace an untold number of Pashtun peasants) to "catch the fish" (the Taliban or any Afghan opposing the US occupation). There couldn't be a better man for the counter-insurgency job assigned by Obama, Petraeus, Clinton and Holbrooke.

Seymour Hersh has detailed how McChrystal directed the "executive assassination wing" of the Pentagon's Joint Special Operations Command (JSOC). No wonder he was a darling of former vice president Dick Cheney and secretary of defense Rumsfeld. The Obama administration's belief in his extreme terrorization methods qualifies as no more than Rumsfeldian foreign policy.

And McChrystal still has the luxury of raising any amount of calibrated hell in neighboring Balochistan to suit Washington's plans—be they to provoke Iranians or incite Balochis to revolt against Islamabad.

According to Pakistani writer Abd Al-Ghafar Aziz, writing for al-Jazeera's Arabic website, Balochistan has been accused by the US for years of "supporting terrorism and harboring the leaders of the Taliban and al-Qaeda." US Predator drones "have been striking 'precious targets', resulting in the death of over 15,000 people." Aziz described Balochis as "orphans without shelter and without protection."

Neighboring Iran is taking no chances; it is testing sophisticated border patrolling techniques this week in its southeast province of Sistan-Balochistan, along the 1,250 kilometers of border with both Afghanistan and Pakistani Balochistan. One of Tehran's ultimate national security nightmares is US cross-border covert ops launched from Pakistani Balochistan, the kind of stuff that's music to McChrystal's ears.

Slouching towards balkanization

There's little doubt Obama's surge will fail. Washington's plan B is also lame—it boils down to some kind of arrangement with the Taliban, something that Saudi Arabia has been frantically mediating.

The problem is the military/Inter-Services Intelligence (ISI) nexus in Islamabad will continue to support the Taliban in Afghanistan—no matter what Washington concocts—because the only possible outcome in their minds is the defeat of the "pro-India" Northern Alliance, which is the de facto power in Kabul with Karzai as a puppet. The Northern Alliance will renege on its alliance with India over their dead bodies. And backed up not only by India but also Iran and Russia, they will never allow the Taliban in power.

In the long run, Obama's AfPak strategy may acquire its own relentless, volatile momentum of addicting the military in Islamabad to make war on their own people—be they Pashtuns or Balochis. So Washington may in fact be setting the slow but inexorable march towards the balkanization of Pakistan. If Pashtun cousins on both sides of the border—26 million in Pakistan, 13 million in Afghanistan—would eventually find an opening to form a long-dreamed-of Pashtunistan, Pakistan as we know it would break up. India might intervene to subdue Sind and Punjab, keeping both under its sphere of influence. Washington for its part would rather concentrate on exploiting the natural wealth and strategic value of an independent Balochistan.

Thus a Pakistan not unlike an Iraq still under US occupation—broke up into three parts—now starts to emerge as a distinct possibility. Unless an improbable Pakistani popular revolt, backed by middle-ranking Pakistani soldiers, rumbles on to make the top heads of the army/security/politico establishment roll. But drones, not guillotines, are the flavor of the moment in AfPak.

May 2009

Pipelineistan goes Iran-Pak

The earth has been shaking for a few days now all across Pipelineistan—with massive repercussions for all the big players in the New Great Game in Eurasia. United States President Barack Obama's AfPak strategists didn't even see it coming.

A silent, reptilian war had been going on for years between the US-favored Turkmenistan-Afghanistan-Pakistan-India (TAPI) pipeline and its rival, the Iran-Pakistan-India (IPI) pipeline, also known as the "peace pipeline." This past weekend, a winner emerged. And it's none of the above: instead, it's the 2,100-kilometer, US$7.5 billion IP (the Iran-Pakistan pipeline), with no India attached. (Please see Pakistan, Iran sign gas pipeline deal, May 27, 2009, *Asia Times Online*.)

This whole saga started way back in 1995—about the time California-based Unocal started floating the idea of building a pipeline crossing Afghanistan. Now, Iran and Pakistan finally signed a deal this week in Tehran, by which Iran will sell gas from its mega South Pars fields to Pakistan for the next 25 years.

According to Iranian energy officials speaking to the ISNA news agency, the final deal will be signed in less than three weeks, slightly after the first round of the Iranian presidential election. The last 250 km of a 900-km pipeline stretch in Iran between Asalouyeh and Iranshahr, near the border with Pakistan, still needs to be built. The whole IP pipeline should be operational by 2014.

The fact that Islamabad has finally decided to move on is pregnant with meaning. For the George W Bush administration IPI was simply anathema; imagine India and Pakistan buying gas from "axis of evil" Iran. The only way to go was TAPI—an extension of the childish neo-conservative belief that the Afghanistan war was winnable.

Now, IP reveals Islamabad's own interests seemed to have prevailed against Washington's (unlike the virtually US-imposed Pakistan army offensive against the Taliban in the Swat Valley). The Barack Obama administration has been mum about IP so far. But it will be very enlightening to hear what former Bush pet Afghan Zalmay Khalilzad—who's been infiltrating himself as the next CEO of Afghanistan—has to say about it. (Please see Slouching towards Balkanization, May 22, 2009, *Asia Times Online*.) Khalilzad's Pipelineistan dream, since the mid-1990s, has always been a trans-Afghan pipeline capable of bypassing both Iran and Russia.

IP, IP, hurrah

India, for a number of reasons (the pricing system, transit fees and above all, security) de facto shelved the IPI idea last year. Had it not been the case, IPI would become a powerful vector in terms of South Asian regional integration—doing more to stabilize India-Pakistan relations than any diplomatic coup. Nevertheless, both Iran and Pakistan still have left an open door to India.

India's (momentary?) loss will be China's gain. Since 2008, with New Delhi having second thoughts, Beijing and Islamabad had set up an agreement—China would import most of this Iranian gas if India dropped out of IPI. China anyway is more than welcome business-wise to both Iran and Pakistan. Only in transit fees, Islamabad could collect as much as $500 million a year.

For Beijing, IP could not be more essential. Iranian gas will flow to the Balochistan province port of Gwadar, in the Arabian Sea (which China itself built, and where it is also building a refinery). And Gwadar is supposed to be connected to a proposed pipeline going north, mostly financed by China, along the Karakoram Highway (which by the way was largely built from the 1960s to the 1980s by Chinese engineers...).

Pakistan is the absolutely ideal transit corridor for China to import oil and gas from Iran and the Persian Gulf. With IP in place and with multibillion-dollar, overlapping Tehran-Beijing gas deals, China can finally afford to import less energy via the Strait of Malacca, which Beijing considers exceedingly dangerous, and subject to Washington's sphere of influence.

With IP, not only China wins; Russia's Gazprom also wins. And by extension, the Shanghai Cooperation Organization (SCO) wins. Russian deputy Energy Minister Anatoly Yankovsky told the Kommersant business daily, "We are ready to join the project as soon as we receive an offer."

The reason is so blatant that Gazprom officials have not even bothered to disguise it. For Russia, IP is a gift-from-above tool in rerouting gas from Iran to South Asia, and away from competing with Russian gas. The big prize, in this case, is the Western European market, dependent almost 30% on Gazprom and the source of 80% of Gazprom's export profits.

The European Union is desperately trying to keep the Nabucco pipeline project—which bypasses Russia—afloat, so it may reduce its dependence on Gazprom. But as anyone in Brussels knows, Nabucco can only work if it is provided enough gas by either Iran or Turkmenistan. The Turkmenistan distribution system is controlled by Russia. And a deal with Iran implies no more US sanctions—still a long way away. With IP in place, Gazprom reasons, Nabucco is deprived of a key supply source.

All eyes on Balochistan

With IP firmly in place, the strategic spotlight focuses even more on Balochistan. (Please see Balochistan is the greatest prize, May 9, 2009, *Asia Times Online*.) First of all, there's an internal Pakistani question to be settled. An editorial in the Pakistani daily *Dawn* has stressed how Islamabad must be serious about hiring indigenous Balochi labor and making sure "the gains of the economic activity... are focused on Balochistan for the benefit of its poverty-stricken people."

The port of Gwadar, in southwest Balochistan, near the Iranian border, is indeed bound to become a new Dubai—but not the way the vice president Dick Cheney and gang in Washington once dreamed of. Gas from the South Pars fields in Iran will definitely flow though it. As for gas from the Daulatabad fields in Turkmenistan, assuming TAPI ever gets built through war-torn Afghanistan, that's much more unlikely.

This all raises the crucial question: how will Islamabad deal with ultra-strategic Balochistan—east of Iran, south of Afghanistan, and boasting three Arabian Sea ports, including Gwadar, practically at the mouth of the Strait of Hormuz?

The New Great Game in Eurasia rules that Pakistan is a key pivot to both NATO and the SCO, of which Pakistan is an observer. Balochistan de facto incorporates Pakistan as a key transit corridor to Iranian gas from the monster South Pars fields, and not to a great deal of the Caspian wealth of "gas republic" Turkmenistan. For the Pentagon, the birth of IP is mega bad news. The ideal Pentagon scenario is the US controlling Gwadar—in yet one more prime confluence of Pipelineistan and the US Empire of Bases.

With Gwadar directly linked to Iran and developed virtually as a Chinese warehouse, the Pentagon also loses the mouth-watering opportunity of a long land route across Balochistan into Helmand, Nimruz, Kandahar or, better yet, all of these three provinces in southwest Afghanistan, where soon, not by accident, there will be another US mega-base in the "desert of death." From a Pentagon/NATO perspective, after the "loss" of the Khyber Pass, that would be the ideal supply route for Western troops in the perennial, now rebranded, GWOT ("global war on terror").

Balochis surging

Islamabad has promised an all-parties conference "within days" to seriously deal with Balochistan. No one is holding their breath. Over a year ago, Balochistan was promised greater control over its immense natural resources—the undisputed, number-one Baloch grievance—and a massive aid package. Not much has happened.

Punjabis derisively refer to Balochistan's "backwardness." But the heart of the matter is systematic, hardcore pillage by Islamabad—combined with hardcore repression and serial Latin America-in-the-1970s-style "disappearances" of political activists and senior Baloch nationalists. Not to mention virtually no investment in health, education and job creation. This Third World dictatorship catalogue of disasters fuels Baloch nationalism and separatism.

Islamabad's paranoia is "foreign involvement" in the different strands of Balochistan's nationalist movements. That would be, in fact, the CIA, MI5 and the Israeli Mossad, all engaged in overlapping agendas which manipulate Balochistan for balkanization of Pakistan purposes and/or as a base for the destabilization of neighboring Iran's southeast. While the Taliban, Afghan or Pakistani, can roam free across Balochistan, Baloch nationalists are intimidated, harassed and killed.

Sanaullah Baloch, a secretary of the Balochistan National Party-Mengal, told *Dawn* how "several Baloch political parties tried to file charges against [former president General Pervez] Musharraf, but the country's institutions lack the will or courage to accept our plea against him." Studies show that rural poverty in Balochistan when Musharraf was in power increased 15% between 1999 and 2005.

Sanaullah Baloch roundly denounces the "civil-military elites" of Pakistan as implicated in the systematic repression going on in Balochistan; "Without their consent, no political regime can undo their policy of continued suppression."

And his analysis of why Islamabad has made a deal with the Taliban in Swat but won't do a deal with Balochis could not be more enlightening: "The establishment in Pakistan has always felt comfortable with religious groups as they do not challenge the centralized authority of the civil-military establishment. The demands of these groups are not political. They don't demand economic parity. They demand centralized religious rule which is philosophically closer to the establishment's version of totalitarianism. Islamabad's elite are stubborn against genuine Baloch demands: governing Balochistan, having ownership of resources, and control over provincial security."

So Islamabad still has all it takes to royally mess up what it has accomplished by approving IP. For the moment, Iran, Pakistan, China and Russia win. The SCO wins. Washington and NATO lose, not to mention Afghanistan (no transit fees). But will Balochistan also win? If not, all hell will break loose, from desperate Balochis sabotaging IP to "foreign interference" manipulating them into creating an even greater, regional, ball of fire.

May 2009

IRAN AND RUSSIA, SCORPIONS IN A BOTTLE

Things get curiouser and curiouser in the Iranian wonderland. Imagine what happened last week during Friday prayers in Tehran, personally conducted by former president Ayatollah Hashemi Rafsanjani, aka "The Shark," Iran's wealthiest man, who made his fortune partly because of Irangate—the 1980s' secret weapons contracts with Israel and the US.

As is well known, Rafsanjani is behind the Mir-Hossein Mousavi-Mohammad Khatami pragmatic conservative faction that lost the most recent battle at the top—rather than a presidential election—to the ultra-hardline faction of Ayatollah Ali Khamenei-Mahmud Ahmadinejad-Iran Revolutionary Guard Corps. During prayers, partisans of the hegemonic faction yelled the usual "Death to America!"—while the pragmatic conservatives came up, for the first time, with "Death to Russia!" and "Death to China!"

Oops. Unlike the United States and Western Europe, both Russia and China almost instantly accepted the contested presidential re-election of Ahmadinejad. Could they then be portrayed as enemies of Iran? Or have pragmatic conservatives not been informed that obsessed-by-Eurasia Zbig Brzezinksi—who has US President Barack Obama's undivided attention—has been preaching since the 1990s that it is essential to break up the Tehran-Moscow-Beijing axis and torpedo the Shanghai Cooperation Organization (SCO)?

On top of it, don't they know that both Russia and China—as well as Iran—are firm proponents of the end of the dollar as global reserve currency to the benefit of a (multipolar) basket of currencies, a common currency of which Russian President Dmitry Medvedev had the gall this month to present a prototype at the Group of Eight (G-8) meeting in Aquila, Italy? By the way, it's a rather neat coin. Minted in Belgium, it sports the faces of the G-8 leaders and also a motto—"Unity in diversity."

"Unity in diversity" is not exactly what the Obama administration has in mind as far as Iran and Russia are concerned—no matter the zillion bytes of lofty rhetoric. Let's start with the energy picture.

Iran is world number two both in terms of proven oil reserves (11.2%) and gas reserves (15.7%), according to the BP Statistical Review of World Energy 2008.

If Iran ever opted towards a more unclenched-fist relationship with Washington, US Big Oil would feast on Iran's Caspian energy wealth. This means that whatever the rhetoric, no US administration will ever want to deal with a hyper-nationalist Iranian regime, such as the current military dictatorship of the mullahtariat.

What really scares Washington—from George W Bush to Obama—is the perspective of a Russia-Iran-Venezuela axis. Together, Iran and Russia hold 17.6% of the world's proven oil reserves. The Persian Gulf petro-monarchies—de facto controlled by Washington—hold 45%. The Moscow-Tehran-Caracas axis controls 25%. If we add Kazakhstan's 3% and Africa's 9.5%, this new axis is more than an effective counter-power to American hegemony over the Arab Middle East. The same thing applies to gas. Adding the "axis" to the Central Asian "stans," we reach 30% of world gas production. As a comparison, the whole Middle East—including Iran—currently produces only 12.1% of the world's needs.

All about Pipelineistan

A nuclear Iran would inevitably turbo-charge the new, emerging multipolar world. Iran and Russia are de facto showing to both China and India that it is not wise to rely on US might subjugating the bulk of oil in the Arab Middle East. All these players are very much aware that Iraq remains occupied, and that Washington's obsession remains the privatization of Iraq's enormous oil wealth.

As Chinese intellectuals are fond of emphasizing, four emerging or re-emerging powers—Russia, China, Iran and India—are strategic and civilizational poles, three of them sanctuaries because they are nuclear powers. A more confident and assertive Iran—mastering the full cycle of nuclear technology—may translate into Iran and Russia increasing their relative weight in Europe and Asia to the distress of Washington, not only in the energy sphere but also as proponents of a multipolar monetary system.

The entente is already on. Since 2008, Iranian officials have stressed that sooner or later Iran and Russia will start trading in rubles. Gazprom is willing to be paid for oil and gas in rubles—and not dollars. And the secretariat of the Organization of Petroleum Exporting Countries (OPEC) has already seen the writing on the wall—admitting for over a year now that OPEC will be trading in euros before 2020.

Not only the "axis" Moscow-Tehran-Caracas, but also Qatar and Norway, for instance, and sooner or later the Gulf emirates, are ready to break up with the petrodollar. It goes without saying that the end of the petrodollar—which won't happen tomorrow, of course—means the end of the dollar as the world's reserve currency; the end of the world paying for America's massive budget deficits; and the end of an Anglo-American finance stranglehold over the world that has lasted since the second part of the 19th century.

The energy equation between Iran and Russia is much more complex: it configures them as two scorpions in a bottle. Tehran, isolated from the West, lacks foreign investment to upgrade its 1970s-era energy installations. That's why Iran cannot fully profit from exploiting its Caspian energy wealth.

Here it's a matter of Pipelineistan at its peak—since the US, still during the 1990s, decided to hit the Caspian in full force by supporting the Baku-Tblisi-Ceyhan (BTC) oil pipeline and the Baku-Tblisi-Supsa (BTS) gas pipeline.

For Gazprom, Iran is literally a goldmine. In September 2008, the Russian energy giant announced it would explore the huge Azadegan-North oilfield, as well as three others. Russia's Lukoil has increased its prospecting and Tatneft said it would be involved in the north. The George W Bush administration thought it was weakening Russia and isolating Iran in Central Asia. Wrong: it only accelerated their strategic energy cooperation.

Putin power play

In February 1995, Moscow committed to finishing construction of a nuclear reactor at Bushehr. This was a project started by that erstwhile, self-proclaimed "gendarme of the Gulf" for the US—the shah of Iran. The shah engaged KWU from Germany in 1974, but the project was halted by the Islamic Revolution in 1979 and hit hard between 1984 and 1988 by Saddam Hussein's bombs. The Russians finally entered the picture proposing to finish the project for $800 million. By December 2001, Moscow also started to sell missiles to Tehran—a surefire way of making extra money offering protection for strategic assets such as Bushehr.

Bushehr is a source of immense controversy in Iran. It should have been finished by 2000. As Iranian officials see it, the Russians seem never to be interested in wrapping it up. There are technical reasons—such as the Russian reactor being too big to fit inside what KWU had already built—as well as a technology deficit on the part of Iranian nuclear engineers.

But most of all there are geopolitical reasons. Former president Vladimir Putin used Bushehr as a key diplomatic peon in his double chessboard match with the West and the Iranians. It was Putin who launched the idea of enriching uranium for Iran in Russia; talk about a strategic asset in terms of managing a global nuclear crisis. Ahmadinejad—and most of all the Supreme Leader—gave him a flat refusal. The Russian response was even more foot-dragging, and even mild support for more US-sponsored sanctions against Tehran.

Tehran got the message—that Putin was not an unconditional ally. Thus, in August 2006, the Russians landed a new deal for the construction and supervision of two new nuclear plants. This all means that the Iranian nuclear dossier simply cannot be solved without Russia. Simultaneously, by Putin's own framework, it's very clear in Moscow that a possible Israeli strike would make it lose a profitable nuclear client on top of a diplomatic debacle. Medvedev for his part is pursuing the same two-pronged strategy; stressing to Americans and Europeans that Russia does not want nuclear proliferation in the Middle East while stressing to Tehran that it needs Russia more than ever.

Another feature of Moscow's chessboard strategy—never spelled out in public—is to keep the cooperation with Tehran to prevent China from taking over the whole project, but without driving the Americans ballistic at the same time. As long as the Iranian nuclear program is not finished,

Russia can always play the wise moderating role between Iran and the West.

Building up a civilian nuclear program in Iran is good business for both Iran and Russia for a number of reasons.

First of all, both are military encircled. Iran is strategically encircled by the US in Turkey, Iraq, Saudi Arabia, Bahrain, Pakistan and Afghanistan, and by US naval power in the Persian Gulf and the Indian Ocean. Russia has seen NATO gobbling up the Baltic countries and threatening to "annex" Georgia and Ukraine; NATO is at war in Afghanistan; and the US is still present, one way or another, across Central Asia.

Iran and Russia share the same strategy as far as the Caspian Sea is concerned. They are in fact opposed to the new Caspian states—Kazakhstan, Turkmenistan and Azerbaijan.

Iran and Russia also face the threat of hardcore Sunni Islam. They have a tacit agreement; for instance, Tehran has never done anything to help the Chechens. Then there's the Armenian issue. A de facto Moscow-Tehran-Erevan axis profoundly irks the Americans.

Finally, in this decade, Iran has become the third-largest importer of Russian weapons, after China and India. This includes the anti-missile system Tor M-1, which defends Iran's nuclear installations.

What's your axis?

So thanks to Putin, the Iran-Russia alliance is carefully deployed in three fronts—nuclear, energy and weapons.

Are there cracks in this armor? Certainly.

First, Moscow by all means does not want a weaponized Iranian nuclear program. This spells out "regional destabilization." Then, Central

Asia is considered by Moscow as its backyard, so for Iran to be ascendant in the region is quite problematic. As far as the Caspian goes, Iran needs Russia for a satisfactory juridical solution (Is it a sea or a lake? How much of it belongs to each border country?)

On other hand, Iran's new military dictatorship of the mullahtariat will react savagely if it ever had Russia fully against it in the UN Security Council. That would spell a rupture in economic relations—very bad for both sides—but also the possibility of Tehran supporting radical Islam everywhere from the southern Caucasus to Central Asia.

Under these complex circumstances, it's not so far-fetched to imagine a sort of polite Cold War going on between Tehran and Moscow.

From Russia's point of view, it all comes back to the "axis"—which would be in fact Moscow-Tehran-Erevan-New Delhi, a counter-power to the US-supported Ankara-Tblisi-Telaviv-Baku axis. But there's ample debate about it even inside the Russian elite. The old guard, like former Prime Minister Yevgeny Primakov, thinks that Russia is back as a great power by cultivating its former Arab clients as well as Iran; but then the so-called "Westernizers" are convinced that Iran is more of a liability.

They may have a point. The key of this Moscow-Tehran axis is opportunism—opposition to US hegemonic designs. Is Obama—via his "unclenched fist" policy—wily enough to try to turn this all upside down; or will he be forced by the Israel lobby and the industrial-military complex to finally strike a regime now universally despised all over the West?

Russia—and Iran—are fully committed to a multipolar world. The new military dictatorship of the mullahtariat in Tehran knows it cannot afford to be isolated; its road to the limelight may have to go through Moscow. That explains why Iran is making all sorts of diplomatic efforts to join the SCO.

As much as progressives in the West may support Iranian pragmatic conservatives—who are far from reformists—the crucial fact remains that Iran is a key peon for Russia to manage its relationship with the US and Europe. No matter how nasty the overtones, all evidence points to "stability" at this vital artery in the heart of the New Great Game.

July 2009

Iran, China and the New Silk Road

Does it make sense to talk about a Beijing-Tehran axis? Apparently no, when one learns that Iran's application to become a full member of the Shanghai Cooperation Organization (SCO) was flatly denied at the 2008 summit in Tajikistan.

Apparently yes, when one sees how the military dictatorship of the mullahtariat in Tehran and the collective leadership in Beijing have dealt with their recent turmoil—the "green revolution" in Tehran and the Uighur riots in Urumqi—reawakening in the West the ghostly mythology of "Asian despotism."

The Iran-China relationship is like a game of Chinese boxes. Amid the turbulence, glorious or terrifying, of their equally millenarian histories, when one sees an Islamic Republic that now reveals itself as a militarized theocracy and a Popular Republic that is in fact a capitalist oligarchy, things are not what they seem to be.

No matter what recently happened in Iran, consolidating the power of the Khamenei-Ahmadinejad-IranianRevolutionary GuardsCorps (IRGC) axis, the relationship will continue to develop within the framework of a clash between US hyperpower—declining as it may be—and the aspiring Chinese big power, allied with the re-emergent Russian big power.

On the road

Iran and China are all about the New Silk Road—or routes—in Eurasia. Both are among the most venerable and ancient of (on the road) partners. The first encounter between the Parthian empire and the Han dynasty was in 140 BC, when Zhang Qian was sent to Bactria (in today's Afghanistan) to strike deals with nomad populations. This eventually led to Chinese expansion in Central Asia and interchange with India.

Trading exploded via the fabled Silk Road—silk, porcelain, horses, amber, ivory, incense. As a serial traveler across the Silk Road over the years, I ended up learning on the spot how the Persians controlled the Silk Road by mastering the art of making oases, thus becoming in the process the middlemen between China, India and the West.

Parallel to the land route there was also a naval route—from the Persian Gulf to Canton (today's Guangzhou). And there was of course a religious route—with Persians translating Buddhist texts and with Persian villages in the desert serving as springboards to Chinese pilgrims visiting India. Zoroastrianism—the official religion of the Sassanid empire—was imported to China by Persians at the end of the 6th century, and Manichaeism during the 7th. Diplomacy followed: the son of the last Sassanid emperor—fleeing the Arabs in 670 AD—found refuge in the Tang court. During the Mongol period, Islam spread into China.

Iran has never been colonized. But it was a privileged theater of the original Great Game between the British Empire and Russia in the 19th century and then during the Cold War between the US and the Soviet Union in the 20th. The Islamic Revolution may at first imply Khomeini's official policy of "neither East nor West." In fact, Iran dreams of bridging both.

That brings us to Iran's key, inescapable geopolitical role at the epicenter of Eurasia. The New Silk Road translates into an energy corridor—the Asian Energy Security Grid—in which the Caspian Sea is an essential node, linked to the Persian Gulf, from where oil is to be transported to Asia. And as far as gas is concerned, the name of the game is Pipelineistan—as in the recently agreed Iran-Pakistan (IP) pipeline and the interconnection between Iran and Turkmenistan, whose end result is a direct link between Iran and China.

Then there's the hyper-ambitious, so-called "North-South corridor"—a projected road and rail link between Europe and India, through Russia, Central Asia, Iran and the Persian Gulf. And the ultimate New Silk Road dream—an actual land route between China and the Persian Gulf via Central Asia (Afghanistan, Tajikistan, Uzbekistan).

The width of the circle

As the bastion of Shi'ite faith, encircled by Sunnis, Iran under what is now a de facto theocratic dictatorship still desperately needs to break out from its isolation. Talk about a turbulent environment: Iraq still under US occupation to the west, the ultra-unstable Caucasus in the northwest, fragile Central Asian "stans" in the northeast, basket cases Afghanistan and Pakistan to the east, not to mention the nuclear neighborhood - Israel, Russia, China, Pakistan and India.

Technological advancement for Iran means fully mastering a civilian nuclear program—which contains the added benefit of turning it into a sanctuary via the possibility of building a nuclear device. Officially, Tehran has declared ad infinitum it has no intention of possessing an "un-Islamic" bomb. Beijing understands Tehran's delicate position and supports its right to the peaceful use of nuclear energy. Beijing would have loved to see Tehran adopt the plan proposed by Russia, the US, Western Europe and, of course, China. Carefully evaluating its vital energy and national security interests, the last thing Beijing wants is for Washington to clench its fist again.

What happened to the George W Bush-declared, post-9/11 "global war on terror" (GWOT), now remixed by Obama as "overseas contingency operations" (OCO)? GWOT's key, shadowy aim was for Washington to firmly plant the flag in Central Asia. For those sorry neo-cons, China was the ultimate geopolitical enemy, so nothing was more enticing than to try to sway a batch of Asian countries against China. Easier dreamed of than done.

China's counter-power was to turn the whole game around in Central Asia, with Iran as its key peon. Beijing was quick to grasp that Iran is a matter of national security, in terms of assuring its vast energy needs.

Of course China also needs Russia—for energy and technology. This is arguably more of an alliance of circumstance—for all the ambitious targets embodied by the SCO—than a long-term strategic partnership. Russia, invoking a series of geopolitical reasons, considers its relationship with Iran as exclusive. China says slow down, we're also in the picture. And as Iran remains under pressure at different levels from both the US and Russia, what better "savior" than China?

Enter Pipelineistan. At first sight, Iranian energy and Chinese technology is a match made in heaven. But it's more complicated than that.

Still the victim of US sanctions, Iran has turned to China to modernize itself. Once again, the Bush/Dick Cheney years and the invasion of Iraq sent an unmistakable message to the collective leadership in Beijing. A push to control Iraq oil plus troops in Afghanistan, a stone's throw from the Caspian, added to the Pentagon's self-defined "arc of instability" from the Middle East to Central Asia—this was more than enough to imprint the message: the less dependent China is on US-subjugated Arab Middle East energy, the better.

The Arab Middle East used to account for 50% of China's oil imports. Soon China became the second-largest oil importer from Iran, after Japan. And since fateful 2003, China also has mastered the full cycle of prospection/exploitation/refining—thus Chinese companies are investing heavily in Iran's oil sector, whose refining capacity, for instance, is risible. Without urgent investment, some projections point to Iran possibly cutting off oil exports by 2020. Iran also needs everything else China can provide in areas like transportation systems, telecom, electricity and naval construction.

Iran needs China to develop its gas production in the gigantic north Pars and south Pars fields—which it shares with Qatar—in the Persian Gulf. So no wonder a "stable" Iran had to become a matter of Chinese national security.

Multipolar we go

So why the stalemate at the SCO? As China is always meticulously seeking to improve its global credibility, it had to be considering the pros and cons of admitting Iran, for which the SCO and its slogan of mutual cooperation for the stability of Central Asia, as well as economic and security benefits, are priceless. The SCO fights against Islamic terrorism and "separatism" in general—but now has also developed as an economic body, with a development fund and a multilateral economic council. The whole idea of it is to curb American influence in Central Asia.

Iran has been an observer since 2005. Next year may be crucial. The race is on to beat the clock, before a desperate Israeli strike, and have Iran accepted by the SCO while negotiating some sort of stability pact with the Barack Obama administration. For all this to happen relatively smoothly, Iran needs China—that is, to sell as much oil and gas as China needs below market prices, while accepting Chinese—and Russian—investment in the exploration and production of Caspian oil.

All this while Iran also courts India. Both Iran and India are focused on Central Asia. In Afghanistan, India is financing the construction of a US$250 million road between Zaranj, at the Iranian border, and

Delaram—which is in the Afghan Ring Road linking Kabul, Kandahar, Herat and Mazar-i-Sharif. New Delhi sees in Iran a very important market. India is actively involved in the construction of a deep-water port in Chabahar—that would be a twin for the Gwadar port built in southern Balochistan by China, and would be very helpful to landlocked Afghanistan (freeing it from Pakistani interference).

Iran also needs its doors to the north—the Caucasus and Turkey—to channel its energy production towards Europe. It's an uphill struggle. Iran has to fight fierce regional competition in the Caucasus; the US-Turkey alliance framed by NATO; the perpetual US-Russian Cold War in the region; and last but not least Russia's own energy policy, which simply does not contemplate sharing the European energy market with Iran.

But energy agreements with Turkey are now part of the picture—after the moderate Islamists of the AKP took power in Ankara in 2002. Now it's not that far-fetched to imagine the possibility of Iran in the near future supplying much-needed gas for the ultra-expensive, US-supported Turkey-to-Austria Nabucco pipeline.

But the fact remains that for both Tehran and Beijing, the American thrust in the "arc of instability" from the Middle East to Central Asia is anathema. They're both anti-US hegemony and US unilateralism, Bush/Cheney style. As emerging powers, they're both pro multipolar. And as they're not Western-style liberal democracies, the empathy is even stronger. Few failed to notice the stark similarities in the degree of repression of the "green revolution" in Tehran and the Uighurs in Xinjiang.

For China, a strategic alliance with Iran is above all about Pipelineistan, the Asian Energy Security Grid and the New Silk Road. For China, a peaceful solution to the Iranian nuclear dossier is imperative. This would lead to Iran being fully opened to (eager) European investment.

Nimble Books LLC

Washington may be reluctant to admit it, but in the New Great Game in Eurasia, the Tehran-Beijing axis spells out the future: multipolarity.

July 2009

JIHAD BLING BLING

The news of Pashtun jihad master Baitullah Mehsud possibly hit by a Predator drone on the roof of his father-in-law's house while undertaking a massage provoked hardly a ripple among the happy few gathered around the table of the appropriately named Pan Dei ("All Gods"), a glitzy multimillion-euro yacht currently anchored at the mythic Mediterranean port of St Tropez.

To start with, the happy few—five toned, tanned, swinging Dolce and Gabbana, model lookalikes—wouldn't even dream of being caught in such a situation, unless the masseuse was a Swedish valkyrie and the tribal setting was a suite of the Pan Dei itself. And they don't deal with drones—only private jets. After all, they are proud enablers of jihad bling bling—post-crisis hypercapitalism's answer to the enduring financial "crisis."

Crisis? What crisis? As much as France remains the number-one destination for mass tourism in the world, St Tropez remains the most coveted spot in the world for jihad bling bling. Forget the Dubai oven with its "artificial islands." Forget the faded California dream. Exclusive St Barth in the Caribbean is too much under the radar. This is not about a Baudelaire remix of luxury, calm and voluptuousness. If we're talking over-the-wall brash and flash, St Tropez is the genuine (gleaming) article.

It's 9pm at the ultra-busy port of St Tropez, the sunset is absolutely smashing, cafes like the swinging Gorilla are bursting at the seams and the gleaming Pan Dei is about to dock—to the speechless amazement of hordes of multinational day trippers in trunks and sandals who packed their ham-and-cheese baguette and diet cola in a plastic bag as their last line of defense against hyper-inflated local prices.

They wouldn't even dream of a fish duo dinner at the perennially cool Cafe des Arts in the Place des Lys, where Chichette—the coolest bartender west of Baghdad—dishes out glasses of fine chilled Cotes de Provence and the patron, an unsmiling summer table warrior who's seen them all, from Brigitte Bardot to the Emir of Qatar, would refuse to get them a table anyway.

Outside, undulating Tropeziennes in impossibly high heels play petanque with hardened veterans sipping pastis, and Bardot replicas in faux Indian chic babble into their golden Motorolas identifying the night's jackpot. A nagging question intervenes. Where are the Russians—aka, the *novi ruski*?

They haven't exactly disappeared from the jihad bling bling planet. Tired of being fleeced, they have partly abandoned St Tropez for more sedate pastures like the wild beaches of Sardinia, where one Silvio Berlusconi, who happens to be Italy's prime minister, keeps his outstanding Tiberian orgy summer digs. For their part, Italians—not all of them horrified by Silvio's erotic antics—are back in St Tropez in full force, escaping the overbuilding devastation of their own Riviera.

Exit the Russians; enter the enigmatic upper bourgeoisie from Latvia, which sends its daughters to London for culture and its sons to Geneva for investment banking; impossibly tanned and fit, they reunite by intermarriage in St Tropez to live la *dolce vita* in style.

The rent-a-yacht lifestyle

Back at the Pan Dei, there couldn't be a more classic jihad bling bling stage. While the five happy few drink (silver) buckets of Krug—served by a stewardess—and hang five to their upcoming wild night, two muscle girls in blue shorts, part of the crew, work their perfect butts off, impeccably landing the boat under the orders of a crew master. The full crew numbers no less than 10.

Jihad bling bling's financial savvy remains merciless. Supporting the local economy is only relatively encouraged—as in landing the best tables in town. But paying taxes is frowned upon. It's not for nothing that virtually every other mega-yacht in St Tropez comes from this magic neverland, Georgetown, in the Cayman Islands, which for all Group of 10 rhetoric to amuse the galleries, will never be subjected to fiscal control.

The jihad bling bling solution to escape the hefty taxes imposed at St Tropez's port is the rent-a-yacht. This means renting only the deck of your yacht for a private dinner (the whole boat, cabins included, is fully locked), when aspiring jihad bling blingers can dazzle the port hordes with their (fake) immunity to the "crisis."

Other, more savvy yachters have come up with an even better solution; they park their gleaming beasts somewhere in the Mediterranean and take a rollicking 10-minute boat ride to shore, where they very excitedly alight in white linen regalia after what is later packaged in conversation as a "sea adventure."

Jihad bling bling as applied to St Tropez could not but be a class society, as in ancient Greece—from the ultra-exclusive multinational yacht crowd and the yacht renters down to the local (European) crew and the multinational hordes of hangers-on. As for the oldest profession in the world... well, talk about crisis.

The current going rate is 2,000 euros (US$2,840) for a live copy of Maria Sharapova rented before 10 pm. At midnight, the rate drops to 1,000 euros. And at 5 am, it all becomes a bargain: only 200 euros. No wonder beach babes are all flocking to Sardinia to do business with Berlusconi. Not only do they get 1,000 euros a night plus immeasurable bonuses, they are elevated to tabloid fodder stardom and show up all over pan-European media telling all about their hot adventure with the insatiable Il Cavaliere.

According to Forbes magazine, now there are "only" 793 billionaires left in the world. A great deal still call St Tropez home. Poor guys. Jihad bling blingers are now more money-conscious than ever. Their newfound, low-cost attitude includes bargaining for every possible free lunch in town, and every available discount in a sales-infested shoposphere. Of course there are exceptions, such as a suspected, lonely Emirati who showed up in an empty St Tropez shop at 10pm and bought 10,000 euros in cashmere.

Where is Chouchou?

It's easy to spot who's really missing in St Tropez; none other than uber-couple "Chouchou" (my little darling) and Carla—or, in plain English, the President of France Nicolas Sarkozy, aka Sarko the First and his belle, Carla Bruni-Sarkozy, the (Italian) priestess of the new French gauche caviar, those specimens who pretend to be impossibly politically correct while dreaming of a star-studded life as jihad bling blingers.

The first couple is currently holed up in the Cap Negre, east of the port of Toulon, far, far away from St Tropez glitz, at the house mansion of mom Bruni-Tedeschi. The definitive bling blinger way back in 2007, the adrenalin junkie Sarko the First is now in full low-cost, low-profile mode—especially after his spectacular collapse while jogging at noon under 35 degrees Celsius. But dedicated Carla still calls him "Chouchou"—a jihad bling bling form of affection if there ever was one.

To the north of Cap Negre lies Provence—which dazzled Van Gogh, Picasso and F Scott Fitzgerald. Not exactly jihad bling bling territory. This is arguably where the essence of the best of real-life France still is—from the vineyards of Chateauneuf-du-Pape to the understated elegance of medieval Bonnieux; from the canyons of Colorado atmosphere of Roussillon to the dazzling hills of the Luberon—mostly a protected national park.

A mere chair on the beach at Pampelone, in St Tropez, rents for a staggering 60 euros a day (and jihad bling blingers get no discount). But arguably the funkiest beach outside the Cote d'Azur is actually in the Camargue—an apex of ecological equilibrium—not far from marshes inhabited by packs of pink flamingos.

The beach, near the salt banks of Saintes-Maries-de-la-Mer, sports a motley crew of gypsies, bikers, dopers, losers, fake rastas, anarchists, trailer park trashers and nudists as if they all had sprung up from *Inherent Vice*, by Thomas Pynchon, the definitive novel of the summer of 2009.

Nostradamus—who was born in Saint-Remy-de-Provence in 1503—didn't bother to predict the arrival of jihad bling bling. Vincent Van Gogh, who lived in Saint-Remy, wouldn't bother to paint them. Jihad bling bling is all about showing who, according to Monty Python, is the Biggus Dickus in town.

In this particular department, few jihad bling blingers may equal former French king Philippe Le Bel. His 13th-century tower still stands at tiny Villeneuve-les-Avignon, on the other side of the river Rhone opposite the legendary city of popes, Avignon. The river used to be the dividing line between the kingdom of France and the Christian kingdom of the papacy. Philippe Le Bel built his fortress/tower on a hill rising above the papal palace on the other side, his way of affirming who had the jihad bling bling Biggus Dickus in town.

And then there are the ruins of the Divine Marquis de Sade's chateau at tiny, hilly Lacoste. Sade, aristocrat-pornographer, the philosopher of transgression in all its nuances, has never been hipper, making the transition from jail in the Bastille to the Pleaiade—the most prestigious of French literary collections. Forever enigmatic, "extreme in everything" according to his self-description, smashing all conventions with his deregulated imagination.

The blueprint of a jihad bling blinger? Hardly. The divine marquis would never dodge taxes on St Tropez's port, or wait for 5am to grab a Russian hooker for 200 euros; he'd keep a non-stop orgy, parked at the port, with all the belles in town.

On the other hand, Sade wrote a detailed eulogy of sodomy. St Tropez locals—men and women—rage about the "weird practices" of selected jihad bling blingers of Middle Eastern extraction. Well, even Nostradamus could not possibly predict the advent of anal hypercapitalism.

August 2009

The glitzy face of Eurabia

Sheikh Hamad bin Khalifa al-Thani, the Emir of Qatar, is a man, to quote rock geopoliticos Mick Jagger and Keith Richards, "of wealth and taste." Not to mention his second wife, the ravishing Sheikh Moza, one of the most powerful women in the Middle East. It goes without saying that the Qatari royal couple had to be bitten by the Francophilia bug, super-villa in Cannes included (not to mention the duplex near Place de la Concorde).

But in terms of global power couples, few rival the complicity between the Emir of Qatar and adrenalin junkie and French President Nicolas Sarkozy. After all, Sarko Le Premier (Sarko the First), as cynics call him in France, could not find a better partner to anchor France's Arab foreign policy. At the Elysee Palace, very cozy relations with a key Persian Gulf actor are considered ultra-strategic. Especially if the actor in question holds the third-largest proven gas reserves in the world, only behind Russia and Iran.

The emir and Sarko are so close that whenever there's business to be done—and that's a lot of business—the emir calls Sarko directly, bypassing the usual diplomatic channels. Not for nothing the Qatari royal couple are regular guests of honor in the traditional French parade of July 14.

The emir is indeed a fascinating character. Faithful to the (previous) empire, he studied at the British military academy in Sandhurst. In June 1995 he applied a bloodless palace coup and snatched power from his own father, who happened to be living *la dolce vita* in Europe. Once again flirting with iconoclasm, the emir then not only famously begged to differ from the House of Saud in virtually all matters but got into no-holds-barred journalism by launching a made in Arabia 24-hour news channel, al-Jazeera.

The emir holds no grudge against the West. Far from it; the best example may be the muscular influence of the Rand Corporation in Qatar. He is now carefully cultivating the profile of an international mediator—as in the Doha accords that led to the 2008 Lebanese presidential election.

When in doubt, invest

The power love affair between the emir and Sarko was born when Sarko was still France's minister of interior—or, critics say, "top cop," at a time when agreements were basically reached under the "war on terror" framework. Now everything is at play—especially Qatari investments in France, such as the renovation of the ultra-chic Hotel Lambert, owned by the emir's brother, as well as the inevitable multitude of villas in the Cote d'Azur. No wonder in February the French parliament approved a bill exempting from taxes any investments made by the emir or his public entities in the French real-estate market.

Inevitably this is a matter of a monster, US$80 billion sovereign fund, the Qatar Investment Authority (QIA), created in 2005 to diversify a monoculture economy until then dominated by oil and gas. QIA simply eschews any opportunities demanding less than 100 million euros (US$142.4 million). Europe accounts for one-third of the investments of Qatari Diar, the company in charge of the financial transactions for the fund.

QIA won't blink to place 7 billion euros to get 25% of Porsche. It already controls 15% of the London Stock Exchange, 8% of Barclays, 2% of Credit Suisse and 8% of the top bank in China, the Industrial and Commercial Bank of China.

Certainly more piles of cash are invested in London, but the emir's heart beats for Paris. Qatar is literally taking over rows and rows of office buildings between Opera and Madeleine in central Paris. Why real estate? It's because what Qataris know best. Even the mayor of Paris, the colorful Bertrand Delanoe, is now in full campaign to make the Qataris invest in other, less pricey, Parisian neighborhoods.

Qatar's dream is not exactly to become a real-estate powerhouse. The emirate wants to be respected as a model of regional development. That's where Moza Bent Nasser al-Misned, the emir's wife, jumps in.

The Qatar Foundation, over which she presides, finances a host of humanitarian and cultural projects—such as the recent ecology awareness global blockbuster *Home*; the movie's director, Yann Arthus-Bertrand, received 1 million euros from the foundation. The emir's wife is now in the French Academy of Beaux-Arts.

She is also vice president of Qatar's Supreme Council for Education, and directs a giant campus (the general plan was designed by superstar architect Arata Isozaki) where six American universities are already shelling out diplomas (60% of them women). Sheikh Moza is an extremely active campaigner for education as the path for feminine emancipation in the Middle East. Quite striking, when one knows how the Qatar peninsula has been for a long time heavily marked by intolerant Wahhabism.

As in all Gulf emirates that have been propelled in less than half a century from a subsistence economy based on fishing to untold oil and gas wealth, culture is not exactly a priority. "Culture" in the region could be defined as the cement of a social cohesion that still has to be invented.

So yes, when they hear the world "culture," Qataris wave their checkbook. Qatar didn't get the new Louvre—it was snatched by Abu Dhabi. But Qatar got the architect of the Grand Louvre.

The architects come from the rich north, the laborers from the poor south. This symbiotic apotheosis is more than evident at the Museum of Islamic Art in Doha, launched in November 2008. Cost: only $350 million. The architect had to be a genius, Chinese-American I M Pei—who, as the emir well knew, built the Louvre Pyramid. The museum is a sensational mix of cubes and curves erected over an artificial island away from the Doha corniche, facing from a distance a spectacular 21st-century skyline. The collection, as a former expert from the Victoria and Albert Museum in London put it, is also spectacular, covering 1,300 years of history in three continents.

And "culture" does not stop here. Qatar is also building a Museum of National History (the architect is another superstar, Jean Nouvel); a Museum of Natural History; a National Library (by superstar architect Arata Isozaki); a Photography Museum (architect Santiago Calatrava); and a Museum of Contemporary Art.

The glass pyramid

Anyway, "culture" in Qatar remains predominantly business. And business is definitely booming for Alcatel, Alstom, Areva, GDF Suez, Total—all the big names of French big business. Vinci, for instance, is building no less than the number one bridge in the world between Doha and Bahrain, 43 kilometers long. GDF Suez is installing a desalinization plant in the middle of the desert.

Business is also booming in European territory. Qatar spent over $2 billion this year on five A-380 Airbus jets, not to mention the $17 billion spent two years ago for 80 A-350s. Add to it the 1.5 billion euros for 20 Tigre military helicopters from Eurocopter—a branch of the giant European consortium European Aeronautic Defence and Space Company (EADS). The French arms industry especially simply can't get enough of

Qatar—betting all its chips on a commercial war against the Americans already doing business with Doha. EADS sold to Qatar their system of border surveillance as well as radars; now the emir wants an anti-missile system.

Qatar is indeed Paradox Central. In the tiny emirate of only 11,000 square kilometers, one finds only 900,000 people—80% of them expatriates—as well as al-Jazeera, a mega-American military base key for the US Central Command and the wife and daughters of Saddam Hussein. On top of it, Qatar finances Hamas in Palestine. Annual per capita gross national product is a ridiculously high $74,000. Crisis? What crisis?

Qatar's love affair with all things French does not exactly include "liberty, equality, fraternity." Everything in what is technically a constitutional monarchy is in the hands of the al-Thani clan. Socially, it's a hardcore pyramid. What's the place of "Western liberal democracy" in all this ocean/desert of cash? The emir and his ultra-pro team have been skillfully projecting Qatar's global image as an extremely modern country. In Qatar everything seems to be diluted in the overwhelming liquid modernity flux of services, banking and smooth efficiency. As much as Dubai in the United Arab Emirates copied to the hilt the Singaporean model, Qatar is re-mixing the Dubai copy. A haven of social justice it ain't.

France—and the European Union for that matter—can live with it. Most of Qatar's gas—the country is the number one exporter of LNG—goes to Asia. Last year, France bought only 85 million euros in oil and 20 million euros in gas from Qatar. The possibilities of expansion, not only for France but the European Union (EU) as a whole, are limitless. Especially because Brussels' dream is to escape from the Russian energy stranglehold. The Holy Grail is North Pars, the largest gas field in the world, which Qatar shares with Iran. Forget about villas in the Cote d'Azur; it's big—energy—business in this node of Eurabia that will be booming for a long time to come.

August 2009

Enduring Freedom until 2050

And it's one, two, three
what are we fighting for?
Don't ask me, I don't give a damn
next stop is Vietnam

- *Country Joe and the Fish, 1969*

After eight long years, now more than ever, the United States invasion and (partial) occupation of Afghanistan is on a roll, courtesy of US President Barack Obama's "new strategy."

This—which Pentagon supremo Robert Gates insists is "working"—includes US and NATO staging mini-Guernicas, *a la* the bombing of Guernica, Spain, by German and Italian warplanes in 1937, as painted by Pablo Picasso.

It also includes General Stanley McChrystal—the former number one hit man for General David Petraeus in Iraq—assaulting Washington to demand (what else is new?) an extra 45,000 US boots on the ground.

Add 52,000 US troops and no less than a staggering 68,000 US contractors as of late March—don't even count NATO—and soon there will be more Americans wallowing in the Afghan mire than Soviets at their occupation peak during the 1980s. In only 450 days, Enduring Freedom plus NATO boots swelled up from 67,000 to 118,000.

Does it matter that, according to a McClatchy/Ipsos survey, almost eight years after the "war on terror" bombing of the Taliban, 54% of

Americans think the US is "losing" the war while 56% are against sending more troops? Of course not.

We want our cut

The latest mini-Guernica is the air strike on two fuel trucks hijacked by the Taliban and stuck in a riverbed near a market in the Ali Abad district in Kunduz province. The strike was ordered by a helpless, intelligence-impaired German colonel under the NATO banner, and has now degenerated into a caustic war of words between Washington and Berlin.

NATO's "mission" in Afghanistan is extremely unpopular in Germany. According to Kunduz locals, the NATO air strike killed more than 100 villagers; NATO says no more than 25; all this while insisting it made sure no civilians were in the area before the hit. It's the same mini-Guernica scenario of Herat in August 2008 and Farah in May 2009.

None of this slows down the relentless Gates/Mullen/McChrystal gravy train—the Pentagon superstar trio obsessed with milking a Vietnam-style escalation of Obama's self-described "necessary war" whose final objective, according to super-envoy Richard Holbrooke, is of the "we'll-know-it-when-we-see-it" kind.

As for USAID, it has just "discovered" that the Taliban—as a protection racket—take a cut from the international development aid pouring into Afghanistan. But the cut pales in comparison to what the Hamid Karzai government and his warlord compadres divert from the European Union coffers under United Nations supervision—via one "Afghan reconstruction" bash after another (Tokyo 2002, Berlin 2004, London 2006, Paris 2008).

Maybe not as much as Americans, European taxpayers are also being fleeced. In a devastating post at the Italian byebyeunclesam blog,

Giancarlo Chetoni explains how Afghanistan is costing Italian taxpayers 1,000 euros (US$1,433) a minute, or 525.6 million euros a year, to "free the country from terrorism and drugs." Surrealism is the norm. Italy famously gave 52 million euros to "reform Afghanistan's judicial system" when, Chetoni notes, "3.5 million penal cases and 5.4 million civil lawsuits are currently pending" in Italy. During the next four years, Italy will practically double its contingent, from 3,250 troops to more than 6,000.

New NATO head, former president George W Bush-friendly Anders Rasmussen from Denmark, has been trying to explain the new "strategy" in pyrotechnic NATOese to skeptical Europeans. But the real plot of the non-stop tragicomedy is never spelled out. The US and its NATO allies will do—and spend—whatever it takes to implant military bases on the doorstep of both Russia and China and—Allah only knows—get their Trans-Afghan Pakistan gas pipeline on track.

From November 2001 to December 2008, the Bush administration burned $179 billion in Afghanistan, while NATO burned $102 billion. Former NATO head Jaap de Hoop Scheffer said the West would keep troops in Central Asia for 25 years. He was corrected by the British army's chief of general staff, General David Richards: it will be 40 years. Expect the "evil," fit Taliban—immune to global warming—to be fighting Enduring Freedom by 2050.

September 2009

Jumpin' Jack Verdi, It's a Gas, Gas, Gas

Oil and natural gas prices may be relatively low right now, but don't be fooled. The New Great Game of the twenty-first century is always over energy and it's taking place on an immense chessboard called Eurasia. Its squares are defined by the networks of pipelines being laid across the oil heartlands of the planet. Call it Pipelineistan. If, in Asia, the stakes in this game are already impossibly high, the same applies to the "Euro" part of the great Eurasian landmass—the richest industrial area on the planet. Think of this as the real political thriller of our time.

The movie of the week in Brussels is: *When NATO Meets Pipelineistan*. Though you won't find it in any headlines, at virtually every recent NATO summit Washington has been maneuvering to involve reluctant Europeans ever more deeply in the business of protecting Pipelineistan. This is already happening, of course, in Afghanistan, where a promised pipeline from Turkmenistan to Pakistan and India, the TAPI pipeline, has not even been built. And it's about to happen at the borders of Europe, again around pipelines that have not yet been built.

If you had to put that Euro part of Pipelineistan into a formula, you might do so this way: Nabucco (pushed by the U.S.) versus South Stream (pushed by Russia). Be patient. You'll understand in a moment.

At the most basic level, it's a matter of the West yet again trying, in the energy sphere, to bypass Russia. For this to happen, however—and it wouldn't hurt if you opened the nearest atlas for a moment—Europe desperately needs to get a handle on Central Asian energy resources, which is easy to say but has proven surprisingly hard to do. No wonder the NATO Secretary General's special representative, Robert Simmons, has been logging massive frequent-flyer miles to Central Asia over these last few years.

Just under the surface of an edgy *entente cordiale* between the EU and Russia lurks the possibility of a no-holds-barred energy war—Liquid War, as I call it. The EU and the US are pinning their hopes on a prospective 3,300-kilometer-long, $10.7 billion pipeline dubbed Nabucco. Planning for it began way back in 2004 and construction is finally expected to start, if all goes well (and it may not), in 2010. So if you're a NATO optimist, you hope that natural gas from the Caspian Sea, maybe even from Iran (barring the usual American blockade), will begin flowing through it by 2015. The gas will be delivered to Erzurum in Turkey and then transported to Austria via Bulgaria, Romania, and Hungary.

Why, you might ask, is the pipeline meant to save Europe named for a Verdi opera? Well, Austrian and Turkish energy executives happened to see the opera together in Vienna in 2002 while discussing their energy dilemmas, and the biblical plight of the Jews exiled by King Nabucco (Nebuchadnezzar), a love story set amid a ferocious struggle for freedom and power, swept them away. Still, it's a stretch to turn steel tubes into dramatic characters.

Of course, the operatic theater here isn't really in the tubing, it's in the politics and strategic implications that surround the pipeline. In Eastern Europe, for instance, Nabucco is seen not as a European economic or energy project, but as a creature of Washington, just like the Baku-Tblisi-Ceyhan (BTC) pipeline from Azerbaijan to Turkey that President Bill Clinton and his crew backed so vigorously in the 1990s and which was finally finished in 2005. For those who have never believed the Cold War is over—the Eastern Europeans among them—once again it's the good guys (the West) against the commies... sorry, the Russians... at an energy-rich OK Corral.

The Great Borderless Gas Bazaar

Russia's answer to Nabucco is the 1,200-kilometer-long, $15 billion South Stream pipeline, also scheduled to be finished in 2015; it is slated to carry Siberian natural gas under the Black Sea from Russia to Bulgaria. From Bulgaria, one branch of the pipeline would then run south through Greece to southern Italy while the other would run north through Serbia and Hungary towards northern Italy.

Now, add another pipeline to the picture, the $9.1 billion Nord Stream that will soon enough snake from Western Russia under the Baltic Sea to Germany, which already imports 41.5% of its natural gas from Russia. The giant Russian energy firm Gazprom holds a controlling 51% of Nord Stream stock; the rest belongs to German and Dutch companies. The chairman of the board is none other than former German Chancellor Gerhard Schroeder.

Put this all together and Russia, with its pipelines running in all directions and firmly embedded in Europe, spells trouble for Nabucco's future and frustration for Washington's New Great Game plans to contain the Russian energy juggernaut. And that's without even mentioning Ukhta which, chances are, you've never heard of. If you aren't in the energy business, why should you have? After all, it's a backwater village in Russia's autonomous republic of Komi, 350 kilometers from the Arctic Circle. Built by forced labor, it was once part of Alexander Solzhenitsyn's Gulag archipelago. By 2030, however, you'll know its name. By then, a pipeline from remote Ukhta will be flooding Europe with natural gas and the village will be one of Nord Stream's key transit nodes.

While Nabucco as well as South Stream remain virtual, Nord Stream is a Terminator on the run. By 2010, it will be tunneling under the Baltic Sea heading for Germany. By 2011, it should be delivering the goods and a second pipe—12 meters long per joint, 100,000 tubes long—will be under construction to double its capacity by 2014. Gazprom CEO Alexei Miller pulls no punches: this, he says, will be "the safest and most modern pipeline in the world."

How can Verdi lovers possibly compete? In the middle of a global recession, Gazprom is spending at least $20 billion to conquer Europe via Nord and South Stream. The strategy is a killer: pump gas under the sea directly to Europe, avoiding messy transit routes across troublesome countries like Ukraine. No wonder Gazprom, which today controls 26% of the European gas market, is expected to have a 33% share by 2020.

In other words, in many ways, the Nabucco versus South Stream energy war already looks settled. Nabucco is, at best, likely to be a secondary pipeline, incapable, as Washington once hoped, of breaking the EU away from energy dependence on Russia.

Brussels, predictably, is in its usual multilingual policy mess. Most bureaucrats at its monster, directive-churning body, the European Commission, publicly bemoan the "pipeline war." On the other hand, Ona Jukneviciene, chairwoman of the committees at the European Parliament dealing with Central Asia, admits that Nabucco cannot be the only option.

As for Reinhard Mitschek, managing director of the Nabucco consortium, he tries to put a brave face on things when he stresses, "we will transport Russian gas, Azeri gas, Iraqi gas." As for the top European official on energy matters, Andris Piebalgs, he can't help being a pragmatist: "We'll continue to work with Russia because Russia has energy resources."

From a business point of view, it's tough to argue with South Stream's selling points. Unlike Nabucco, it will offer cheaper, all-Russian natural gas that won't have to transit through potential war zones, and while Nabucco will always deliver limited amounts of Caspian natural gas to market, South Stream, given Russian resources, will have plenty of room to increase its output.

The fact is that, as of now, Nabucco still has no guaranteed sources of gas. In order for the gas to come from energy-rich Turkmenistan, to take but one example, the Turkmen leadership would have to break a deal they've already made with Russia, which now buys all of that country's export gas. There's no way that Moscow is likely to let one of the former Soviet Republics do that easily. In addition, both Russia and Iran could well be capable of blocking any pipeline straddling the floor of the Caspian Sea.

Gazprom will pay to build South Stream, and then distribute and sell gas it already controls to Europe; Nabucco, on the other hand, has to rely on a messy consortium of six countries (Austria, Hungary, Romania, Bulgaria, Turkey, and Germany) simply to finance one-third of its prospective costs, and then convince wary international bankers to shell out the rest.

The Pentagon does the Black Sea

So what does Washington want out of this mess? That's easy. Rewind to then-prospective Secretary of State Hillary Clinton in her Senate confirmation hearings on January 13, 2009. There, she decried Europe's dependence on Russian natural gas and issued an urgent call for "investments in the Trans-Caspian energy sector." Think of it as a signal: The new Obama administration would be as committed to Nabucco as the Bush administration had been.

What is never spelled out is why. Enter the Black Sea, that crucial geostrategic stage where Europe meets the Middle East, the Caucasus, and Central Asia. Enter, thus, Bulgaria, home to a new Pentagon air base in Bezmer, one of six new strategic bases being built outside the US and as potentially important to Washington's future games as the stalwart air bases in Incirlik, Turkey, and Aviano, Italy have been in the past. (Aviano was the key U.S./NATO base for the bombing of the Bosnian Serbs in 1995 and the 78-day bombing campaign against Serbia in 1999.)

With the Pentagon's bases already creeping within a stone's throw of Southwest and Central Asia, it doesn't take a genius to imagine the role Bezmer might play in any future attack on Iran (something the Russian defense establishment has already taken careful note of). With both Romania and Bulgaria now part of NATO, Article 5 of the alliance's charter now applies. NATO can take action "in the event of crises which jeopardize Euro-Atlantic stability and could affect the security of Alliance members."

In this way, Pipelineistan meets the American Empire of Bases.

Young Turks and Wily Russians

Why is everyone so damn hooked on Central Asian oil and gas? Elshad Nasirov, deputy chairman of the state-owned Azerbaijani oil company SOCAR, sums the addiction up succinctly enough: "This is the place where there is oil and gas in abundance. It is not Arab, not Persian, not Russian, and not OPEC."

It's the Caspian and, unfortunately for Europe, the region could, in energy terms, turn out to be not the caviar for which it's renowned but so many rotten fish eggs. No one knows, after all, whether the EU will ever be able to buy Iranian gas via Nabucco. No one knows whether the Central Asian "stans" have enough gas to supply Russia, China, and Turkey, not to mention India and Pakistan. No one knows whether any of their leaders will have the nerve to renege on their deals with Gazprom.

Ever since a 2008 British study determined that Turkmenistan may have natural gas reserves second only to Russia on the planet, the European Commission has been on a no-holds-barred tear to lure that country into delivering some of its future gas directly to Europe—and not through the Russian pipeline system either. Turkmenistan's inscrutable leader, the spectacularly named Gurbanguly Berdymukhammedov, just has to say the word, but despite the claims of EU officials that he has agreed to send some gas Europe-wards, he's never offered a public word of confirmation. No wonder: with Nabucco unbuilt and a pipeline from his country to China still under construction, Turkmenistan can play Pipelineistan games only with Russia and Iran. In fact, Russia essentially controls the flow of Turkmen gas for the next 15 years.

Should Gurbanguly someday say the magic word—and assuming the Russians don't throw a monkey wrench into the works—he can marry Turkey, as the key transit country, with the EU and let them all sing Verdi till the sheep come home. In the meantime, angst is the name of the game in Europe (and so in Washington).

A declassified dossier from the *Federal'naya sluzhba bezopasnosti Rossiyskoy Federatsii* (FSB), the Russian heir to the KGB, is adamant: considering Nabucco's shortcomings, "Russia will remain the primary supplier of energy to Europe for the foreseeable future." Call it a matter of having your gas and processing it, too. Prime Minister Vladimir Putin has been making the point for years. If Europe tries to snub it, Russia will simply build its own LNG plants, to facilitate storage and transport, and sell its LNG all over the world.

Anyway it's worth paying attention to what the St. Petersburg State Mining Institute (where Putin earned his doctorate) has to say. According to the institute, Russia has only 20 years' worth of its own natural gas reserves left. Since Russia plans to sell up to 40% of its gas abroad, "Russian" gas may in the future actually mean Central Asian gas. All the more reason for the Russians to make sure that those massive Turkmen and other reserves flow north, not west.

Whatever Washington thinks, the Europeans know that energy independence from Russia is, in reality, inconceivable. Bottom line when it comes to natural gas: Europe needs everything—Nord Stream, South Stream, *and* Nabucco. The bulk of the natural gas in this Pipelineistan maze may well turn out to be Central Asian anyway and a substantial part could be Iranian, if the Obama administration ever normalizes relations with Iran.

That, then, is the current state of play in the European wing of Pipelineistan. Russia seems to have virtually guaranteed its status as the top gas supplier to Europe for the foreseeable future. But that brings us to Turkey, a key regional power for both the US and the EU. As President Obama has recognized, Turkey is both a real and a metaphorical bridge between the Christian and Muslim worlds. It is also an ideal transit country for carrying non-Russian gas to Europe and is now playing its own suitably complex Pipelineistan game.

Chances are that, like Ukhta in far off Siberia, you've never heard of Yumurtalik either. It's a fishing port squeezed between the Mediterranean Sea and the Taurus mountains, very close to Ceyhan, the terminal for two key nodes of Pipelineistan: the Kirkuk-Ceyhan pipeline from Iraq and the monster BTC pipeline. Turkey wants to turn Yumurtalik-Ceyhan into nothing less than the Rotterdam of the Mediterranean.

Even as it dreams of future EU membership, however, Turkey worries about antagonizing Moscow. And yet, being aboard the Nabucco Express and already fully committed to the functioning BTC pipeline puts the country on a potential collision course with Russia, its largest trading partner. Of course, this does not displease Washington.

On the other hand, the Turkish leadership draws ever closer to Iran, which provides 38% of Turkey's oil and 25% of its natural gas. Ankara and Tehran also have geopolitical affinities (especially in fighting Kurdish separatism). Together, they offer the best alternative to the Caucasus (Azerbaijan, Georgia) in terms of supplying Europe with Iranian natural gas. All this, of course, drives Washington nuts.

Needless to say, the Nabucco consortium itself would kill to have Iran as a gas supplier for the pipeline. They are also familiar with realpolitik: this could happen only with a Washington-blessed solution to the Iranian nuclear dossier. Iran, for its part, knows well how to seduce Europe. Mohammad Reza Nematzadeh, managing director of the National Iranian Oil Company (NIOC), has insisted Iran is Europe's "sole option" for the success of Nabucco.

Is Russia just watching all this gas go by? Of course not. In October 2007, Putin signed a key agreement with Iranian President Mahmoud Ahmadinejad: If Iran cannot sell its gas to Nabucco—a likelihood given the turbulence of American domestic politics and its foreign policy—Russia will buy it. Translation: Iranian gas could end up, like Central Asian gas, heading for Europe as more "Russian" gas. With its European and Iranian policies at cross-purposes, Washington will not be amused.

When Turkish Prime Minister Recep Tayyip Erdogan threatened to "rethink Nabucco" if the tricky negotiations for Turkey to enter the EU drag on forever, EU leaders got the message (as much as France and Germany may be against a "Europe without borders"). Pragmatically, most EU leaders know very well that they need excellent relations with Turkey to one day have access to the Big Prize, Iranian gas; and that puts Europe's energy and EU membership inclinations at loggerheads.

Last July in Ankara, Nabucco was formally launched by an intergovernmental agreement. The representatives of Turkey, Austria, Bulgaria, Romania and Hungary were there. Obama's special Eurasian envoy, Richard Morningstar (a veteran of the BTC adventure), was there as well. The Central Asian stans were not there.

But crucially, Gurbanguly, ever the showman, finally made an entrance without ever leaving Turkmenistan, (almost) uttering the magic words in a meeting with his ministers in the capital, Ashgabat, on July 10th: "Turkmenistan, staying committed to the principles of diversification of supply of its energy resources to the world markets, is going to use all available opportunities to participate in major international projects—such as, for example, [the] Nabucco project."

At the Vienna headquarters of Nabucco the mantra remains: this is "no anti-Russian project." Still, everyone knows that Russia's leaders are eager to kill it, and not a soul from Brussels to Vienna, Washington to Ashgabat, knows how to link Central Asia to Europe via a non-Russian pipeline, at the cost of more than $10 billion, without some assurance that Turkmeni, Kazakh, Azerbaijani, and/or Iranian natural gas will be fully (or even partially) on board. Who would be foolish enough to invest that kind of money without some guarantee that hundreds of miles of steel tubes won't remain empty? You don't need Verdi to tell you this is one hell of a quirky plot for a global opera.

October 2009. Originally at TomDispatch.com

IRAQ'S OIL AUCTION HITS THE JACKPOT

Former US Vice President Dick Cheney, ex-secretary of defense Donald Rumsfeld and assorted US neo-cons will have plenty of time to nurse their apoplexy. One of their key reasons to unleash the war on Iraq in 2003 was to seize control of its precious oilfields and thus shape a great deal of the New Great Game in Eurasia—the energy front—by restricting the access of Europe and Asia to Iraq's staggering 115 billion barrels of proven oil reserves.

After at least US$2 trillion spent by Washington and arguably more than a million dead Iraqis, it has come to this: a pipe dream definitely buried this past weekend in Baghdad with round two of bids to exploit a number of vast and immensely profitable oil fields.

The bids, supervised by the Oil Ministry, were presented on a live TV game show. Instead of *American Idol*, Iraqis got "Oil Idol." In a raucous carpet bazaar atmosphere, the ministry played "my way or the highway" and forced 44 foreign Big Oil corporations to cut to the max the fee they collect on every barrel extracted in Iraq and submit to 20-year contracts. These multinationals were not given a share in Iraqi oil production; they will be paid a $2 fee per barrel for raising output above a mutually agreed level.

Still, for Big Oil, the possibility of having a crack at all those megagiant fields in Shi'ite-controlled southeast Iraq—the largest concentration of its kind in the world—led all players to yell, "It's raining oil!" Once you've paid the ticket, you're inside the theater. And what a theater... The Iraqi government may end up paying foreign Big Oil as much as $50 billion for its know-how. All these "service" deals will dodge Iraq's parliament—which might throw a wrench in the works. And Big Oil will still get $2 for each barrel of extra crude above a minimum production target.

In June, Iraq held its first oil auction, offering foreign companies the chance to increase production at already-pumping fields. The latest auction was the first time foreign firms could bid on untapped fields. Of the ten groups of fields available, seven were awarded.

Win-win for Russia and China

Cheney's and Rumsfeld's script was never supposed to develop like this. Instead of US Big Oil getting the lion's share, strategic competitors Russia and China turned out to be big winners. Dick Cheney's "consolation prize" was an ExxonMobil-Shell alliance getting the phase 1 of West Qurna in early November. ExxonMobil had been the favorite to also win Rumaila (17.8 billion barrels of reserves). But a BP-CNPC (China National Petroleum Corporation) alliance got it in the end because unlike ExxonMobil they agreed to cut their fee per barrel down to the Oil Ministry-enforced $2.

CNPC (50%), along with partners Total from France (25%) and Petronas from Malaysia (25%), was also a big winner for Halfaya (4.1 billion barrels of reserves, projected output of 535,000 barrels per day (bpd)), southeast of Amara.

Petronas again (with 60%), and the Japan Petroleum Exploration Company (Japex), with 40%, will invest a cool $7 billion to develop Gharaf (reserves of around 860 million barrels, projected output of 230,000 bpd). Bidding was fierce. Losers were a joint Turkish-Indian bid, a Kazakh/South Korean/Italian consortium, and Pertamina from Indonesia.

A Petronas-Shell alliance got the highly coveted Majnoon (reserves of more than 12 billion barrels, projected output of 1.8 million bpd), near the Iranian border. Russia's Lukoil (85%), with junior partner Statoil (15%), got phase 2 of the immense West Qurna (located 65 kilometers northwest of Basra; about 12 billion barrels of reserves; projected production of 1.8 million bpd)—which in theory it had already bagged under Saddam Hussein. When Lukoil was stripped of its contract by Saddam, it blamed US-instigated UN sanctions, while Saddam blamed Lukoil itself.

West Qurna's phase 1 (8.7 billion barrels of reserves, with a projection to increase output from 300,000 bpd to 2.3 million bpd before 2016) was won in November by the aforementioned Exxon Mobil-Shell alliance. Losers were Total from France, a consortium of Petronas, Pertamina and Petrovietnam, and a BP-CNPC alliance.

Gazprom (40%), with junior partners TPAO, Kogas and Petronas, got Badra (projected production of 170,000 bpd). Unlike the mad scramble for the southern fields, no one even bid for the East Baghdad field, for obvious reasons: it's located in a virtual war zone. [1]

The Shi'ites are coming!

Iraq nationalized its oil industry in 1972. Now Big Oil is back with a vengeance. Iraqi Oil Minister Hussain al-Shahristani made no bones about Iraq's ambitions, saying, "Our principal objective is to increase our oil production from 2.4 million barrels per day to more than four million in the next five years." Iraq is at present exporting less oil than under Saddam, but it aims to export seven million barrels a day by 2016. Shahristani also insists "our country will have total control over production."

---

[1] To see which companies got what in detail, go here: http://www.iraqoilreport.com-/oil/production-exports/complete-round-2-results-3371/

That is enormously debatable.

For the moment, Prime Minister Nuri al-Maliki's government in Baghdad is obviously a winner. Iraq currently gets only $60 billion a year in oil revenues. It's not enough to rebuild a country destroyed by the Iran-Iraq war of the 1980s, UN sanctions and the American occupation. Arguably, Iraq's oil industry would not have sufficient funds, equipment and technical people to get back on its feet alone.

Whether with more oil revenues Baghdad will be able to impose law and order—starting with the capital—and fully equip its 275,000 military plus police forces, that's an open question. No one knows for sure who will be in control of Iraq in the near future, with parliamentary elections due early next year. A new government may be tempted to renegotiate these contracts, or even invalidate them.

In the next few years, with Iraq being able to reach the target of producing at least four million barrels a day, it's fair to argue this won't substantially influence the price of oil; but it will prevent it from shooting up out of proportion. China is now importing over four million bpd—and this will continue to rise. China by itself will be gobbling up any output increase in the global oil market.

What the early 2010s will definitely see is the rise of a relatively wealthy, Shi'ite-controlled Iraq friendly with Iran and Lebanon's Hezbollah. Essentially, Shi'ite Islam on the rise. The US-friendly autocracies and dictatorships in the Gulf will cry again, "It's the return of the Shi'ite crescent!" USt think-tanks may be tempted to define Maliki as the new Saddam. The only difference is that by then, Cheney and company will be safely ensconced in the dustbin of history.

December 2009

Welcome, comrade Maobama

Dear comrade Maobama,

It's such an honor to receive you here in the northern capital of the Middle Kingdom as you pay tribute to the hub of the already developing 21st-century multipolar world.

Excuse us if we may diverge for a while from the outlines of established diplomatic finesse, but as we fully admire your integrity, honesty and magnificent intellectual accomplishments, allow us to address you with a measured degree of frankness.

First of all, we congratulate you for the auspicious sales of *The Audacity of Hope* in the Chinese market—140,000 to date, and counting. But please excuse us as you won't be able to bask in the glow of wide-eyed, "audacity of hope" crowds as in Berlin, Ghana, Cairo, London or Paris. Certainly Sasha and Malia would be thrilled if you had the chance to snap up a commemorative comrade Maobama T-shirt in Houhai for a few undervalued yuan. You'd definitely look handsome in an olive-green Cultural Revolution suit and cap.

We are otherwise very pleased that you have just described yourself as "America's first Pacific president"—even boasting a half-brother living in our gloriously booming special economic zone, Shenzhen.

We find a remarkable convergence between "Pacific" and our own doctrine of *heping jueqi*—"sudden peaceful emergence." We are all pacifists at heart; if you're familiar with our doctrine you will know how it fully spells out why China is not a "threat" to the US. After all, our military budget is less than 20% of your military budget, and much less than the combined military budgets of Japan, India and Russia.

About our pacifist strain, President Hu Jintao—with whom you will have very detailed discussions—made it all very clear already during the administration of your predecessor George W Bush, when he announced his "four Nos" (no to hegemony; no to the politics of force; no to the politics of blocks; no to an arms race) and his "four Yes's" (yes to building trust; yes to attenuating difficulties; yes to developing cooperation; yes to avoiding confrontation).

We noticed you have also chosen to define us as "an essential partner" as well as a "competitor." Yes, we are very competitive. It's kind of built into your DNA when you have been a major economic power in the world for 18 of the past 20 centuries. If the "strategic reassurance" doctrine devised by your think-tanks works in the sense of respecting our competitive spirit as well as our views and customs, we certainly have no problems with that.

By the way, we're extremely pleased that you chose Tokyo, Japan, this past Saturday to finally reassure us that "the United States does not seek to contain China." But we were just wondering whether your generals—avid practitioners of the fullspectrumdominance doctrine—were listening.

Dear comrade, there are some things that we must clarify at once. We definitely won't bow to US pressure on our currency policy. Please listen to Liu Mingkang, chairman of the China Banking Regulatory Commission. He has just pressed the fact at a forum here in Beijing that the very weak US dollar and low US interest rates are creating "unavoidable risks for the recovery of the global economy, especially emerging economies," and this is "seriously impacting global asset prices and encouraging speculation in stock and property markets." We're afraid you're more part of the problem than the solution. If you had the chance to meet average Chinese in the streets of Beijing—oh, those pesky security arrangements—they would ask you why China should listen to US hectoring, when the US prints dollars like crazy and expects China to prop them up?

For our part of the world, we hope you have the opportunity to appreciate how sound are our economic fundamentals—with rising industrial production, retail sales and investments in fixed capital, and moderate deflation, as outlined by Sheng Laiyun, spokesman for the National Bureau of Statistics. Our economy will grow by 8% in 2009. Why? Because we have spent the past 11 months working 24-hours a day, investing productively in our economy, honing up our monetary policy and launching fiscal measures to support selected industrial sectors. We are forecasting a consumer boom lasting up to the next Chinese New Year on February 14, 2010. So our priority is to keep on growing; later we may think about devaluing the yuan.

Dear comrade, we're sure you'd marvel at the power of our three main industrial clusters. It's a pity you won't have time to visit the Pearl River Delta, the factory of the world, our hub of manufacturing and endless assembly lines. You might catch a glimpse of the Yang-Tze Delta—the hub of our capital-intensive industry and production of cars, semiconductors and computers. But if only you had enough time for a stroll in Zhongguancun, just outside of Beijing—our Silicon Valley.

A glimpse of just one of our immense info-tech malls, bursting with small businesses and eager, industrious, very well-educated youth, would imprint to you how technology has become China's new opium (without a war attached, as the British Empire imposed it on us in the 19th century). It makes us dream of a time when technological innovations originate in China and then swarm the world. Yes, we may have a cheap workforce—but most of all we have an extraordinarily motivated workforce, which is regimented under good health and education standards, has immense self-discipline and is fully mobilized for non-stop productive ends.

Dear comrade, now onwards to some more controversial matters. About that little war of yours in Afghanistan. You may have realized by now that it was China that actually won the "war on terror." And that explains in great measure why China is so much more influential now in East Asia—and around many parts of the world—than the US.

You may realize that as long as the Pentagon is fully deployed in West Asia we must be extremely careful. We closely follow the strategies deployed by your think-tanks. We are particularly amused by the strategy of our old friend Dr. Henry Kissinger, who proposes to integrate China in a reformed world order still revolving around a US axis—after all, this still translates as US hegemony. There are far more worrying aspects in-built in the encircling of China by a system of military bases and a strategic military alliance controlled by the US—a new Cold War in fact. We cannot abide by it, as it will only lead to the fragmentation of Asia and the Global South.

Rest assured that we can deal with both North Korea and Iran on our own—not confrontationally but harmoniously. And coming back to Afghanistan, we believe the best solution should be worked out within the cadre of the Shanghai Cooperation Organization (SCO)—of which ourselves and Russia are the key co-founders. This is an Asian problem—in terms of drug trafficking as much as religious fundamentalism—that should be debated and solved among Asian powers.

Dear comrade, you may have noticed that the Washington Consensus is for all purposes dead. What has emerged is what we might call the Beijing Consensus. China has shown the Global South that "there is an alternative"—a "third way" of independent economic development and integration to the global order. We have shown that unlike the Washington Consensus "one-size-fits-all" package, economic development has to be "local" in every case. Our beloved Little Helmsman Deng Xiaoping would have called it "development with local characteristics."

We have shown that developing states in the Global South must unite, not to hail US unilateralism but to organize a new world order based on economic independence and at the same time respectful of cultural and political differences. We have embarked on a yellow BRIC road—and it's not only us, Brazil, Russia, India and China, who are on to it; everybody else in the Global South is. Yet we are also aware that the rich North will always be trying to co-opt certain countries in the South to prevent that hierarchical change the world can believe in—which, as you may already know, is incarnated by China.

You may also have realized why China has consistently beaten hands down the elitist economic and financial institutions controlled by the North. After all, we offer countries all over the Global South much better deals to access their natural resources. We have been engaged in vast, complex infrastructure projects that invariably end up costing less than half the price charged by countries in the North. Our loans are more carefully targeted; they are impervious to political misunderstandings; and they don't come with exorbitant consultant fees attached.

You may have realized that key oil-producing countries have re-routed their excess capacity towards the South. Oil-wealthy countries from West Asia have started to heavily invest in East and South Asia some of the surplus that they normally would have directed to the US and Europe.

You may have noticed, comrade, that the monetarist counter-revolution is dead. So the question now is not whether Asia, and the Global South as a whole, will continue to use the US dollar as their exchange currency—that, of course, will go on for years. The key long-term question is whether they will continue to place their excess current account balances at the mercy of institutions controlled by the North, or if they will instead work towards the emancipation of the South. Your egalitarian instincts may agree with the latter, but we are certain the US ruling class will fight it tooth and nail.

Forgive us what may be perceived as impertinence, comrade. Of course—taking a leaf from the great master Lao Tzu—we are also aware of our shortcomings. We well know that it would be suicidal for even one-quarter of our population of 1.3 billion to adopt the mode of production and consumption known as the American way of life. We know that we must do more to protect the environment. Our 2006-2010 Five-Year Plan, for example, has made it a target to reduce energy consumption by 20%, and our industrial policy has shut down nearly 400 industrial sub-sectors and restricted a further 190. We well know what's at stake if, up to 2025, no less than 300 million peasants transfer themselves to our cities, where cars, including your American Buicks, already dwarf the number of bicycles.

We even acknowledge know many distortions may be implicit in our blind reproduction of the Western development model. To give you an example, when our foreign visitors go to The Place megamall in the central business district in Beijing and watch the largest suspended screen saver on Earth—featuring computer-generated images—they complain what a waste of energy this is. It's an addiction for which we still have no cure. We just can't get enough of malls—and SUVs, and Hummers and Ferrari dealerships on Jinbao Dajie...

We are well aware of hundreds of strikes and widespread social turmoil happening here every single month, involving especially the new Chinese working class—young internal migrants—that are the backbone of our enviable export industry. You may not believe it in the US, but of course there is a worker's movement in China—not one, but many, spontaneous and relatively unarticulated, all extremely active in virtually every city in the country.

We pay attention, and we are doing our best to attend to their grievances. Chairman Mao always alerted about *luan*—chaos—and nothing worries us more than social revolt in urban and rural areas. That's why we changed our policies, trying to correct development inequalities and passing new legislation offering more rights to workers.

At the same time, we always remember how comrade Deng Xiaoping's reforms first and foremost had to deal with the agricultural sector. That's why President Hu today is so concentrated on the development of education, health protection and social aid in the countryside. That's how we see the development of a "harmonious society."

To sum it all up, comrade Maobama. We really hope you appreciate the fabulous Peking duck in the company of comrade Hun Jintao, and that you conduct a frank exchange of views. And by the way, if you need a crash course on Chinese politics, don't bother to listen to your think-tanks; send a diplomat to a DVD shop to buy you a (pirate) copy of Zhang Yimou's *Curse of the Golden Flower*, with Chow Yun-fat and our gorgeous Gong Li. It's all there; the cult of secrecy and dissimulation; the logic and cruelty of competing clans; the sense of political tragedy; and how, in China, the *raison d'etat* trumps everything. Yes, we may be a violent society after all, but our violence is internalized. Chairman Mao's *luan* is our deepest fear; we fear most what ill we can inflict on ourselves. If we master our self-control, then we can be a true Middle Kingdom—between heaven and Earth. "Global superpower" is just an afterthought.

Anyway, as comrade Deng said, to get rich is glorious—the more so when you become the banker of the current global superpower. We will always be here for you when you need it—just please refrain from asking us to devalue the yuan. May you be blessed to conduct an auspicious and prosperous administration, and may you and your family live a long and fruitful life.

Respectfully yours,

The People's Republic of China

November 2009

CHINA PLAYS PIPELINEISTAN

For all the rhapsodies on the advent of the New Silk Road, it may have come into effect for good last week, when China and Central Asia got together to open a crucial Pipelineistan node linking Turkmenistan to China's Xinjiang.

By 2013, Shanghai, Guangzhou and Hong Kong will be cruising to ever more dizzying heights courtesy of gas supplied by the 1,833-kilometer Central Asia Pipeline from Turkmenistan—operating at full capacity. The pipeline will even help China achieve its goals in terms of curbing carbon emissions.

And in a few years China's big cities will also be cruising courtesy of oil from Iraq. (See Iraq's oil auction hits the jackpot *Asia Times Online*, December 16.)

China needs Iraqi oil. But instead of spending more than US$2 trillion on an illegal war, Chinese companies got some of the oil they needed from Iraq by bidding in a legal Iraqi oil auction. And in the New Great Game in Eurasia, instead of getting bogged down in Afghanistan, they made a direct deal with Turkmenistan, built a pipeline, profited from Turkmenistan's disagreements with Moscow (Gazprom stopped buying Turkmen gas last April, which cost the Central Asian "stan" $1 billion a month), and will get most of the gas they need.

The running myth is that China is addicted to oil. Coal would be more like it. The No. 1 global emitter of greenhouse gases, China still produces more than 70% of its energy from coal. Beijing will inevitably get deeper into biogas or solar energy, but in the short term most of the "factory of the world" runs on coal. Of its verified energy reserves, 96% are coal.

This does not imply that China's shortage of raw materials such as oil and iron ore does not have the possibility of materializing Beijing's planners' worst nightmare—making the country a hostage to foreign raw-material producers (iron ore plays a significant part in China's strategic relationship with Brazil). But diversifying oil supplies is a matter of extreme national security. When oil reached $150 a barrel in 2008—before the US-unleashed financial crisis—China's media accused foreign Big Oil of being "international petroleum crocodiles," and insinuated that the West's hidden agenda was ultimately to stop China's relentless development dead in its tracks.

Have sanctions won't travel

Twenty-eight percent of the world's total proven oil reserves are in the Arab world. China badly needs this oil—with its factories churning out everything from sneakers to laptops, its car market booming like there's no tomorrow (last month alone it produced 1.34 million vehicles), and Beijing constantly increasing its strategic oil reserves.

Few may know that China is actually the world's fifth largest oil producer, at 3.7 million barrels per day (bpd), just below Iran and slightly over Mexico. In 1980, China consumed only 3% of the world's oil. Now it's already around 10%—the world's second-largest consumer, overtaking Japan but still way behind the US at 27%.

According to the International Energy Agency (IEA), China will account for more than 40% of the increase in global oil demand up to 2030. And this assumes that China's gross domestic product will grow at "only" 6%. In 2009, even with the global financial crisis, China's GDP is expected to have grown 8%.

Saudi Arabia controls 13% of the world's oil production. It is the only swing producer capable of substantially increasing output. Not by accident, until recently it was China's main supplier—with 500,000 bpd.

China will get increasingly more oil from Iraq starting from 2013 or 2014. So from now on China National Petroleum Corp (CNPC) will be very well positioned. But it's the Iranian equation that's really complex.

Chinese companies committed to investing no less than a staggering $120 billion in Iran's energy sector over the past five years. Iran is already China's No 2 oil supplier. Sinopec has just signed another memorandum of understanding with the National Iranian Oil Refining and Distribution Co to invest an additional $6.5 billion to build oil refineries in Iran. Despite sanctions, trade between China and Iran grew 35% in 2009, to $27 billion.

Saudi Arabia—harboring extreme paranoia about the Iranian nuclear program—has offered to supply the Chinese the same amount of oil it currently imports from Iran, at much lower prices. Beijing scotched the deal. Then US President Barack Obama warned President Hu Jintao during his November visit to Beijing that the US would not be able to keep Israel from attacking Iran—as a tactic to persuade Beijing to agree to harsher sanctions.

Arguably nothing will happen in January, when China takes over the presidency of the UN Security Council. No matter what's spun in the US, Russia as well as China won't agree to more sanctions against Iran. But France takes over in February, and will definitely press the council to be harsher.

So many escape routes

From Beijing's point of view, both the US vs Iran conflict and the simmering US vs China strategic competition boil down to what could be called "escape from Hormuz and Malacca."

The Strait of Hormuz—the only entry to the Persian Gulf—at its narrowest is only 36km wide, with Iran to the north and Oman to the south. Roughly 20% of China's oil imports travel through it. Beijing frets at the sight of US aircraft carriers patrolling nearby.

The Strait of Malacca—very busy and very dangerous—at its narrowest is only 2.8km wide, with Singapore to the north and Indonesia to the south. As much as 80% of China's oil imports may travel through it.

The "escape" logic explains China's foray into Africa. China went to Africa because that continent is home to the few oilfields not owned by foreign Big Oil. When Chinese state oil companies buy equity stakes in African oilfields, they are protecting China from increases in oil prices, with the added bonus of no hassle—as happened in 2005 when China National Offshore Oil Corp (CNOOC) tried to buy Unocal in the US.

Hu Jintao goes to Africa every single year. Angola even overtook Saudi Arabia as China's main oil supplier in 2006. CNPC is extremely active in Sudan, owning equity in a number of oilfields. There are no fewer than 10,000 Chinese workers in Sudan building refineries and pipelines to the Red Sea. Beijing showers Khartoum with loans to build infrastructure. Sudan already is China's sixth oil supplier, responsible for about 6% of oil imports.

There are problems, of course. China's refineries deal mainly with low-sulfur sweet crude (predominant in African oilfields) rather than high-sulfur sour crude (predominant in Saudi Arabia). So more Chinese demand at first glance would mean the necessity to import more African oil. But that will change in time. China is building new refineries to process sour crude, some even financed by Saudi Arabia.

The road goes on forever

China's Central Asia strategy could be summed up as bye-bye Hormuz, bye-bye Malacca, and welcome to the New Silk Road.

Kazakhstan has 3% of the world's proven oil reserves. Its largest oilfields are not far from the Chinese border. China sees Kazakhstan as a key alternative oil supplier—with Pipelineistan linking Kazakh oilfields to Chinese refineries.

CNPC financed the Kazakh-China pipeline in 2005 (with a capacity of 400,000 bpd) and bought two-thirds of formerly Canadian PetroKazakhstan, which controls the Kumkol fields in the Turgai basin (the other third is owned by the Kazakh government) for $4.18 billion. And China Investment Corp, a sovereign wealth fund, bought 11% of KazMunaiGas Exploration Production (KMG), the oil production subsidiary of the national energy company, for $1 billion.

China's first transnational Pipelineistan adventure was the China-Kazakhstan oil link. But this does not detract at all from China-Russia Pipelineistan—in both oil and gas. Russian Prime Minister Vladimir Putin recently sealed more than $5 billion in deals with China, mostly on energy, advancing the agreement on a gas pipeline that will deliver up to 70 billion cubic meters of gas a year from Russia to China, according to Gazprom's Aleksey Miller.

But the Russia vs China chapter of Pipelineistan may be very tricky. Russia can at times behave as a strategic competitor. For example, the Kazakhstan-China pipeline operates with no hassle only for seven months a year. In winter the crude oil must be mixed with less viscous oils so it won't freeze. Russia supplies them. But Transneft delayed delivery of these additives in the winter of 2006, arguing that its own pipeline was already operating at the limit. CNPC was forced to transport the additives by rail from another part of Kazakhstan for a lot of money.

Central Asia—via Turkmenistan—will definitely be China's major supplier of gas, but on the oil front, it's much more complex. Even if all the "stans" sold China every barrel of oil they currently pump, the total would be less than half of China's daily needs.

This means that ultimately only the Middle East can placate China's thirst for oil. According to the IEA, China's oil demand will rise to 11.3 million barrels a day by 2015, even with its domestic production peaking. Compare that with what some of China's alternative suppliers are producing: Angola at 1.4 million bpd, Kazakhstan at 1.4 million as well, and Sudan at 400,000.

On the other hand, Saudi Arabia produces 10.9 million bpd, the United Arab Emirates 3.0 million, Kuwait 2.7 million—and then there's Iraq, bound to reach 4 million by 2015. But Beijing is still not convinced—not with all those US "forward operating sites" in the United Arab Emirates (UAE), Bahrain, Kuwait, Qatar and Oman, plus a naval battle group in the Persian Gulf.

China may also count on a South Asia option. China spent $200 million on the first phase of construction of the deep-water port of Gwadar in Balochistan. It wanted—and it got from Islamabad—"sovereign guarantees to the port's facilities." Gwadar is only 400km from Hormuz. From Gwadar, China can easily monitor traffic in the strait.

But Gwadar is infinitely more crucial as the pivot of the virtual Pipelineistan war between TAPI and IPI. TAPI is the Turkmenistan-Afghanistan-Pakistan-India pipeline, which will never be built as long as a US/NATO foreign occupation is fighting the Taliban in Afghanistan. IPI is the Iran-Pakistan-India pipeline, also known as the "peace pipeline" (TAPI would be the "war pipeline" then?). Iran and Pakistan have already agreed to build it, much to Washington's distress.

In this case, Gwadar will be a key node. And if India pulls out, China already has made it clear it wants in; China would build another Pipelineistan node from Gwadar across the Karakoram highway towards Xinjiang. That would be a classic case of close energy cooperation among Iran, Pakistan and China—and a major strategic Pentagon defeat in the New Great Game in Eurasia.

An additional complicating factor is that India harbors infinite suspicion about a Chinese "string of pearls"—ports along China's key oil supply routes, from Pakistan to Myanmar. Washington still believes that if TAPI is built, India will refrain from breaking the US-enforced embargo on Iran. But for India it would be a much safer—and strategically sounder—deal to align with IPI than with TAPI.

A Maoist drenched in oil

For China there's also an "escape to South America" option. In the Venezuelan overall strategy it's essential to sell more oil to China so as to lower its heavy dependence on the US market. According to the existing terms of the China-Venezuela partnership, four tankers and at least two refineries will be built—one in the immensely oil-rich Orinoco Belt in Venezuela and the other in Guangdong. State-owned Petroleos de Venezuela (PDVSA) will be responsible for shipping the oil to China.

The Venezuelan target is to export 500,000bpd in 2009—already reached—and 1 million by 2012. President Hugo Chavez—who in typical colorful manner described himself as a "Maoist" during his last visit to China—wants Venezuela to be no less than China's top oil supplier. China's energy analysts take this partnership extremely seriously; it means that Venezuela could replace Angola. Currently, according to China's Ministry of Commerce, Angola, Saudi Arabia and Iran are its top three oil suppliers.

Meanwhile, China has retrofitted many of its coal-fired plants in the past few years, and is accelerating moves to bypass high-intensity carbon-emitting technology, rebuilding its steel and cement industries. The country spends $9 billion a month on clean energy. There are plenty of wind farms across the countryside. A Shenzhen company is the world leader in lithium-ion battery technology. The first affordable, global electric car is bound to be made in China.

According to the China Greentech Initiative, the potential green market in China could reach a staggering $1 trillion a year by 2013—that is, 15% of China's gross domestic product by then.

But for the moment, Beijing's strategic priority has been to develop an extremely meticulous energy supply policy—with sources in Russia, the South China Sea, Central Asia, the East China Sea, the Middle East, Africa and South America.

As masterly as China may be able to play Pipelineistan, it will stride ever more confidently into a green future.

December 2009

STARING AT THE ABYSS

As far as precious little corners of paradise in Southeast Asia go, one could hardly ask for more. An isolated octagonal house with a beautiful garden, owned by a retired couple from California, facing a volcanic rock beach to the north of the tropical island of Bali, with the only locals being fishermen who at night set out on a *junkuh*—the elegant, wooden predecessor of the catamaran—to scour the calm, warm waters for tuna and barracuda.

The night is mostly pitch black—courtesy of punctual power shortages from the grid in distant Java. The sound is the usual, cacophonous tropical jungle "silence"—deafened by the inevitable daily storm. There's not much to do except sit at the seaside bale, pinpoint the kerosene lamps identifying the *junkuh*, and stare at the Bali sea.

But this being Bali, where everything is a matter of *sekala* and *niskala*, soon I saw myself staring at the abyss.

Sekala is the fabulous, fascinating Balinese world of ritual, ceremony, dance, drama and endless daily offerings to the spirit world. But the real action is in *niskala*—the occult, the magic underlining it all. In Bali definitely what you see is not what you get.

So while staring at the sea I was actually thinking about the late, great Howard Zinn, American historian, author and activist who died on January 27 this year, and his take on this sorry world of non-stop war and infinite injustice; Zinn asked how can we "stay socially engaged," committed to a struggle for justice and truth, and still keep our sanity and not become resigned or cynical, or turn into a vegetable, or totally burn out.

Did I miss much while staring at the Bali sea? Oh, the usual shop of horrors. The ghost of Osama bin Laden released a new audio hit blasting the US for global warming and inciting everyone to dump the US dollar (the ghost is right on both counts). Pakistani Taliban supremo Hakeemullah Mehsud may or may not have been blasted to bits by a US drone (who cares? His replacement is already in business). US President Barack Obama's surge duly proceeds as a Kill Bill-style killing spree on both sides of the AfPak border. The CIA swears al-Qaeda will try another hit inside the US within the next six months. There was a corporate takeover of American democracy (so why not "elect" US politicians by auction, once and for all?) and neo-cons are now rehashing the mantra "Bomb, Bomb Iran" as the only way for Obama to save his presidency.

So the moment I laid my eyes on the Internet, borrowing the satellite dish signal of my neighbor Hans, a Dutch architect who wisely said byebye to cranky, fearful, priced-out and reactionary Europe—the Bali sea instantly vanished. It was not only a matter of *niskala* taking over *sekala*. It was a matter of being sucked back into the realm of the hungry ghosts—and all that's left in this case is the abyss, as in the Pentagon's "long war."

Ghosts in regalia

Last weekend, the Pentagon told the Obama administration to tell the whole of US media that it was stepping up its war machine (from extra Patriot missile batteries in Bahrain, Kuwait, Qatar and the UAE to Aegisclass cruisers on permanent patrol) against possible missile attacks by Iran on those helpless peons to democracy—the Arab Gulf petromonarchies.

The operative word is "possible." Former president George W Bush's preventive war ethos rules more than ever in Washington. It does not matter that the possibility of Tehran launching a first strike on any US Arab ally is as high as corporations not owning US democracy. And by the way, what happened to missile defense in Eastern Europe, also supposed to protect it from those same evil Tehran missiles?

So Pentagon logic now totally rules. The Pentagon assumes Iran will now prop up its own defenses. Thus the Pentagon may claim that Iran is "threatening its neighbors"—and deploy even more military might. It's the logic of an arms race, which Tehran obviously cannot keep up with, that may give the Pentagon the "defensive" excuse it's been waiting for, so one more war can be marketed to the battered US populace.

Pentagon hawks, always oblivious to internal political subtleties of "The Other"—the developing world enemy *du jour*—obviously ignore that for the regime in Tehran the key existential threat now is the internal opposition movement. The military dictatorship of the mullahtariat has better fish to fry than to launch a missile at Dubai's Burj Khalifa, the tallest man-made structure ever built.

The whole thing still qualifies as a tragicomedy when added to the fact that the Pentagon was forced to admit its attempt to shoot down a mimicked Iran ballistic missile miserably failed, courtesy of a "rogue" Raytheon radar.

To top it all, tragicomedy finally melts into farce as US Secretary of State Hillary Clinton "warns" China that it must support more sanctions against Iran—as if Beijing would agree to what amounts to an act of war against one of its key energy partners, especially after the Obama-approved US$6.4 billion arms sale to US client Taiwan, which includes 60 Black Hawk helicopters, Patriot missiles and advanced Harpoon missiles that can be used against land or ship targets, all of them obviously mainland Chinese.

The US Senate also approved a bill that would punish companies for exporting gasoline to Iran or helping Iran to expand its oil refining capability—by the way, this is another act of war. All these moves obviously have to be seen within the "grand chessboard" (copyright Dr. Zbigniew Brzezinski, former US national security advisor) of the New Great Game in Eurasia and the irreversible decline of the American empire/ascension of China. The Beijing collective leadership is not exactly quaking in their Ferragamos.

What does it take for Washington elites to realize that mini-acts of war simply won't intimidate a military dictatorship of the mullahtariat, which is now fighting internally for its own survival? President Mahmud Ahmadinejad himself—for all his outbursts—has been wily enough to defuse the whole nuclear issue, saying on Iranian state TV the country would have "no problem" to send its low-enriched uranium abroad at 3.5% for further enrichment at 20% and taking it back four or five months later, as dictated by the UN. This voids any possible rationale for an attack on Iran by the US, Israel, or both. But it does not mean the attack won't happen.

The Islamic regime's short-term strategy is to lump all internal opponents as lackeys of the US and Israel and at the same time beef up its already considerable prestige in the Arab street as well as around the Muslim world as resisters to American imperialism. Meanwhile, in the US, the Israel lobby, industrial-military hawks, the Republican right and corporate media will keep up relentless pressure on Obama to "act." The abyss scenario for 2010 reads like a crescendo series of Washington ultimatums against an already cornered military dictatorship of the mullahtariat. There can only be one terrible outcome; Tehran surrenders, or the dogs of war will be unleashed.

Barry does Indonesia

And all this is still part of a larger—warring—picture. This week, Pentagon supremo Robert Gates released two new key documents—the Quadrennial Defense Review (QDR in Pentagon-speak), and the Pentagon's 2011 defense budget proposal, at a staggering $708.2 billion (plus a request for $3 billion to help pay for the AfPak war).

The QDR (one year in redaction, full support of the Joint Chiefs of Staff) may have, at least in theory, finished off with Bush's pre-emptive war doctrine. But still it paints a Hieronymus Bosch-like picture of Hobbesian hell—including everything from suicide bombers attacking inside the US to waves of attacks against the worldwide US Empire of Bases, biological terrorist attacks and even Taiwan being attacked by—what else?—Chinese missiles.

The new arsenal of weapons Gates needs was immaculately described by a top Pentagon civilian strategist as "a broad portfolio of military capabilities with maximum versatility across the widest possible spectrum of conflict." Problem is, all those masses of supremely equipped American soldiers will still have no ground intelligence and won't be able to speak a single "hello" in a foreign language. So much for conquering the hearts and minds of the inscrutable "other."

The hungry ghosts are having a ball. Early this week, the US launched Cobra Gold—its mega-military exercise in the Pacific in cooperation with allies Thailand, Japan, South Korea, Singapore and Indonesia. The Pentagon, industrial-military and political elites, and their courtiers in the American corporate media would rather crave then abandon the mindset of a "long war" for global hegemony.

Obama will come to Indonesia next month to relive his "Little Barry" 1967-1971 Jakarta years and practice his Bahasa Indonesia vocabulary. It might do him some good to skip Java for a while and go Balinese. Maybe staring at the sea will make him see *niskala*—and prevent him from being permanently engulfed by the realm of the hungry ghosts.

February 2010

Happy Birthday, Comrade Kim

It's a cold, crisp, sunny morning in the capital of the Democratic People's Republic of Korea (DPRK), and there could not be a more important game in town. Billboards bearing the numbers "2.16 [February 16]"—usually decorated with huge red flowers—are all over the place. The flowers are the only splashes of full color against drab grays and browns. They are of course kimjongilia, a modified begonia programmed to bloom exactly on—when else—2.16.

For Pyongyang's 2 million or so residents, it's time to party. Today is the 68th birthday of the general secretary of the Worker's Party of Korea, chairman of the DPRK National Defense Commission and Supreme Commander of the Korean People's Army—comrade Kim Jong-il.

Kim Jong-il, aka the Dear Leader, has been the maximum leader of North Korea for almost 12 years now. But he's not the president (the titular head of state is the chairman of the presidium of the Supreme People's Assembly, Kim Yong-nam.) A key reason is that he's not very fond of the endless, obligatory diplomatic round of meeting foreign heads of state.

The relentlessly apocalyptic Western media narrative would lead one to believe that on this eventful day the citizens of what is routinely depicted as a "Stalinist/communist/terrorist/totalitarian/insane/rogue/axis of evil gulag" would be one step short of showering a battery of commemorative missiles over South Korea, Japan or the west coast of the US for that matter, not to mention conduct another nuclear test. Reality though bears no "axis of evil" overtones.

Holiday on ice

The day starts with an early morning visit to the imposing bronze statue of president Kim Il-sung—aka the Great Leader, the father of the nation—on top of Mansu hill. It is officially 20 meters high (and certainly looks bigger). At the end of the Japanese colonial period, this site housed the largest Shinto shrine in Pyongyang; thus the Great Leader's statue had to be no-holds-barred imposing.

Everyone and his neighbor seems to have come, bringing flowers, bowing respectfully, and always arriving in neatly arranged groups, from soldiers and high-ranking officials to village elders and the very good-looking traffic ladies in their blue winter jackets. Higher ups arrive with their wives in black Mercedes or Audis, the men in black suits, the women sporting extremely elegant and colorful versions of the Korean national dress.

Then it's off to an international figure skating exhibition—not competition—that includes athletes from England, Switzerland, Ukraine, Belarus and even a Russian, who was a bronze medalist in the 2006 Turin Winter Olympics, a favorite of the crowd. Call it Pyongyang's counterpart to the 2010 Vancouver Winter Olympics. The real stars though are the locals skaters, kids included, and their apotheosis routine bearing the North Korean flag and the *Juche* flag—with its hammer, sickle and flame, symbolizing workers, peasants and intellectuals who, according to Kim Il-sung, are "the true masters of society," as "creators of both material and spiritual wealth."

Next stop is the 14th Kimjongilia Festival—a wacky, dazzling flower extravaganza with arrangements offered by everyone from military organs, ministries, national agencies and cooperatives to businesses, overseas Koreans, international organizations and foreign embassies, all featuring the hybrid red begonia (not the national flower of North Korea though; that's the magnolia). The "flower of Kim Jong-il" was created by a Japanese botanist in 1988, symbolizing, according to the official narrative, "wisdom, love, justice, and peace." The Great Leader Kim Il-sung, of course, has his own flower, the Kimilsungia.

The hall is absolutely packed. Everyone seems to have a portable digital camera that somehow materialized from China, and whole families and reams of schoolchildren are eager to pose for a flowery photo of ruby red Kimjongilias enveloping globes, displayed under depictions of high-speed trains, under emblems of the Dear Leader himself and even flanked by mini-replicas of Taepodong missiles.

Then it's time for a mass open-air dance in a square flanked by government buildings—well, not really "mass"; a few hundred couples, the men in dark suits and the women in white, jade green, light pink, cream or black *chima* (skirt) and *jogori* (blouse), the "evocative of the fairies in the heavens" Korean national dress. They are all dancing to traditional songs blared to ear-splitting level by what could be dubbed the North Korean version of the Jamaican sound system.

The few steps are very simple, involving a bit of handclapping; the few gaping foreigners are welcomed to join the fun. The locals perform it all stone-faced, although not robotically. Sex in North Korea is not exactly in the air. Schools are segregated by sex. Even holding hands in public is considered very improper behavior. Unmarried single mothers are virtually non-existent (but if it happens, the newborn is meticulously taken care of by the state—just as Korea war orphans were.)

The highlight of the day is synchronized swimming—in an arena in the sports village. The elaborate ballets, performed by dozens of teenagers, rival China's. Kimjongilia panels adorn the arena. Party elders and higher ups get the best seats. The foreign figure skating stars are also attending. The highlight is a stunning aquatic socialist ballet featuring a native siren in red swimsuit.

That's it; then socialist formalism dissolves, and the locals are off to dinner with relatives, mostly using the metro (two lines), or the aging, mobile works of socialist realism that are the local buses and trams. Some folk may eventually go bowling in the state-of-the-art Pyongyang Golden Lane Bowling Alley (45 lanes in fact; a detailed diagram on the wall shows the itinerary followed by Kim Il-sung on its inauguration day, and even all the spots where he stood). One fact though stands out; all through these merry proceedings, the Dear Leader Kim Jong-il himself was nowhere to be seen.

To be or not to be

Kim Jong-il was born on February 16, 1942, in an anti-Japanese guerrilla camp near Khabarovsk, just across the border from Manchukuo in occupied China. By this time, both his parents had been fighting the Japanese occupation for no less than 10 years.

All trap doors in secretive North Korea seem eventually to lead to what is in fact the royal Kim family—whose Shakespearean saga, if ever brought to a TV mini-series (maybe a Chinese or Hong Kong investor?) would undoubtedly enthrall a global audience.

The Dear Leader's father Kim Il-sung, over six feet tall and sporting a broad forehead (a big thing among Korean mothers), was charisma personified. His mother, Kim Chong-suk, widely revered as the ultimate anti-Japanese heroine, was less than five feet tall, pear-shaped, always in guerrilla fatigues, with a round, wide, smiling face, friendly but not very well educated. Kim Jong-il looks more like mom. And to put it mildly, that has made him extremely uneasy all his life.

While he was still a boy, Kim Jong-il suffered two terrible traumas; the accidental drowning of his younger brother in 1947, and the death of his mother in childbirth in 1949. That's when—sporting a state-issued polyester summer uniform and plastic shoes—he started going to gender-segregated elementary school.

Fast forward, and the plot thickens. The focus now is on Kim Jong-nam, Kim Jong-il's son—and until recently heir not-so-apparent (for years he's been living in China on and off). And also on Li Nam-ok, Kim Jong-il's daughter, adopted by him to tutor and play with his beloved son. She is from an aristocratic landowning family from, well, the enemy, South Korea. And although she was born—and lived—with a silver spoon in her mouth, inevitably there would come a day when she would rebel.

The great love of Kim Jong-il's life is and has always been his mistress, the ravishing—and also Southern aristocrat—Sung Hae-rim, the absolute top North Korean movie star. She happens to double as Li Nam-ok's aunt. And it gets even juicier—she is Kim Jong-nam's mother. This means Kim Jong-nam, a possible future DPRK leader (but by now bypassed by his youngest half-brother Kim Jong-un) is technically an illegitimate son.

Kim Jong-nam, tall and handsome like his grandfather Kim Il-sung, grew up much like Pu Yi—the last emperor of China; hyper-protected, hyper-pampered and in fact cloistered in the most cloistered society on the planet. At first he was educated by palace tutors, and had a court attending to his every whim. Meanwhile Li Nam-ok was developing different roles; at first she was his playmate, then his teacher, till finally she became his sister.

And here lies a crucial plot twist; these brother-and-sister royals lived virtually their whole early life as strangers in their own land. That's definitely, deeply imprinted in the psyche of a possible future North Korean leader.

Later as teenagers, both Kim Jong-nam and Li Nam-ok were sent to expensive secondary schools in Geneva—with the inevitable corollary of partying with the rich and famous in Paris. That's when *la dolce vita* made Li Nam-ok "betray" North Korea. Now she believes that even Kim Jong-il himself regards as nonsense the monolithic official narrative of post-1912 North Korea—the year the father of the nation, Kim Il-sung, was born.

Arguably the best informed source available anywhere on Kim Jong-il is Li Nam-ok herself, through her *Breaking North Korean Silence: Kim Jong-il's Daughter, A Memoir*, written by Imogen O'Neill. Here one learns that the Dear Leader is very intelligent and very sensitive—a prudish and rather shy guy who'd rather stay at home and work in his pyjamas, as indeed he does.

He is not the socializing type—he'd probably rather drop dead than join Facebook. That in itself would explain why he didn't make a public appearance on "2.16." Like a grand maestro, Kim Jong-il apparently orchestrates all manner of North Korean spectaculars but is bored to tears to show up. He also seems to have a sharp comment about everything—solutions included—and is capable of mimicking virtually anyone. And—very important—he loves to laugh.

He apparently quit smoking a few years ago and drinks basically at formal occasions. Surprisingly for many, he is said to be not at all fond of the non-stop hero worship. In a very Korean manner, he's a family man, whose company he prefers to anybody else's. He seems to keep Joseph Stalin's timetable—waking up in the middle of the night, working through the early morning and sleeping before noon. He used to like partying, when his 20 or so preferred guests indulged in beer, imported

French cognac and ginseng whisky. But then the system's elite can do the same in selected Pyongyang hotels.

As much as he may dislike the DPRK's massive bureaucracy, he could not but be acutely aware of his own—and the state's—security; he only trusts his close relatives. The top commanders in charge of Pyongyang's security are four brothers who are in-laws to Kim Jong-il's sister. In a nutshell, Kim Jong-il seems not to suffer fools, nor sycophants, gladly; he'd rather listen to honest straight-shooters, a rare commodity in his circle.

It comes as no surprise that Kim Jong-il could never be immune from the seductive soft power of American and Western mass culture. He's an inveterate fan of Western post-modernity. Thus the array of Sony LED televisions in every room of his many palatial abodes, which means that Kim Jong-il may tune in to every trashy offering on Japanese, South Korean and American cable. He surfs the Internet every day and is very well informed in a variety of issues. He's a collector with an immense video and DVD library, especially from Hollywood. He loves classical music but also the Rolling Stones, the Beach Boys and Pink Floyd (there's a fabulous black and white photo of Kim Jong-il in 1977 with rebel hair and dark glasses. What would be his Western role model then? Joe Strummer of The Clash? Would he be listening to *White Riot*?)

And then there's his fleet of over 20 cars, including American brands but most of all his now iconic black armored Mercedes S-600 with tinted windows, sometimes glimpsed in Pyongyang's boulevards (but not on this 2.16).

Whether or not he's the Dr. Evil portrayed by Western corporate media, what is certain is that Kim Jong-il urgently has to sort out plenty of turbulence rattling the DPRK.

The house the Great Leader built

Close observation of Pyongyang reveals that the North Korean system may be now like an overlapping maze of Chinese boxes—some more elaborate than others, but all very circumscribed in trying to defeat the law of gravity and keep their relative privileges. The "law of gravity" in this case is an economy that's been in chronic crisis for the past two decades.

Kim Jong-il's official "military-first" policy means heavy weaponry benefits from 25% to 30% of North Korea's annual budget (well, the US shifts 19% of federal spending and 44% of tax revenues to the Pentagon; the Iraq and AfPak wars, both funded by borrowing from foreign powers, have cost each American family $25,000, according to Canadian media). But the crucial problem is that the army now has become more important than the Worker's Party, which in a socialist system spells certified disaster for the toiling, loyal masses. The party still regiments no less than over a third of the DPRK's adult population.

The massive bureaucracy has acquired a life of its own. The historically centralized, and bureaucratically planned, supply of goods and services by the state sometimes breaks down to a halt at the local level. There's a tremendous generation gap/shock between the old Korean War (1950-1953) revolutionaries and the baby boomers—the North Korean version.

The only Great Leader that North Korea ever had has been dead for almost 16 years—and the official narrative can be seen as a perpetual meditation/mourning of this loss. And there's one confrontation after another with the United States.

Kim Jong-il must think that North Korea definitely is not Somalia; this is a much more developed and modern economy. But what is it, exactly?

The house the Great Leader Kim Il-sung built from scratch could possibly be described as an ultra-nationalist, family values, Confucian corporate state. It is Confucian in its profound respect for the family and its respect for a supposedly enlightened, learned elite. Chu Hsi, the founder of neo-Confucianism during the Song Dynasty (960-1279) would arguably feel at home in the DPRK.

As for nationalism, it manifested himself, for instance, by the choice of a "pure" indigenous language, based on an alphabet invented by King Sejong in the early 15th century, and thus not contaminated by either English or Japanese.

But the most striking aspect of North Korea's official narrative is that no less than five millennia of very rich history are condensed and everything is telescoped to April 15, 1912, the birth date of Kim Il-sung ("the day of the Sun") and the ground zero of the *juche* (pronounced chuch'e) idea.

Juche was Kim Il-sung's indigenous remix of Marxism/Leninism/Stalinism inflected with heavy boosts of Confucianism and metaphysics. On face value, *juche* means "self-reliance" and independence, not only in ideology and politics but also in all matters economic. *Juche* was in action already in 1955, when the DPRK declared its independence from the USSR, and again in the mid-1960s, when it reaffirmed its independence from both the USSR and China. It was to a great extent by formalizing *juche* that Kim Il-sung was revered all over the developing world as one of the great 1950s icons of decolonization.

Bruce Cumings, arguably the best American scholar on North Korea, gets straight to the point: "The term is really untranslatable; the closer one gets to its meaning, the more the meaning slips away. For a foreigner its meaning is ever-receding, into a pool of everything that makes Koreans Korean, and therefore ultimately inaccessible to the non-Korean. *Juche* is the opaque core of North Korean national solipsism."

In his own book *On the Juche Idea* (1982), a perennial best-seller at the Foreign Languages Publishing House in Pyongyang, Kim Jong-il seems to break away from the DPRK's irredeemable solipsism to trace a surefire path for economic development. He writes that "heavy industry with the machine-building industry as its backbone is the pillar of an independent national economy." This in turn will "accelerate the development of light industry and agriculture," and it must be coupled with "solving the problem of food on one's own through successful farming."

In sum: "If one is to be economically self-sufficient and develop the economy on a safe basis and with a long-term perspective, one must depend on one's own raw materials and fuel sources."

Is it working? Not exactly. Kim Jong-il has roughly a little over two years to turn things around—amid insistent rumors about his health and his succession—and, in official terminology, "open the gate to a thriving nation in 2012," when there will be a massive national party to celebrate the centenary of the birth of Great Leader Kim Il-sung.

So no wonder in the end he had better things to do than show up for his own birthday party. But a few nagging questions remain. Considering his background and his tastes, does he ever feel like escaping from his own fortress? Does this certified recluse harbor the subversive thought of going to a mall somewhere in the West and watching a disaster movie in a cineplex, just like anybody else? Or ultimately would this movie buff— author of the quite decent *On the Art of the Cinema* (1973)—rather be the star in an alternative plot?

February 2010

THE BRIC POST-WASHINGTON CONSENSUS

The BRIC countries (Brazil, Russia, India and China) got together in the Brazilian capital, Brasilia, on Thursday with a bang. After meeting Chinese President Hu Jintao, and once again condemning an "asymmetric, dysfunctional globalization," Brazilian President Luiz Inacio Lula da Silva was at his ebullient best: "A new global economic geography has been born." Well, not quite. Not yet.

Anyone across the world fed up with Somali pirates in Zegna suits disrupting global trade is interested in what the BRICs are (potentially) up to. The world's largest developing countries, bound to be the engine of the global economy for the next four decades, are essentially up to what then Russian President Vladimir Putin outlined in his famous speech in Munich in 2007; forming a new global consensus. Call it the rise of the periphery (the "Second" and "Third" worlds). Call it the dawn of the post-Washington Consensus.

It's nothing short of ironic that major players in the current global financial architecture are being forced to acknowledge that the global "economic and political tectonic plates are shifting." No, that was not Lula, but the George W Bush-appointed head of the World Bank, Robert Zoellick. Zoellick even felt compelled to deliver the coup de grace to the patronizing concept of "Third World."

Is the World Bank finally waking up to the real world(s)? The BRICs met in Brazil roughly one week before the World Bank and International Monetary Fund annual love fest in Washington. The old order may resent it, but the BRIC voice is and will continue to be ever more insistent.

No wonder; they are shelling more funds to the International Monetary Fund (IMF), thus they should have more say on where the money is going. They want an antithesis of Wall Street: transparency. The 2008 financial crisis—which by no means is over—was unleashed by a Wall Street-biased financial casino.

Strategic and transparent

The BRICs officially met for the first time in Yekaterinburg, Russia, in June 2009. At the time they delved deep into discussing the global financial crisis and advanced the possibility of dumping the US dollar as the world's reserve currency.

Now their common strategy is much more subtle. The leaders in these four countries know it's still too early to think about a common currency; first they need a potent unifying ideal. The inevitable outcome will be a common market, and then a common currency. The euro took 50 years to be born.

So no wonder, at the moment, as China's Foreign Ministry would put it, the mood is still kind of mellow, with plenty of rhetoric about "South-South cooperation," "strategic partnerships," "common development" and "common understanding." But the call for "more transparency" is very substantial; it will be hammered over and over again at the Americans and Europeans during the next Group of 20 (G-20) meeting in Canada in June.

Unlike the US, the BRICs' health is sound; no lingering financial crisis, decent growth rates. All of these countries are regional leaders. Unlike the US—and the rest of the world has noticed it—they have all preserved a very privileged role for public investment in their development model.

The BRICs may represent 42% of the world's population, roughly 15% of the world's gross domestic product, and almost 30% of world trade. But they're not even constituted as a commercial bloc such as the European Union or Mercosur trade blocs. At least not yet.

So the road will be long. BRICs are starting by getting their commercial act together—like setting up closer cooperation between development banks in Brazil, India and China for an array of partnership projects.

In Brasilia, experts for example discussed the Brazil-Argentina experience of trading in local currencies, the real and the peso—and not in US dollars. The next stage, as Russian President Dmitry Medvedev has enthusiastically pointed out, includes multiple cooperation deals on agricultural technology, nuclear energy, aircraft engineering, space exploration and nanotechnology.

The new world order

BRIC is rife in internal contradictions. China and India are on a collision course in terms of Asian preeminence. China is not exactly fond of India trying to get a seat at the UN Security Council. China and India fiercely compete to get as much oil and gas from Central Asia as possible. Russia is acutely aware of Chinese expansion in Siberia. India is not exactly fond of Brazil—one of the world's top food exporters—wanting to slash tariffs on agricultural products. Brazilian Finance Minister Guido Mantega sounds like a US Treasury official when he calls for the yuan to be revalued; cheap imports are killing Brazilian manufacturers as much as it killed America's.

But these internal contradictions pale compared to the BRICs' common agenda of being very careful not to antagonize Washington. As much as they know that the new multipolar world cannot have a center—

which at the moment is in a Washington that, with the exception of military hegemony, is largely impotent—China, for instance, has built an economy battling with Japan to become the world's second-largest economy by profiting from the current US-centered system.

The BRICs may complement each other in many aspects (Brazil and China are the best example; China has toppled the US as Brazil's largest trading partner). But a key problem is that they cannot speak for the rest of the developing and undeveloped world—as much as China will keep successfully exporting its "model" of soft power, belief in multipolarity, non-political interference, integrated development and technology transfer.

The world anyway will never become "flat"—this is a silly neoliberal, simplistic fantasy. A new global political consensus would have to be formulated by the UN—but not a UN dominated by the US; ideally this should be under a reformed UN, with an expanded and fully representative UN Security Council. One thing is certain; entrenched elites in both the US and Europe (which for all practical purposes is now a midget in the global arena) will fight the dilution of their power tooth and nail.

BRICs anyway will keep insisting on remaking the global financial architecture—and that starts with profound reforms at the Bretton Woods institutions. They will be increasingly more powerful inside the G-20—and that has already reduced the Group of Eight to irrelevancy. It's very enlightening to see how they have evolved their common position on burning issues such as the Iranian nuclear dossier: once again they have stressed in Brasilia they want dialogue, not confrontation, sanctions and threats.

So the BRIC name of the game may be evolution—not revolution. But the game itself is clear; full speed ahead towards the post-Washington Consensus.

April 2010

IRAN, SUN TZU AND THE DOMINATRIX

Let's face it: Hillary Clinton is one hell of a dominatrix.

At first the US Secretary of State said the Brazil-Turkey mediation to get Iran to accept a nuclear fuel swap was destined to fail. Then the US State Department said it was the "last chance" for an agreement without sanctions. And finally, less than 24 hours after a successful agreement in Tehran, Hillary whips the UN Security Council into submission and triumphantly proclaims to the world a draft resolution for a fourth UN round of sanctions against Iran has been reached.

She framed the drive towards sanctions as "an answer to the efforts undertaken in Tehran over the last few days." Wait a minute. Immediately after a genuine—and fruitful—mediation on a very sensitive dossier by two emerging powers—and honest brokers—in the multipolar world, Brazil and Turkey, Washington and its two European Union allies at the Security Council, France and Britain, torpedo it. Is this what passes for global "diplomacy"?

No wonder key US allies Brazil and Turkey, both non-permanent members of the Security Council, and both key regional powers, were fuming after such a public slapping. Brazil at first said it would not even discuss sanctions at the UN. Then Brazil and Turkey sent a formal letter to the UN, asking to be part of the negotiations of the "Iran Six" about the sanctions "to prevent the adoption of measures going against a peaceful solution."

Brazilian President Luiz Inacio Lula da Silva—who had personally told Clinton earlier this year that it was "not prudent to push Iran against a wall"—could not help but blast the outdated Security Council, stressing it was not predisposed to negotiations after all. Turkish Foreign Minister Ahmet Davutoglu warned the new sanctions package would "spoil the atmosphere."

And Turkish Prime Minister Recep Tayyip Erdogan stressed the move seriously damaged the credibility of the Security Council—not failing to wryly remind everyone of the absurd notion of five nuclear-armed permanent Security Council members seeking to dismantle the legal civilian nuclear program of a developing country.

As for "US credibility," it's biting the dust once again not only as far as Lula and Erdogan are concerned, but across the developing world—the real, flesh and blood "international community" following this interminable charade.

Whipping enrichment to a frenzy

Over the past few months, dominatrix Clinton relentlessly accused Iran of rejecting a similar fuel swap agreement proposed by the US last October. That's part of the usual Washington script—to behave with textbook deviousness, insisting sanctions "have nothing to do" with enrichment when only a few weeks ago it was the lack of an enrichment deal that was the key reason for more sanctions.

And it gets worse. As Gareth Porter has revealed (Washington burns its bridges with Iran *Asia Times Online*, May21, 2010) Washington only proposed a fuel swap last October because it wanted from the start to force Iran to agree to suspend all its uranium enrichment (to which it has a right as per the nuclear Non-Proliferation Treaty—NPT). But this was never announced publicly.

Iran anyway will continue to produce 20%-enriched uranium (it has a right to it, according to the NPT), and will start the construction of a new enrichment plant about the same size as Natanz's. This is part of a plan to build 10 new plants, announced last year by the Mahmud Ahmadinejad government. Moreover, the Russian-built Bushehr nuclear power plant is under final testing and will be inaugurated this summer. These are irreversible facts on the ground.

Secretary of Iran's Supreme National Security Council Saeed Jalili, the de facto top Iranian nuclear negotiator, may soon meet with the European Union foreign policy chief Catherine Ashton in Turkey. Ashton, the "international community's" designated negotiator, is as representative of global public opinion as a BP press release on the Gulf of Mexico oil spill. Specially because the EU is bound to issue its own unilateral sanctions against Iran. Same for the US Congress, as Senator Chris Dodd, a Democrat from Connecticut, has confirmed this week. So apart from the Security Council, Iran will also have to face extra sanctions from the US-led coalition of the willing right-wing, mired-in-decay European poodles.

China and Russia pull a Sun Tzu

Ancient Chinese military general, strategist, philosopher and author of *The Art of War*, Sun Tzu said, "Allow your enemy to make his own mistakes, and don't correct them." China and Russia, both master strategists, are applying this maxim with panache regarding the US.

The current 10-page UN draft sanctions resolution was already diluted to death by permanent members Russia and China—and whatever bellicose language remains will be further shot down at the Security Council by non-permanent members Brazil, Turkey and Lebanon (without unanimity at the Security Council new sanctions are for all practical purposes dead). There's no way Washington can coerce the rest of the

Security Council to sign up for a new sanctions round when Iran is actually engaged in cooperation.

As it stands, the current sanctions package punishes Iran's import of conventional arms; curbs imports related to ballistic missiles; freezes assets of key members of the Islamic Revolutionary Guards Corps; and sets up cargo inspections in seaports and on international waters. Most of these sanctions are voluntary—or non-binding—and will have zero interference on Iran's global trade of oil and gas.

Beijing and Moscow are not exactly licking Clinton's whip. Immediately after her bombastic announcement, the Chinese ambassador at the UN, Li Badong, said the draft resolution "did not close the doors on diplomacy," once again emphasizing "dialogue, diplomacy and negotiations."

And Russian Foreign Minister Sergei Lavrov made sure to talk to Clinton over the phone arguing for a deeper analysis of the fuel swap deal mediated by Brazil-Turkey. Lavrov also stressed Russia didn't like one bit the extra US and EU unilateral sanctions. The Russian Foreign Ministry said the unilateral sanctions would include measures "of an extraterritorial nature, beyond the agreed decisions of the international community and contradicting the principle of the rule of the international law, enshrined in the UN charter."

So we have come to a situation whereby a real, Iran-approved nuclear fuel swap is on the table at the International Atomic Energy Agency while an offensive towards sanctions on Iran is ongoing at the UN. Who is the real "international community" going to trust? Erdogan could not have put it better; "This is the time to discuss whether we believe in the supremacy of law or the law of the supremes and superiors..."

Most of all, what the developing world sees is the past—US, France, Britain, Germany—fighting against the advance of the future—China, India, Brazil, Turkey, Indonesia. The global security architecture—policed by a bunch of fearful, self-appointed Western guardians—is in a coma. The "Atlanticist" West is sinking Titanic-style.

We want war and we want it now

Only the powerful pro-infinite war lobby in the US is capable of framing a first step towards a full nuclear agreement with Iran as a disaster. That includes the largely discredited pro-Iraq war *New York Times* (the Brazil-Turkey mediation is "complicating sanctions talk") and *Washington Post* (Iran "creates illusion of progress in nuclear negotiations").

For the pro-war lobby the Brazil-Turkey-mediated fuel swap is a "threat" because it is on a direct collision course with an attack on Iran (initiated by Israel, then dragging the US) and "regime change"—the never-reneged Washington desire.

At a recent Council on Foreign Relations speech in Montreal, luminary Dr. Zbigniew "let's conquer Eurasia" Brzezinski warned that a "global political awakening," along with infighting among the global elite, was something to be deeply feared. The former US national security advisor remarked that "for the first time in all of human history mankind is politically awakened—that's a total new reality—it has not been so for most of human history."

Who do these politically awakened upstarts such as Brazil and Turkey think they are—daring to disturb "our" rule of the world? And then uninformed Americans keep asking themselves "Why do they hate us?" Be cause, among other reasons, unilateral to the core, Washington does not hesitate to lift its middle finger even to its closest friends.

May 2010

Mistah McChrystal—He Dead

Mistah Kurtz—he dead.

—Joseph Conrad, *Heart of Darkness*

When it comes to American wars, history has a kinky habit of repeating itself as farce over and over again. So now the Pentagon has been plunged into turmoil because General Stanley McChrystal, former US and NATO commander in Afghanistan, was featured unplugged in a *Rolling Stone* magazine interview.

Those were the days when the Washington Post used to bring down a president (now the Post, as well as the *New York Times*, prefer war, on Iraq, on AfPak, on Iran). Gonzo master Hunter S Thompson anyway must be celebrating with heavenly tequila shots in his wild and crazy tomb; *Rolling Stone* after all managed to bring down a general—to the sound of *The End* by The Doors.

Which brings us to Francis Ford Coppola using The Doors to start *Apocalypse Now*—or the US winning the Vietnam War (only) on film. McChrystal could be portrayed as a mix of Captain Willard and the original Mistah Kurtz of Conrad's masterpiece, the literary model for Marlon Brando's Colonel Kurtz. Both warrior-intellectuals—one about to cross to the heart of darkness, the other already there.

Although hailed by a wildly sycophantic media as a hero, McChrystal, like Willard, is essentially a trained killer, the head of a killing squad in Iraq active way before the "surge," the same "surge" which was sculpted in stone in Washington as paving the way for an American "victory" (while generating profitable side products such as Oscar winner for Best Picture *The Hurt Locker*).

Sooner or later a Kurtzean McChrystal character will end up in a Hollywood blockbuster. The US lost the war in Vietnam but won it on screen. The US is losing the war in Iraq but it's already winning it on screen. And the US will lose the war in AfPak and will win it on screen.

TS Eliot used "Mistah Kurtz—he dead" as the epigraph of *The Hollow Men*. According to the *Rolling Stone* interview, McChrystal's band of brothers is a "handpicked collection of killers, spies, geniuses, patriots, political operators and outright maniacs" who refer to themselves as the South Park-esque Team America. Well, Team America is more like a Facebook version of Eliot's *Hollow Men*:

> *Our dried voices, when we whisper together are quiet and meaningless as wind in dry grass or rats' feet over broken glass.*

No wonder President Barack Obama looked "uncomfortable and intimidated" by a roomful of Pentagon brass when he met McChrystal. Obama is a progressive urban intellectual. He could not but mistrust McChrystal, his band of brothers, in fact much of the coterie of killers and functionaries who populate the sprawling industrial-military complex. What's ironic is that at the same time the functionaries of empire could not but mistrust the phalanx of Obama advisors who didn't and don't have a clue about "the mission."

So what's "the mission" in AfPak? For the Obama team it's rather to use Afghanistan as a pawn to expand the already abysmal fissure between the US and Iran, and to throw Shi'ite Iran and Sunni Wahhabi Saudi Arabia at each other's throats.

But for the industrial-military complex it goes way beyond. It's about the New Great Game in Eurasia. It's about the Pentagon's Full Spectrum

Dominance doctrine, which presupposes setting up strategic Afghan bases to control and survey strategic competitors Russia and China very close to their borders. It's still about the late 1990s all over again; to isolate or crush or bribe the Taliban so the ultimate pipe dream—the Trans-Afghan Pipeline (TAP)—can be built to carry Turkmen gas to Western markets, and not the rival, anathema IP (Iran-Pakistan) pipeline. In a nutshell, it's about infinite war.

It's easy to forget—as much of US corporate media do—that in the midst of all the "runaway general" hoopla, McChrystal's own COIN (counter-insurgency) strategy in Afghanistan had already been reduced, according to his own neologism, to "Chaos-istan" for quite some time. To apply counter-insurgency en masse against Pashtun brothers and cousins is a foolish recipe for failure. Washington does not even know who the "enemy" is; Afghans on the other hand see it as a war of Christian foreign invaders against the Pashtun nation.

The recipe was originally "designed" by the new general in AfPak, McChrystal's boss, Central Command chief David "I'm always positioning myself to 2012" Petraeus, the conceptual hero of the "surge" in Iraq. Meet the new general, (not quite the) same as the old general; let's say Petraeus is a silkier version of Captain Willard, without the Kurtzean overtones of McChrystal. Cue that Peter Townshend power chord: "Won't be fooled again." Or will we?

The McChrystal goes rogue/McChrystal gets fired story is yet one more classic Pentagon non-event magnified to dementia. What the general unplugged to *Rolling Stone* was basically a collection of generic, mild and milder insults to US civilians. The "warrior-intellectual" never gave any sign he was engaging in specific, detailed criticism of the overall military strategy; after all, the Pentagon's Full Spectrum Dominance cannot be really sold for what it is. And even Obama has stated on the record that replacing a general with another general does not mean a change in strategy. Is there a strategy? Yes—infinite war; but the Pentagon won't allow it to be spelled out.

It's been a long time since the immense, absurdly expensive, the-road-goes-on-forever American war obsession bore any relation whatsoever to politics and reality. It pertains to fiction—as the dance of the generals goes on, as Eliot would say, "in this hollow valley." And these fictional steps are dead certain to punctuate "this broken jaw of our lost kingdoms" for years and years to come.

June 2010

ON THE ROAD IN PATAGONIA

This is a place where men come to be shocked and awed. The discovery of Patagonia is still a work in progress. Patagonia may be an enigma wrapped in a riddle of glaciers, mountain lakes, forests and wind-beaten steppes—and as such is impervious to fiction; reality is infinitely more powerful.

Forget Kashmir, the Himalayas, the Silk Road; this is reality secreting magic, legend and fantasy. Had he ever been to Patagonia straight out of Ireland, Irish poet W B Yeats would have marveled at its "violent," not "terrible," beauty.

The end of the world is immense, but inevitably some boundaries apply; the Colorado River to the north; the Atlantic Ocean to the east; Tierra del Fuego to the south; and the Pacific Ocean to the west.

From the Atlantic across the central steppes/altiplano and up to the Cordillera (the Andes) along the Argentina-Chile border in the west, most is still virgin, pristine land—and water. Silence is vast and liquid. Invisible to man, *anchimallen* (demons) patrol the central *meseta* (plains). Lagoons play host to flamingos and black-necked swans. Glaciers swell up to the point of forming dams between lakes—and then start breaking up with a bang, like they have done for millennia.

If there was ever a role model for the true spirit of a Patagonian trip, that would have been crack Argentine writer Roberto Arlt (1900-1942), who in the summer of 1934, as a columnist for the daily newspaper El Mundo, set out to travel in Neuquen (in northern Patagonia), the Cordillera, the lake region north of Bariloche (he described the Nahuel Hapi as "the most beautiful lake in the world") and "I don't know, maybe discover a new continent."

He carried boots, a leather bag and "an enigmatic pistol." In this austral winter of 2010, minus the pistol, I actually set out the other way, starting in Ushuaia, the southernmost city in the world, heading north along the Cordillera and then the Patagonian desert (minus the ferocious winds, absent in winter), and ending at Neuquen wine country.

The Patagonian narrative has been spun for centuries by bold navigators and adventurers, hydrologists, royal mariners from Spain, Portugal and Britain, scientific investigation bulletins, devoted settlers, fierce pirates.

In the early 21st century, as the Global South is trying to reclaim its rights, what was most interesting was to blend this narrative with the new wealthy North's take on how this "arid, desert, windy, abandoned" Patagonia has become an open space and "a sea of opportunities" for foreign occupation.

Terra manuscrita ahead

Driving miles on end without seeing anyone on Ruta 40—the mythical asphalt spinal cord of Argentina; navigating pristine lakes; trekking towards glaciers on sunset; trying to spot an elusive *huemul* (the Andean cerf, close to extinction), it's not hard to comprehend how Patagonia inhabits humanity's dreams. But it's also easy to understand why Patagonia right from the beginning made the transition from *terra incognita* to *terra manuscrita*.

It all started with Cavalier Antonio Pigafetta, the scribe on Portuguese explorer Ferdinand Magellan's psychedelic 1519-1522 circumnavigation of the globe who first put down Patagonia on manuscript as he described "a man of giant stature... almost naked, singing and dancing and throwing sand over his head."

This "giant" was christened as a Pathagon—the mythical giant in the wildly popular Spanish courtly novel *Primaleon*, published in Salamanca in 1512. Fiction also applied to the description of a *guanaco* (a Patagonian cousin of the llama)—an animal "with the head and ears of a mule, the body of a camel, the legs of a deer and the tail of a horse."

The Portuguese court was sure what was later baptized as the Magellan Strait did exist—based on maps drawn in 1507 by cosmographer Martin Waldseemuller, who was inspired by notes from Amerigo Vespucci; America's "discoverer" was sure there was a continent, or *mundus novus*; he had navigated the coast of Patagonia and identified—or dreamed—of a strait uniting the Atlantic and the Pacific.

Anyway, reality as legend always prevailed. Patagonia was the target of countless expeditions searching for the City of the Caesars—or Trapalanda, a splendorous abode full of treasures supposed to be somewhere in South America ever since Francisco Cesar, in 1529, offered a very imprecise description of the wealth of the Incas.

But most of all, for centuries Patagonia was an immense battlefield for greedy European colonial powers. It took the Spanish crown no less than two centuries to wake up to the designs of England, France and Holland—and evolve its own breed of colonization as self-defense. Spain never bothered to colonize Patagonia. They wanted to find a naval pass towards the Spice Islands. Then gold and silver mines were discovered in Peru—and they lost the plot completely. As much as Spain was keen to protect the monopoly of its American colonies, its sea power was risible.

In 1764-1766, John Byron—grandfather of the poetic lord—carefully explored the Patagonian shores, the Magellan Strait, the Malvinas islands, circumnavigated Tierra del Fuego and reached the Pacific around Cape Horn. Also in 1764, French navigator Louis Antoine Bougainville settled the islands he named Malouines, then Malvinas (but for English neo-colonialists they will always be the Falklands).

Ten years later, Jesuit Thomas Falkner warned, "Any great power could secretly invade Patagonia." The English got the message; Spaniards were so incompetent that fabulous Patagonia was up for grabs. It was only in the 19th century that the Viceroyalty of the Rio de la Plata (River Plate) and then the government of Buenos Aires took serious steps to colonize the land, sending travelers, adventurers, explorers—and then the guns.

Beat the *Beagle*

In a never-ending narrative of Patagonian reality transmuted into fiction—and legend—it's impossible to understand the present without retracing Charles Darwin's legendary 1832 trip on the *Beagle*, when he was still an unknown 23-year-old naturalist. Arguably the most important characters on the trip were the Tierra del Fuego natives who Captain Robert Fitz Roy took to England with the first *Beagle* expedition in 1826 (he paid for all their expenses).

Before colonization, these *fueguinos*—living between the islands south of the Magellan Strait and Cape Horn—were around 10,000 in the 19th century, divided into four groups speaking different languages; two were sea nomads—the *yamanas* and the *alacalufes*, and two others were non-navigators, the *onas* and the *haush*. On the spot, Darwin met only *yamanas* and *haush*.

Of the captured *fueguinos* by Fitz Roy, three were *alacalufes* and one was a *yamana*. One of the *alacalufes*, christened Boat Memory, died in England in 1830. In December 1831, before setting out to sea, Darwin met the two remaining *alacalufes*—York Minster, a 26-year-old man, and Fuegia Basket, a 10-year-old girl—as well as the *yamana*, Jemmy Button (15); legend says Fitz Roy bought him for a mother-of-pearl button). They had become so famous in England they had been received by King William IV; Fuegia Basket got a complete wedding outfit from Queen Adelaide.

At first, Darwin seems not to have learned much from the *fueguinos*—basically the *yamanas*, describing them as "atrophied," "miserable" or "infected savages." But he was not a racist—as Californian anthropologist Anne Chapman, among other authorities, has been arguing for years. He got along very well with both Jemmy and Fuegia Basket. But he thought the *tehuelche* Indians—the so-called "patagons"—were superior.

Darwin anyway was hostage to what British anthropologists developed as a mid-19th century paradigm—the notion that human race had evolved from brute primitives such as the *fueguinos* to the complex sophistication of Victorian, imperial Britain, ladies and gentlemen. Darwin's cultural ranking, from the bottom (the *fueguinos*) to the top (the English gentleman) eventually softened up as he rebelled against the concept of progress applied to biology. No wonder he did not refer to "evolution" but to "descent with modification."

What Jemmy and Fuegia certainly taught Darwin (while they were aboard the *Beagle* and also in England) is that "savages" could in no time become "civilized." Darwin's merit is that he started imperfectly by mixing cultural evolution with some instant impressions of the *fueguinos* and only later carried out a profound investigation leading to his revolutionary theory of natural processes.

It would be enlightening—for them—if planeloads of US creationists took the trouble to follow Darwin's steps in Tierra del Fuego. Navigating tempests around Cape Horn or marveling at the landscape ("impossible to imagine anything more beautiful than the admirable blue of these glaciers"), Darwin was hooked by Patagonia and Tierra del Fuego.

And so was Fitz Roy—who named "Darwin" some of these "great mountains" stretching from a bay west of Ushuaia to Isla Grande in Chilean Patagonia (unfortunately it's impossible to navigate this whole region, including the impeccably named Fjords of Fuegia, during a harsh winter). And already, Darwin described what takes place forever as the glaciers melt—"the canal with its mountains of ice looks like a polar sea in miniature."

Wanna buy a strait?

In Patagonia, reality always beat fiction hands down. In 1845, an unnamed Irishman who worked as a harbor pilot actually bought the Magellan Strait. Chileans had maltreated the *tehuelche* Indians, who then commissioned legendary chief Casimiro Bigua to go for it; after all, the *tehuelches* considered themselves the rightful owners of the strait and its surrounding areas. The sale was later annulled in Buenos Aires.

Tired of being oppressed by the English since annexation in 1536, the Welsh embarked on a worldwide diaspora—towards the US, Canada, Brazil, Australia. But some actually elected Patagonia as their promised land. This could have come straight out of a Jorge Luis Borges short story. Picture a sailor, Love Jones-Parry, Baron of Madryn, plus a typographer, Lewis Jones, telling Minister Rawson from the Mitre government, through an interpreter (none of them spoke Spanish) they wanted to found a Welsh nation in Argentina.

Rawson—today the name of a town in eastern Patagonia—went for it. As Welsh writer Horwell Jones would put it, "Being Celts they have the fortune—or is it the curse?—of having a vivid imagination..." So all 151 of them left Liverpool on May 1865. It took them decades to overcome all odds—the hostile land, the ultra-hardcore winters, the arid desert, the merciless winds, floods, and the not useless detail they were above all miners who had no idea about farming.

But then the *tehuelche* Indians set up camp near the first Welsh colony and this unlikely indigenous/settler coupling soon started trading and exchanging knowledge. This stands on its own as one of the very few significant examples of peaceful coexistence in four centuries of colonization of the Americas.

The Welsh ended up operating a total fusion with the Argentine nation. Ever since boundary problems with Chile in the early 20th century, they always wanted to live under the Argentine flag. Not to mention they also had the guts to cross the whole Patagonian desert to the west and settle down in lovely Trevelin, at the feet of the Cordillera, and close to the spectacular Los Alerces national park and the Chilean border. Trevelin at night looks like a ghost Welsh town at the end of the world. But it's reality—not fiction.

Feel free to bask in my glow

It also seems that every reality in Patagonia is interchangeable with a heroic, larger-than-life character.

Think of French lawyer Orllie-Antoine de Tounens, who on November 1860 founded, under his authority, the Constitutional Monarchic Kingdom of Araucania, then annexed Patagonia. His title was King Orllie-Antoine I. He tried the trick twice more and eventually was jailed and deported out of Buenos Aires. When he died, the crown was inherited by his cousin, who without even moving from Europe conducted a lot of business to colonize "the new France." The Arauco-Patagonian throne even had its own flag, shield and currency—billing themselves as fierce defenders of indigenous peoples' rights. Even former US president Dwight Eisenhower was honored with a royal medal in 1966.

Yet few Patagonian characters can be as larger-than-life than Romanian engineer Julius Popper, a clever public relations man who went to Argentina in 1886 determined to find gold in Patagonia and literally moved if not mountains but steppes to get it.

Witty, sarcastic, a fine linguist and a darling of the Buenos Aires high society circles, not to mention dictatorial and imbued with imperial fantasies—some sort of enlightened tyrant—Popper set up a trend which would be fully replicated in the late 20th century; getting loads of precious, valuable Patagonian land in concession, without red tape, and always under his own terms.

Darwin would have applauded Popper's experience of Tierra del Fuego. He regarded the *yamanas* and *alacalufes*, "who live in canoes and fish as a way of survival," as "doomed to extinction" (that's exactly what happened).

On the other hand, he compared the *onas* to the *tehuelches* and even to the North American Indians—a race "that fully represents the primitive man in its maximum expression of moral and physical evolution" (but that did not also prevent them from being virtually extinct).

Darwin also would have agreed that Popper's expression of what Tierra del Fuego is all about at a July 1891 conference is still matchless: "It is a country full of surprises; it is the land where the polar animals greet those of the tropics; where the call of the Antarctic penguin meets the prattle of the Equator parrot; it is the country of many topographic varieties, which has, in proportion, more vegetation than Mexico; more views and landscapes than Norway and Switzerland; in an extension smaller than that of

Portugal it concentrates more contrasts of geography and hydrography, of meteorology and ethnography than in all the continent of Australia."

The last yamana

Double-trouble colonization—religious and civilian, the latter accelerated in 1870—exterminated virtually all indigenous Patagonians. In Ushuaia, stretching east-west along the Beagle Channel, 3,220 kilometers south of Buenos Aires, it is easy to note why the merciless austral weather and isolation would not dissuade northern Europeans—English, Scots, Danish, Dutch—to migrate during the 18th and 19th centuries in search of whale oil, seal skin, pastures for cattle, timber and strategic positioning to trade with the rest of the world. Then came industry—especially related to marine products. And finally, mass tourism.

Generations of global schoolchildren have been in awe of the lighthouse at the end of the world in the famous 1905 Jules Verne book of the same name. The lighthouse was real—built in the Isla de los Estados in 1884. In 1998, France donated a symbolic reconstruction to Argentina—and it's right down there, in the same spot, not to be confused with Les Eclaireurs lighthouse, which can be easily navigated around, not far from Ushuaia. Navigating the Beagle Channel at sunset in a small boat, one certainly feels touched by Infinite grace (anti-Darwin creationists would insist on a "hand from above").

By 1933, there were only 40 *yamanas* left in Patagonia, including mixed race. Ushuaia had a few dozen Argentine men by 1884, some *yamanas*, missionaries and their families, for a total of 200 inhabitants. Now the population is close to 70,000. Ushuaia thrives in the self-described "end of the world" industry (not exactly true; nearby Puerto Williams, in Chilean Tierra del Fuego, at the Beagle southern margin, is actually the southernmost city in the world). It also thrives as "the most active gateway to Antarctica" (true, and the closest as well, at only 1,000 km).

The only remaining authentic *yamana*—an anthropological treasure—is octogenarian Cristina Calderon, a daughter of *yamanas* who speaks the language fluently. She lives in Puerto Williams, along with some mestizos who work in the fishing industry. Darwin might have loved her as much as he was fascinated by Fuegia Basket, as she is perhaps the last living human link with Patagonia's Arcadian past.

The end of the world is on sale

"Desert and sterile" Patagonia (in Charles Darwin's initial assessment) boasts no less than 230,000 square kilometers of river basins flowing into the Atlantic. It holds 4,000 square kilometers of continental ice and glaciers—as well as one of the largest reserves of fresh water on the planet.

We are currently in the advanced stages of a relentless global war for oil and gas (Patagonia, by the way, has both). A crucial 2000 report by the United Nations Economic and Social Organisation (UNESCO) already warned that in the next 50 years, problems related to lack of water or contamination of masses of water would affect practically everyone on the planet. It's when the Great Water Wars explode—perhaps as early as around 2020—that this Patagonia of crystal-clear blue lakes and millenarian glaciers will be at a premium price; possession of water will be infinitely more valuable than possession of oil and gas.

Analytical/warring minds at the Pentagon and the CIA cannot possibly block the wet dream of a secessionist Patagonia as the definitive Liquid Saudi Arabia; sparsely populated (less than 2 million people), with all that water, plenty of hydroelectric energy and 80% of Argentina's reserves of oil and natural gas. The degree of neglect felt by most residents of Patagonia in relation to Buenos Aires can be reasonably compared to what is felt by the Baloch in Pakistan in relation to Islamabad. Recent polls have shown the desire for an independent Patagonia to be always over 50% (with 78% among the young and unemployed).

A crash course on four centuries of Patagonian "development" would go something like this. In the beginning were the indigenous peoples. Then came the Iberian navigators, the English pirates, the all-European science buffs, the religious missionaries, the exiles who dreamed of making it in America, the austral version. Then came the landlords—from Chile or Holland, Wales or Poland, Scotland or Denmark. Getting rid of the indigenous populations was a colonialism no-brainer; northern Patagonians were exterminated by the infamous, euphemistic, 1879 Conquest of the Desert; southern Patagonians were forced to become the workforce for agribusiness. And then, in the 1990s, came the First World billionaires.

As every wildlife-loving billionaire plus rows of sharp-dressed corporate executives duly know, the sale of Patagonia started in 1996, under the ultra-neoliberal Carlos Menem government. Menem, in his own words, wanted to sell "surplus land" of the country he presided. There's no federal law in Argentina regulating the sale of land to foreigners. Only in the late 1990s, more than 8 million hectares were sold. According to the Argentine army, more than 10% of the national land is foreign-owned—and counting. The problem is not the sale itself; it's the absence of virtually any control over proposed investment projects.

If you're flush, you can still buy whatever you want anywhere—even inside spectacular national parks. Each province sets its own rules. If you reach the right functionary with the right cash-filled Samsonite, the world—Tony Montana-style—is yours. No wonder virtually every resident of Rio Negro or Santa Cruz provinces say the local mayor's offices are always the top real-estate agency in town. And these same residents will inevitably lament that Patagonia is being gobbled up by foreigners—from Ted Turner to the Benetton family. Moreover, two of Patagonia's largest oil companies are also foreign-owned; one of them, state-owned, was sold to Spain, and the other, private, to Brazil's Petrobras.

Walking on water

The Four Horsemen of the Apocalypse—the End of the World version—are known as Tompkins, Turner, Lewis and Benetton. They are the 21st-century breed of Patagonia's conquistadores, adventurers and pirates—from Francis Drake and George Newbery to Butch Cassidy and the Sundance Kid (their ranch is still there in Cholilla, a dejected pueblo which would be at home in the more dejected parts of New Mexico). Foreigners have always dreamed of the end of the world. And its violent beauty—as we'll see—makes grown man cry.

Californian green guru Doug Tompkins, former founder of both The North Face and Esprit, is known in Patagonia as the "owner of the water." He's the biggest private owner of natural resources in Chilean Patagonia as well as the Corrientes region in Argentina, and owns a number of strategically placed haciendas. When Tompkins first saw southern Patagonia, on the Chilean side, and then northwest Patagonia, on the Argentine side, in 1961, he cried like a baby. Then he came back—and started buying.

Trout-fishing fanatic and CNN founder Ted Turner has a spectacular 5,000 hectare villa in the south of Neuquen province and controls most access to one of Patagonia's most pristine rivers. He has another 35,000 hectares in the same province plus another 5,000 in Tierra del Fuego. Outside of the US, Ted only bought in Patagonia.

Villa Traful is a green, hilly private valley bordering the spectacular homonymous lake. It's virtually empty in winter—projecting the sensation this is what Shangri-La must have been all about, before the advent of Facebook. Buying land in Traful during the 1990s was a piece of cake. Those in the know quickly grabbed public land around the lake. Now the dream is over. Jorge Sobisch, the Croatian-family former governor of Neuquen province who wants to become president, is basically selling it all for huge mass tourism groups.

But above all this is Ted Turner land. Turner is the owner of La Primavera, a spectacular 5,000 hectare estancia right on the mouth of the Traful river, where he can blissfully fish for the best trout and salmon nature can manufacture. Jane Fonda was a sucker for La Primavera. Tompkins was a guest, as well as George Bush senior and Henry Kissinger. Intruders are monitored by satellite. As this was winter and everything was dead, I could not even afford the pleasure of navigating on Turner waters. And of course Ted never shows up on Vila Traful himself—although he visits La Primavera a few times a year.

La Primavera was actually founded by an American, odontologist and former vice US consul in Buenos Aires George Newbery, in 1894. George and Ralph Newbery (father of famous aviator Jorge, whose name now graces one of Buenos Aires's airports) were convinced that Patagonia should be populated with cowboys imported from Texas.

So already in the early 20th century there was widespread fear in northern Patagonia of a yankee colonization drive. The Texas cowboy exile route soon dried up. La Primavera was sold to an Englishman, then a Frenchman, then an Argentine and finally fell on Ted's lap as he was deeply involved in a 2 million hectare conservation project—or territorial expansion—in Montana, New Mexico and Nebraska. But Patagonian Ted has always been adamant; this is only about fishing.

1, 2, 1,000 Shangri-Las

Brit Joseph Lewis, the 6th largest fortune in the United Kingdom, known in northern Patagonia as Uncle Joe because of his overdrive philanthropy, controls all the 14,000 hectares of land bordering sublime Lake Escondido ("Hidden Lake"), 92 km out of Bariloche on the Chile border, as well as the basin of the prized Azur river. Ultra-discreet Lewis, who lives between London, Orlando, the Bahamas and Patagonia, is a big shark on financial speculation as well as genetic investigation, and the hands of his Tavistock Group are in everything from oil and gas in Siberia to Puma and Gottex outfits.

Lewis' Andean-Patagonian Shangri-La is not far from El Bolson, the Argentine hippie Mecca of the 1970s transmogrified into the country's first ecological municipality in the early 1990s. Its Tolkien-style forests are filled with prized alerces, or lahuan wood—the oldest living organism in Argentina, third-oldest in the world. Almost as ubiquitous as the alerces are mixed feelings over Lewis' push to actually do the work expected from provincial and national authorities—establishing what is a de facto state within a state.

In just a few years, Lewis bought land equivalent to three-quarters of the city of Buenos Aires—but in the form of millenarian forests, glaciers, crystal-clear lakes and rivers. Lewis stopped short of buying the lake itself—because the law does not allow it. But what he did was to buy the whole land surrounding the lake, so if you want to reach the border you have to cross 18 km of his private property. Seeing Shangri-La live thus can only be done with a helping hand from above—that is, Lewis' minions. Lewis is also suspected of trying to buy the nascent of numerous rivers in the region. And considering Tavistock is heavily involved in genetic investigation and biotechnology, there's also ample suspicion it is extracting and exporting very rare species out of the Cordillera.

There are many other players in the Great Patagonian Sale. There's Jacobo Suchard (the owner of Nestle). There's the Swarowsky jewelry family. There's french fries king Ward Lay, who also got into the wine business with the Rutini family and usually brags that "Patagonia reminds me of Texas in the 1950s" (it actually does, in terms of unlimited opportunities; landscape-wise, it would be more like a cross between Montana and New Mexico). Lay owns the 80,000 hectare Alicura estancia, a valley crisscrossed by three rivers and precious wild animals and fleeting former abode of Butch Cassidy and the Sundance Kid.

There's Belgian group Burco, owner of the Dubai crowd-style country club Arelauquen near Bariloche—a sort of de luxe agrarian reform project in reverse, pristine forest turned into a polo-and-golf gated condo. There's a group led by Frenchman Michel Biquard, which has built a lone five-star hotel right in front of Argentina's most famous glacier.

But among all these the big sharks are undoubtedly the Benetton brothers—Carlo and Luciano, who control 1 million hectares of productive land under the Compania de Tierras Sud Argentino (CTSA), originally founded by the British as the Argentine Southern Land Co. in 1889 and now the most important agribusiness in the country. The Benetton brothers are the biggest private owners of land in Argentina—apart from the state.

It's the same old story. When Carlo and Luciano first trekked on ice over the Perito Moreno glacier in 2004—sealed off for the occasion, as if they were the Emir of Qatar and his wife shopping at Harrods—they also cried. But they had been right on the money since 1991, when they started buying haciendas. CTSA, a huge agribusiness corporation spanning the Andes to the Atlantic Ocean, owns at least 16,000 head of cattle and 260,000 sheep—producing up to 1.3 million tons of wool a year, all exported to Italy.

It didn't help that ultra-politically correct United Colors of Benetton got involved in a nasty conflict with "delocalized" *Mapuche* families in the early 2000s—leading it to be known in many progressive quarters as United Colors of Land Grab. Suffice to say that the Benetton spokesman in Argentina at the time used to be the governor of Chubut province, politician Mario das Neves. The corporation pulled no punches buying media and unleashing a lavish public relations exercise in both Argentina and Italy. A *Mapuche* committee was received by Luciano Benetton in a Rome palazzo. But they didn't get their property back.

For the *Mapuches* this was just another step in the invasion of Patagonia. First by the Spanish in 1492; then by the 1879 Conquest of the Desert, the Buenos Aires-conducted ethnic cleansing sold as taking "civilization" to a "desert" peopled by Indians; and finally by big corporations and foreign billionaires.

Austral *tehuelches* used to live between the Magellan Strait and the Santa Cruz River. They were cousins to the *onas* of Tierra del Fuego. There were two other *tehuelche* tribes more to the north, one of them fusioned with Araucans from Chile. This *"araucanization"* led to the forming of the *Mapuche* nation—a single territory spanning parts of Argentina and Chile. Nowadays, there are around 76,000 *Mapuches* in Argentina, compared to 350,000 in Chile.

Right inside the enormous Benetton-owned Leleque estancia in Chubut province, the *Mapuche* controversy reaches its peak in the form of a museum. The museum's lavish catalogue, boasting detailed historiography, aims to basically prove that the *Mapuches* were not Argentine Patagonia's original inhabitants; ergo, they cannot possibly claim ownership of a land now occupied by the immaculate, vertically integrated Benetton sheep. Make no mistake, the war between Indians and wealthy foreigners is still on.

Patagonia as Pandora's box

El Chalten—not more than 700 people at the foot of the Andes, the starting point for trekking to the spectacular Torre and Fitz Roy peaks, is the youngest pueblo in Argentina. But it is above all the Holy Grail for politicians from Santa Cruz province who now rule the country, everyone very cosy with former president Nestor Kirchner and the current president, his wife Cristina Fernandez de Kirchner. The local economy is virtually dollarized. When Tompkins first visited, in 1968—no Paris barricades for him—El Chalten was not even on the map.

Tompkins' own Shangri-La is actually in Pumalin, on the Chilean Cordillera—300,000 hectares of land declared a nature sanctuary in 2005 by the Chilean government after 10 years of tough negotiations, complete with glaciers, snow-capped volcanoes, pumas and wild horses. Pumalin is now a national park with public access—but private control.

Ever since the mid-1990s, there had been rumors about a mysterious American ecological guru who was the sole owner of Patagonia. Although far from it, Tompkins finally struck gold in Argentina with Monte Leon in Santa Cruz province, which the World Wildlife Fund duly includes among the 237 top conservation regions on the planet—as it mixes the species-wealthy Mar Argentino (including a 60,000 strong colony of Magellan penguins) with the oil-and-gas-rich Patagonia steppe.

When the Gulfstreams of foreign billionaires started landing in Patagonia during the 1990s, the Menem government did recognize the remaining Indians as original peoples. But that did not solve many problems as most are still enmeshed in fierce territorial disputes with dodgy landowners not as famous as the Benetton. The problem is that the tandem real-estate agencies/provincial state functionaries are bound to keep indulging in a perpetual Patagonia-on-sale party.

Everywhere I went I had the feeling that the Cordillera is on sale. The price of a hectare depends on the timeless mantra—location, location, location. In Villa La Angostura, north of Bariloche—an aspiring cousin of Aspen and Vail—buying and selling land is a more popular topic of conversation over a bottle of Malbec than soccer.

Same in more austral Patagonia, in Calafate, Santa Cruz province, an historic crossroads for selling cattle and sheep, a magnet for dodgy adventurers in search of limitless estancias, and today a boutique pueblo with a totally dollarized economy. A humongous—and empty—casino dominates Main Street.

I stayed very close to the Kirchner couple's mansion (they usually show up on weekends). The FOK (Friends of Kirchner—the austral equivalent to good old Friends of Bill, or Friends of Bush) control everything, with a special mention to Jorge Fernandez Campbell, owner of the sole monopoly exploiting the ultra-profitable navigation around the spectacular glaciers in Lago Argentino, the largest mass of continental ice in the world. The Glaciers National Park ends only 500 meters from the Magellan Peninsula, where the glacier touches the earth; from there onwards, all land is subjected to market valuation.

All over the place, from the Beagle Channel to the empty steppes, I was told that Patagonia was colonized with cattle and sheep—and not with people. So there were always very few land ownership titles flying around. Tough questions though remain—and they apply to virtually all the developing world. How to "develop" Patagonia? How to preserve it from serious environmental contamination? There is a necessity for a clear policy setting serious targets for responsible tourism, and the necessity for a clear policy regarding industrial development.

As Argentina is a country of immigrants—a sort of austral Europe—foreign ownership may not be such a problem per se; the question is how the land should be used or developed. It's up to the state to delimit the rules; if there is enough land for wealthy foreigners, there must be enough land for aboriginal peoples as well. And even for Argentines. As much as the striking beauty of Patagonia may be financially off-limits for a typical Argentine middle-class family, it is also Argentines who are indiscriminately selling land to foreigners.

And still the verdict on this spectacular land that makes grown men cry is open. Will it be the ultimate, pristine gated condo for the globe's ultra-wealthy? Will it be the granary for those lucky enough to escape the disasters about to engulf the developed North? Will it be the Pandora's box of natural treasures that will unleash the next world wars?

August 2010

China's Pipelineistan "War"

Future historians may well agree that the twenty-first century Silk Road first opened for business on December 14, 2009. That was the day a crucial stretch of pipeline officially went into operation linking the fabulously energy-rich state of Turkmenistan (via Kazakhstan and Uzbekistan) to Xinjiang Province in China's far west. Hyperbole did not deter the spectacularly named Gurbanguly Berdymukhamedov, Turkmenistan's president, from bragging, "This project has not only commercial or economic value. It is also political. China, through its wise and farsighted policy, has become one of the key guarantors of global security."

The bottom line is that, by 2013, Shanghai, Guangzhou, and Hong Kong will be cruising to ever more dizzying economic heights courtesy of natural gas supplied by the 1,833-kilometer-long Central Asia Pipeline, then projected to be operating at full capacity. And to think that, in a few more years, China's big cities will undoubtedly also be getting a taste of Iraq's fabulous, barely tapped oil reserves, conservatively estimated at 115 billion barrels, but possibly closer to 143 billion barrels, which would put it ahead of Iran. When the Bush administration's armchair generals launched their Global War on Terror, this was not exactly what they had in mind.

China's economy is thirsty, and so it's drinking deeper and planning deeper yet. It craves Iraq's oil and Turkmenistan's natural gas, as well as oil from Kazakhstan. Yet instead of spending more than a trillion dollars on an illegal war in Iraq or setting up military bases all over the Greater Middle East and Central Asia, China used its state oil companies to get some of the energy it needed simply by bidding for it in a perfectly legal Iraqi oil auction.

Meanwhile, in the New Great Game in Eurasia, China had the good sense not to send a soldier anywhere or get bogged down in an infinite quagmire in Afghanistan. Instead, the Chinese simply made a direct commercial deal with Turkmenistan and, profiting from that country's disagreements with Moscow, built itself a pipeline which will provide much of the natural gas it needs.

No wonder the Obama administration's Eurasian energy czar Richard Morningstar was forced to admit at a congressional hearing that the US simply cannot compete with China when it comes to Central Asia's energy wealth. If only he had delivered the same message to the Pentagon.

That Iranian Equation

In Beijing, they take the matter of diversifying oil supplies very, very seriously. When oil reached $150 a barrel in 2008—before the U.S.-unleashed global financial meltdown hit—Chinese state media had taken to calling foreign Big Oil "international petroleum crocodiles," with the implication that the West's hidden agenda was ultimately to stop China's relentless development dead in its tracks.

Twenty-eight percent of what's left of the world's proven oil reserves are in the Arab world. China could easily gobble it all up. Few may know that China itself is actually the world's fifth largest oil producer, at 3.7 million barrels per day (bpd), just below Iran and slightly above Mexico. In 1980, China consumed only 3% of the world's oil. Now, its take is around 10%, making it the planet's second-largest consumer. It has already surpassed Japan in that category, even if it's still way behind the U.S., which eats up 27% of global oil each year. According to the IEA, China will account for over 40% of the increase in global oil demand un-

187

til 2030. And that's assuming China will grow at "only" a 6% annual rate which, based on present growth, seems unlikely.

Saudi Arabia controls 13% of world oil production. At the moment, it is the only swing producer—one, that is, that can move the amount of oil being pumped up or down at will—capable of substantially increasing output. It's no accident, then, that, pumping 500,000 bpd, it has become one of Beijing's major oil suppliers. The top three, according to China's Ministry of Commerce, are Saudi Arabia, Iran, and Angola. By 2013-2014, if all goes well, the Chinese expect to add Iraq to that list in a big way, but first that troubled country's oil production needs to start cranking up. In the meantime, it's the Iranian part of the Eurasian energy equation that's really nerve-racking for China's leaders.

Chinese companies have invested a staggering $120 billion in Iran's energy sector over the past five years. Already Iran is China's number two oil supplier, accounting for up to 14% of its imports; and the Chinese energy giant Sinopec has committed an additional $6.5 billion to building oil refineries there. Due to harsh UN-imposed and American sanctions and years of economic mismanagement, however, the country lacks the high-tech know-how to provide for itself, and its industrial structure is in a shambles. The head of the National Iranian Oil Company, Ahmad Ghalebani, has publicly admitted that machinery and parts used in Iran's oil production still have to be imported from China.

Sanctions can be a killer, slowing investment, increasing the cost of trade by over 20%, and severely constricting Tehran's ability to borrow in global markets. Nonetheless, trade between China and Iran grew by 35% in 2009 to $27 billion. So while the West has been slamming Iran with sanctions, embargos, and blockades, Iran has been slowly evolving as a crucial trade corridor for China—as well as Russia and energy-poor India. Unlike the West, they are all investing like crazy there because it's easy to get concessions from the government; it's easy and relatively cheap to build infrastructure; and being on the inside when it comes to Iranian energy reserves is a necessity for any country that wants to be a crucial player in Pipelineistan, that contested chessboard of crucial energy pipelines over which much of the New Great Game in Eurasia takes place. Undoubtedly, the leaders of all three countries are offering thanks to whatever gods they care to worship that Washington continues to make it so easy (and lucrative) for them.

Few in the US may know that last year Saudi Arabia—now (re)arming to the teeth, courtesy of Washington, and little short of paranoid about the Iranian nuclear program—offered to supply the Chinese with the same amount of oil the country currently imports from Iran at a much cheaper price. But Beijing, for whom Iran is a key long-term strategic ally, scotched the deal.

As if Iran's structural problems weren't enough, the country has done little to diversify its economy beyond oil and natural gas exports in the past 30 years; inflation's running at more than 20%; unemployment at more than 20%; and young, well-educated people are fleeing abroad, a major brain drain for that embattled land. And don't think that's the end of its litany of problems. It would like to be a full member of the Shanghai Cooperation Organization (SCO)—the multi-layered economic/military cooperation union that is a sort of Asian response to NATO—but is only an official SCO observer because the group does not admit any country under UN sanctions. Tehran, in other words, would like some great power protection against the possibility of an attack from the US or Israel. As much as Iran may be on the verge of becoming a far more influential player in the Central Asian energy game thanks to Russian and Chinese investment, it's extremely unlikely that either of those countries would actually risk war against the US to "save" the Iranian regime.

The Great Escape

From Beijing's point of view, the title of the movie version of the intractable US v. Iran conflict and a simmering US v. China strategic competition in Pipelineistan could be: "Escape from Hormuz and Malacca."

The Strait of Hormuz is the definition of a potential strategic bottleneck. It is, after all, the only entryway to the Persian Gulf and through it now flow roughly 20% of China's oil imports. At its narrowest, it is only 36 kilometers wide, with Iran to the north and Oman to the south. China's leaders fret about the constant presence of US aircraft carrier battle groups on station and patrolling nearby.

With Singapore to the north and Indonesia to the south, the Strait of Malacca is another potential bottleneck if ever there was one—and through it flow as much as 80% of China's oil imports. At its narrowest, it is only 54 kilometers wide and like the Strait of Hormuz, its security is also of the made-in-USA variety. In a future face-off with Washington, both straits could quickly be closed or controlled by the US Navy.

Hence, China's increasing emphasis on developing a land-based Central Asian energy strategy could be summed up as: bye-bye, Hormuz! Bye-bye, Malacca! And a hearty welcome to a pipeline-driven new Silk Road from the Caspian Sea to China's Far West in Xinjiang.

Kazakhstan has 3% of the world's proven oil reserves, but its largest oil fields are not far from the Chinese border. China sees that country as a key alternative oil supplier via future pipelines that would link the Kazakh oil fields to Chinese oil refineries in its far west. In fact, China's first transnational Pipelineistan adventure is already in place: the 2005 China-Kazakhstan oil project, financed by Chinese energy giant CNPC.

Much more is to come, and Chinese leaders expect energy-rich Russia to play a significant part in China's escape-hatch planning as well. Strategically, this represents a crucial step in regional energy integration, tightening the Russia/China partnership inside the SCO as well as at the UN Security Council.

When it comes to oil, the name of the game is the immense Eastern Siberia-Pacific Ocean (ESPO) pipeline. Last August, a 4,000-kilometer-long Russian section from Taishet in eastern Siberia to Nakhodka, still inside Russian territory, was begun. Russian Premier Vladimir Putin hailed ESPO as "a really comprehensive project that has strengthened our energy cooperation." And in late September, the Russians and the Chinese inaugurated a 999-kilometer-long pipeline from Skovorodino in Russia's Amur region to the petrochemical hub Daqing in northeast China.

Russia is currently delivering up to 130 million tons of Russian oil a year to Europe. Soon, no less than 50 million tons may be heading to China and the Pacific region as well.

There are, however, hidden tensions between the Russians and the Chinese when it comes to energy matters. The Russian leadership is understandably wary of China's startling strides in Central Asia, the former Soviet Union's former "near abroad." After all, as the Chinese have been doing in Africa in their search for energy, in Central Asia, too, the Chinese are building railways and introducing high-tech trains, among other modern wonders, in exchange for oil and gas concessions.

Despite the simmering tensions between China, Russia, and the U.S., it's too early to be sure just who is likely to emerge as the victor in the

New Great Game in Central Asia, but one thing is clear enough. The Central Asian "stans" are becoming ever more powerful poker players in their own right as Russia tries not to lose its hegemony there, Washington places all its chips on pipelines meant to bypass Russia (including the Baku-Tbilisi-Ceyhan (BTC) pipeline that pumps oil from Azerbaijan to Turkey via Georgia) and China antes up big time for its Central Asian future. Whoever loses, this is a game that the "stans" cannot but profit from.

Recently, our man Gurbanguly, the Turkmen leader, chose China as his go-to country for an extra $4.18 billion loan for the development of South Yolotan, his country's largest gas field. (The Chinese had already shelled out $3 billion to help develop it.) Energy bureaucrats in Brussels were devastated. With estimated reserves of up to 14 trillion cubic meters of natural gas, the field has the potential to flood the energy-starved European Union with gas for more than 20 years. Goodbye to all that?

In 2009, Turkmenistan's proven gas reserves were estimated at a staggering 8.1 trillion cubic meters, fourth largest in the world after Russia, Iran, and Qatar. Not surprisingly, from the point of view of Ashgabat, the country's capital, it invariably seems to be raining gas. Nonetheless, experts doubt that the landlocked, idiosyncratic Central Asian republic actually has enough blue gold to supply Russia (which absorbed 70% of Turkmenistan's supply before the pipeline to China opened), China, Western Europe and Iran, all at the same time.

Currently, Turkmenistan sells its gas to: China via the world's largest gas pipeline, 7,000 kilometers long and designed for a capacity of 40 billion cubic meters per year; Russia (10 billion cubic meters per year, down from 30 billion per year until 2008); and Iran (14 billion cubic meters per year). Iranian President Mahmoud Ahmadinejad always gets a red-carpet welcome from Gurbanguly, and the Russian energy giant Gazprom, thanks to an improved pricing policy, is treated as a preferred customer.

At present, however, the Chinese are atop the heap, and more generally, whatever happens, there can be little question that Central Asia will be China's major foreign supplier of natural gas. On the other hand, the fact that Turkmenistan has, in practice, committed its entire future gas exports to China, Russia, and Iran means the virtual death of various trans-Caspian Sea pipeline plans long favored by Washington and the European Union.

IPI vs. TAPI All Over Again

On the oil front, even if all the "stans" sold China every barrel of oil they currently pump, less than half of China's daily import needs would be met. Ultimately, only the Middle East can quench China's thirst for oil. According to the IEA, China's overall oil needs will rise to 11.3 million barrels per day by 2015, even with domestic production peaking at 4.0 million bpd. Compare that to what some of China's alternative suppliers are now producing: Angola, 1.4 million bpd; Kazakhstan, 1.4 million as well; and Sudan, 400,000.

On the other hand, Saudi Arabia produces 10.9 million bpd, Iran around 4.0 million, the UAE 3.0 million, Kuwait 2.7 million—and then there's Iraq, presently at 2.5 million and likely to reach at least 4.0 million by 2015. Still, Beijing has yet to be fully convinced that this is a safe supply, especially given all those US "forward operating sites" in the UAE, Bahrain, Kuwait, Qatar, and Oman, plus those roaming naval battle groups in the Persian Gulf.

On the gas front, China definitely counts on a South Asian game changer. Beijing has already spent $200 million on the first phase in the construction of a deep-water port at Gwadar in Pakistan's Balochistan

Province. It wanted, and got from Islamabad, "sovereign guarantees to the port's facilities." Gwadar is only 400 kilometers from Hormuz. With Gwadar, the Chinese Navy would have a homeport that would easily allow it to monitor traffic in the strait and someday perhaps even thwart the US Navy's expansionist designs in the Indian Ocean.

But Gwadar has another infinitely juicier future role. It could prove the pivot in a competition between two long-discussed pipelines: TAPI and IPI. TAPI stands for the Turkmenistan-Afghanistan-Pakistan-India pipeline, which can never be built as long as US and NATO occupation forces are fighting the resistance umbrella conveniently labeled "Taliban" in Afghanistan. IPI, however, is the Iran-Pakistan-India pipeline, also known as the "peace pipeline" (which, of course, would make TAPI the "war pipeline"). To Washington's immeasurable distress, last June, Iran and Pakistan **finally closed** the deal to build the "IP" part of IPI, with Pakistan assuring Iran that either India or China could later be brought into the project.

Whether it's IP, IPI, or IPC, Gwadar will be a key node. If, under pressure from Washington, which treats Tehran like the plague, India is forced to pull out of the project, China already has made it clear that it wants in. The Chinese would then build a Pipelineistan link from Gwadar along the Karakoram highway in Pakistan to China via the Khunjerab Pass—another overland corridor that would prove immune to US interference. It would have the added benefit of radically cutting down the 20,000-kilometer-long tanker route around the southern rim of Asia.

Arguably, for the Indians it would be a strategically sound move to align with IPI, trumping a deep suspicion that the Chinese will move to outflank them in the search for foreign energy with a "string of pearls" strategy: the setting up of a series of "home ports" along its key oil supply routes from Pakistan to Myanmar. In that case, Gwadar would no longer simply be a "Chinese" port.

As for Washington, it still believes that if TAPI is built, it will help keep India from fully breaking the U.S.-enforced embargo on Iran. Energy-starved Pakistan obviously prefers its "all-weather" ally China, which might commit itself to building all sorts of energy infrastructure within that flood-devastated country. In a nutshell, if the unprecedented energy cooperation between Iran, Pakistan, and China goes forward, it will signal a major defeat for Washington in the New Great Game in Eurasia, with enormous geopolitical and geoeconomic repercussions.

For the moment, Beijing's strategic priority has been to carefully develop a remarkably diverse set of energy-suppliers—a flow of energy that covers Russia, the South China Sea, Central Asia, the East China Sea, the Middle East, Africa, and South America. If China has so far proven masterly in the way it has played its cards in its Pipelineistan "war," the US hand—bypass Russia, elbow out China, isolate Iran—may soon be called for what it is: a bluff.

October 2010. Originally at TomDispatch.com

Have (Infinite) War, Will Travel

Anyone aware enough to think that Washington's goal is not to "win" the unwinnable AfPak quagmire but to keep playing its bloody infinite war game forever is now eligible for a personal stimulus package (in gold).

Let's review the recent evidence. All of a sudden, the White House, the Pentagon and the United States House of Representatives have all embarked on a new narrative: forget major US troop withdrawal from Afghanistan in 2011; let's move the goalpost to 2014.

Then wily Afghan President Hamid Karzai tells the Washington Post he does not want all these US troops roaming around "his" country no more, adding please, stop killing my people with Special Forces night ops—a euphemism for Pentagon terrorism.

General David "I'm always positioning myself for 2012" Petraeus is "astonished." How could he not be? After all, Karzai wanted to give the boot to private contractors—undisputed AfPak champions of false-flag black ops—then he gave up, as he might give up again on the night raids. As for Petraeus, he only wants the best of both worlds; kick up the hell-raising, as in drone hits and night ops (who cares about collateral damage?) and sit back and talk with the Pakistani ISI-created Taliban.

Incidentally, Petraeus' counter-insurgency myth has been buried in the plains south of the Hindu Kush (not that many in the US noted). The counter-insurgency (COIN) myth implies that Washington, NATO and what passes for "Afghan security forces" could "take, clear, hold and build" areas previously controlled by the Taliban. They could not accomplish any of this even in Marjah, insistently sold by the Pentagon and compliant corporate media as a success, not to mention much bigger Kandahar.

Former US Secretary of State Colin Powell has just weighed in on CNN, admitting the US won't be "pulling out 100,000 troops. I don't know how many troops we'll pull out." Powell also said that "inside the national security team," the whole thing is "conditions-based." Thus "conditions" may be bent to suit any narrative. Sharp noses may immediately detect a whiff of Vietnam, and Powell had to insist that Afghanistan is not that country. Well, whether Karzai is increasingly becoming the new Ngo Dinh Diem is beside the point; his assassination would not solve anything anyway.

And all this while a 71-page Council on Foreign Relations report written by 25 "experts" gets a lot of traction in Washington. The report finds that the war costs a fortune, may not serve US interests and it's not "clear that the effort will succeed." Do people get paid to conclude this? The report also meekly suggests that depending on President Barack Obama's December strategic AfPak review, the US "should move quickly to recalculate its military presence in Afghanistan." It won't.

Let's try following the money. The AfPak war costs roughly US $7 billion a month—money that Washington needs to borrow from Beijing. Afghanistan in itself costs $65 billion a year—not counting NATO and humanitarian aid. Afghanistan's gross domestic product is only $22 billion. So Washington is spending three times the wealth of a whole country just to occupy it. Money for nothing. Properly invested, by this time Afghanistan would be the new Singapore.

AfPak costs nearly $100 billion a year. Surrealist as it may seem, polls indicate that for most Americans the US federal budget deficit is not a priority. No wonder no election candidates on November 2 emitted a peep about the ridiculously expensive quagmire.

Let's face it. Whoever is writing this screenplay deserves an Oscar.

All you need is NATO

According to the official narrative, technically NATO only left its (cavernous) building in Europe for Afghanistan under the organization's Article 5 (emphasizing collective defense) to help Washington fight George W Bush's "war on terror" against al-Qaeda. Yet even somnolent diplomats in Brussels know that Osama bin Laden and his deputy Ayman al-Zawahiri crossed from eastern Afghanistan to Pakistan in early December 2001, and disappeared into a black void.

This would never prevent NATO chief Anders Fogh Rasmussen—ahead of the NATO summit this weekend in Lisbon—stressing that the war, well, goes on forever, as in "there is no alternative to continuing military operations." NATO's council secretary Edmund Whiteside didn't mince his words, "Afghanistan will be a very long military venture." And German Brigadier General Josef Blotz insists: "No timetable has been set for withdrawal of coalition troops."

The "strategy" of the 152,000-soldier, 50-nation, NATO-led International Security Assistance Force in Afghanistan ranks as a thesis on Monty Python geopolitics; to pledge a tsunami of euros for Karzai's shenanigans while forcing member countries to unleash ever more troops into the Taliban meat grinder—even though public opinion all across Europe says out loud "we can't take this anymore."

At least the commander of British forces in southern Afghanistan, Major-General Nick Carter, was sensible enough to stress that NATO would only know if it was "winning" by June 2011, "when the fighting season begins again" and everyone can "compare Taliban attacks with this year." Wait for another eight months and pray for 2014; that's the "strategy." Talk about on-the-ground intelligence.

NATO is absolutely useless at infiltrating the historic Taliban—also known as the Quetta shura, based in Balochistan (they cannot even point a drone to where Mullah Omar is). NATO cannot infiltrate the Haqqani network in North Waziristan. And NATO cannot infiltrate the Hezb-i-Islami network, controlled by former prime minister and bomber of Kabul (in the mid-1990s) Gulbuddin Hekmatyar, based in and around the strategic Khyber Pass.

The Pakistani ISI will always align with the Taliban under any circumstances—because this is Islamabad's way of protecting its "strategic depth" against India. The ISI will always insist on having the Taliban at the same table with Washington, otherwise any semblance of "talks" will be dead on arrival.

Islamabad's dream scenario is the Taliban, the Haqqanis and Hezb-i-Islami controlling southern and eastern Afghanistan. That would also be instrumental in preventing another one of Islamabad's primal fears—that disgruntled Pashtuns will unite and go all-out to form an across-the-artificial-border Pashtunistan.

The key to all this mess is not Obama, Karzai, the Pentagon or NATO. It's which way General Ashfaq Parvez Kiani, number 29 on Forbes' list of the most powerful people in the world, will see the wind blowing. As much as during the Bush "war on terror" years, when Islamabad was ruled from Washington, during the Obama AfPak years the White House is a hostage of Islamabad.

But for the Pentagon/NATO axis, Pakistan is just a drop in the ocean. Next Friday and Saturday, at the Lisbon summit, the world will be presented with a NATO-goes-global narrative. Team Pentagon/NATO will be convinced to abandon its privileged outpost of infinite war—Afghanistan—over its dead nuclear bombs. After all, Washington/Brussels has implanted a precious foothold in the heart of Eurasia—arguably for life.

The Lisbon summit, moreover, will see NATO formally adopting a new strategic concept—which essentially means keeping its nuclear arsenal in perpetuity, including US nuclear bombs stationed in Europe. You know, those nuclear bombs that Iran does not have (but Pakistan and India, not to mention Israel, do). Paraphrasing the great Burt Bacharach, what the world needs now, is NATO sweet NATO.

November 2010

US A KID IN A NATO CANDY STORE

As clinically on target as a pat-down in a major US airport, the Pentagon got a fabulous box of chocolates—and then some—from its 27 NATO allies at last weekend's Lisbon summit.

The chocolates come in a full spectrum of flavors.

One: NATO's new "Strategic Concept," complete with European-wide cyber-warfare subordinated to a "meet the old boss, same as the old boss" pattern—the Pentagon's new Cyber Command, euphemistically defined as "centralized cyber protection."

Two: The promise of the whole of Europe—in theory—enveloped by a missile defense dome ("missile defense will become an integral part of our overall defense posture").

Three: US tactical nuclear weapons indefinitely stationed in five bases scattered across European soil.

Four: 20 NATO "partners" still shelling out troops for the Afghan war for, well, forever. (At least the Lisbon summit declaration did not beat around the bush: "Transition will be conditions-based, not calendar-driven, and will not equate to withdrawal of ISAF [International Security Assistance Force] troops.")

NATO has also acquired what seems to be a new missile-defense "partner" all across Eurasia—from the Baltic to the Pacific Ocean: Russia. But contrary to the Western corporate-media narrative, Russia has only agreed to a study of "possible" missile threats and to engage in a vague "dialogue" before a possible joint decision by defense ministers from NATO countries in June 2011.

The Pentagon/NATO Star Wars remake has been relentlessly spun as defense against a highly hypothetical full-scale ballistic missile attack by either Iran or North Korea. Even assuming this is not a Marvel Comics stunt, such a system would rely on Airborne Warning and Control Systems, which even a moderately skilled hacker could jam. And all this assumes that the respective leaderships of "axis of evil" members Iran and North Korea are in the business of committing *seppuku*—ritual suicide.

So, essentially, the "dome" is a public-relations myth. But if this Star Wars remake is interpreted as a sort of large-scale improvised explosive device conceived to "contain" strategic competitor China in a not-so-distant future, then the script gets much juicier.

A prodigy of intelligence

NATO pledged to hand over security in Afghanistan to Afghans by the end of 2014. But, just in case, it also pledged to keep occupying it indefinitely. Even 2014 (anybody remember 2011?) is an "aspirational" goal, according to Pentagon spokesman Geoff Morrell. As to how many US/NATO troops will be getting a piece of the action from 2015 onwards, that's a classic example of one of former US defense secretary Donald Rumsfeld's "known unknowns."

As far as a "known known" goes, nothing beats the Fake Mullah Dude gambit.

A diplomat told the *New York Times* that Mullah Akhtar Muhammad Mansour, the alleged number two to invisible Taliban leader Mullah Omar involved in discussions with the Karzai government, is not the real mullah: he is a fake. General David Petraeus had to run to the rescue—if not for cover—saying that the Pentagon suspected something was off. NATO was involved in the discussions—which have been going on for a few months now. The fake mullah did not fail to bag a lot of cash in the process. And obviously Mullah Omar's gang in Quetta must be laughing their turbans off.

Once again, NATO's fabled multilingual skills don't mean that you can dust up your Polish when you need to think in Pashto. File this one as another spectacular triumph of Pentagon/NATO intelligence.

NATO's self-described "mission" since 2001 has been to fight against "international terrorism." Even low-level CIA operatives know there are no "al-Qaeda" in Afghanistan, apart from 20 or 30 invisible jihadi trainers. So this war is not about al-Qaeda.

On the other hand, Pashtuns comprise 42% of Afghanistan's population.

NATO is attacking anyone from the Gulbuddin Hekmatyar faction to the Jalaluddin Haqqani network, and all the disgruntled tribal guerrilla factions in between. The Pentagon/NATO "strategy" has been essentially to take out mid-level Taliban or guerrilla commanders. Problem is, most are Pashtun tribal leaders. Inevitably their tribes rebel en masse, be they Taliban-affiliated or not, and vow to kill the invaders. The bottom line: Afghanistan is nothing but a Western war against Pashtuns.

In yet one more spectacular PR failure, Pentagon/NATO even forgot to inform the Pashtuns about it. A report by a International Council on Security and Development (ICOS) think-tank has just showed that 92% of Pashtuns in Helmand and Kandahar provinces know absolutely nothing about 9/11. The report noted that the "relationship gap" between Afghans and the "international community" was "dramatic." File this one as understatement of the decade.

So a bunch of angry Pashtuns are in fact the ultimate threat to NATO and its global, non-stop expansionist drive from the Balkans to the former Soviet Union—instilling supreme fear in NATO's 36 divisions, 120 brigades, 11,000 tanks, 23,000 artillery pieces and 4,500 fighter jets (and that's only what's stationed in Europe).

If NATO is scared to death of Pashtuns, imagine when it turns its attention to the nomadic Tuareg—the indigenous population of most of central Sahara and the Sahel, with impressive numbers in the north of both Niger and Mali. In the current, concerted Western campaign to define them as pawns of "evil" al-Qaeda in the Maghreb (AQIM), NATO should be warned that the Tuareg can be every bit the bad asses that the Pashtuns are. God help the white man's burden.

NATO did make a deal with Moscow to send logistical support to Afghanistan through Russia—and not Pakistan. That does put Islamabad on the spot. Next time Washington won't even ask permission to ramp up the drone war. In fact, this game is already on.

The operative mood now is not only bomb the tribal areas (especially after the Haqqani network scattered northwards, from North Waziristan to Kurram); it is also bomb Quetta, Balochistan's capital—where Taliban leader Mullah Omar may be hiding (and laughing his turban off).

Pakistan's Ministry of Interior duly denies everything—even as the CIA and Pakistan's ISI "increase their cooperation." So one should expect major upcoming "collateral damage" in and around Quetta; and the Balochistan separatist movements will be having a ball. The bottom line: real men go to Quetta.

The war boutique

Whatever the drama quotient involved, one may be certain that NATO's nuclear/cyber-warfare/missile-defense embrace will be striving to include the whole white world. As the Lisbon summit declaration proclaimed: "The promotion of Euro-Atlantic security is best assured through a wide network of partner relationships with countries and organizations around the globe." Translation: Europe, apart from posing as an oversized boutique seducing the Asian consuming hordes, now exists primarily as a forward operating base for war around the globe.

In fact, the US, NATO and the European Union are now on the way to becoming essentially the same entity—as in the president of the EU's European Council, faceless Belgian bureaucrat Herman Van Rompuy, telling NATO leaders in Lisbon: "The ability of our two organizations to shape our future security environment would be enormous if they worked together. It is time to break down the remaining walls between them." Pashtuns of the world unite; if you keep rocking, these walls will definitely crumble.

November 2010

The Odyssey Dawn top 10

War is peace. Protesters are now off-camera, missile diplomacy is on camera. Packaged in moral uprightness, Tomahawks, Typhoons, Tornados, Rafales, Mirages, B-2s and F-18s—not to mention sexy European Storm Shadow cruise missiles and possible guest star the F-22 Raptor radar-evading stealth jet—now speak the language of democracy. These "military assets," displaying their "unique capabilities," are now "protecting the Libyan people." Run for cover—or become collateral damage.

And now for our top ten list:

10. The return of Ulysses. Operation "Odyssey Dawn"? Gotta hand it to Pentagon ghost writers. Homer's Odyssey is the archetype of all travel writing. So Odysseus/Ulysses roams the Med again. The return of the heroes who conquered Troy is now the return of the heroes who gave you Shock and Awe. Benghazi is Ithaca, with Tripoli in the waiting list. Muammar Gaddafi plays the Cyclops. But who's Circe? Hillary Clinton? Homeric Ulysses was upgraded from a fishing boat to the *USS Mount Whitney*, the flagship of the US Navy's 6th Fleet. So one must assume that, for now, Ulysses is commander Samuel Locklear III, who's in charge of the bombing.

As for Homer revised by Shakespeare, the trophy goes to chairman of the US Joint Chief of Staff, Admiral Mike Mullen. He told CNN Operation Odyssey Dawn "isn't about seeing him [Gaddafi] go." But then he told the National Broadcasting Corporation (NBC) Gaddafi could stay, as in "it's very uncertain on how this ends." No wonder no one in this Odyssey has yet claimed to be Penelope.

9. The invisible Africa Command (AFRICOM). There's total radio silence about the commander of the US AFRICOM, General Carter Ham. He's in charge of all those Tomahawks, from his office in Stuttgart, Germany; after all, none among 53 African countries offered to host AFRICOM. After the current phase 1, the command switches from AFRICOM to the Anglo-French duo, or to NATO in Brussels. AFRICOM's main business is to guarantee the rapid deployment of "highly mobile troops"—to fight the never-extinct "war on terror"; laser in on all those oil fields; try to offset China's business drive in Africa; talk about an open-ended mission. In short: AFRICOM is about the Pentagon's militarization of Africa—suavely sold as "bringing peace and security." It's all part of the time-tested Pentagon's Full Spectrum Dominance doctrine.

8. The R2P enigma. Top American humanitarian imperialists—or liberal hawks—include US Secretary of State Hillary Clinton, US ambassador to the UN Susan Rice, and National Security Council senior directors Samantha Power and Gayle Smith. They are all suckers for R2P—"responsibility to protect," the new international norm that supposedly prevents and stops genocides, war crimes, ethnic cleansing and crimes against humanity.

R2P is still hazy. How many civilians must be killed before R2P kicks in? A few thousand? (a fair estimate of Gaddafi's victims before Odyssey Dawn). And where next for R2P? Here's a list of candidates. Yemen. Bahrain. Saudi Arabia. Israel. Uzbekistan. Ivory Coast. Sudan. Somalia. North Korea. Myanmar. Iran. Pakistan. And—remember Xinjiang and Tibet—China. Don't count on the UN to "protect" civilians in any of these destinations.

7. The new Obama doctrine, or Bush 2.0. The Obama administration turned George W Bush's wars in Iraq and Afghanistan into open-ended occupations; started an air/counter-insurgency war in Pakistan; bolstered

a war in Somalia; bolstered a war in Yemen; and now started a war in Libya. The Western/Arab League war in Libya perfectly fits the new, two-pronged Obama doctrine of US outreach/regime alteration; outreach (former "regime change") for "evil dictators," alteration for "our" bastards.

That accounts for Washington desperately trying to position itself on the right side of history at least in one chapter of the great 2011 Arab revolt—amid all the geostrategic imperatives of trying to somewhat control the course of the Arab revolutions, and to keep an eye on the oil.

Gaddafi for his part labeled the US/Anglo-French bombing a "crusader aggression" and his regime's resistance, a "long war." He thus managed to mix the Pentagon with al-Qaeda in one sweep. And we always thought they were fighting each other. His Bab al-Azizia compound in Tripoli has already been bombed. At least his family is not featured in a Pentagon deck of cards—yet.

6. No R2P for Israel. In late 2008, while no one was watching, Israel bombed Gaza, killed 1,300 people, the absolute majority civilians, and destroyed at least 20,000 buildings. The UN didn't bother to invoke R2P, or impose a no-fly zone over Gaza to protect its civilians (50% of them children). Israel never respected any of countless UN Security Council resolutions. By the way, George W Bush invaded Iraq in 2003 without a UN Security Council resolution.

5. No R2P for Yemen. President Ali Abdullah Saleh is a "valuable ally" in the "war on terror"—against al-Qaeda in the Arabian Peninsula (AQAP); although he is the Yemeni Gaddafi, he falls into the privileged "regime alteration" category. President Barack Obama said he "strongly condemn[s]" snipers killing Yemeni civilians and says those responsible "must be held accountable." This means Saleh's government. Bit of a

problem though; these are the people getting US cash and weapons to fight "terror."

4. The oh so democratic Arab League. The voting at the Arab League calling for a no-fly zone over Libya was unanimous. But at first, Algeria and Syria were strongly against it. Damascus publicly justified itself as against another Western intervention in Arab affairs.

This never deterred the six Gulf Cooperation Council (GCC) dictatorships (Saudi Arabia, Bahrain, Kuwait, Oman, Qatar and UAE), which lobbied hard for no-fly. American and European diplomats are desperate for the Arab League—and not NATO—to do something, like flying the odd jet and paying most of the bill to provide the illusion that the West is not attacking another Muslim country.

Washington explicitly requested that from Qatar, the UAE and Jordan. Qatar and UAE—which helped Saudi Arabia to invade Bahrain—are now invoked to secure "democracy" for Libya. The UAE will support democracy with 24 Mirage 2000-9s and F-16s and Qatar with up to six Mirage 2000-5s.

The Arab League first warned against an "attack" on Libya—as if a no-fly zone could be imposed by broomsticks, not bombs. Then supreme opportunist Amr Moussa, head of the Arab League, criticized Odyssey Dawn because of the inevitable collateral damage. And then he backtracked. No one cares, as long as the Arab League rubber stamps Odyssey Dawn to make it look like an Arab decision.

3. No R2P for Bahrain. The House of Saud invasion of Bahrain to help Sunni "cousins" the al-Khalifa dynasty—with pitiful coverage by otherwise progressive al-Jazeera—smells like a deal between the House of Saud and the Emir of Qatar, which implies Washington behind it as well; the immensely corrupt and fearful House of Saud does absolutely nothing

without Washington's approval. al-Jazeera reports have called for a "dialogue" between government and opposition in Bahrain; no such calls for Libya.

The GCC dictatorships are basically Pentagon annexes. Since 2007, they've bought no less than $70 billion in weapons—and counting. Libya is part of the African Union (AU). Gaddafi requested support from the AU against his internal opposition; that's exactly the same as Bahrain asking for support from the GCC. The difference is the AU did not vote for a no-fly zone—nor invaded a neighbor, a la Saudi Arabia.

The al-Khalifas in Bahrain have been so scared by the protest movement that they had to physically demolish the Pearl monument at the center of the homonymous square in Manama, with its six white curved beams topped with a huge pearl. This implies also destroying Bahrain's history; before becoming "business-friendly," Bahrain was a pearl diving center. Now it's just "bullet-friendly Bahrain."

2. How good was my dictator. Just yesterday Italian Prime Minister Silvio "Bunga Bunga" Berlusconi was literally kissing Gaddafi's hand—and allowing him to pose this tent in Rome. He dropped him like a stone. Same with the Brits who were merrily selling loads of weapons to the colonel.

As for neo-Napoleonic French President Nicolas Sarkozy, Gaddafi was a godsend—allowing Sarko to officially pose as the new Arab nationalist hero. France in effect prohibited NATO from intervening at the start of Odyssey Dawn, so Sarko's dashing Mirages could get all the glory. Carla Bruni—who calls his husband Chou Chou—must be very impressed; who needs bunga bunga when you can actually bang, bang?

1. Democratic Saudi Arabia. To have the Holy Grail of medievalism and repression—the House of Saud—voting in the Arab League to bring

democracy to Libya while quashing any progressive moves inside the kingdom (and invading a neighbor) will forever live in infamy as the Top Hypocrisy of the Great 2011 Arab Revolt. King Abdullah's billionaire package of "reforms," ie bribes, essentially bolster the House of Saud's two strategic pillars; the security/repression establishment (60,000 new jobs for the Interior Ministry), and the religious clerics (more money to the Commission for the Promotion of Virtue and Prevention of Vice). Even if they have successfully preempted the kingdom's "Day of Rage," this proves how scared they really are.

What many don't know is that Operation Odyssey Dawn is personal—and has nothing to do with Greek heroism but Bedouin hatred. It revolves around the extremely bad blood between King Abdullah and Gaddafi since 2002, in the run-up to the war on Iraq, when Gaddafi accused Abdullah of selling out the Arab world to Washington. So this is not Operation Odyssey Dawn; it's Operation House of Saud Takes Out Gaddafi. With all the heavy lifting subcontracted to the West, of course, and the eastern Libya protesters posing as extras.

Odyssey Dawn—a "just war"—started exactly eight years after the Iraq war. In 2003, at the start of Operation Enduring Freedom—still ongoing, having "liberated" over a million Iraqis from life—George W Bush said, "American and coalition forces are in the early stages of military operations to disarm Iraq, to free its people and to defend the world from grave danger."

This Saturday, at the start of Operation Odyssey Dawn, Barack Obama said, "Today we are part of a broad coalition. We are answering the calls of a threatened people. And we are acting in the interests of the United States and the world."

Maybe we should call this whole thing Operation Enduring Odyssey—and send the bill to the House of Saud.

March 2011

THERE'S NO BUSINESS LIKE WAR BUSINESS

Lies, hypocrisy and hidden agendas. This is what US President Barack Obama did not dwell on when explaining his Libya doctrine to America and the world. The mind boggles with so many black holes engulfing this splendid little war that is not a war (a "time-limited, scope-limited military action," as per the White House)—compounded with the inability of progressive thinking to condemn, at the same time, the ruthlessness of the Muammar Gaddafi regime and the Anglo-French-American "humanitarian" bombing.

UN Security Council resolution 1973 has worked like a Trojan horse, allowing the Anglo-French-American consortium—and NATO—to become the UN's air force in its support of an armed uprising. Apart from having nothing to do with protecting civilians, this arrangement is absolutely illegal in terms of international law. The inbuilt endgame, as even malnourished African kids know by now, but has never been acknowledged, is regime change.

Lieutenant General Charles Bouchard of Canada, NATO's commander for Libya, may insist all he wants that the mission is purely designed to protect civilians. Yet those "innocent civilians" operating tanks and firing Kalashnikovs as part of a rag-tag wild bunch are in fact soldiers in a civil war—and the focus should be on whether NATO from now on will remain their air force, following the steps of the Anglo-French-American consortium. Incidentally, the "coalition of the wiling" fighting Libya consists of only 12 NATO members (out of 28) plus Qatar. This has absolutely nothing to do with an "international community."

The full verdict on the UN-mandated no-fly zone will have to wait for the emergence of a "rebel" government and the end of the civil war (if it ends soon). Then it will be possible to analyze how Tomahawking and bombing was ever justified; why civilians in Cyrenaica were "protected" while those in Tripoli were Tomahawked; what sort of "rebel" motley crew was "saved"; whether this whole thing was legal in the first place; how the resolution was a cover for regime change; how the love affair between the Libyan "revolutionaries" and the West may end in bloody divorce (remember Afghanistan); and which Western players stand to immensely profit from the wealth of a new, unified (or balkanized) Libya.

For the moment at least, it's quite easy to identify the profiteers.

The Pentagon

Pentagon supremo Robert Gates said this weekend, with a straight face, there are only three repressive regimes in the whole Middle East: Iran, Syria and Libya. The Pentagon is taking out the weak link—Libya. The others were always key features of the neo-conservative take-out/evil list. Saudi Arabia, Yemen, Bahrain, etc are model democracies.

As for this "now you see it, now you don't" war, the Pentagon is managing to fight it not once, but twice. It started with AFRICOM—established under the George W Bush administration, beefed up under Obama, and rejected by scores of African governments, scholars and human rights organizations. Now the war is transitioning to NATO, which is essentially Pentagon rule over its European minions.

This is AFRICOM's first African war, conducted up to now by General Carter Ham out of his headquarters in un-African Stuttgart. AFRICOM, as Horace Campbell, professor of African American studies and political science at Syracuse University puts it, is a scam; "fundamentally a front for US military contractors like Dyncorp, MPRI and KBR operating in Africa. US military planners who benefit from the revolving door of privatization of warfare are delighted by the opportunity to give AFRICOM credibility under the facade of the Libyan intervention."

AFRICOM's Tomahawks also hit—metaphorically—the African Union (AU), which, unlike the Arab League, cannot be easily bought by the West. The Arab Gulf petro-monarchies all cheered the bombing—but not Egypt and Tunisia. Only five African countries are not subordinated to AFRICOM; Libya is one of them, along with Sudan, Ivory Coast, Eritrea and Zimbabwe.

NATO

NATO's master plan is to rule the Mediterranean as a NATO lake. Under these "optics" (Pentagon-speak) the Mediterranean is infinitely more important nowadays as a theater of war than AfPak.

There are only three out of 20 nations on or in the Mediterranean that are not full members of NATO or allied with its "partnership" programs: Libya, Lebanon and Syria. Make no mistake; Syria is next. Lebanon is already under a NATO blockade since 2006. Now a blockade also applies to Libya. The US—via NATO—is just about to square the circle.

Saudi Arabia

What a deal. King Abdullah gets rid of his eternal foe Gaddafi. The House of Saud—in trademark abject fashion—bends over backwards for the West's benefit. The attention of world public opinion is diverted from the Saudis invading Bahrain to smash a legitimate, peaceful, pro-democracy protest movement.

The House of Saud sold the fiction that "the Arab League" as a whole voted for a no-fly zone. That is a lie; out of 22 members, only 11 were present at the vote; six are members of the Gulf Cooperation Council (GCC), of which Saudi Arabia is the top dog. The House of Saud just needed to twist the arms of three more. Syria and Algeria were against it. Translation; only nine out of 22 Arab countries voted for the no-fly zone.

Now Saudi Arabia can even order GCC head Abdulrahman al-Attiyah to say, with a straight face, "the Libyan system has lost its legitimacy." As for the "legitimate" House of Saud and the al-Khalifas in Bahrain, someone should induct them into the Humanitarian Hall of Fame.

Qatar

The hosts of the 2022 soccer World Cup sure know how to clinch a deal. Their Mirages are helping to bomb Libya while Doha gets ready to market eastern Libya oil. Qatar promptly became the first Arab nation to recognize the Libyan "rebels" as the only legitimate government of the country only one day after securing the oil marketing deal.

The "rebels"

All the worthy democratic aspirations of the Libyan youth movement notwithstanding, the most organized opposition group happens to be the National Front for the Salvation of Libya—financed for years by the House of Saud, the CIA and French intelligence. The rebel "Interim Transitional National Council" is little else than the good ol' National Front, plus a few military defectors. This is the elite of the "innocent civilians" the "coalition" is "protecting."

Right on cue, the "Interim Transitional National Council" has got a new finance minister, US-educated economist Ali Tarhouni. He disclosed that a bunch of Western countries gave them credit backed by Libya's sovereign fund, and the British allowed them to access $1.1 billion of Gaddafi's funds. This means the Anglo-French-American consortium—and now NATO—will only pay for the bombs. As war scams go this one is priceless; the West uses Libya's own cash to finance a bunch of opportunist Libyan rebels to fight the Libyan government. And on top of it the Americans, the Brits and the French feel the love for all that bombing. Neo-cons must be kicking themselves; why couldn't former US deputy defense secretary Paul Wolfowitz come up with something like this for Iraq 2003?

The French

Oh la la, this could be material for a Proustian novel. The top spring collection in Paris catwalks is President Nicolas Sarkozy's fashion show— a no-fly zone model with Mirage/Rafale air strike accessories. This fashion show was masterminded by Nouri Mesmari, Gaddafi's chief of protocol, who defected to France in October 2010. The Italian secret service leaked to selected media outlets how he did it. The role of the Direction Générale de la Sécurité Extérieure (DGSE), the French secret service, has been more or less explained on paid website Maghreb Confidential.

Essentially, the Benghazi revolt *coq au vin* had been simmering since November 2010. The cooks were Mesmari, air force colonel Abdullah Gehani, and the French secret service. Mesmari was called "Libyan WikiLeak," because he spilled over virtually every one of Gaddafi's military secrets. Sarkozy loved it—furious because Gaddafi had cancelled juicy contracts to buy Rafales (to replace his Mirages now being bombed) and French-built nuclear power plants.

That explains why Sarkozy has been so gung-ho into posing as the new Arab liberator, was the first leader of a European power to recognize the "rebels" (to the disgust of many at the European Union), and was the first to bomb Gaddafi's forces.

This busts open the role of shameless self-promoting philosopher Bernard Henri-Levy, who's now frantically milking in the world's media that he phoned Sarkozy from Benghazi and awakened his humanitarian streak. Either Levy is a patsy, or a convenient "intellectual" cherry added to the already-prepared bombing cake.

Terminator Sarkozy is unstoppable. He has just warned every single Arab ruler that they face Libya-style bombing if they crack down on protesters. He even said that the Ivory Coast was "next." Bahrain and Yemen, of course, are exempt. As for the US, it is once again supporting a military coup (it didn't work with Omar "Sheikh al-Torture" Suleiman in Egypt; maybe it will work in Libya).

Al-Qaeda

The oh so convenient bogeyman resurfaces. The Anglo-French-American consortium—and now NATO—are (again) fighting alongside al-Qaeda, represented by al-Qaeda in the Maghreb.

Libyan rebel leader Abdelhakim al-Hasidi—who has fought alongside the Taliban in Afghanistan—extensively confirmed to Italian media that he had personally recruited "around 25" jihadis from the Derna area in eastern Libya to fight against the US in Iraq; now "they are on the front lines in Adjabiya."

This after Chad's president Idriss Deby stressed that AQM had raided military arsenals in Cyrenaica and may be now holding quite a few surface-to-air missiles. In early March, AQM publicly supported the "rebels." The ghost of Osama bin Laden must be pulling a Cheshire cat; once again he gets the Pentagon to work for him.

The water privatizers

Few in the West may know that Libya—along with Egypt—sits over the Nubian Sandstone Aquifer; that is, an ocean of extremely valuable fresh water. So yes, this "now you see it, now you don't" war is a crucial water war. Control of the aquifer is priceless—as in "rescuing" valuable natural resources from the "savages."

This Water Pipelineistan—buried underground deep in the desert along 4,000 km—is the Great Man-Made River Project (GMMRP), which Gaddafi built for $25 billion without borrowing a single cent from the

IMF or the World Bank (what a bad example for the developing world). The GMMRP supplies Tripoli, Benghazi and the whole Libyan coastline. The amount of water is estimated by scientists to be the equivalent to 200 years of water flowing down the Nile.

Compare this to the so-called three sisters—Veolia (formerly Vivendi), Suez Ondeo (formerly Generale des Eaux) and Saur—the French companies that control over 40% of the global water market. All eyes must imperatively focus on whether these pipelines are bombed. An extremely possible scenario is that if they are, juicy "reconstruction" contracts will benefit France. That will be the final step to privatize all this—for the moment free—water. From shock doctrine to water doctrine.

Well, that's only a short list of profiteers—no one knows who'll get the oil—and the natural gas—in the end. Meanwhile, the (bombing) show must go on. There's no business like war business.

March 2011

Exposed: The US-Saudi Libya deal

You invade Bahrain. We take out Muammar Gaddafi in Libya. This, in short, is the essence of a deal struck between the Barack Obama administration and the House of Saud. Two diplomatic sources at the UN independently confirmed that Washington, via Secretary of State Hillary Clinton, gave the go-ahead for Saudi Arabia to invade Bahrain and crush the pro-democracy movement in their neighbor in exchange for a "yes" vote by the Arab League for a no-fly zone over Libya—the main rationale that led to UN Security Council resolution 1973.

The revelation came from two different diplomats, a European and a member of the BRIC group, and was made separately to a US scholar and *Asia Times Online*. According to diplomatic protocol, their names cannot be disclosed. One of the diplomats said, "This is the reason why we could not support resolution 1973. We were arguing that Libya, Bahrain and Yemen were similar cases, and calling for a fact-finding mission. We maintain our official position that the resolution is not clear, and may be interpreted in a belligerent manner."

As *Asia Times Online* has reported, a full Arab League endorsement of a no-fly zone is a myth. Of the 22 full members, only 11 were present at the voting. Six of them were Gulf Cooperation Council (GCC) members, the US-supported club of Gulf kingdoms/sheikhdoms, of which Saudi Arabia is the top dog. Syria and Algeria were against it. Saudi Arabia only had to "seduce" three other members to get the vote.

Translation: only nine out of 22 members of the Arab League voted for the no-fly zone. The vote was essentially a House of Saud-led operation, with Arab League secretary general Amr Moussa keen to polish his CV with Washington with an eye to become the next Egyptian President.

Thus, in the beginning, there was the great 2011 Arab revolt. Then, inexorably, came the US-Saudi counter-revolution.

Profiteers rejoice

Humanitarian imperialists will spin en masse this is a "conspiracy," as they have been spinning the bombing of Libya prevented a hypothetical massacre in Benghazi. They will be defending the House of Saud—saying it acted to squash Iranian subversion in the Gulf; obviously R2P—"responsibility to protect" does not apply to people in Bahrain. They will be heavily promoting post-Gaddafi Libya as a new—oily—human rights Mecca, complete with US intelligence assets, black ops, Special Forces and dodgy contractors.

Whatever they say won't alter the facts on the ground—the graphic results of the US-Saudi dirty dancing. *Asia Times Online* has already reported on who profits from the foreign intervention in Libya (see There's no business like war business, March 30). Players include the Pentagon (via AFRICOM), NATO, Saudi Arabia, the Arab League's Moussa, and Qatar. Add to the list the al-Khalifa dynasty in Bahrain, assorted weapons contractors, and the usual neoliberal suspects eager to privatize everything in sight in the new Libya—even the water. And we're not even talking about the Western vultures hovering over the Libyan oil and gas industry.

Exposed, above all, is the astonishing hypocrisy of the Obama administration, selling a crass geopolitical coup involving northern Africa and the Persian Gulf as a humanitarian operation. As for the fact of another US war on a Muslim nation, that's just a "kinetic military action."

There's been wide speculation in both the US and across the Middle East that considering the military stalemate—and short of the "coalition of the willing" bombing the Gaddafi family to oblivion—Washington, London and Paris might settle for the control of eastern Libya; a northern African version of an oil-rich Gulf Emirate. Gaddafi would be left with a starving North Korea-style Tripolitania.

But considering the latest high-value defections from the regime, plus the desired endgame ("Gaddafi must go," in President Obama's own words), Washington, London, Paris and Riyadh won't settle for nothing but the whole kebab. Including a strategic base for both AFRICOM and NATO.

Round up the unusual suspects

One of the side effects of the dirty US-Saudi deal is that the White House is doing all it can to make sure the Bahrain drama is buried by US media. BBC America news anchor Katty Kay at least had the decency to stress, "they would like that one [Bahrain] to go away because there's no real upside for them in supporting the rebellion by the Shi'ites."

For his part the Emir of Qatar, Sheikh Hamad bin Khalifa al-Thani, showed up on al-Jazeera and said that action was needed because the Libyan people were attacked by Gaddafi. The otherwise excellent al-Jazeera journalists could have politely asked the emir whether he would send his Mirages to protect the people of Palestine from Israel, or his neighbors in Bahrain from Saudi Arabia.

The al-Khalifa dynasty in Bahrain is essentially a bunch of Sunni settlers who took over 230 years ago. For a great deal of the 20th century they were obliging slaves of the British empire. Modern Bahrain does not live under the specter of a push from Iran; that's an al-Khalifa (and House of Saud) myth.

Bahrainis, historically, have always rejected being part of a sort of Shi'ite nation led by Iran. The protests come a long way, and are part of a true national movement—way beyond sectarianism. No wonder the slogan in the iconic Pearl roundabout—smashed by the fearful al-Khalifa police state—was "neither Sunni nor Shi'ite; Bahraini."

What the protesters wanted was essentially a constitutional monarchy; a legitimate parliament; free and fair elections; and no more corruption. What they got instead was "bullet-friendly Bahrain" replacing "business-friendly Bahrain," and an invasion sponsored by the House of Saud.

And the repression goes on—invisible to US corporate media. Tweeters scream that everybody and his neighbor are being arrested. According to Nabeel Rajab, president of the Bahrain Center for Human Rights, over 400 people are either missing or in custody, some of them "arrested at checkpoints controlled by thugs brought in from other Arab and Asian countries—they wear black masks in the streets." Even blogger Mahmood Al Yousif was arrested at 3 am, leading to fears that the same will happen to any Bahraini who has blogged, tweeted, or posted Facebook messages in favor of reform.

Globocop is on a roll

Odyssey Dawn is now over. Enter Unified Protector—led by Canadian Charles Bouchard. Translation: the Pentagon (as in AFRICOM) transfers the "kinetic military action " to itself (as in NATO, which is nothing but the Pentagon ruling over Europe). AFRICOM and NATO are now one.

The NATO show will include air and cruise missile strikes; a naval blockade of Libya; and shady, unspecified ground operations to help the "rebels." Hardcore helicopter gunship raids a la AfPak—with attached "collateral damage"—should be expected.

A curious development is already visible. NATO is deliberately allowing Gaddafi forces to advance along the Mediterranean coast and repel the "rebels." There have been no surgical air strikes for quite a while.

The objective is possibly to extract political and economic concessions from the defector and Libyan exile-infested Interim National Council (INC)—a dodgy cast of characters including former Justice minister Mustafa Abdel Jalil, US-educated former secretary of planning Mahmoud Jibril, and former Virginia resident, new "military commander" and CIA asset Khalifa Hifter. The laudable, indigenous February 17 Youth movement—which was in the forefront of the Benghazi uprising—has been completely sidelined.

This is NATO's first African war, as Afghanistan is NATO's first Central/South Asian war. Now firmly configured as the UN's weaponized arm, Globocop NATO is on a roll implementing its "strategic concept" approved at the Lisbon summit last November (see Welcome to NATO-stan, *Asia Times Online*, November 20, 2010).

Gaddafi's Libya must be taken out so the Mediterranean—the *mare nostrum* of ancient Rome—becomes a NATO lake. Libya is the only nation in northern Africa not subordinated to AFRICOM or Centcom or any one of the myriad NATO "partnerships." The other non-NATO-related African nations are Eritrea, Sawahiri Arab Democratic Republic, Sudan and Zimbabwe.

Moreover, two members of NATO's "Istanbul Cooperation Initiative"—Qatar and the UAE—are now fighting alongside AFRICOM/NATO for the fist time. Translation: NATO and Persian Gulf partners are fighting a war in Africa. Europe? That's too provincial. Globocop is the way to go.

According to the Obama administration's own official doublespeak, dictators who are eligible for "US outreach"—such as in Bahrain and Yemen—may relax, and get away with virtually anything. As for those eligible for "regime alteration," from Africa to the Middle East and Asia, watch out. Globocop NATO is coming to get you. With or without dirty deals.

April 2011

Obama/Osama Rock the Casbah

The Sheikh he drove his Cadillac
He went a-cruisin' down the ville
The Muezzin was a-standin'
On the radiator grill

—The Clash, *Rock the Casbah*

It's irrelevant. It may be a rockin' Hollywood thriller—an Osama/Obama double bill (directed by Kathryn "Hurt Locker" Bigelow). But the targeted assassination—allegedly with an iconic American bullet to the head—of Osama bin Laden on Monday in fact only matches the irrelevancy the larger-than-life jihadi Godfather had sunk into.

US President Barack Obama may have turned the boogie sound on his 2012 re-election—bookmakers are giving him 1.75—way beyond the reach of a circus freak show featuring specimens such as mama grizzly Sarah Palin and billionaire bully (with a fox in his head) Donald Trump.

But was it "justice"—as Obama claimed? Justice—up to the age of the drone—implied a crime scene, evidence, courts, due process, a jury, a judge and a sentence. Former President George "war on terror" W Bush, in his bluntness, was closer to the mark: this was more like "US revenge."

Fundamentally he can't take it

At first sight, Bin Laden was not a casualty of war. He was a casualty of an irresistible push for democracy and social equity—the great 2011 Arab revolt. Bin Laden, the proponent of a restored Caliphate, shunned parliamentary democracy. History had made him irrelevant as much as al-Qaeda had been made irrelevant even before the Arab revolt—in geographic, political, cultural and social terms.

American exceptionalism and Western hysteria notwithstanding—the *in crowd say it's cool/to dig this chanting thing*—al-Qaeda and its declination of affiliates, off-shots and copycats are condemned to remain dwelling like ghosts in the periphery of the Muslim world, with a new generation of leaders directing the odd shoe or underwear bomber.

What's spookier is how the al-Qaeda narrative has been resuscitated as a specter hovering over the collective unconscious of the West. With the dangerous poetic metaphor of Bin Laden's body now rockin' an aquatic Casbah at the bottom of the Arabian Sea. The White House/Pentagon/CIA did not want a "shrine"; the shrine now happens to be diluted in waters patrolled by the US and not far from those shores where the House of Saud is conducting a harsh counter-revolution against the yearning for a better life.

It's as if the carefully staged, too good to be true, non-martyrdom of bin Laden was in fact opening the doors to a new breed of hell—with Washington and the West betting on their self-fulfilling prophecy; al-Qaeda will react "with a vengeance" (American style?), there will be blood, a lot more blood, and the Arab world will revert to barbarism instead of dreaming of democracy, as in *the crowd caught a whiff/of that crazy Casbah jive.*

Welcome to the resurrection of al-Qaeda as a death blow to the great 2011 Arab revolt.

We ban that boogie sound

There are plenty of reasons not to take at face value what may eventually be revealed as one of the most sophisticated psy-ops of the young 21st century.

A 14-member, four-helicopter, elite navy SEALs team, under the command of CIA director Leon Panetta, may have taken Bin Laden out. But the Pentagon narrative of an American golden bullet is as wobbly as *the King telling the boogie man/you have to let that raga drop*. Bin Laden had always said he would die as a *shaheed*—a martyr, fighting for his cause, and he would not surrender. One of his bodyguards would have come up with the bullet, under his command, when Bin Laden concluded that *by order of the Prophet* he would have to *ban that boogie sound*.

Spinning crossfire in Washington in the early hours led to the usual "US officials" stressing the Pakistani Inter-Services Intelligence (ISI) was kept out of the loop—as they would certainly tip Bin Laden about the operation, while Pentagon types insisted Bin Laden was killed a week ago in a drone strike (*the jet pilots tuned/to the cockpit radio blare*). Others spun that leads from the ISI itself led US Special Forces to the site—and then Washington used its own sources to confirm, "receive clearance to strike from Pakistan" and well, rock the Casbah.

GEO TV in Pakistan played a completely different mix. ISI types spun that the operation was in fact Pakistani—conducted after an army helicopter was shot down (Pentagon types also mentioned it) and a search party then got involved in a firefight. Pakistani troops helped cordon off the compound. They arrested a few Arab women, kids and armed Arabs who then confessed Bin Laden was there; that led to another firefight in which Bin Laden was killed. Two US helicopters then flew to the site and carried away the body of Bin Laden. According to this version, the fire in the compound was caused by the crashed helicopter.

The US "firefight" account is also murky. According to Obama's description, there were no US casualties; that doesn't sound like much of a "firefight." This may have been a heavily defended compound, or just a compound where US forces were holding Bin Laden.

The CIA is spinning this was a kill operation. That's also shaky. Capturing Bin Laden alive—just as with Saddam Hussein—would have been the ultimate minaret of humiliation, and a much juicier public relations coup for the White House. That may explain Washington's zeal to dispose of his body in the Arabian Sea as soon as possible—to the despair of many a sharia law specialist.

The compound was burned to the ground. Conveniently—just as in 9/11—there is no crime scene, and no body. This would be rejected in any CSI script conference. The whole world awaits an incontrovertible photo of the body as well as the results of the DNA test.

And sooner rather than later—as with Saddam—some informant will reveal there was nothing Hollywood about the kill; it all came about as an enterprising individual decided to finally bag the $50 million reward. There's only one destination this almighty leak may have come from: the Pakistani ISI. And if that is the case, army chief General Ashfaq Kiani—a Pentagon darling—had to issue the final imprimatur. His "reward" will be the stuff legends are made of.

Degenerate the faithful

Bin Laden was the quintessential product of Cold War US foreign policy; the unholy alliance of Washington, Pakistan and Saudi Arabia. Bin Laden was never charged by the Federal Bureau of Investigation

(FBI) as guilty of perpetrating 9/11; there was never any direct evidence. Even uber-neocon former Vice President Dick Cheney over the years admitted on and off that Bin Laden was not connected to 9/11.

Talk about on the ground "intelligence." It took Washington no less than 3,519 days since 9/11 to find Bin Laden "dead or alive," as John Wayne Bush promised, only 240 kilometers east of the mountains of Tora Bora, his last confirmed location in December 2001. Bin Laden would have been a really otherworldly entity if suffering from kidney disease, diabetes and low blood pressure, and in need of dialysis, he had managed to survive in a musty cave for almost a decade.

Abbottabad, a two-hour drive north of Islamabad, in Khyber Pakhtunkhwa province, is a hill station in a valley very close to Azad ("free") Kashmir. It's a sort of mini-Colorado Springs, complete with a cinema (the Taj) and, more crucially, the Pakistani equivalent of West Point. No caves around it, and, also crucially, no raucous tribal areas—where the CIA drone campaign is spraying a lot of "collateral damage" under the pretext of fighting "al-Qaeda."

The capture of Bin Laden could have happened in fact as early as August 2001. At the time, back from Afghanistan, I had heard in Peshawar that a US commando was ready to go inside Afghanistan and snatch Bin Laden in his compound in Kandahar. As much as Bush lobbied for it, then-president Pervez Musharraf vetoed it, saying he would not want to be responsible for a civil war in Pakistan.

Then, after 9/11, Washington practically ordered the Taliban to hand over Bin Laden. As the Taliban ambassador in Islamabad told us at the time, Mullah Omar asked for proof of Bin Laden's guilt. Bush refused—after all, as the FBI knew, there was no concrete evidence. Subsequent Bin Laden videos "accepting" responsibility for 9/11 were revealed to be fakes.

The Taliban even agreed to hand over Bin Laden to Saudi Arabia—one of the three Taliban sponsors alongside Pakistan and the United Arab Emirates (UAE). King Abdullah refused. It's in fact Khalid Sheikh Muhammad—arrested by Pakistani intelligence, and who will spend the rest of his life in Guantanamo—who has claimed total responsibility for 9/11; and he never accused Bin Laden of anything.

That crazy Casbah sound

The more we look at it, the targeted assassination of Bin Laden shows facets of that famous children's toy, the jack-in-the-box.

Major powers playing this game—the US and Saudi Arabia—have finally decided they no longer needed a bogeyman conveniently resurfaced on and off to justify anything, from lack of democracy to brutal crackdowns or even drone attacks gone wrong. But why right now?

Let's start with the power vacuum in Pakistan. There's a serious split inside the ISI, between the ISI and part of the army, and between the army and the government. That can only mean chaos. What the Pentagon might dub Operation Osama Sunset marks the crucial shift of the top "war on terror" theater from Afghanistan to Pakistan. The "war on terror" goes on, ramped up, bound to rock all Casbahs. A bewildered Islamabad doesn't seem to know how to profit from it, especially now that it burned the precious Bin Laden card.

Then there's the House of Saud. Bin Laden was taken out just as Saudi Arabia was bending the uplifting narrative of the great 2011 Arab revolt to profit a counter-revolution narrative of a Sunni/Shi'ite sectarian war, a de facto renewed Cold War between "good" Saudi Arabia and "evil" Iran. Washington was playing all along with the House of Saud.

This House of Saud diversionist tactic is a serious attempt to shift the focus from the fact that the great 2011 Arab revolt threatens exactly medieval regimes such as Bahrain's and the House of Saud's. The corrupt, Western lackey House of Saud was the key motivator of Bin Laden's anger and outrage that shaped his ideology.

Yet under the current Bin Laden hysteria, the House of Saud can easily sing *The King called up his jet fighters/he said you better earn your pay/drop your bombs between the minarets/down the Casbah way*, ramping up its hardcore repression in the eastern provinces and in Bahrain and lavishly bribing tribal leaders in Yemen to form a next pro-Saudi government.

Washington for its part also used the diversionist tactic to distract/puzzle Arab popular opinion as an Anglo-French-American intervention, marketed as "humanitarian," struck yet another oil-rich Muslim country, Libya. Besides, Washington also applied new polish to the old tactic of isolating/containing Iran.

As for the pathetic CIA-infested, al-Qaeda-linked Libyan "rebels" who have hijacked Cyrenaica's legitimate protests—and who welcome NATO bombing of their own country—they now want the US to take out Muammar Gaddafi (NATO is already working on it). Rock the Casbah is the way to go.

Pious Saudi Arabian millionaires have always been a key source of bundles of cash for al-Qaeda. No wonder there may be a horde of new breed Bin Ladens ready to rock the Casbah in Saudi Arabia—and they will, hopefully inside the kingdom.

Al-Qaeda's ideology is based on two pillars; the current governments in Muslim lands are un-Islamic and oppressive; and they are pro-American (correct on both counts). Where al-Qaeda got it wrong was the method to reverse this situation; thus its strategic defeat by the great 2011 Arab revolt.

General David Petraeus, who was the Pentagon supremo in Afghanistan, is about to become CIA supremo—with Bin Laden's head as trophy and his hands free to rock multiple Casbahs via all-out targeted assassinations and assorted black ops. The whole reason for the US to invade Afghanistan in 2001 was to get Bin Laden "dead or alive." He's now dead and in the bottom of the Arabian Sea.

Yet the US won't leave Afghanistan. US Secretary of State Hillary Clinton is already monopolizing the narrative saying the war on al-Qaeda, as in "war on terror," goes on forever. Official US policy as the best jihadi recruiter Bin Laden could have hoped for goes on unabated—as in the same panoply of soldiers, mercenaries, CIA killer teams, killer drones, contractors and "diplomats" costing trillions of dollars.

There would be only one realistic way of possibly bringing this madness to a close, as in *the oil in the desert way/has been shaken to the top*; killer drones or targeted assassinations of the whole House of Saud. Pity that unlike bin Laden, who went rogue, the sheikhs will always take cover by posing as "our" fanatic bastards.

May 2011

THE COUNTER-REVOLUTION CLUB

They are a shish kebab of hereditary monarchies, emirates and outright theocracies. Most sit on oceans of oil (45% of the world's reserves). They are addicted to the West's glitter and glamour—from London to Monte Carlo, from the delicacies of Paris to the weaponized delicacies of NATO. They abhor democracy like they abhor poverty. Some would be glad to topple their own people—as indeed they do. And they view Shi'ite Iran as worse than the anti-Christ.

Welcome to the Gulf Cooperation Council (GCC), formed in 1981 by top dog Saudi Arabia plus the United Arab Emirates (UAE), Qatar, Kuwait, Bahrain and Oman. A more appropriate denomination would be Gulf Counter-Revolutionary Council—or club; a Gulf club to end all golf clubs. As far as the GCC is concerned, the great 2011 Arab revolt will triumph over their (wealthy) dead bodies.

How can they be so sure? Republican dynasties as in Tunisia or Egypt may be toppled; Libya may be bombed to the Stone Age; Syria may be threatened. But nothing will happen to the GCC because the enlightened West—not Allah—is their supreme guardian.

New members welcome

It's instructive to note that those 3,000-plus bombing raids on Libya since NATO took over the war on March 31 were conducted mostly by monarchies (Britain, Denmark, the Netherlands, Norway, Qatar and the UAE), apart from republican France, and before that, via AFRICOM, the United States.

Only a few hours before US President Barack Obama and British Prime Minister David Cameron were enjoying a special relationship barbecue this week, NATO was turning 19 Libyan civilians into, well, barbecue, and slightly roasting at least 130 others. The GCC merrily applauded.

The European Union (EU) and the GCC have issued a joint declaration forcing Colonel Muammar Gaddafi to go, not before handing over power to the Libyan Transitional National Council—which happens to be financed and armed exactly by NATO and the GCC.

Now the GCC has declared it would love the idea of Jordan joining the club—and the same applies to Morocco. As for Yemen—which has yearned to be a member since 1999—forget it; it's not a monarchy, and "unstable" to boot, with al those unruly people protesting. The best the GCC can do is to allegedly "mediate" into what is in effect regime change—fully supported by the US and the EU.

Apart from tiny Oman, whose Sultan Qabus follows the Ibadi school, all GCC members are hardcore Sunnis. There are plenty of Jordanian "advisors" among the Bahraini/Saudi repression machine.

Jordan and Morocco may get to become GCC members not only because they're monarchies—but most of all because they hate Iran like the plague (even though they are not exactly located in the Persian Gulf.)

Jordan's King Playstation, sorry, Abdullah II, invented the murky concept of the "Shi'ite crescent" way back in 2004, a conspiracy according to which Shi'ites from Iran and Iraq to Lebanon and Syria would violently take over the Middle East. Morocco's King Muhammad VI for his part cut off diplomatic relations with Tehran in 2009.

The GCC's top moment of counter-revolutionary glory, so far, happened less than two days after US Defense Secretary Robert Gates left

Bahrain—when Saudi Arabia, with a minor contribution from the UAE, invaded Bahrain in support of their cousins, the Sunni al-Khalifa dynasty, and against the overwhelming majority of the peaceful, protesting Bahraini population. The GCC's secretary general, Abdullatif al-Zayani, happens to be an al-Khalifa-aligned Bahraini.

There were no US, UN or EU sanctions, much less a NATO bombing spree to "celebrate" this invasion. Instead, earlier this week, EU foreign ministers slapped even more sanctions against Belarus, Iran, Libya and Syria. Not by accident all of them have been Washington targets for regime change, since the time of the neo-conservatives.

Let us play in your courtyard

Neo-colonial NATO and monarchic/theocratic GCC is a match made in weapons contractor heaven. The GCC will be incorporated into the global US missile shield system. Soon, there'll be that juicy $60 billion weapons deal with Saudi Arabia—the largest in American history.

Western idolatry practitioners that they are, GCC members also wanna have fun and be part of the real post-modern action—neo-colonial war. After all, NATO itself can be interpreted as a professional mercenary neo-colonial army, ready to intervene anywhere from Central Asia to Northern Africa.

Take Qatar. Qatar was the first country to recognize that dodgy bunch, the Libyan "rebels"; the first GCC member to supply NATO with French Mirage fighter jets and American C-17 Globemasters; it set up satellite Ahrar TV for the Transitional Council; showered them with MI-LAN missile launchers; and most of all immediately started to "supervise" oil exports from Cyrenaica.

The reward was inevitable; on April 14, Obama hosted the Emir of Qatar, Sheikh Hamad bin Khalifa al-Thani, at the White House, and lavishly praised him for his "leadership" in promoting "democracy in the Middle East"—a reference to Qatar's role in Libya.

As for Salman al-Khalifa, the Crown Prince of Bahrain, on May 19 he glowingly posed for a photo-op on the steps of 10 Downing Street in London with Prime Minister Cameron, proving that slaughtering civilian, unarmed protesters and giving a green light for the House of Saud to invade his country was definitely good for business.

But no one beats the UAE in the deadly toy realm. President Nicolas Sarkozy opened France's first military base in the Middle East in Abu Dhabi. The UAE has sent fighter jets to NATO in Libya. They are a "troop-contributing nation" for NATO in Afghanistan. And they will be the first GCC and Arab nation to send an ambassador to NATO headquarters in Brussels.

Along with Qatar, Kuwait and Bahrain, the UAE is a member of one of NATO's myriad "partnerships"—the Istanbul Cooperation Initiative military partnership. Translation: NATO encroaching on the Persian Gulf, positioning itself to raise any amount of hell against Iran.

And then there's Zayed Military City; a secluded training camp in the desert for a secret army of mercenaries, to be deployed not only in the UAE but throughout the Middle East and Northern Africa.

Off with their heads!

Milking the GCC's burning desire to outsource mercenaries; that's the latest high-value-added scam of former navy SEALs and former Blackwater supremo Erik Prince (in 2009 Blackwater was rebranded Xe Services.)

It was in Abu Dhabi that Prince—through a joint venture called Reflex Responses—signed a first contract of $529 million on July 13, 2010, to deliver his services to "progressive" Sheik Mohamed bin Zayed al-Nahyan. The idea was Zayed's.

The *New York Times* may have had its kicks depicting, in a May 14 story, Colombians entering the UAE posing as construction workers, with special visas stamped by the UAE's military intelligence branch, so they could clear customs and immigration with no questions asked; yes, Prince wants battalions of Colombian and Central American mercenaries; he won't recruit Muslims to kill their own cousins and be faced with malfunctioning units.

At least the paper pointed that Prince "is hoping to build an empire in the desert, far from the trial lawyers, congressional investigators and Justice Department officials"—without asking any hard questions about it.

The mercenary army's agenda contains everything one needs to know; they will be involved in special ops inside and outside the UAE; "urban combat"; the "securing of nuclear and radioactive materials"; "humanitarian missions" (?); the defense of oil pipelines and sleek glass towers from "terrorist attacks"; and most significant of all, "crowd-control operations," where the crowd "is not armed with firearms but does pose a risk using improvised weapons [clubs and stones]."

There it is, spelled out; internal repression all across the Persian Gulf, as against the sprawling labor camps housing tens of thousands of South Asian workers; or in case citizens of the UAE get the Bahrain pro-democracy fever. The excuse for all these ops could not be less original: the Iranian bogeyman, or "aggression."

Prince had always wanted Blackwater to be a mercenary army deployable anywhere in Africa, Asia and the Middle East. He even wanted the

CIA to use it for global special ops—before the CIA decided to laser on drones as a more cost-effective method. Now Prince has a wealthy Sheikh—a Pentagon fan who's in favor of bombing Iran—to bankroll his "vision."

The first battalion boasts 580 mercenaries. Zayed's men have promised that if they prove themselves in a "real-world mission," the Emirate will pay Prince for a whole brigade of several thousand men, to the tune of billions of dollars. Prince could then move to his dream of a desert mercenary training complex modeled after Blackwater's compound in Moyock, North Carolina.

So expect another "House of Saud does Bahrain" scenario. Like the mercenary army beating to death Pakistanis, Nepalis, Bangladeshis and Filipinos who want better working conditions in the UAE.

Or expect covert special ops in Egypt and Tunisia to ensure their next governments align themselves with the US and the EU. Or expect boots on the ground in Libya to "provide humanitarian aid to civilians" (oops, that was two months ago; even Obama now says it's all about regime change).

Still, all those Libyan "oil facilities" must be in the safe hands of US and EU multinationals (and not Russian, Indian and Chinese). Still, Gaddafi's inner circle must be "neutralized." And still Libya must be kept subdued, according to the age-old imperial tenets of divide and rule.

So when the goin' gets tough, who you're gonna call? Definitely Xe Services' "innovative solutions," brought to you by Sheikh Zayed. No wonder the GCC club is the talk of the (counter-revolutionary) town.

May 2011

Disaster capitalism swoops over Libya

Think of the new Libya as the latest spectacular chapter in the Disaster Capitalism series. Instead of weapons of mass destruction, we had R2P ("responsibility to protect"). Instead of neo-conservatives, we had humanitarian imperialists.

But the target is the same: regime change. And the project is the same: to completely dismantle and privatize a nation that was not integrated into turbo-capitalism; to open another (profitable) land of opportunity for turbocharged neoliberalism. The whole thing is especially handy because it is smack in the middle of a nearly global recession.

It will take some time; Libyan oil won't totally return to the market within 18 months. But there's the reconstruction of everything NATO bombed (well, not much of what the Pentagon bombed in 2003 was reconstructed in Iraq.)

Anyway—from oil to rebuilding—in thesis juicy business opportunities loom. France's neo-Napoleonic Nicolas Sarkozy and Britain's David of Arabia Cameron believe they will be especially well positioned to profit from NATO's victory. Yet there's no guarantee the new Libyan bonanza will be enough to lift both former colonial powers (neo-colonials?) out of recession.

President Sarkozy in particular will milk the business opportunities for French companies for all they're worth—part of his ambitious agenda of "strategic redeployment" of France in the Arab world. A compliant French media are gloating that this was "his" war—spinning that he decided to arm the rebels on the ground with French weaponry, in close cooperation with Qatar, including a key rebel commando unit that went by sea from Misrata to Tripoli last Saturday, at the start of "Operation Siren."

Well, he certainly saw the opening when Muammar Gaddafi's chief of protocol defected to Paris in October 2010. That's when the whole regime change drama started to be incubated.

Bombs for oil

As previously noted (see Welcome to Libya's 'democracy', *Asia Times Online*, August 24) the vultures are already circling Tripoli to grab (and monopolize) the spoils. And yes—most of the action has to do with oil deals, as in this stark assertion by Abdeljalil Mayouf, information manager at the "rebel" Arabian Gulf Oil Company; "We don't have a problem with Western countries like the Italians, French and UK companies. But we may have some political issues with Russia, China and Brazil."

These three happen to be crucial members of the BRICS group of emerging economies (Brazil, Russia, India, China and South Africa), which are actually growing while the Atlanticist, NATO-bombing economies are either stuck in stagnation or recession. The top four BRICs also happen to have abstained from approving UN Security Council resolution 1973, the no-fly zone scam that metamorphosed into NATO bringing regime change from above. They saw right through it from the beginning.

To make matters worse (for them), only three days before the Pentagon's AFRICOM launched its first 150-plus Tomahawks over Libya, Colonel Gaddafi gave an interview to German TV stressing that if the country were attacked, all energy contracts would be transferred to Russian, Indian and Chinese companies.

So the winners in the oil bonanza are already designated: NATO members plus Arab monarchies. Among the companies involved, British Petroleum (BP), France's Total and the Qatar national oil company. For Qatar—which dispatched jet fighters and recruiters to the front lines, trained "rebels" in exhaustive combat techniques, and is already managing oil sales in eastern Libya—the war will reveal itself to be a very wise investment decision.

Prior to the months-long crisis that is in its end game now with the rebels in the capital, Tripoli, Libya was producing 1.6 million barrels per day. Once resumed, this could reap Tripoli's new rulers some US$50 billion annually. Most estimates place oil reserves at 46.4 billion barrels.

The "rebels" of new Libya better not mess with China. Five months ago, China's official policy was already to call for a ceasefire; if that had happened, Gaddafi would still control more than half of Libya. Yet Beijing—never a fan of violent regime change—for the moment is exercising extreme restraint.

Wen Zhongliang, the deputy head of the Ministry of Trade, willfully observed, "Libya will continue to protect the interests and rights of Chinese investors and we hope to continue investment and economic cooperation." Official statements are piling up emphasizing "mutual economic cooperation."

Last week, Abdel Hafiz Ghoga, vice president of the dodgy Transitional National Council (TNC), told Xinhua that all deals and contracts agreed with the Gaddafi regime would be honored—but Beijing is taking no chances.

Libya supplied no more than 3% of China's oil imports in 2010. Angola is a much more crucial supplier. But China is still Libya's top oil customer in Asia. Moreover, China could be very helpful in the infrastructure rebuilding front, or in technology export—no less than 75 Chinese companies with 36,000 employees were already on the ground before the outbreak of the tribal/civil war, swiftly evacuated in less than three days.

The Russians—from Gazprom to Tafnet—had billions of dollars invested in Libyan projects; Brazilian oil giant Petrobras and the construction company Odebrecht also had interests there. It's still unclear what will happen to them. The director general of the Russia-Libya Business Council, Aram Shegunts, is extremely worried: "Our companies will lose everything because NATO will prevent them from doing business in Libya."

Italy seems to have passed the "rebel" version of "you're either with us or without us." Energy giant ENI apparently won't be affected, as Premier Silvio "Bunga Bunga" Berlusconi pragmatically dumped his previous very close pal Gaddafi at the start of the AFRICOM/NATO bombing spree.

ENI's directors are confident Libya's oil and gas flows to southern Italy will resume before winter. And the Libyan ambassador in Italy, Hafed Gaddur, reassured Rome that all Gaddafi-era contracts will be honored. Just in case, Berlusconi will meet the TNC's prime minister, Mahmoud Jibril, this Thursday in Milan.

Bin Laden to the rescue

Turkey's Foreign Minister Ahmet Davutoglu—of the famed "zero problems with our neighbors" policy—has also been gushing praise on the former "rebels" turned powers-that-be. Eyeing the post-Gaddafi business bonanza as well, Ankara—as NATO's eastern flank—ended up helping to impose a naval blockade on the Gaddafi regime, carefully cultivated the TNC, and in July formally recognized it as the government of Libya. Business "rewards" loom.

Then there's the crucial plot; how the House of Saud is going to profit from having been instrumental in setting up a friendly regime in Libya, possibly peppered with Salafi notables; one of the key reasons for the Saudi onslaught—which included a fabricated vote at the Arab League—was the extreme bad blood between Gaddafi and King Abdullah since the run-up towards the war on Iraq in 2002.

It's never enough to stress the cosmic hypocrisy of an ultra-regressive absolute monarchy/medieval theocracy—which invaded Bahrain and repressed its native Shi'ites—saluting what could be construed as a pro-democracy movement in Northern Africa.

Anyway, it's time to party. Expect the Saudi Bin Laden Group to reconstruct like mad all over Libya—eventually turning the (looted) Bab al-Aziziyah into a monster, luxury Mall of Tripolitania.

August 2011

HOW AL-QAEDA GOT TO RULE IN TRIPOLI

His name is Abdelhakim Belhaj. Some in the Middle East might have, but few in the West and across the world would have heard of him.

Time to catch up. Because the story of how an al-Qaeda asset turned out to be the top Libyan military commander in still war-torn Tripoli is bound to shatter—once again—that wilderness of mirrors that is the "war on terror," as well as deeply compromising the carefully constructed propaganda of NATO's "humanitarian" intervention in Libya.

Muammar Gaddafi's fortress of Bab-al-Aziziyah was essentially invaded and conquered last week by Belhaj's men—who were at the forefront of a militia of Berbers from the mountains southwest of Tripoli. The militia is the so-called Tripoli Brigade, trained in secret for two months by US Special Forces. This turned out to be the rebels' most effective militia in six months of tribal/civil war.

Already last Tuesday, Belhaj was gloating on how the battle was won, with Gaddafi forces escaping "like rats" (note that's the same metaphor used by Gaddafi himself to designate the rebels).

Abdelhakim Belhaj, aka Abu Abdallah al-Sadek, is a Libyan jihadi. Born in May 1966, he honed his skills with the mujahideen in the 1980s anti-Soviet jihad in Afghanistan.

He's the founder of the Libyan Islamic Fighting Group (LIFG) and its de facto *emir*—with Khaled Chrif and Sami Saadi as his deputies. After the Taliban took power in Kabul in 1996, the LIFG kept two training camps in Afghanistan; one of them, 30 kilometers north of Kabul—run by Abu Yahya—was strictly for al-Qaeda-linked jihadis.

After 9/11, Belhaj moved to Pakistan and also to Iraq, where he befriended none other than ultra-nasty Abu Musab al-Zarqawi—all this before al-Qaeda in Iraq pledged its allegiance to Osama bin Laden and Ayman al-Zawahiri and turbocharged its gruesome practices.

In Iraq, Libyans happened to be the largest foreign Sunni jihadi contingent, only losing to the Saudis. Moreover, Libyan jihadis have always been superstars in the top echelons of "historic" al-Qaeda—from Abu Faraj al-Libi (military commander until his arrest in 2005, now lingering as one of 16 high-value detainees in Guantanamo) to Abu al-Laith al-Libi (another military commander, killed in Pakistan in early 2008).

Time for an extraordinary rendition

The LIFG had been on the CIA's radars since 9/11. In 2003, Belhaj was finally arrested in Malaysia—and then transferred, extraordinary rendition-style, to a secret Bangkok prison, and duly tortured.

In 2004, the Americans decided to send him as a gift to Libyan intelligence—until he was freed by the Gaddafi regime in March 2010, along with other 211 "terrorists," in a public relations coup advertised with great fanfare.

The orchestrator was no less than Saif Islam al-Gaddafi—the modernizing/London School of Economics face of the regime. LIFG's leaders—Belhaj and his deputies Chrif and Saadi—issued a 417-page confession dubbed "corrective studies" in which they declared the jihad against Gaddafi over (and illegal), before they were finally set free.

A fascinating account of the whole process can be seen in a report called "Combating Terrorism in Libya through Dialogue and Reintegration."[2] Note that the authors, Singapore-based terrorism "experts" who were wined and dined by the regime, express the "deepest appreciation to Saif al-Islam Gaddafi and the Gaddafi International Charity and Development Foundation for making this visit possible."

Crucially, still in 2007, then al-Qaeda's number two, Zawahiri, officially announced the merger between the LIFG and al-Qaeda in the Islamic Mahgreb (AQIM). So, for all practical purposes, since then, LIFG/AQIM have been one and the same—and Belhaj was/is its *emir*.

In 2007, LIFG was calling for a jihad against Gaddafi but also against the US and assorted Western "infidels."

Fast forward to last February when, a free man, Belhaj decided to go back into jihad mode and align his forces with the engineered uprising in Cyrenaica.

Every intelligence agency in the US, Europe and the Arab world knows where he's coming from. He's already made sure in Libya that himself and his militia will only settle for *sharia* law.

There's nothing "pro-democracy" about it—by any stretch of the imagination. And yet such an asset could not be dropped from NATO's war just because he was not very fond of "infidels."

The late July killing of rebel military commander General Abdel Fattah Younis—by the rebels themselves—seems to point to Belhaj or at least people very close to him.

It's essential to know that Younis—before he defected from the regime—had been in charge of Libya's special forces fiercely fighting the LIFG in Cyrenaica from 1990 to 1995.

---

[2] http://www.rsis.edu.sg/wp-content/uploads/2014/07/RSIS_Libya14.pdf

The Transitional National Council (TNC), according to one of its members, Ali Tarhouni, has been spinning Younis was killed by a shady brigade known as Obaida ibn Jarrah (one of the Prophet Mohammed's companions). Yet the brigade now seems to have dissolved into thin air.

Shut up or I'll cut your head off

Hardly by accident, all the top military rebel commanders are LIFG, from Belhaj in Tripoli to one Ismael as-Salabi in Benghazi and one Abdelhakim al-Assadi in Derna, not to mention a key asset, Ali Salabi, sitting at the core of the TNC. It was Salabi who negotiated with Saif al-Islam Gaddafi the "end" of LIFG's jihad, thus assuring the bright future of these born-again "freedom fighters."

It doesn't require a crystal ball to picture the consequences of LIFG/AQIM—having conquered military power and being among the war "winners"—not remotely interested in relinquishing control just to please NATO's whims.

Meanwhile, amid the fog of war, it's unclear whether Gaddafi is planning to trap the Tripoli Brigade in urban warfare; or to force the bulk of rebel militias to enter the huge Warfallah tribal areas.

Gaddafi's wife belongs to the Warfallah, Libya's largest tribe, with up to 1 million people and 54 sub-tribes. The inside word in Brussels is that NATO expects Gaddafi to fight for months if not years; thus the Texas George W Bush-style bounty on his head and the desperate return to NATO's plan A, which was always to take him out.

Libya may now be facing the specter of a twin-headed guerrilla Hydra; Gaddafi forces against a weak TNC central government and NATO boots on the ground; and the LIFG/AQIM nebula in a jihad against NATO (if they are sidelined from power).

Gaddafi may be a dictatorial relic of the past, but you don't monopolize power for four decades for nothing, and without your intelligence services learning a thing or two.

From the beginning, Gaddafi said this was a foreign-backed/al-Qaeda operation; he was right (although he forgot to say this was above all neo-Napoleonic French President Nicolas Sarkozy's war, but that's another story).

He also said this was a prelude for a foreign occupation whose target was to privatize and take over Libya's natural resources. He may—again—turn out to be right.

The Singapore "experts" who praised the Gaddafi regime's decision to free the LIFG's jihadis qualified it as "a necessary strategy to mitigate the threat posed to Libya."

Now, LIFG/AQIM is finally poised to exercise its options as an "indigenous political force."

Ten years after 9/11, it's hard not to imagine a certain decomposed skull in the bottom of the Arabian Sea boldly grinning to kingdom come.

August 2011

THE DECLINE AND FALL OF JUST ABOUT EVERYONE

More than 10 years ago, before 9/11, Goldman Sachs was predicting that the BRIC countries (Brazil, Russia, India, China) would make the world economy's top ten—but not until 2040. Skip a decade and the Chinese economy already has the number two spot all to itself, Brazil is number seven, India 10, and even Russia is creeping closer. In purchasing power parity, or PPP, things look even better. There, China is in second place, India is now fourth, Russia sixth, and Brazil seventh.

No wonder Jim O'Neill, who coined the neologism BRIC and is now chairman of Goldman Sachs Asset Management, has been stressing that "the world is no longer dependent on the leadership of the US and Europe." After all, since 2007, China's economy has grown by 45%, the American economy by less than 1%—figures startling enough to make anyone take back their predictions. American anxiety and puzzlement reached new heights when the latest IMF projections indicated that, at least by certain measurements, the Chinese economy would overtake the US by 2016. (Until recently, Goldman Sachs was pointing towards 2050 for that first-place exchange.)

Within the next 30 years, the top five will, according to Goldman Sachs, likely be China, the U.S., India, Brazil, and Mexico. Western Europe? Bye-bye!

A system stripped to its essence

Increasing numbers of experts agree that Asia is now leading the way for the world, even as it lays bare glaring gaps in the West's narrative of civilization. Yet to talk about "the decline of the West" is a dangerous proposition. A key historical reference is Oswald Spengler's 1918 essay with that title. Spengler, a man of his times, thought that humanity functioned through unique cultural systems, and that Western ideas would not be pertinent for, or transferable to, other regions of the planet. (Tell that howler to the young Egyptians in Tahrir Square.)

Spengler, of course, captured the Western-dominated *zeitgeist* of another century. He saw cultures as living and dying organisms, each with a unique soul. The East or Orient was "magical," while the West was "Faustian." A reactionary misanthrope, he was convinced that the West had already reached the supreme status available to a democratic civilization—and so was destined to experience the "decline" of his title.

If you're thinking that this sounds like an *avant la lettre* Huntingtonesque "clash of civilizations," you can be excused, because that's exactly what it was.

Speaking of civilizational clashes, did anyone notice that "maybe" in a recent *Time* cover story picking up on Spenglerian themes and headlined "The Decline and Fall of Europe (and Maybe the West)"? In our post-Spenglerian moment, the "West" is surely the United States, and how could that magazine get it so wrong? Maybe? After all, a Europe now in deep financial crisis will be "in decline" as long as it remains inextricably intertwined with and continues to defer to "the West"—that is, Washington—even as it witnesses the simultaneous economic ascent of what's sometimes derisively referred to as "the South."

Think of the present global capitalist moment not as a "clash," but a "cash of civilizations."

If Washington is now stunned and operating on autopilot, that's in part because, historically speaking, its moment as the globe's "sole superpower" or even "hyperpower" barely outlasted Andy Warhol's notorious 15 minutes of fame—from the fall of the Berlin Wall and collapse of the Soviet Union to 9/11 and the Bush doctrine. The new American century was swiftly throttled in three hubris-filled stages: 9/11 (blowback); the invasion of Iraq (pre-emptive war); and the 2008 Wall Street meltdown (casino capitalism).

Meanwhile, one may argue that Europe still has its non-Western opportunities, that, in fact, the periphery increasingly dreams with European—not American—subtitles. The Arab Spring, for instance, was focused on European-style parliamentary democracies, not an American presidential system. In addition, however financially anxious it may be, Europe remains the world's largest market. In an array of technological fields, it now rivals or outpaces the U.S., while regressive Persian Gulf monarchies splurge on euros (and prime real estate in Paris and London) to diversify their portfolios.

Yet, with "leaders" like the neo-Napoleonic Nicolas Sarkozy, David (of Arabia) Cameron, Silvio ("bunga bunga") Berlusconi, and Angela ("Dear Prudence") Merkel largely lacking imagination or striking competence, Europe certainly doesn't need enemies. Decline or not, it might find a whole new lease on life by sidelining its Atlanticism and boldly betting on its Euro-Asian destiny. It could open up its societies, economies, and cultures to China, India, and Russia, while pushing southern Europe to connect far more deeply with a rising Turkey, the rest of the Middle East, Latin America, and Africa (and not via further NATO "humanitarian" bombings either).

Otherwise, the facts on the ground spell out something that goes well beyond the decline of the West: it's the decline of a system in the West that, in these last years, is being stripped to its grim essence. Historian Eric Hobsbawm caught the mood of the moment when he wrote in his book *How to Change the World* that "the world transformed by capitalism," which Karl Marx described in 1848 "in passages of dark, laconic eloquence is recognizably the world of the early twenty-first century."

In a landscape in which politics is being reduced to a (broken) mirror reflecting finance, and in which producing and saving have been superseded by consuming, something systemic comes into view. As in the famous line of poet William Butler Yeats, "the center cannot hold"—and it won't either.

If the West ceases to be the center, what exactly went wrong?

Are You With Me or Against Me?

It's worth remembering that capitalism was "civilized" thanks to the unrelenting pressure of gritty working-class movements and the ever-present threat of strikes and even revolutions. The existence of the Soviet bloc, an alternate model of economic development (however warped), also helped. To counteract the USSR, Washington's and Europe's ruling groups had to buy the support of their masses in defending what no one blushed about calling "the Western way of life." A complex social contract was forged, and it involved capital making concessions.

No more. Not in Washington, that's obvious. And increasingly, not in Europe either. That system started breaking down as soon as—talk about total ideological triumph!—neoliberalism became the only show in town. There was a single superhighway from there and it swept the most fragile strands of the middle class directly into a new post-industrial proletariat, or simply into unemployable status.

If neoliberalism is the victor for now, it's because no realist, alternative developmental model exists, and yet what it has won is ever more in question. Meanwhile, except in the Middle East, progressives the world over are paralyzed, as if expecting the old order to dissolve by itself. Unfortunately, history teaches us that, at similar crossroads in the past, you are as likely to find the grapes of wrath, right-wing populist-style, as anything else—or worse yet, outright fascism.

"The West against the rest" is a simplistic formula that doesn't begin to describe such a world. Imagine instead, a planet in which "the rest" are trying to step beyond the West in a variety of ways, but also have absorbed that West in ways too deep to describe. Here's the irony, then: Yes, the West will "decline," Washington included, and still it will leave itself behind everywhere.

Sorry, Your Model Sucks

Suppose you're a developing country, shopping in the developmental supermarket. You look at China and think you see something new—a consensus model that's turning on the lights everywhere—or do you? After all, the Chinese version of an economic boom with no political freedom may not turn out to be much of a model for other countries to follow. In many ways, it may be more like an inapplicable lethal artifact, a cluster bomb made up of shards of the Western concept of modernity married to a Leninist-based formula where a single party controls personnel, propaganda, and—crucially—the People's Liberation Army.

At the same time, this is a system evidently trying to prove that, even though the West unified the world—from neocolonialism to globalization—that shouldn't imply it's bound to rule forever in material or intellectual terms.

For its part, Europe is hawking a model of supra-national integration as a means of solving problems and conflicts from the Middle East to Africa. But any shopper can now see evidence of a European Union on the verge of cracking amid non-stop inter-European bickering that includes national revolts against the euro, discontent over NATO's role as a global Robocop, and a style of ongoing European cultural arrogance that makes it incapable of recognizing, to take one example, why the Chinese model is so successful in Africa.

Or let's say our shopper looks to the United States, that country still being, after all, the world's number one economy, its dollar still the world's reserve currency, and its military still number one in destructive power and still garrisoning much of the globe. That would indeed seem impressive, if it weren't for the fact that Washington is visibly on the decline, oscillating wildly between a lame populism and a stale orthodoxy, and shilling for casino capitalism on a side street in its spare time. It's a giant power enveloped in political and economic paralysis for all the world to see, and no less visibly incapable of coming up with an exit strategy.

Really, would you buy a model from any of them? In fact, where in a world in escalating disarray is anyone supposed to look these days when it comes to models?

One of the key reasons for the Arab Spring was out-of-control food prices, driven significantly by speculation. Protests and riots in Greece, Italy, Spain, France, Germany, Austria, and Turkey were direct consequences of the global recession. In Spain, nearly half of 16- to 29-year-olds—an overeducated "lost generation"—are now out of jobs, a European record.

That may be the worst in Europe, but in Britain, 20% of 16- to 24-year-olds are unemployed, about average for the rest of the European

Union. In London, almost 25% of working-age people are unemployed. In France, 13.5% of the population is now officially poor—that is, living on less than $1,300 a month.

As many across Western Europe see it, the state has already breached the social contract. The *indignados* of Madrid have caught the spirit of the moment perfectly: "We're not against the system, it's the system that is against us."

This spells out the essence of the abject failure of neoliberal capitalism, as David Harvey explained in his latest book, *The Enigma of Capital*. He makes clear how a political economy "of mass dispossession, of predatory practices to the point of daylight robbery, particularly of the poor and the vulnerable, the unsophisticated and the legally unprotected, has become the order of the day."

Will Asia Save Global Capitalism?

Meanwhile Beijing is too busy re-mixing its destiny as the global Middle Kingdom—deploying engineers, architects, and infrastructure workers of the non-bombing variety from Canada to Brazil, Cuba to Angola—to be much distracted by the Atlanticist travails in MENA (aka the region that includes the Middle East and Northern Africa).

If the West is in trouble, global capitalism is being given a reprieve—how brief we don't know—by the emergence of an Asian middle class, not only in China and India, but also in Indonesia (240 million people in boom mode) and Vietnam (85 million). I never cease to marvel when I compare the instant wonders and real-estate bubble of the present moment in Asia to my first experiences living there in 1994, when such countries were still in the "Asian tiger," pre-1997-financial-crisis years.

In China alone 300 million people—"only" 23% of the total population—now live in medium-sized to major urban areas and enjoy what's always called "disposable incomes." They, in fact, constitute something like a nation unto themselves, an economy already two-thirds that of Germany's.

The McKinsey Global Institute notes that the Chinese middle class now comprises 29% of the Middle Kingdom's 190 million households, and will reach a staggering 75% of 372 million households by 2025 (if, of course, China's capitalist experiment hasn't gone off some cliff by then and its potential real-estate/finance bubble hasn't popped and drowned the society).

In India, with its population of 1.2 billion, there are already, according to McKinsey, 15 million households with an annual income of up to $10,000; in five years, a projected 40 million households, or 200 million people, will be in that income range. And in India in 2011, as in China in 2001, the only way is up (again as long as that reprieve lasts).

Americans may find it surreal (or start packing their expat bags), but an annual income of less than $10,000 means a comfortable life in China or Indonesia, while in the United States, with a median household income of roughly $50,000, one is practically poor.

Nomura Securities predicts that in a mere three years, retail sales in China will overtake the US and that, in this way, the Asian middle class may indeed "save" global capitalism for a time—but at a price so steep that Mother Nature is plotting some seriously catastrophic revenge in the form of what used to be called climate change and is now more vividly known simply as "weird weather."

Back in the USA

Meanwhile, in the United States, Nobel Peace Prize laureate President Barack Obama continues to insist that we all live on an American planet, exceptionally so. If that line still resonates at home, though, it's an ever harder sell in a world in which the first Chinese stealth fighter jet goes for a test spin while the American Secretary of Defense is visiting China. Or when the news agency Xinhua, echoing its master Beijing, fumes against the "irresponsible" Washington politicians who starred in the recent debt-ceiling circus, and points to the fragility of a system "saved " from free fall by the Fed's promise to shower free money on banks for at least two years.

Nor is Washington being exactly clever in confronting the leadership of its largest creditor, which holds $3.2 trillion in US currency reserves, 40% of the global total, and is always puzzled by the continued lethal export of "democracy for dummies" from American shores to the AfPak war zones, Iraq, Libya, and other hot spots in the Greater Middle East. Beijing knows well that any further U.S.-generated turbulence in global capitalism could slash its exports, collapse its property bubble, and throw the Chinese working classes into a pretty hardcore revolutionary mode.

This means—despite rising voices of the Rick Perry/Michele Bachmann variety in the U.S.—that there's no "evil" Chinese conspiracy against Washington or the West. In fact, behind China's leap beyond Germany as the world's top exporter and its designation as the factory of the world lies a significant amount of production that's actually controlled by American, European, and Japanese companies. Again, the decline of the West, yes—but the West is already so deep in China that it's not going away any time soon. Whoever rises or falls, there remains, as of this moment, only a one-stop-shopping developmental system in the world, fraying in the Atlantic, booming in the Pacific.

If any Washington hopes about "changing" China are a mirage, when it comes to capitalism's global monopoly, who knows what reality may turn out to be?

Wasteland Redux

The proverbial bogeymen of our world—Osama, Saddam, Gaddafi, Ahmadinejad (how curious, all Muslims!)—are clearly meant to act like so many mini-black holes absorbing all our fears. But they won't save the West from its decline, or the former sole superpower from its comeuppance.

Yale's Paul Kennedy, that historian of decline, would undoubtedly remind us that history will sweep away American hegemony as surely as autumn replaces summer (as surely as European colonialism was swept away, NATO's "humanitarian" wars notwithstanding). Already in 2002, in the run-up to the invasion of Iraq, world-system expert Immanuel Wallerstein was framing the debate this way in his book *The Decline of American Power*: the question wasn't whether the United States was in decline, but if it could find a way to fall gracefully, without too much damage to itself or the world. The answer in the years since has been clear enough: no.

Who can doubt that, 10 years after the 9/11 attacks, the great global story of 2011 has been the Arab Spring, itself certainly a subplot in the decline of the West? As the West wallowed in a mire of fear, Islamophobia, financial and economic crisis, and even, in Britain, riots and looting, from Northern Africa to the Middle East, people risked their lives to have a crack at Western democracy.

Of course, that dream has been at least partially derailed, thanks to the medieval House of Saud and its Persian Gulf minions barging in with a ruthless strategy of counter-revolution, while NATO lent a helping hand by changing the narrative to a "humanitarian" bombing campaign meant to reassert Western greatness. As NATO's secretary general Anders Fogh Rasmussen put the matter bluntly, "If you're not able to deploy troops beyond your borders, then you can't exert influence internationally, and then that gap will be filled by emerging powers that don't necessarily share your values and thinking."

So let's break the situation down as 2011 heads for winter. As far as MENA is concerned, NATO's business is to keep the US and Europe in the game, the BRICS members out of it, and the "natives" in their places. Meanwhile, in the Atlantic world, the middle classes barely hang on in quiet desperation, even as, in the Pacific, China booms, and globally the whole world holds its breath for the next economic shoe to drop in the West (and then the one after that).

Pity there's no neo-T.S. Eliot to chronicle this shabby, neo-medievalist wasteland taking over the Atlanticist axis. When capitalism hits the intensive care unit, the ones who pay the hospital bill are always the most vulnerable—and the bill is invariably paid in blood.

September 2011. Originally at TomDispatch.com

THE US POWER GRAB IN AFRICA

Beware of strangers bearing gifts. Post-modern Amazon and US Secretary of State Hillary Clinton finally landed in Tripoli—on a military jet—to lavish praise on the dodgy Transitional National Council (TNC), those opportunists/defectors/Islamists formerly known as "NATO rebels."

Clinton was greeted on Tuesday "on the soil of free Libya" (her words) by what the *New York Times* quaintly described as an "irregular militia" (translation: a heavily armed gang that is already raising hell against other heavily armed gangs), before meeting TNC chairman Mustafa Abdel-NATO (formerly known as Jalil).

The bulk of the US gifts—US$40 million—on top of the $135 million already disbursed since February (most of it military "aid") is for a missile scramble conducted by "contractors" (ie mercenaries) trying to track the tsunami of mobile anti-aircraft rockets that by now are already conveniently ensconced in secret Islamist warehouses.

Clinton told students at the University of Tripoli, "We are on your side." She could not possibly connect the dots and note that the *shabab* (young people) who started demonstrating against Muammar Gaddafi in February have absolutely nothing to do with the TNC's opportunists/defectors/Islamists who hijacked the protests. But she did have time to unveil another US foreign policy "secret"—that the US wants Gaddafi "dead or alive," George W Bush-style (or as the beneficiary of targeted assassination, Barack Obama-style).

The new Fallujah

In her exhausting six-and-a-half hours on "free Libya" soil, Clinton couldn't possibly find the time to hitch a helicopter ride to Sirte and see for herself how NATO is exercising R2P ("responsibility to protect" civilians).

A few hundred soldiers and no less than 80,000 civilians have been bombed for weeks by NATO and the former "rebels." Only 20,000 civilians have managed to escape. There's no food left. Water and electricity have been cut off. Hospitals are idle. The city—under siege—is in ruins. Sirte *imams* have issued a *fatwa* allowing survivors to eat cats and dogs.

What Gaddafi never did to Benghazi—and there's no evidence he might have—the TNC is doing to Sirte, Gaddafi's home town. Just like the murderous US offensive in Fallujah in the Iraqi Sunni triangle in late 2004, Sirte is being destroyed in order to "save it." Sirte, the new Fallujah, is brought to you by NATO rebels. R2P, RIP.

It gets much nastier. Libya is just one angle of a multi-vector US strategy in Africa. Wacko presidential candidate Michelle Bachmann, during Tuesday's Republican debate in Las Vegas, may have inadvertently nailed it. Displaying her geographical acumen as she referred to Obama's new US intervention in Uganda, Bachmann said, "He put us in Libya. Now he's putting us in Africa." True, Libya is not in Africa anymore; as the counter-revolutionary House of Saud would want it, Libya has been relocated to Arabia (ideally as a restored monarchy).

As for Obama "putting us in Africa" (see Obama, King of Africa *Asia Times Online*, October 18, 2011), those 100 special forces in Uganda billed as "advisors" should be seen as a liquid modernity remix of Vietnam in the early 1960s; that also started with a bunch of "advisors"—and the rest is history.

Murderous mystic crackpot Joseph Kony's Lord's Resistance Army (LRA) is now a rag-tag bunch of no more than 400 warriors (they used to be over 2,000). They are on the run—and not even based in Uganda, but in South Sudan (now a Western protectorate), the Central African Republic and the long border with the Democratic Republic of Congo.

So why Uganda? Enter London-based Heritage Oil, and its chairman Tony Buckingham, a former—you guessed it—"contractor" (ie mercenary). Here's Heritage's *modus operandi*, described by Buckingham himself; they deploy "a first mover strategy of entering regions with vast hydrocarbon wealth where we have a strategic advantage."

Translation: wherever there's foreign invasion, civil war, total breakdown of social order, there are big bucks to be made. Thus Heritage's presence in Iraq, Libya and Uganda.

Profiting from post-war fog, Heritage signed juicy deals in Iraqi Kurdistan behind the back of the central government in Baghdad. In Libya, Heritage bought a 51% stake in a local company called Sahara Oil Services; this means it's now directly involved in operating oil and gas licenses. Pressed about it, TNC honchos have tried to change the conversation, alleging that nothing is approved yet.

What's certain is that Heritage barged into Libya via a former Special Air Service (SAS) commando, John Holmes, founder of Erinys, one of the top mercenary outfits in Iraq apart from Xe Services, former Blackwater. Holmes cunningly shipped the right bottles of Johnnie Walker Blue Label to Benghazi for the right TNC crooks, seducing them with Heritage's mercenary know-how of enforcing "oil field security."

Got contractor, will travel

Obama's Uganda surge is also a classic Pipelineistan gambit. The possibly "billions of barrels" of oil reserves discovered recently in sub-Saharan Africa are located in the sensitive cross-border of Uganda, South Sudan, the Central African Republic and the Democratic Republic of Congo.

Believe it or not, Heritage was the top oil company in Uganda up to 2009, drilling on Lake Albert—between Uganda and the Democratic Republic of Congo—and playing one country against another. Then they sold their license to Tullow Oil, essentially a spin-off, also owned by Buckingham, bagging $1.5 billion in the process and crucially not paying 30% of profits to Washington's bastard, the government of Ugandan President Yoweri Museveni.

Enter Libya's state oil company, Tamoil, which was part of a joint venture with the Ugandans to build a crucial oil pipeline to Kenya; Uganda is landlocked, and badly needs the pipeline when oil exports start next year. The NATO war on Libya paralyzed the Pipelineistan gambit. Now everything is open for business again. Tamoil may be out of the picture—but so may be other players.

Trying to sort out the mess, the parliament in Uganda—slightly before Obama's announcement—decided to freeze all oil contracts, hitting France's Total and the China National Offshore Oil Corporation, but especially Tullow oil.

But now, with Obama's special forces "advising" not only Uganda but also the neighbors, and linking up with Heritage—which is essentially a huge oil/mercenary outfit—it's not hard to fathom where Uganda's oil contracts will eventually land.

The Amazon rules

Unified Protector, Odyssey Dawn and all other metaphors Homeric or otherwise for the AFRICOM/NATO 40,000-plus bombing of Libya have yielded the desired result; the destruction of the Libyan state (and much of the country's infrastructure, to the delight of disaster capitalism vultures). It also delivered the lethal unintended consequence of those anti-aircraft missiles appropriated by Islamists—a supremely convincing reason for the "war on terror" in northern Africa to become eternal.

Washington couldn't care less about R2P; as the Libyan Clinton hop shows, the only thing that matters is the excuse to "securitize" Libya's arsenal—the perfect cover story for US contractors and Anglo-French intel ops to take over Libyan military bases.

The iron rule is that "free" Libya should be under the control of the "liberators." Tell that to the "irregular militias," not to mention the Abdelhakim Belhaj gang and his al-Qaeda assets now in military control of Tripoli.

It's useful to remember that last Friday, the same day the US State Department announced it was sending "contractors" to Libya, was the day Obama announced his Uganda surge. And only two days later, Kenya invaded Somalia—once again under the R2P excuse of protecting civilians from Somali jihadis and pirates.

The US adventure in Somalia looks increasingly like a mix of Sophocles and the Marx Brothers. First there was the Ethiopian invasion (it failed miserably). Then the thousands of Ugandan soldiers sent by Museveni to fight al-Shabaab (partially failed; after all the Washington-backed "government" barely controls a neighborhood in Mogadishu).

Now the Kenyan invasion. A measure of the CIA's brilliance is that operatives have been on the ground for months alongside bundles of mercenaries. Soon some counter-insurgency hotshot in Washington praying in the altar of new CIA head David Petraeus will conclude that the only solution is an army of MQ-9 Reapers to drone Somalia to death.

The big picture remains the Pentagon's AFRICOM spreading its militarized tentacles against the lure of Chinese soft power in Africa, which goes something like this: in exchange for oil and minerals, we build anything you want, and we don't try to sell you "democracy for dummies."

The Bush administration woke up to this "threat" a bit too late—at AFRICOM's birth in 2008. Under the Obama administration, the mood is total panic. For Petraeus, the only thing that matters is "the long war" on steroids—from boots on the ground to armies of drones; and who are the Pentagon, the White House and the State Department to disagree?

Italian geographer and political scientist Manlio Dinucci is one of the few to point out how neocolonialism 2.0 works; one just needs to look at the map. In Central Africa, the objective is US military supremacy—on air and in intel—over Uganda, South Sudan, the Central African Republic and the Democratic Republic of Congo.

In Libya, the objective is to occupy an absolutely strategic crossroads between the Mediterranean, northern Africa and the Middle East, with the added (nostalgic?) benefit of the West—as in Paris, London and Washington—finally getting to hold military bases as when King Idris was in power (1951 to 1969). As a whole, control must be established over northern Africa, central Africa, eastern Africa and—more problematically—the Horn of Africa.

The trillion-dollar question ahead is how China—which plots strategic moves years in advance—is going to react. As for Amazon Clinton, she must be beaming. In Iraq, Washington meticulously destroyed a whole country over two long decades just to end up with nothing—not even a substantial oil contract. Clinton at least got a private army—the "advisors" who will be stationed in the bigger-than-the-Vatican US Embassy in Baghdad.

And considering that Obama's new African "advisors" will be paid by the State Department, now Clinton's also got her own African private army. After November 2012, Clinton might well consider a move into the contractor business. In the sacred name of R2P, naturally.

October 2011

The Dead Drone sketch

(Hats off, of course, to Monty Python)

A group of journalists attend a CIA press conference in a nondescript room in Langley, Virginia.

Journalist 1 [approaching the podium]: Excuse me, I wish to register a complaint.

[CIA spokesman/spook does not respond.]

Journalist 1: 'Ello, Miss?

CIA spook: What do you mean "miss"? I'm no Victoria Nuland, buddy.

Journalist 1: I'm sorry, I thought this was the State Department. I wish to make a complaint.

CIA spook: We're closin' for now, gotta move forward with our shadow war in Iran.

Journalist 1: Precisely. I wish to complain about this spy drone of yours that disappeared this week in eastern Iran.

CIA spook: Oh yes, the, uh, the RQ-170... And your information is incorrect, that was in eastern Afghanistan. What's, uh... What's wrong with it?

Journalist 1: I'll tell ya what's wrong with it, buddy. It's dead, that's what's wrong with it.

CIA spook: No, no, it's uh... it's resting.

Journalist 1: In the freaking Iranian desert? Look, buddy, we all know a dead drone when we see one, and I'm looking at one—in Iran—right now.

CIA spook: No, no, it's not dead, it's... it's restin'! Remarkable drone, the RQ-170, ain't it? Beautiful radar-evading piece of technology, right? Can't tell you more about it because it's classified.

Journalist 1: "Classified" doesn't cut it. It's stone dead.

CIA spook: Nononono, no, no! It's resting!

Journalist 1: All right then, if it's restin', I'll wake it up! [Shouting at a joystick] 'Ello, Mister Dodo Drone! I've got a lovely fresh IRGC] target for you if you just show...

[CIA spook hits the joystick]

CIA spook: There, it beeped!

Journalist 1: No, it didn't, that was you hitting the remote control!

CIA spook: I never!!

Journalist 1: Yes, you did!

CIA spook: I never, never did anything...

Journalist 1: [Yelling and hitting the joystick repeatedly] 'Ello!!!!! Dronie Boy! Testing! Testing! Testing! Testing! This is the god damned CIA calling!

[Thumps joystick on the CIA spook's lectern. Throws it up in the air and watches it plummet to the floor.]

Journalist 1: Now that's what I call a dead drone.

CIA spook: No, no... No, it's stunned!

Journalist 1: STUNNED?!?

CIA spook: Yeah! You stunned it, just as it was wakin' up! RQ-170s stun easily.

Journalist 1: Um... now look, buddy, I've definitely 'ad enough of this. That drone is definitely deceased, and when you guys issued a press statement a while ago, you assured us all that its total lack of movement was due to it bein' tired because of its prolonged secret mission.

CIA spook: There is no indication, I repeat, no indication, that Iran shot it down.

Journalist 1: But you're missing a drone. It was on a secret mission. It crash-landed in Iran. And Iran says they shot the bloody thing down.

CIA spook: Well, it's... it's, ah... it probably thought it was in the Nevada desert.

Journalist 1: NEVADA DESERT?!?!?!? What kind of crap is that? Look, why did it fall flat on its back in Iran, of all places? By now the Revolutionary Guards must be throwing a party to the Russians, the Chinese, the Pakistanis, the North Koreans for God's sake, so everyone can rip your technology apart, for a price...

CIA spook: The RQ-170 prefers keepin' on its back! Hey, remarkable drone! Lovely tech features, radar evasion, portable...

Journalist 1: Look, the IRNA news agency took the liberty of examining that drone after it crash-landed, they discovered that, yes, it was nailed to the soil of eastern Iran. [Pause]

CIA spook: Well, o'course we nailed it over there! If we hadn't nailed that drone down, it would have flown away and VOOM! Feeweeweewee!

Journalist 1: "VOOM"?!? Buddy, this drone wouldn't "voom" if you sent the navy SEALs Team Six to give it an electric shock. It's bleedin' demised!

CIA spook: No no! It's a trick! It's a top-secret counter-insurgency trick to fool the enemy!

Journalist 1: It's not a bloody trick! It's passed on! This drone is no more! It has ceased to be! It's expired and gone to meet its industrial-military complex maker! It's a stiff! Bereft of life, it rests in peace in a Shi'ite paradise! Its metabolic processes are now history! It's off the twig! It's kicked the bucket, it's shuffled off its mortal coil, run down the curtain and joined the bleedin' choir invisible!! THIS IS AN EX-DRONE!! [Pause]

CIA spook: Well, we'd better replace it, then. (he takes a quick peek behind the lectern). Sorry sir, I talked to our boss, General David Petraeus and uh, we're right out of secret drones.

Journalist 1: I see. I see, I get the picture.

CIA spook: We got loads of bunker-buster bombs though. [Pause]

Journalist 1: Do they spy?

CIA spook: Nnnnot really.

Journalist 1: WELL THAT'S HARDLY A BLOODY REPLACEMENT, AIN'T THAT RIGHT?!!???!!?

CIA spook: N-no, I guess not. [Acts stiff, looks at his feet]

Journalist 1: Well. [Pause]

CIA spook: [Quietly] D'you... d'you want to go visit the Pentagon and take a peek at their... contingency plans?

Journalist 1: [Looks around] Yeah, all right, sure.

(And now for something completely different…NOT! Monty Python's Terry Jones' latest piece on the war drums beating for an attack on Iran: Here)

December 2011

The Myth of "Isolated" Iran

Let's start with red lines. Here it is, Washington's ultimate red line, straight from the lion's mouth. Only last week Secretary of Defense Leon Panetta said of the Iranians, "Are they trying to develop a nuclear weapon? No. But we know that they're trying to develop a nuclear capability. And that's what concerns us. And our red line to Iran is do not develop a nuclear weapon. That's a red line for us."

How strange, the way those red lines continue to retreat. Once upon a time, the red line for Washington was "enrichment" of uranium. Now, it's evidently an actual nuclear weapon that can be brandished. Keep in mind that, since 2005, Iranian Supreme Leader Ayatollah Khamenei has stressed that his country is not seeking to build a nuclear weapon. The most recent National Intelligence Estimate on Iran from the US Intelligence Community has similarly stressed that Iran is not, in fact, developing a nuclear weapon (as opposed to the breakout capacity to build one someday).

What if, however, there is no "red line," but something completely different? Call it the petrodollar line.

Banking on Sanctions?

Let's start here: In December 2011, impervious to dire consequences for the global economy, the US Congress—under all the usual pressures from the Israel lobby (not that it needs them)—foisted a mandatory sanctions package on the Obama administration (100 to 0 in the Senate and with only 12 "no" votes in the House). Starting in June, the US will have to sanction any third-country banks and companies dealing with Iran's Central Bank, which is meant to cripple that country's oil sales. (Congress did allow for some "exemptions.")

The ultimate target? Regime change—what else?—in Tehran. The proverbial anonymous US official admitted as much in the *Washington Post*, and that paper printed the comment. ("The goal of the US and other sanctions against Iran is regime collapse, a senior US intelligence official said, offering the clearest indication yet that the Obama administration is at least as intent on unseating Iran's government as it is on engaging with it.") But oops! The newspaper then had to revise the passage to eliminate that embarrassingly on-target quote. Undoubtedly, this "red line" came too close to the truth for comfort.

Former chairman of the Joint Chiefs of Staff Admiral Mike Mullen believed that only a monster shock-and-awe-style event, totally humiliating the leadership in Tehran, would lead to genuine regime change—and he was hardly alone. Advocates of actions ranging from air strikes to invasion (whether by the U.S., Israel, or some combination of the two) have been legion in neocon Washington. (See, for instance, the Brookings Institution's 2009 report Which Path to Persia.)

Yet anyone remotely familiar with Iran knows that such an attack would rally the population behind Khamenei and the Revolutionary Guards. In those circumstances, the deep aversion of many Iranians to the military dictatorship of the mullahtariat would matter little.

Besides, even the Iranian opposition supports a peaceful nuclear program. It's a matter of national pride.

Iranian intellectuals, far more familiar with Persian smoke and mirrors than ideologues in Washington, totally debunk any war scenarios. They stress that the Tehran regime, adept in the arts of Persian shadow play, has no intention of provoking an attack that could lead to its obliteration. On their part, whether correctly or not, Tehran strategists assume that Washington will prove unable to launch yet one more war in the Greater Middle East, especially one that could lead to staggering collateral damage for the world economy.

In the meantime, Washington's expectations that a harsh sanctions regime might make the Iranians give ground, if not go down, may prove to be a chimera. Washington spin has been focused on the supposedly disastrous mega-devaluation of the Iranian currency, the rial, in the face of the new sanctions. Unfortunately for the fans of Iranian economic collapse, Professor Djavad Salehi-Isfahani has laid out in elaborate detail the long-term nature of this process, which Iranian economists have more than welcomed. After all, it will boost Iran's non-oil exports and help local industry in competition with cheap Chinese imports. In sum: a devalued rial stands a reasonable chance of actually reducing unemployment in Iran.

More Connected Than Google

Though few in the US have noticed, Iran is not exactly "isolated," though Washington might wish it. Pakistani Prime Minister Yusuf Gilani has become a frequent flyer to Tehran. And he's a Johnny-come-lately compared to Russia's national security chief Nikolai Patrushev, who only recently warned the Israelis not to push the US to attack Iran. Add in as well US ally and Afghan President Hamid Karzai. At a Loya Jirga (grand council) in late 2011, in front of 2,000 tribal leaders, he stressed that Kabul was planning to get even closer to Tehran.

On that crucial Eurasian chessboard, Pipelineistan, the Iran-Pakistan (IP) natural gas pipeline—much to Washington's distress—is now a go. Pakistan badly needs energy and its leadership has clearly decided that it's unwilling to wait forever and a day for Washington's eternal pet project—the Turkmenistan-Afghanistan-Pakistan-India (TAPI) pipeline—to traverse Talibanistan.

Even Turkish Foreign Minister Ahmet Davutoglu recently visited Tehran, though his country's relationship with Iran has grown ever edgier. After all, energy overrules threats in the region. NATO member Turkey is already involved in covert ops in Syria, allied with hardcore fundamentalist Sunnis in Iraq, and—in a remarkable volte-face in the wake of the Arab Spring(s)—has traded in an Ankara-Tehran-Damascus axis for an Ankara-Riyadh-Doha one. It is even planning on hosting components of Washington's long-planned missile-defense system, targeted at Iran.

All this from a country with a Davutoglu-coined foreign policy of "zero problems with our neighbors." Still, the needs of Pipelineistan do set the heart racing. Turkey is desperate for access to Iran's energy resources, and if Iranian natural gas ever reaches Western Europe—something the Europeans are desperately eager for—Turkey will be the privileged transit country. Turkey's leaders have already signaled their rejection of further US sanctions against Iranian oil.

And speaking of connections, last week there was that spectacular diplomatic *coup de théâtre*, Iranian President Mahmoud Ahmadinejad's Latin American tour. US right-wingers may harp on a Tehran-Caracas axis of evil—supposedly promoting "terror" across Latin America as a springboard for future attacks on the northern superpower—but back in real life, another kind of truth lurks. All these years later, Washington is still unable to digest the idea that it has lost control over, or even influence in, those two regional powers over which it once exercised unmitigated imperial hegemony.

Add to this the wall of mistrust that has only solidified since the 1979 Islamic Revolution in Iran. Mix in a new, mostly sovereign Latin America pushing for integration not only via leftwing governments in Venezuela, Bolivia, and Ecuador but through regional powers Brazil and Argentina. Stir and you get photo ops like Ahmadinejad and Venezuelan President Hugo Chavez saluting Nicaraguan President Daniel Ortega.

Washington continues to push a vision of a world from which Iran has been radically disconnected. State Department spokesperson Victoria Nuland is typical in saying recently, "Iran can remain in international isolation." As it happens, though, she needs to get her facts straight.

"Isolated" Iran has $4 billion in joint projects with Venezuela including, crucially, a bank (as with Ecuador, it has dozens of planned projects from building power plants to, once again, banking). That has led the Israel-first crowd in Washington to vociferously demand that sanctions be slapped on Venezuela. Only problem: how would the US pay for its crucial Venezuelan oil imports then?

Much was made in the US press of the fact that Ahmadinejad did not visit Brazil on this jaunt through Latin America, but diplomatically Tehran and Brasilia remain in sync. When it comes to the nuclear dossier in particular, Brazil's history leaves its leaders sympathetic. After all, that country developed—and then dropped—a nuclear weapons program. In May 2010, Brazil and Turkey brokered a uranium-swap agreement for Iran that might have cleared the decks on the U.S.-Iranian nuclear imbroglio. It was, however, immediately sabotaged by Washington. A key member of the BRICS, the club of top emerging economies, Brasilia is completely opposed to the US sanctions/embargo strategy.

So Iran may be "isolated" from the United States and Western Europe, but from the BRICS to NAM (the 120 member countries of the Non-Aligned Movement), it has the majority of the global South on its side. And then, of course, there are those staunch Washington allies, Japan and South Korea, now pleading for exemptions from the coming boycott/embargo of Iran's Central Bank.

No wonder, because these unilateral US sanctions are also aimed at Asia. After all, China, India, Japan, and South Korea, together, buy no less than 62% of Iran's oil exports.

With trademark Asian politesse, Japan's Finance Minister Jun Azumi let Treasury Secretary Timothy Geithner know just what a problem Washington is creating for Tokyo, which relies on Iran for 10% of its oil needs. It is pledging to at least modestly "reduce" that share "as soon as possible" in order to get a Washington exemption from those sanctions, but don't hold your breath. South Korea has already announced that it will buy 10% of its oil needs from Iran in 2012.

Silk Road Redux

Most important of all, "isolated" Iran happens to be a supreme matter of national security for China, which has already rejected the latest Washington sanctions without a blink. Westerners seem to forget that the Middle Kingdom and Persia have been doing business for almost two millennia. (Does "Silk Road" ring a bell?)

The Chinese have already clinched a juicy deal for the development of Iran's largest oil field, Yadavaran. There's also the matter of the delivery of Caspian Sea oil from Iran through a pipeline stretching from Kazakhstan to Western China. In fact, Iran already supplies no less than 15% of China's oil and natural gas. It is now more crucial to China, energy-wise, than the House of Saud is to the U.S., which imports 11% of its oil from Saudi Arabia.

In fact, China may be the true winner from Washington's new sanctions, because it is likely to get its oil and gas at a lower price as the Iranians grow ever more dependent on the China market. At this moment, in fact, the two countries are in the middle of a complex negotiation on the pricing of Iranian oil, and the Chinese have actually been ratcheting up the pressure by slightly cutting back on energy purchases. But all this should be concluded by March, at least two months before the latest round of US sanctions go into effect, according to experts in Beijing. In the end, the Chinese will certainly buy much more Iranian gas than oil, but Iran will still remain its third biggest oil supplier, right after Saudi Arabia and Angola.

As for other effects of the new sanctions on China, don't count on them. Chinese businesses in Iran are building cars, fiber optics networks, and expanding the Tehran subway. Two-way trade is at $30 billion now and expected to hit $50 billion in 2015. Chinese businesses will find a way around the banking problems the new sanctions impose.

Russia is, of course, another key supporter of "isolated" Iran. It has opposed stronger sanctions either via the UN or through the Washington-approved package that targets Iran's Central Bank. In fact, it favors a rollback of the existing UN sanctions and has also been at work on an alternative plan that could, at least theoretically, lead to a face-saving nuclear deal for everyone.

On the nuclear front, Tehran has expressed a willingness to compromise with Washington along the lines of the plan Brazil and Turkey suggested and Washington deep-sixed in 2010. Since it is now so much clearer that, for Washington—certainly for Congress—the nuclear issue is secondary to regime change, any new negotiations are bound to prove excruciatingly painful.

This is especially true now that the leaders of the European Union have managed to remove themselves from a future negotiating table by shooting themselves in their Ferragamo-clad feet. In typical fashion, they have meekly followed Washington's lead in implementing an Iranian oil embargo. As a senior EU official told National Iranian American Council President Trita Parsi, and as EU diplomats have assured me in no uncertain terms, they fear this might prove to be the last step short of outright war.

Meanwhile, a team of International Atomic Energy Agency inspectors has just visited Iran. The IAEA is supervising all things nuclear in Iran, including its new uranium-enrichment plant at Fordow, near the holy city of Qom, with full production starting in June. The IAEA is positive: no bomb-making is involved. Nonetheless, Washington (and the Israelis) continue to act as though it's only a matter of time—and not much of it at that.

Follow the Money

That Iranian isolation theme only gets weaker when one learns that the country is dumping the dollar in its trade with Russia for rials and rubles—a similar move to ones already made in its trade with China and Japan. As for India, an economic powerhouse in the neighborhood, its leaders also refuse to stop buying Iranian oil, a trade that, in the long run, is similarly unlikely to be conducted in dollars. India is already using the yuan with China, as Russia and China have been trading in rubles and yuan for more than a year, as Japan and China are promoting direct trading in yen and yuan. As for Iran and China, all new trade and joint investments will be settled in yuan and rial.

Translation, if any was needed: in the near future, with the Europeans out of the mix, virtually none of Iran's oil will be traded in dollars.

Moreover, three BRICS members (Russia, India, and China) allied with Iran are major holders (and producers) of gold. Their complex trade ties won't be affected by the whims of a US Congress. In fact, when the developing world looks at the profound crisis in the Atlanticist West, what they see is massive US debt, the Fed printing money as if there's no tomorrow, lots of "quantitative easing," and of course the eurozone shaking to its very foundations.

Follow the money. Leave aside, for the moment, the new sanctions on Iran's Central Bank that will go into effect months from now, ignore Iranian threats to close the Strait of Hormuz (especially unlikely given that it's the main way Iran gets its own oil to market), and perhaps one key reason the crisis in the Persian Gulf is mounting involves this move to torpedo the petrodollar as the all-purpose currency of exchange.

It's been spearheaded by Iran and it's bound to translate into an anxious Washington, facing down not only a regional power, but its major strategic competitors China and Russia. No wonder all those carriers are heading for the Persian Gulf right now, though it's the strangest of showdowns—a case of military power being deployed against economic power.

In this context, it's worth remembering that in September 2000 Saddam Hussein abandoned the petrodollar as the currency of payment for Iraq's oil, and moved to the euro. In March 2003, Iraq was invaded and the inevitable regime change occurred. Libya's Muammar Gaddafi proposed a gold dinar both as Africa's common currency and as the currency of payment for his country's energy resources. Another intervention and another regime change followed.

Washington/NATO/Tel Aviv, however, offers a different narrative. Iran's "threats" are at the heart of the present crisis, even if these are, in fact, that country's reaction to non-stop US/Israeli covert war and now, of course, economic war as well. It's those "threats," so the story goes, that are leading to rising oil prices and so fueling the current recession, rather than Wall Street's casino capitalism or massive US and European debts. The cream of the 1% has nothing against high oil prices, not as long as Iran's around to be the fall guy for popular anger.

As energy expert Michael Klare pointed out recently, we are now in a new geo-energy era certain to be extremely turbulent in the Persian Gulf and elsewhere. But consider 2012 the start-up year as well for a possibly massive defection from the dollar as the global currency of choice. As perception is indeed reality, imagine the real world—mostly the global South—doing the necessary math and, little by little, beginning to do business in their own currencies and investing ever less of any surplus in US Treasury bonds.

Of course, the US can always count on the Gulf Cooperation Council (GCC)—Saudi Arabia, Qatar, Oman, Bahrain, Kuwait and the UAE—which I prefer to call the Gulf Counter-Revolution Club (just look at their performances during the Arab Spring). For all practical geopolitical purposes, the Gulf monarchies are a US satrapy. Their decades-old promise to use only the petrodollar translates into them being an appendage of Pentagon power projection across the Middle East. Centcom, after all, is based in Qatar; the US Fifth Fleet is stationed in Bahrain. In fact, in the immensely energy-wealthy lands that we could label Greater Pipelineistan—and that the Pentagon used to call "the arc of instability"—extending through Iran all the way to Central Asia, the GCC remains key to a dwindling sense of US hegemony.

If this were an economic rewrite of Edgar Allan Poe's story, "The Pit and the Pendulum," Iran would be but one cog in an infernal machine slowly shredding the dollar as the world's reserve currency. Still, it's the cog that Washington is now focused on. They have regime change on the brain. All that's needed is a spark to start the fire (in—one hastens to add—all sorts of directions that are bound to catch Washington off guard).

Remember Operation Northwoods, that 1962 plan drafted by the Joint Chiefs of Staff to stage terror operations in the US and blame them on Fidel Castro's Cuba. (President Kennedy shot the idea down.) Or recall the Gulf of Tonkin incident in 1964, used by President Lyndon Johnson as a justification for widening the Vietnam War. The US accused North Vietnamese torpedo boats of unprovoked attacks on US ships. Later, it became clear that one of the attacks had never even happened and the president had lied about it.

It's not at all far-fetched to imagine hardcore Full-Spectrum-Dominance practitioners inside the Pentagon riding a false-flag incident in the Persian Gulf to an attack on Iran (or simply using it to pressure Tehran into a fatal miscalculation). Consider as well the new US military strategy just unveiled by President Obama in which the focus of Washington's attention is to move from two failed ground wars in the Greater Middle East to the Pacific (and so to China). Iran happens to be right in the middle, in Southwest Asia, with all that oil heading towards an energy-hungry modern Middle Kingdom over waters guarded by the US Navy.

So yes, this larger-than-life psychodrama we call "Iran" may turn out to be as much about China and the US dollar as it is about the politics of the Persian Gulf or Iran's non-existent bomb. The question is: What rough beast, its hour come round at last, slouches towards Beijing to be born?

January 2012. Originally at TomDispatch.com

WAR, PIPELINEISTAN-STYLE

US Secretary of State Hillary "We came, we saw, he died" Clinton's message to Pakistan was stark; try to go ahead with the IP (Iran-Pakistan) gas pipeline, and we're going to take you out financially.

Islamabad, its economy in tatters, living in power-cut land, and desperate for energy, tried to argue. Pakistan's top official in the Petroleum and Natural Resources Ministry, Muhammad Ejaz Chaudhry, stressed that the 2,775-km, $1.5 billion IP was absolutely crucial for Pakistan's energy security.

That fell on deaf ears. Clinton evoked "particularly damaging" sanctions—tied to Washington's push to isolate Iran by all means available and the no-holds-barred campaign to force particularly India, China and Turkey to cut off their imports of Iranian oil and gas.

So as Washington has been impotent to disrupt Pipelineistan moves in Central Asia—by isolating Iran and bypassing Russia—it's now going ballistic to prevent by all means the crucial integration of Southwest Asia and South Asia, from Iran's giant South Pars gas field to Pakistan's Balochistan and Sindh provinces.

IP, it should be remembered, is the original, $7 billion IPI; Iran-Pakistan-India, also known as the "peace pipeline." India dropped out in 2009 after non-stop harassment by the George W Bush and then Barack Obama administrations; India was offered access to civilian nuclear technology.

China, for its part, is still eyeing the possibility of extending IP out of Gwadar port, then crossing to Pakistan's north alongside the Karakoram

Highway all the way to Xinjiang. China is already helping Islamabad to build civilian nuclear reactors—as part of Pakistan's energy security policy.

ICBC, China's largest bank and the world's number one lender, was already positioned as financial advisor to IP. But then, contemplating the (sanctions) writing on the wall, it started to "show less interest," as Islamabad chose to spin it. Is ICBC totally out? Not exactly. At least according to the Pakistani Ministry of Petroleum's spokesman, Irfan Ashraf Qazid; "ICBC is still engaged in the IP project and the negotiations are still going on."

A mega-bank such as ICBC, with myriad global interests, may be wary of defying the Washington sanction machine; but other financing options may be found, as in other banks or government-level agreements with China or Russia. Pakistan's Foreign Minister Hina Rabbani Khar has just made it very clear. Pakistan badly needs gas that should start flowing by December 2014.

Islamabad and Tehran have already agreed on pricing. Iran's 900-km stretch of IP is already built; Pakistan's is starting, via ILF Engineering from Germany. Iran's IRNA agency said Pakistan has announced that the IP is still on; predictably, Western media spin is that the Chinese got scared and backed out.

IPC, anyone?

For Washington, the only way to go is another Pipelineistan gambit—the perennially troubled TAPI (Turkmenistan-Afghanistan-Pakistan-India). Even assuming it will find financing; even assuming the Taliban will be taking their cut (that was, in fact, why negotiations between them and the Bill Clinton then Bush administrations failed); and even assuming it would not be bombed routinely by mujahideen, TAPI would only be ready, optimistically, by 2018. And Islamabad simply can't wait that long.

Predictably, Washington's anti-IP campaign has been relentless—including, of course, shadow war. Islamabad is convinced that the CIA, the Indian intel agency RAW, the Israeli Mossad and the British MI-6 have been actively conspiring to get some sort of Greater Balochistan to secede from the central government. They have been, a la Libyan model, financing and weaponizing selected Baloch fighters. Not because they love their independent spirit—but as a means to balkanize Pakistan.

To compound Washington's fury, "isolated" Iran, by the way, is about to start exporting an extra 80,000 barrels of oil a day to Pakistan; and has already committed $250 million to the Pakistani stretch of IP.

This has got the potential of becoming much, much uglier. Washington won't be deterred from its intent to smash IP. For an Iran under pressure and a strangled Pakistani economy—as well as China—this is all about the Asian Energy Security Grid.

ICBC may be out—sort of. But the whole thing could become even juicier if Beijing decides to step in for good, and turn it from IP to IPC. Will Washington have the guts to defy Beijing head on?

March, 2012

WAR PORN: THE NEW SAFE SEX

The early 21st century is addicted to war porn, a prime spectator sport consumed by global couch and digital potatoes. War porn took the limelight on the evening of September 11, 2001, when the George W Bush administration launched the "war on terror"—which was interpreted by many of its practitioners as a subtle legitimization of state terror against, predominantly, Muslims.

This was also a war OF terror—as in a manifestation of state terror pitting urban high-tech might against basically rural, low-tech cunning. The US did not exercise this monopoly; Beijing practiced it in Xinjiang, its far west, and Russia practiced it in Chechnya.

Like porn, war porn cannot exist without being based on a lie—a crude representation. But unlike porn, war porn is the real thing; unlike crude, cheap snuff movies, people in war porn actually die—in droves.

The lie to finish all lies at the center of this representation was definitely established with the leak of the 2005 Downing Street memo, in which the head of the British MI6 confirmed that the Bush administration wanted to take out Iraq's Saddam Hussein by linking Islamic terrorism with (non-existent) weapons of mass destruction (WMD). So, as the memo put it, "The intelligence and facts were being fixed around the policy."

In the end, George "you're either with us or against us" Bush did star in his own, larger-than-life snuff movie—that happened to double as the invasion and destruction of the eastern flank of the Arab nation.

EMPIRE OF CHAOS

The new Guernica

Iraq may indeed be seen as the Star Wars of war porn—an apotheosis of sequels. Take the (second) Fallujah offensive in late 2004. At the time I described it as the new Guernica. I also took the liberty of paraphrasing Jean-Paul Sartre, writing about the Algerian War; after Fallujah no two Americans shall meet without a corpse lying between them. To quote Coppola's *Apocalypse Now*, there were bodies, bodies everywhere.

The Francisco Franco in Fallujah was Iyad Allawi, the US-installed interim premier. It was Allawi who "asked" the Pentagon to bomb Fallujah. In Guernica—as in Fallujah—there was no distinction between civilians and guerrillas: it was the rule of "*Viva la muerte!*"

Marine commanders said on the record that Fallujah was the house of Satan. Franco denied the massacre in Guernica and blamed the local population—just as Allawi and the Pentagon denied any civilian deaths and insisted "insurgents" were guilty.

Fallujah was reduced to rubble, at least 200,000 residents became refugees, and thousands of civilians were killed, in order to "save it" (echoes of Vietnam). No one in Western corporate media had the guts to say that in fact Fallujah was the American Halabja.

Fifteen years before Fallujah, in Halabja, Washington was a very enthusiastic supplier of chemical weapons to Saddam, who used them to gas thousands of Kurds. The CIA at the time said it was not Saddam; it was Khomeinist Iran. Yet Saddam did it, and did it deliberately, just like the US in Fallujah.

Fallujah doctors identified swollen and yellowish corpses without any injuries, as well as "melted bodies"—victims of napalm, the cocktail of polystyrene and jet fuel. Residents who managed to escape told of bombing by "poisonous gases" and "weird bombs that smoke like a mushroom cloud... and then small pieces fall from the air with long tails of smoke behind them. The pieces of these strange bombs explode into large fires that burn the skin even when you throw water over them."

That's exactly what happens to people bombed with napalm or white phosphorus. The UN banned the bombing of civilians with napalm in 1980. The US is the only country in the world still using napalm.

Fallujah also provided a mini-snuff movie hit; the summary execution of a wounded, defenseless Iraqi man inside a mosque by a US Marine. The execution, caught on tape, and watched by millions on YouTube, graphically spelled out the "special" rules of engagement. Marine commanders at the time were telling their soldiers to "shoot everything that moves and everything that doesn't move"; to fire "two bullets in every body"; in case of seeing any military-aged men in the streets of Fallujah, to "drop 'em"; and to spray every home with machine-gun and tank fire before entering them.

The rules of engagement in Iraq were codified in a 182-page field manual distributed to each and every soldier and issued in October 2004 by the Pentagon. This counter-insurgency manual stressed five rules; "protect the population; establish local political institutions; reinforce local governments; eliminate insurgent capabilities; and exploit information from local sources."

Now back to reality. Fallujah's population was not protected: it was bombed out of the city and turned into a mass of thousands of refugees. Political institutions were already in place: the Fallujah Shura was running the city. No local government can possibly run a pile of rubble to be recovered by seething citizens, not to mention be "reinforced." "Insurgent capabilities" were not eliminated; the resistance dispersed around the 22 other cities out of control by the US occupation, and spread up north all the way to Mosul; and the Americans remained without intelligence "from local sources" because they antagonized every possible heart and mind.

Meanwhile, in the US, most of the population was already immune to war porn. When the Abu Ghraib scandal broke out in the spring of 2004, I was driving through Texas, exploring Bushland. Virtually everybody I spoke to either attributed the humiliation of Iraqi prisoners to "a few bad apples," or defended it on patriotic grounds ("we must teach a lesson to "terrorists").

I love a man in uniform

In thesis, there is an approved mechanism in the 21st century to defend civilians from war porn. It's the R2P—"responsibility to protect" doctrine. This was an idea floated already in 2001—a few weeks after the war on terror was unleashed, in fact—by the Canadian government and a few foundations. The idea was that the concert of nations had a "moral duty" to deploy a humanitarian intervention in cases such as Halabja, not to mention the Khmer Rouge in Cambodia in the mid-1970s or the genocide in Rwanda in the mid-1990s.

In 2004, a panel at the UN codified the idea—crucially with the Security Council being able to authorize a "military intervention" only "as a last resort." Then, in 2005, the UN General Assembly endorsed a resolution supporting R2P, and in 2006 the UN Security Council passed resolution 1674 about "the protection of civilians in armed conflict"; they should be protected against "genocide, war crimes, ethnic cleansing and crimes against humanity."

Now fast forward to the end of 2008, early 2009, when Israel—using American fighter jets to raise hell—unleashed a large-scale attack on the civilian population of the Gaza strip.

Look at the official US reaction; "Israel has obviously decided to protect herself and her people," said then-president Bush. The US Congress voted by a staggering 390-to-5 to recognize "Israel's right to defend itself against attacks from Gaza." The incoming Barack Obama administration was thunderously silent. Only future Secretary of State Hillary Clinton said, "We support Israel's right to self-defense."

At least 1,300 civilians—including scores of women and children—were killed by state terror in Gaza. Nobody invoked R2P. Nobody pointed to Israel's graphic failure in its "responsibility to protect" Palestinians. Nobody called for a "humanitarian intervention" targeting Israel.

The mere notion that a superpower—and other lesser powers—make their foreign policy decisions based on humanitarian grounds, such as protecting people under siege, is an absolute joke. So already at the time we learned how R2P was to be instrumentalized. It did not apply to the US in Iraq or Afghanistan. It did not apply to Israel in Palestine. It would eventually apply only to frame "rogue" rulers that are not "our bastards"—as in Muammar Gaddafi in Libya in 2011. "Humanitarian" intervention, yes; but only to get rid of "the bad guys."

And the beauty of R2P was that it could be turned upside down anytime. Bush pleaded for the "liberation" of suffering Afghans—and especially *burqa*-clad Afghan women—from the "evil" Taliban, in fact configuring Afghanistan as a humanitarian intervention.

And when the bogus links between al-Qaeda and the non-existent WMDs were debunked, Washington began to justify the invasion, occupation and destruction of Iraq via... R2P; "responsibility to protect" Iraqis from Saddam, and then to protect Iraqis from themselves.

The killer awoke before dawn

The most recent installment in serial episodes of war porn is the Kandahar massacre, when, according to the official Pentagon version (or cover up) an American army sergeant, a sniper and Iraqi war veteran—a highly trained assassin—shot 17 Afghan civilians, including nine women and four children, in two villages two miles apart, and burned some of their bodies.

Like with Abu Ghraib, there was the usual torrent of denials from the Pentagon—as in "this is not us" or "we don't do things these way"; not to mention a tsunami of stories in US corporate media humanizing the hero-turned-mass killer, as in "he's such a good guy, a family man." In contrast, not a single word about The Other—the Afghan victims. They are faceless; and nobody knows their names.

A—serious—Afghan enquiry established that some 20 soldiers may have been part of the massacre—as in My Lai in Vietnam; and that included the rape of two of the women. It does make sense. War porn is a lethal, group subculture—complete with targeted assassinations, revenge killings, desecration of bodies, harvesting of trophies (severed fingers or ears), burning of Korans and pissing on dead bodies. It's essentially a collective sport.

US "kill teams" have deliberately executed random, innocent Afghan civilians, mostly teenagers, for sport, planted weapons on their bodies, and then posed with their corpses as trophies. Not by accident they had been operating out of a base in the same area of the Kandahar massacre.

And we should not forget former top US commander in Afghanistan, General Stanley McChrystal, who in April 10, 2010, admitted, bluntly, "We've shot an amazing number of people" who were *not* a threat to the US or Western civilization.

The Pentagon spins and sells in Afghanistan what it sold in Iraq (and even way back in Vietnam for that matter); the idea that this is a "population-centric counter-insurgency"—or COIN, to "win hearts and minds," and part of a great nation-building project.

This is a monumental lie. The Obama surge in Afghanistan—based on COIN—was a total failure. What replaced it was hardcore, covert, dark war, led by "kill teams" of Special Forces. That implies an inflation of air strikes and night raids. No to mention drone strikes, both in Afghanistan and in Pakistan's tribal areas, whose favorite targets seem to be Pashtun wedding parties.

Incidentally, the CIA claims that since May 2010, ultra-smart drones have killed more than 600 "carefully selected" human targets—and, miraculously, not a single civilian.

Expect to see this war porn extravaganza celebrated in an orgy of upcoming, joint Pentagon-Hollywood blockbusters. In real life, this is spun by people such as John Nagl, who was on General David Petraeus' staff in Iraq and now runs the pro-Pentagon think-tank Center for New American Security.

The new stellar macho, macho men may be the commandos under the Joint Special Operations Command (JSOC). But this a Pentagon production, which has created, according to Nagl, an "industrial strength counter-terrorism killing machine."

Reality, though, is much more prosaic. COIN techniques, applied by McChrystal, relied on only three components; 24-hour surveillance by drones; monitoring of mobile phones; and pinpointing the physical location of the phones from their signals.

This implies that anyone in an area under a drone watch using a cell phone was branded as a "terrorist," or at least "terrorist sympathizer."

And then the focus of the night raids in Afghanistan shifted from "high-value targets"—high-level and mid-level al-Qaeda and Taliban—to anyone who was branded as helping the Taliban.

In May 2009, before McChrystal arrived, US Special Forces were carrying 20 raids a month. By November, they were 90 a month. By the spring of 2010, they were 250 a month. When McChrystal was fired—because of a story in *Rolling Stone* (he was competing with Lady Gaga for the cover; Lady Gaga won)—and Obama replaced him with Petraeus in the summer of 2010, there were 600 a month. By April 2011, they were more than 1,000 a month.

So this is how it works. Don't even think of using a cell phone in Kandahar and other Afghan provinces. Otherwise, the "eyes in the sky" are going to get you. At the very least you will be sent to jail, along with thousands of other civilians branded as "terrorist sympathizers"; and intelligence analysts will use your data to compile their "kill/capture list" and catch even more civilians in their net.

As for the civilian "collateral damage" of the night raids, they were always presented by the Pentagon as "terrorists." Example; in a raid in Gardez on February 12, 2010, two men were killed; a local government prosecutor and an Afghan intelligence official, as well as three women (two of them pregnant). The killers told NATO command in Kabul that the two men were "terrorists" and the women had been found tied up and gagged. Then the actual target of the raid turned himself in for questioning a few days later, and was released without any charges.

That's just the beginning. Targeted assassination—as practiced in Afghanistan—will be the Pentagon's tactic of choice in all future US wars.

Pass the condom, darling

Libya was a major war porn atrocity exhibition—complete with a nifty Roman touch of the defeated "barbarian" chief sodomized in the streets and then executed, straight on YouTube.

This, by the way, is exactly what Secretary of State Hillary Clinton, in a lightning visit to Tripoli, had announced less than 48 hours before the fact. Gaddafi should be "captured or killed." When she watched it in the screen of her BlackBerry she could only react with the semantic earthquake "Wow!"

From the minute a UN resolution imposed a no-fly zone over Libya under the cover of R2P, it became a green card to regime change. Plan A was always to capture and kill Gaddafi—as in an Afghan-style targeted assassination. That was the Obama administration official policy. There was no plan B.

Obama said the death of Gaddafi meant, "the strength of American leadership across the world." That was as "We got him" (echoes of Saddam captured by the Bush administration) as one could possibly expect.

With an extra bonus. Even though Washington paid no less than 80% of the operating costs of those dimwits at NATO (roughly $2 billion), it was still pocket money. Anyway, it was still awkward to say, "We did it," because the White House always said this was not a war; it was a "kinetic" something. And they were not in charge.

Only the hopelessly naïve may have swallowed the propaganda of NATO's "humanitarian" 40,000-plus bombing which devastated Libya's infrastructure back to the Stone Age as a Shock and Awe in slow motion. This never had anything to do with R2P.

This was R2P as safe sex—and the "international community" was the condom. The "international community," as everyone knows, is composed of Washington, a few washed-up NATO members, and the democratic Persian Gulf powerhouses of Qatar and the United Arab Emirates (UAE), plus the House of Saud in the shade. The EU, which up to extra time was caressing the helm of Gaddafi's gowns, took no time to fall over themselves in editorials about the 42-year reign of a "buffoon."

As for the concept of international law, it was left lying in a drain as filthy as the one Gaddafi was holed up in. Saddam at least got a fake trial in a kangaroo court before meeting the executioner (he ended up on YouTube as well). Osama bin Laden was simply snuffed out, assassination-style, after a territorial invasion of Pakistan (no YouTube—so many don't believe it). Gaddafi went one up, snuffed out with a mix of air war and assassination. They are The Three Graceful Scalps of War Porn.

Sweet emotion

Syria is yet another declination of war porn narrative. If you can't R2P it, fake it.

And to think that all this was codified such a long time ago. Already in 1997, the US Army War College Quarterly was defining what they called "the future of warfare." They framed it as "the conflict between information masters and information victims."

They were sure "we are already masters of information warfare... Hollywood is 'preparing the battlefield'... Information destroys traditional jobs and traditional cultures; it seduces, betrays, yet remains invulnerable ... Our sophistication in handling it will enable us to outlast and outperform all hierarchical cultures... Societies that fear or otherwise cannot manage the flow of information simply will not be competitive. They might master the technological wherewithal to watch the videos, but we will be writing the scripts, producing them, and collecting the royalties. Our creativity is devastating."

Post-everything information warfare has nothing to do with geopolitics. Just like the proverbial Hollywood product, it is to be "spawned" out of raw emotions; "hatred, jealousy, and greed—emotions, rather than strategy."

In Syria this is exactly how Western corporate media has scripted the whole movie; the War College "information warfare" tactics in practice. The Syrian government never had much of a chance against those "writing the scripts, producing them, and collecting the royalties."

For example, the armed opposition, the so-called Free Syrian Army (a nasty cocktail of defectors, opportunists, jihadis and foreign mercenaries) brought Western journalists to Homs and then insisted to extract them, in extremely dangerous condition, and with people being killed, via Lebanon, rather than through the Red Crescent. They were nothing else than writing the script for a foreign-imposed "humanitarian corridor" to be opened to Homs. This was pure theater—or war porn packaged as a Hollywood drama.

The problem is Western public opinion is now hostage to this brand of information warfare. Forget about even the possibility of peaceful negotiations among adult parties. What's left is a binary good guys versus bad guys plot, where the Big Bad Guy must be destroyed at all costs (and on top of it his wife is a snob bitch who loves shopping!)

Only the terminally naïve may believe that jihadis—including Libya's NATO rebels—financed by the Gulf Counter-revolution Club, also know as Gulf Cooperation Council (GCC) are a bunch of democratic reformists burning with good intentions. Even Human Rights Watch was finally forced to acknowledge that these armed "activists" were responsible for "kidnapping, detention, and torture," after receiving reports of "executions by armed opposition groups of security force members and civilians."

What this (soft and hard) war porn narrative veils, in the end, is the real Syrian tragedy; the impossibility for the much-lauded "Syrian people" to get rid of all these crooks—the Assad system, the Muslim Brotherhood-controlled Syrian National Council, and the mercenary-infested Free Syrian Army.

Listen to the sound of chaos

This—very partial—catalogue of sorrows inevitably brings us to the current supreme war porn blockbuster—the Iran psychodrama.

2012 is the new 2002; Iran is the new Iraq; and whatever the highway, to evoke the neocon motto, real men go to Tehran via Damascus, or real men go to Tehran non-stop.

Perhaps only underwater in the Arctic we would be able to escape the cacophonous cortege of American right-wingers—and their respective European poodles—salivating for blood and deploying the usual festival of fallacies like "Iran wants to wipe Israel off the map," "diplomacy has run its course," "the sanctions are too late," or "Iran is within a year, six months, a week, a day, or a minute of assembling a bomb." Of course these dogs of war would never bother to follow what the International Atomic Energy Agency is actually doing, not to mention the National Intelligence Estimates released by the 17 US intelligence agencies.

Because they, to a great extent, are "writing the scripts, producing them, and collecting the royalties" in terms of corporate media, they can get away with an astonishingly toxic fusion of arrogance and ignorance—about the Middle East, about Persian culture, about Asian integration, about the nuclear issue, about the oil industry, about the global economy, about "the Rest" as compared to "the West."

Just like with Iraq in 2002, Iran is always dehumanized. The relentless, totally hysterical, fear-inducing "narrative" of "should we bomb now or should we bomb later" is always about oh so very smart bunker-buster bombs and precision missiles that will accomplish an ultra clean large-scale devastation job without producing a single "collateral damage." Just like safe sex.

And even when the voice of the establishment itself—the *New York Times*—admits that neither US nor Israeli intelligence believe Iran has decided to build a bomb (a 5-year-old could reach the same conclusion), the hysteria remains inter-galactic.

Meanwhile, while it gets ready—"all options are on the table," Obama himself keeps repeating—for yet another war in what it used to call "arc of instability," the Pentagon also found time to repackage war porn. It took only a 60-second video now on YouTube, titled *Toward the Sound of Chaos*, released only a few days after the Kandahar massacre. Just look at its key target audience: the very large market of poor, unemployed and politically very naïve young Americans.

Let's listen to the mini-movie voice over: "Where chaos looms, the Few emerge. Marines move toward the sounds of tyranny, injustice and despair—with the courage and resolve to silence them. By ending conflict, instilling order and helping those who can't help themselves, Marines face down the threats of our time."

Maybe, in this Orwellian universe, we should ask the dead Afghans urinated upon by US Marines, or the thousands of dead in Fallujah, to write a movie review. Well, dead men don't write. Maybe we could think about the day NATO enforces a no-fly one over Saudi Arabia to protect the Shi'ites in the eastern province, while Pentagon drones launch a carpet of Hellfire missiles over those thousands of arrogant, medieval, corrupt House of Saud princes. No, it's not going to happen.

Over a decade after the beginning of the war on terror, this is what the world is coming to; a lazy, virtually worldwide audience, jaded, dazed and distracted from distraction by distraction, helplessly hooked on the shabby atrocity exhibition of war porn.

March 2012

A HISTORY OF THE WORLD, BRIC BY BRIC

Goldman Sachs—via economist Jim O'Neill—invented the concept of a rising new bloc on the planet: BRICS (Brazil, Russia, India, China, South Africa). Some cynics couldn't help calling it the "Bloody Ridiculous Investment Concept."

Not really. Goldman now expects the BRICS countries to account for almost 40% of global GDP by 2050, and to include four of the world's top five economies.

Soon, in fact, that acronym may have to expand to include Turkey, Indonesia, South Korea and, yes, nuclear Iran: BRIIICTSS? Despite its well-known problems as a nation under economic siege, Iran is also motoring along as part of the N-11, yet another distilled concept. (It stands for the next 11 emerging economies.)

The multitrillion-dollar global question remains: Is the emergence of BRICS a signal that we have truly entered a new multipolar world?

Yale's canny historian Paul Kennedy (of "imperial overstretch" fame) is convinced that we either are about to cross or have already crossed a "historical watershed" taking us far beyond the post-Cold War unipolar world of "the sole superpower." There are, argues Kennedy, four main reasons for that: the slow erosion of the US dollar (formerly 85% of global reserves, now less than 60%), the "paralysis of the European project," Asia rising (the end of 500 years of Western hegemony), and the decrepitude of the United Nations.

The Group of Eight (G-8) is already increasingly irrelevant. The G-20, which includes the BRICS, might, however, prove to be the real thing. But there's much to be done to cross that watershed rather than simply be swept over it willy-nilly: the reform of the UN Security Council, and above all, the reform of the Bretton Woods system, especially those two crucial institutions, the IMF and the World Bank.

On the other hand, willy-nilly may prove the way of the world. After all, as emerging superstars, the BRICS have a ton of problems. True, in only the last seven years Brazil has added 40 million people as middle-class consumers; by 2016, it will have invested another $900 billion—more than a third of its GDP—in energy and infrastructure; and it's not as exposed as some BRICS members to the imponderables of world trade, since its exports are only 11% of GDP, even less than the U.S.

Still, the key problem remains the same: lack of good management, not to mention a swamp of corruption. Brazil's brazen new monied class is turning out to be no less corrupt than the old, arrogant, comprador elites that used to run the country.

In India, the choice seems to be between manageable and unmanageable chaos. The corruption of the country's political elite would make Shiva proud. Abuse of state power, nepotistic control of contracts related to infrastructure, the looting of mineral resources, real estate property scandals—they've got it all, even if India is not a Hindu Pakistan. Not yet anyway.

Since 1991, "reform" in India has meant only one thing: unbridled commerce and getting the state out of the economy. Not surprisingly then, nothing is being done to reform public institutions, which are a scandal in themselves. Efficient public administration? Don't even think about it. In a nutshell, India is a chaotic economic dynamo and yet, in some sense, not even an emerging power, not to speak of a superpower.

Russia, too, is still trying to find the magic mix, including a competent state policy to exploit the country's bounteous natural resources, extraordinary space, and impressive social talent. It must modernize fast as, apart from Moscow and St. Petersburg, relative social backwardness prevails. Its leaders remain uneasy about neighboring China (aware that any Sino-Russian alliance would leave Russia as a distinctly junior partner). They are distrustful of Washington, anxious over the depopulation of their eastern territories, and worried about the cultural and religious alienation of their Muslim population.

Then again the Putinator is back as president with his magic formula for modernization: a strategic German-Russian partnership that will benefit the power elite/business oligarchy, but not necessarily the majority of Russians.

Dead in the Woods

The post-World War II Bretton Woods system is now officially dead, totally illegitimate, but what are the BRICS planning to do about it?

At their summit in New Delhi in late March, they pushed for the creation of a BRICS development bank that could invest in infrastructure and provide them with back-up credit for whatever financial crises lie down the road. The BRICS know perfectly well that Washington and the European Union (EU) will never relinquish control of the IMF and the World Bank. Nonetheless, trade among these countries will reach an impressive $500 billion by 2015, mostly in their own currencies.

However, BRICS cohesion, to the extent it exists, centers mostly around shared frustration with the Masters of the Universe-style financial speculation that nearly sent the global economy off a cliff in 2008. True, the BRICS crew also has a notable convergence of policy and opinion when it comes to embattled Iran, an Arab Sprung Middle East, and

Northern Africa. Still, for the moment the key problem they face is this: they don't have an ideological or institutional alternative to neoliberalism and the lordship of global finance.

As Vijay Prashad has noted, the Global North has done everything to prevent any serious discussion of how to reform the global financial casino. No wonder the head of the G-77 group of developing nations (now G-132, in fact), Thai ambassador Pisnau Chanvitan, has warned of "behavior that seems to indicate a desire for the dawn of a new neocolonialism."

Meanwhile, things happen anyway, helter-skelter. China, for instance, continues to informally advance the yuan as a globalizing, if not global, currency. It's already trading in yuan with Russia and Australia, not to mention across Latin America and in the Middle East. Increasingly, the BRICS are betting on the yuan as their monetary alternative to a devalued US dollar.

Japan is using both yen and yuan in its bilateral trade with its huge Asian neighbor. The fact is that there's already an unacknowledged Asian free-trade zone in the making, with China, Japan, and South Korea on board.

What's ahead, even if it includes a BRICS-bright future, will undoubtedly be very messy. Just about anything is possible (verging on likely), from another Great Recession in the US to European stagnation or even the collapse of the euro zone, to a BRICS-wide slowdown, a tempest in the currency markets, the collapse of financial institutions, and a global crash.

And talk about messy, who could forget what Dick Cheney said, while still Halliburton's CEO, at the Institute of Petroleum in London in 1999: "The Middle East, with two-thirds of the world's oil and the lowest cost, is still where the prize ultimately lies." No wonder when, as vice president, he came to power in 2001, his first order of business was to "liberate" Iraq's oil. Of course, who doesn't remember how that ended?

Now (different administration but same line of work), it's an oil-embargo-cum-economic-war on Iran. The leadership in Beijing sees Washington's whole Iran psychodrama as a regime-change plot, pure and simple, having nothing to do with nuclear weapons. Then again, the winner so far in the Iran imbroglio is China. With Iran's banking system in crisis, and the US embargo playing havoc with that country's economy, Beijing can essentially dictate its terms for buying Iranian oil.

The Chinese are expanding Iran's fleet of oil tankers, a deal worth more than $1 billion, and that other BRICS giant, India, is now purchasing even more Iranian oil than China. Yet Washington won't apply its sanctions to BRICS members because these days, economically speaking, the US needs them more than they need the U.S.

The World Through Chinese Eyes

Which brings us to the dragon in the room: China.

What's the ultimate Chinese obsession? Stability, stability, stability.

The usual self-description of the system there as "socialism with Chinese characteristics" is, of course, as mythical as a gorgon. In reality, think hardcore neoliberalism with Chinese characteristics led by men who have every intention of saving global capitalism.

At the moment, China is smack in the middle of a tectonic, structural shift from an export/investment model to a services/consumer-led model. In terms of its explosive economic growth, the last decades have been almost unimaginable to most Chinese (and the rest of the world), but according to the *Financial Times*, they have also left the country's richest

1% controlling 40%-60% of total household wealth. How to find a way to overcome such staggering collateral damage? How to make a system with tremendous inbuilt problems function for 1.3 billion people?

Enter "stability-mania." Back in 2007, Prime Minister Wen Jiabao was warning that the Chinese economy could become "unstable, unbalanced, uncoordinated, and unsustainable." These were the famous "Four Uns."

Today, the collective leadership, including the next Prime Minister, Li Leqiang, has gone a nervous step further, purging "unstable" from the Party's lexicon. For all practical purposes, the next phase in the country's development is already upon us.

It will be quite something to watch in the years to come.

How will the nominally "communist" princelings—the sons and daughters of top revolutionary Party leaders, all immensely wealthy, thanks, in part, to their cozy arrangements with Western corporations, plus the bribes, the alliances with gangsters, all those "concessions" to the highest bidder, and the whole Western-linked crony-capitalist oligarchy—lead China beyond the "Four Modernizations"? Especially with all that fabulous wealth to loot.

The Obama administration, expressing its own anxiety, has responded to the clear emergence of China as a power to be reckoned with via a "strategic pivot"—from its disastrous wars in the Greater Middle East to Asia. The Pentagon likes to call this "rebalancing" (though things are anything but rebalanced or over for the US in the Middle East).

Before 9/11, the Bush administration had been focused on China as its future global enemy number one. Then 9/11 redirected it to what the Pentagon called "the arc of instability," the oil heartlands of the planet extending from the Middle East through Central Asia. Given Washington's distraction, Beijing calculated that it might enjoy a window of roughly two decades in which the pressure would be largely off. In those years, it could focus on a breakneck version of internal development, while the US was squandering mountains of money on its nonsensical "Global War on Terror."

Twelve years later, that window is being slammed shut as from India, Australia, and the Philippines to South Korea and Japan, the US declares itself back in the hegemony business in Asia. Doubts that this was the new American path were dispelled by Secretary of State Hillary Clinton's November 2011 manifesto in *Foreign Policy* magazine, none too subtly labeled "America's Pacific Century." (And she was talking about this century, not the last one!)

The American mantra is always the same: "American security," whose definition is: whatever happens on the planet. Whether in the oil-rich Persian Gulf where Washington "helps" allies Israel and Saudi Arabia because they feel threatened by Iran, or Asia where similar help is offered to a growing corps of countries that are said to feel threatened by China, it's always in the name of US security. In either case, in just about any case, that's what trumps all else.

As a result, if there is a 33-year Wall of Mistrust between the US and Iran, there is a new, growing Great Wall of Mistrust between the US and China. Recently, Wang Jisi, Dean of the School of International Studies at Peking University and a top Chinese strategic analyst, offered the Beijing leadership's perspective on that "Pacific Century" in an influential paper he coauthored.

China, he and his coauthor write, now expects to be treated as a first-class power. After all, it "successfully weathered… the 1997-98 global financial crisis," caused, in Beijing's eyes, by "deep deficiencies in the US economy and politics. China has surpassed Japan as the world's second-largest economy and seems to be the number two in world politics, as well... Chinese leaders do not credit these successes to the United States or to the U.S.-led world order."

The U.S., Wang adds, "is seen in China generally as a declining power over the long run... It is now a question of how many years, rather than how many decades, before China replaces the United States as the largest economy in the world... part of an emerging new structure." (Think: BRICS.)

In sum, as Wang and his coauthor portray it, influential Chinese see their country's development model providing "an alternative to Western democracy and experiences for other developing countries to learn from, while many developing countries that have introduced Western values and political systems are experiencing disorder and chaos."

Put it all in a nutshell and you have a Chinese vision of the world in which a fading US still yearns for global hegemony and remains powerful enough to block emerging powers—China and the other BRICS—from their twenty-first century destiny.

Dr. Zbig's Eurasian Wet Dream

Now, how does the US political elite see that same world? Virtually no one is better qualified to handle that subject than former national security advisor, BTC pipeline facilitator, and briefly Obama ghost advisor, Dr. Zbigniew ("Zbig") Brzezinski. And he doesn't hesitate to do so in his latest book, *Strategic Vision: America and the Crisis of Global Power.*

If the Chinese have their strategic eyes on those other BRICS nations, Dr. Zbig remains stuck on the Old World, newly configured. He is now arguing that, for the US to maintain some form of global hegemony, it must bet on an "expanded West." That would mean strengthening the Europeans (especially in energy terms), while embracing Turkey, which he imagines as a template for new Arab democracies, and engaging Russia, politically and economically, in a "strategically sober and prudent fashion."

Turkey, by the way, is no such template because, despite the Arab Spring, for the foreseeable future, there are no new Arab democracies. Still, Zbig believes that Turkey can help Europe, and so the U.S., in far more practical ways to solve certain global energy problems by facilitating its "unimpeded access across the Caspian Sea to Central Asia's oil and gas."

Under the present circumstances, however, this, too, remains something of a fantasy. After all, Turkey can only become a key transit country in the great energy game on the Eurasian chessboard I've long labeled Pipelineistan if the Europeans get their act together. They would have to convince the energy-rich, autocratic "republic" of Turkmenistan to ignore its powerful Russian neighbor and sell them all the natural gas they need. And then there's that other energy matter that looks unlikely at the moment: Washington and Brussels would have to ditch counterproductive sanctions and embargos against Iran (and the war games that go with them) and start doing serious business with that country.

Dr. Zbig nonetheless proposes the notion of a two-speed Europe as the key to future American power on the planet. Think of it as an upbeat version of a scenario in which the present eurozone semi-collapses. He would maintain the leading role of the inept bureaucratic fat cats in Brussels now running the EU, and support another "Europe" (mostly the southern "Club Med" countries) outside the euro, with nominally free movement of people and goods between the two. His bet—and in this he reflects a key strand of Washington thinking—is that a two-speed Europe, a Eurasian Big Mac, still joined at the hip to America, could be a globally critical player for the rest of the twenty-first century.

And then, of course, Dr. Zbig displays all his Cold Warrior colors, extolling an American future "stability in the Far East" inspired by "the role Britain played in the nineteenth century as a stabilizer and balancer of Europe." We're talking, in other words, about this century's number one gunboat diplomat. He graciously concedes that a "comprehensive American-Chinese global partnership" would still be possible, but only if Washington retains a significant geopolitical presence in what he still calls the "Far East"—"whether China approves or not."

The answer will be "not."

In a way, all of this is familiar stuff, as is much of actual Washington policy today. In his case, it's really a remix of his 1997 magnum opus *The Grand Chessboard* in which, he once again certifies that "the huge Trans-Eurasian continent is the central arena of world affairs." Only now reality has taught him that Eurasia can't be conquered and America's best shot is to try to bring Turkey and Russia into the fold.

Robocop Rules

Yet Brzezinski looks positively benign when you compare his ideas to Hillary Clinton's recent pronouncements, including her address to the tongue-twistingly named World Affairs Council 2012 NATO Conference. There, as the Obama administration regularly does, she highlighted "NATO's enduring relationship with Afghanistan" and praised negotiations between the US and Kabul over "a long-term strategic partnership between our two nations."

Translation; despite being outmaneuvered by a minority Pashtun insurgency for years, neither the Pentagon nor NATO have any intention of rebalancing out of their holdings in the Greater Middle East. Already negotiating with President Hamid Karzai's government in Kabul for staying rights through 2024, the US has every intention of holding onto three major strategic Afghan bases: Bagram, Shindand (near the Iranian border), and Kandahar (near the Pakistani border). Only the terminally naïve would believe the Pentagon capable of voluntarily abandoning such sterling outposts for the monitoring of Central Asia and strategic competitors Russia and China.

NATO, Clinton added ominously, will "expand its defense capabilities for the twenty-first century," including the missile-defense system the alliance approved at its last meeting in Lisbon in 2010.

It will be fascinating to see what the possible election of socialist François Hollande as French president might mean. Interested in a deeper strategic partnership with the BRICS, he is committed to the end of the US dollar as the world's reserve currency. The question is: Would his victory throw a monkey wrench into NATO's works, after these years under the Great Liberator of Libya, that neo-Napoleonic image-maker Nicolas Sarkozy (for whom France was just mustard in Washington's steak tartar).

No matter what either Dr. Zbig or Hillary might think, most European countries, fed up with their black-hole adventures in Afghanistan and Libya, and with the way NATO now serves US global interests, support Hollande on this. But it will still be an uphill battle. The destruction and overthrow of Muammar Gaddafi's Libyan regime was the highpoint of the recent NATO agenda of regime change in MENA (the Middle East-Northern Africa). And NATO remains Washington's plan B for the future, if the usual network of think-tanks, endowments, funds, foundations, NGOs, and even the UN fail to provoke what could be described as YouTube regime change.

In a nutshell: after going to war on three continents (in Yugoslavia, Afghanistan, and Libya), turning the Mediterranean into a virtual NATO lake, and patrolling the Arabian Sea non-stop, NATO will be, according to Hillary, riding on "a bet on America's leadership and strength, just as we did in the twentieth century, for this century and beyond." So 21 years after the end of the Soviet Union—NATO's original raison d'etre—this could be the way the world ends; not with a bang, but with NATO, in whimpering mode, still fulfilling the role of perpetual global Robocop.

We're back once again with Dr. Zbig and the idea of America as the "promoter and guarantor of unity" in the West, and as "balance and conciliator" in the East (for which it needs bases from the Persian Gulf to Japan, including those Afghan ones). And don't forget that the Pentagon has never given up the idea of attaining Full Spectrum Dominance.

For all that military strength, however, it's worth keeping in mind that this is distinctly a New World (and not in North America either). Against the guns and the gunboats, the missiles and the drones, there is economic power. Currency wars are now raging. BRICS members China and Russia have cordilleras of cash. South America is uniting fast. The Putinator has offered South Korea an oil pipeline. Iran is planning to sell all its oil and gas in a basket of currencies, none dollars. China is paying to expand its blue-water navy and its anti-ship missile weaponry. One day, Tokyo may finally realize that, as long as it is occupied by Wall Street and the Pentagon, it will live in eternal recession. Even Australia may eventually refuse to be forced into a counterproductive trade war with China.

So this twenty-first century world of ours is shaping up right now largely as a confrontation between the U.S./NATO and the BRICS, warts and all on every side. The danger: that somewhere down the line it turns into a Full Spectrum Confrontation. Because make no mistake, unlike Saddam Hussein or Muammar Gaddafi, the BRICS will actually be able to shoot back.

April 2012. Originally at TomDispatch.com

Drone Me Down on the Killing Floor

Lord knows, I should'a been gone
Lord knows, I should'a been gone
And I wouldn't've been here,
down on the killin' floor

- Howlin' Wolf, *Killing Floor*

As convenient as it is for someone in a cubicle in the Nevada desert to press a button and incinerate a Pashtun wedding party in North Waziristan, now, with only a click, anyone can download a 359 KB file available on Amazon for only $8.99—including free wireless delivery—and learn everything there is to learn about All Things Drone.

It's fitting that *Terminator Planet: The First History of Drone Warfare, 2001-2050* has been put together by Tom Engelhardt—editor, MC of the TomDispatch website and "a national treasure," in the correct appraisal of University of Michigan professor Juan Cole—and TomDispatch's associate editor Nick Turse, author of the seminal 2008 study The Complex: How the Military Invades Our Everyday Lives.

This is essentially Tom and Nick's revised and updated body of work detailing the uber-dystopian Dronescape over the past few years—spanning everything from secret Drone Empire bases to offshore droning; a Philip Dick-style exercise on a more than plausible drone-on-drone war off East Africa in 2050; and a postscript inimitably titled, "America as a Shining Drone Upon a Hill." It does beat fiction because it's all fact-based.

An MQ-1 Predator or an MQ-9 Reaper to go?

This digital file becomes even more crucial now that US and world public opinion knows US President Barack Obama is the certified Droner-in-Chief; the final judge, jury and digital Grand Inquisitor on which suspicious Muslim (for the moment, at least, they are all Muslims) will get his paradise virgins via targeted assassination.

Obama owns his newspeak-drenched "kill list." He decides on a "personality strike" (a single suspect) or a "signature strike" (a group). "Nominations" are scrutinized by Obama and his associate producer, counter-terrorism czar John Brennan. The logic is straight from Kafka; anyone lurking around an alleged "terrorist" is a terrorist. The only way to know for sure is after he's dead.

And the winner of the Humanitarian Oscar for Best Targeted Assassination with No Collateral Damage goes to... the Barack Obama White House death squad.

Targeted—and dissolved—throughout this grim process are also a pile of outdated concepts such as national sovereignty, set-in-stone principles of US and international law, and any category which until the collapse of the Soviet Union used to define what is war and what is peace. Anyway, those categories started to be dissolved for good already during the Bush administration—which "legalized" widespread CIA and Special Ops torture sessions and death squads.

Any self-respecting jurist would have to draw the inevitable conclusion; the United States of America is now outside international law—as rogue a state as they come, with The Drone Empire enshrined as the ultimate expression of shadow war.

Incinerate the faithful

Reading Terminator Planet inevitably evokes the incestuous interaction between Hollywood and the Pentagon. Even discounting the trademark wacky paranoia of Hollywood screenwriters and producers, a simple rerun of both the *Robocop* and *Terminator* series reveals this may end up badly.

And we're not even talking about a Revolt of the Drones—yet. In 2010 there was already a hint of juicy possibilities to come, when a RQ-170 Sentinel crash-landed in Western Iran via sophisticated jamming, and was duly reverse-engineered, to the delight of Iranians, Russians and the Chinese. The Pentagon hysterically denied it had been outmaneuvered.

The notion that a Drone Empire may win definitive control over what the Pentagon used to call the "arc of instability" between the Middle East and Central Asia—at the behest of Big Oil—is eminently laughable.

As laughable as the notion that a Drone Empire active in AfPak, Yemen, Somalia and soon in all points across the "arc of instability" will save the homeland from jihad, sharia law, a new Caliphate set up by a bunch of fanatics, and all of the above.

Especially now that the Pentagon itself ditched the rhetoric—and is focused on a "pivoting" to face the potential peer competitor that really counts, China.

And US Army brigades (and Special Ops commandos) from 2013 onwards will be rotated all around the world—with an emphasis in Africa—according to a Pentagonese "regionally aligned force concept."

And Southcom has announced that Predator, Reaper and Global Hawk drones will be deployed in Central and South America for "anti-drug operations, counter-insurgency and naval vigilance."

As much as The Drone Empire is global, drones can only be effective if ground intelligence is effective. A simple example is enough. Ultimately, in AfPak, it's not Obama that decides on his "kill list." It's the Pakistani ISI—which relies the info that suits its contingencies to the CIA. And this while the Pentagon and the CIA keep working under the galactic illusion of absolute supremacy of American technology—when they cannot even neutralize an inflation of cheap, ultra low-tech IEDs.

Uncle Sam wants your ass

Americans must also worry about the Inland Drone Empire—as the pitifully unpopular US Congress and President Obama have now fully authorized their "integration" into American airspace by 2015; by 2020, they will number at least 30,000. For the moment, the Pentagon has "only" 7,000 drones (ten years ago there were less than 50).

Predictably, massive corporate lobbying by drone manufacturers such as General Atomics was key for the approval of the new legislation. There's even a drone caucus, with 55 Congressmen (and expanding), and a global lobby with 507 corporate members in 55 countries, the Association for Unmanned Vehicles International, which essentially sets the rules.

The Orwellian—and Philip Dick—overtones are inescapable; this is all about 24/7 drone surveillance of large swathes of the US population via radar, infrared cameras, thermal imaging, wireless "sniffers" and, crucially, crowd-control weapons. You better monitor the skies very closely before you even start thinking about protesting. And wait for the imminent arrival of nuclear-powered drones, which can go on non-stop for months, and not only days.

Tom and Nick's digital file is absolutely essential reading for contextualizing the lineaments of an already de facto surveillance state, where everyone is a suspect by definition, and the only "winner" is the military-industrial complex. Welcome to Motown as Dronetown: "Nowhere to run to, baby, nowhere to hide…" Obama and the Dronellas, anyone?

June 2012

Let's party like it's ... 1997

It was 15 years ago today. General China taught the Brits to play. That was, of course, the Hong Kong handover—a milestone in Little Helmsman Deng Xiaoping's "crossing the river while feeling the stones" strategy. First, command "to get rich is glorious." Then develop the special economic zones. Get Hong Kong back from the Brits. Then, one day, annex Taiwan. And perhaps, by 2040, evolve to some variant of Western parliamentary democracy.

Those were heady days. There were only faint rumblings about a possible financial crisis in Asia. Mainland China media carped about the "humiliations" of the past—including heavy promotion for a blockbuster telling the real story of the Opium Wars. In Hong Kong island, daily showers thundered with fear. Will the People's Liberation Army (PLA) cross the border at midnight in a blitzkrieg and militarize all the malls in Kowloon? Will we be duly indoctrinated as model communists?

For a foreign correspondent, there was nowhere else to be. The Foreign Correspondents Club buzzed like in a perpetual rock concert. At the hip Shanghai Tang store, a waving Deng wristwatch was all the rage. The days went by with plenty of huffing and puffing around to find interviews and gauge the prospects of doom from residents and analysts. Then the long, sweaty nights partying at the Club 1997 in Lan Kwai Fong—and having to beat the hangover back at the hotel to write copy solid enough to fill two newspaper pages a day.

In the end, the proceedings were as normal as Deng would have thought. Chris Patten—the last governor—left in an anti-climax. The

British Empire was over. There was no PLA "invasion." The party at Club 1997 was monstrous. The day after, massive hangover included, the real celebration began. I boarded a plane to China.

Beyond the pale

Little did I know that the Asian financial crisis had just exploded—with a monster devaluation of the Thai baht. Well, on the first of July itself, some of us may have suspected this could be a minor problem—but no one was foreseeing the financial tsunami ahead.

My agenda was to plunge into deep China—the entrails of that beast which was now lording over Hong Kong. Robert Plant was on my flight to Xian. Yes, *the* Robert Plant—minus Jimmy Page. I resisted the temptation to address him with the opening bars of Kashmir. It turns out we were at the same hotel in Xian—and kept meeting for breakfast. He was traveling with his son and his manager. And yes—we were about to do the same thing. Get our kicks not on Route 66—but on the mother of all them routes.

I have always been a Silk Road fanatic. The "Silk Road" is not only the great, open highway of Eurasia—from lethal deserts such as the Taklamakan to snowy mountain peaks—but also waves and waves of cultural history connecting Asia to Europe. It's about forgotten empires such as the Sogdians, fabulous cities like Merv, Bukhara and Samarkand, fabled oasis like Kashgar. It's not "a" road but a maze of "roads"—extensions branching out to Afghanistan and Tibet.

I had to start at the beginning, in Xian, formerly Chang'an—though most of China's silk came from further south. Xian was a former capital of China during the Han dynasty, when Rome got a hard-on for Chinese silk. And was a capital again during the Tang dynasty—when the Buddhist connection with India solidified the Silk Road.

Hong Kong galleries were filled with copies of Tang terracotta figures such as Yang Guifei, aka the "fat concubine," the most famous femme fatale in Chinese history. Turks, Uyghurs, Sogdians, Arabs and Persians all lived in this Chinese Rome—and built their own temples (the mosque is still the most beautiful in China; but the three Zoroastrian temples are all gone).

It would take me a few more years—in successive trips—to finally do most of the core of the Silk Road, in separate stretches, an obsession I carried since I was in high school. This time though, I wanted to concentrate on the Chinese Silk Road.

It started with a painter/calligrapher rendering sublime copies in Mandarin of the Buddha's heart sutra to monks living for years in huts in the mountains north of Chang'an. It was supremely hard to resist both temptations; bye-bye journalism, why not become a calligrapher, or a monk? Then I started moving west, through Lanzhou—with a deviation to the immaculate Tibetan enclave of Xiahe and, on the way, an enormous concentration of Hui—Chinese Muslims. Everything by train, local bus, local trucks.

From Lanzhou I even went to Chengdu, in Sichuan, by bus and then to Lhasa in Tibet by plane, and all the way back. That was a classic Silk Road branch-out. But what was really driving me was to go "beyond the pale." To follow the westernmost spur of the Great Wall and finally reach Jiayuguan—the "First and Greatest Pass under Heaven."

It was everything I expected it to be; sort of like the desolate setting for the end of the empire. The (literal) end of the Great Wall. To the west was "beyond the pale"; Chinese who were banned to go west would never return. Still in 1997 I was met with incredulous stares when I said I wanted to keep going further into Gansu towards the deserts of Xinjiang. "Why? There's nothing there."

This was still two years before Beijing launched its official "Go West" policy. The turbocharged neo-colonization of "beyond the pale"—a Xinjiang extremely rich in natural resources but populated (till then) mostly by Muslim Uyghurs—hadn't yet started.

Death, also known as Taklamakan

Through the Gansu corridor I finally reached the caves of Dunhuang—one of the great Buddhist centers in China for over six centuries; a feast of wall-paintings and stucco images excavated in caves carved from a cliff on the eastern edge of the Lop desert and the southern edge of the Gobi desert. Dazzling doesn't even began to describe it.

One of my all-time heroes, the great Buddhist pilgrim Xuanzang (602-664), had a stop over in Dunhuang on his way to India—where he collected holy texts for translation into Chinese (that explains that calligrapher back in Xian).

Xuanzang's own account of his absolutely epic travels, *Xiyuji* ("Record of the Western Regions") remains matchless. He started—where else—in Chang'an. Everything happened, including being "tortured by hallucinations" and driving away "all sorts of demon shapes and strange goblins." But he did manage to get back to China 16 years later, carrying a wealth of Buddha statues and books.

Around Dunhuang, the Silk Road split. I had to make up my mind. The northern route follows the southern edge of the spectacular Tian Shan mountains—running along the north of the terrifying Taklamakan desert (whose name, in Uyghur, means "you may get in but you never get out"). Along the way, there are plenty of oasis towns—Hami, Turfan, Aksu—before reaching Kashgar.

That's the route I took, under temperatures hovering around 50 degrees Celsius, riding a battered Land Rover with a monosyllabic Hui who negotiated the desert track like Ayrton Senna. And this was the "easier" route—compared to the southern one. I had in mind the Buddhist monks doing it by camel, branching out to head through the Karakoram mountains to Leh (in Ladakh) and Srinagar (in Kashmir) and then down into India.

It's absolutely impossible to even try to battle the horrifying sandstorms of the Taklamakan. The best one can do is to circumvent it. Certainly not the option chosen by the coolest cat among the Silk Road modern giants, Sven Hedin (1865-1952), the author of *My Life as an Explorer* (1926) and a man of huge brass balls who faced certain death countless times and left behind him a long trail of ponies, camels and yes, dead men.

In one of his adventures, when Hedin was hoping to cross the southwestern corner of the Taklamakan in less than a month, the camels died one after another; the caravan was hit by a sandstorm; his last servant died; yet he was the only one who made it, "as though led by an invisible hand."

Guided by my very visible Hui, I finally made it to Kashgar—a hallucinating throwback to medieval Eurasia; once again, at the time the forced Han neo-colonization was just beginning, around the Mao statue at People's Square. The Sunday market sprang up straight from the 10th century. There was not a single Han Chinese even around the pale green Id Kah mosque at early morning prayers.

From Kashgar the Silk Road did another major branching out. Buddhist monks would travel through the Hindu Kush past Tashkurgan to the Buddhist kingdoms of Gandhara and Taxila in contemporary Pakistan. I did it the China-Pakistan motorized friendship way—that is, taking the fabulous Karakoram highway from Kashgar through the Khunjerab Pass, by jeep and local bus, all the way to Islamabad, stopping on the way in the idyllic Hunza valley. Northern Pakistan was all quiet in those pre-war on terror days; although the Taliban were in power in Afghanistan, there was virtually no hardcore Islamist in sight.

Silk road traders would have done it differently. They would go north of the Pamir mountains to Samarkand and Bukhara, or south of the Pamirs to Balkh (in contemporary Afghanistan) and then to Merv (in Iran). From Merv, a maze of Silk Roads would go all the way to the Mediterranean via Baghdad to Damascus, Antioch or Constantinople (Istanbul). It would still take me a few more years to follow stretches of most of these routes.

So suddenly I was in an Islamabad duly doing business with the Taliban while all financial hell was breaking loose all across Asia. I made it back to Singapore and then Hong Kong. Thailand, Indonesia, South Korea were braking up. But Hong Kong, once again was surviving—now under close inspection by Beijing.

Motherland knows best

Fifteen years later, none of those Western bogeymen predictions about Chinese heavy-handedness in Hong Kong came true. The third smooth transition of power in Hong Kong under China is already on. Chinese Vice President Xi Jinping—the next Dragon Emperor—has given it his full blessing.

Here's the key Xi quote; "Fifteen years after the handover, Hong Kong has gone through storms. Overall, the principle of 'one country, two systems' has made enormous strides… Hong Kong's economy has developed well and citizens' livelihoods have improved. Progress has been made in democratic development, and society has become harmonious."

Well, not that harmonious. True, Hong Kong is the IPO capital of the world. It's the top offshore center in the world for yuan trading. It's a matchless world city—in many aspects putting even New York to shame; the best the world has to offer in an ultra-compact environment. The city's economy grew every year except in 2009—during the world economy abyss. Annual GDP growth has been 4.5% on average. Unemployment is never higher than 6%.

But Hong Kong still has not made the transition towards a high-value-added, knowledge-based economy. The outgoing administration by Donald Tsang bet on "six new pillar industries" which should have "clear advantages" for growth; cultural and creative industries, medical services, education, innovation and technology, testing and certification services, and environmental industries.

But their development, so far, has been negligible. Hong Kong still relies basically on its four core industries; financial services, tourism, professional services, and trading. Over 36 million tourists a year won't turn Hong Kong into a knowledge-based society. Most of them are from—where else—the mainland. The backlash is immense; most Hong Kongers deride them as "locusts"—country bumpkins with suitcases overflowing with yuan buying everything cash. And this while inside Hong Kong itself the wealth gap is widening dramatically.

As far as Beijing is concerned, it all comes down to "crossing the river while feeling the stones." Here's Xi, once again; "The SAR [Special Administrative Region] government has united various social sectors under the strong support of the central government and the motherland." The motherland has its own ideas on reviving the Silk Road—and perhaps Hong Kong could be part of it, a least on the financial services side. Maybe it's time to party like it's 1997 and hit the Taklamakan again. Well, you can take the boy our of the Silk Road, but you can't take the Silk Road out of the boy.

June 2012

THE MYTH OF A FREE HONG KONG ECONOMY

with Eddie Leung

Open any standard economic textbook and look for the definition of a free economy; its key characteristic is the lack of government intervention. Less state intervention means a freer market.

On this standard, Hong Kong has been hailed as the world's freest economy for more than two decades. But is this the whole truth? What if the main sectors of the whole economy are dominated by a few oligopolies or even a virtual monopoly?

Let's look at the hypothetical case of Mr and Mrs Chan, an average Hong Kong household. Both Mr and Mrs Chan are senior-level employees of the Hong Kong government and earn a total monthly salary of HK$85,000 (US$10,900).

The Chan family bought a 800 square feet (74 square meters) flat from Cheung Kong (owned by the richest local tycoon, Li Ka-Shing) and has to pay a mortgage of HK$30,000 a month. The couple subscribes to the 3shop mobile phone service, a subsidiary of Hutchison Whampoa (also owned by Li) and pay a monthly service fee of HK$2,000.

Wherever they go to buy their daily necessities, they use Park'n Shop (a supermarket chain owned by Li), where they spend about HK$5,000 every month.

Whenever the Chan family pays their electricity bill (HK$1,000 per month), it goes to Hong Kong Electricity (again owned by Li). For pharmaceutical products, they go to Watsons (again owned by Li), and they spend HK$2,000.

Let's say the couple wants to purchase the latest LCD monitor for their son; they buy it from Fortress (still owned by Li). The couple subscribes to the paid TV service of NOW for HK$1,000 a month. This time the service is not owned by Li himself, but rather Richard Li, his youngest son.

One might ask: how come that almost half of what Mr and Mrs Chan earn contribute to the coffers of Li Ka-shing? Do we really want to call this the freest economy in the world, or even a free economy?

A gilded cage?

In every poll, Hong Kong is invariably ranked as among or the most expensive city in Asia—usually behind Japanese megalopolises like Tokyo and Osaka. It's at least the fifth-priciest in the world to own a home;[3] the second priciest to rent an apartment;[4] and Queen's Road Central and Canton Road are the second costliest for retail space. [5]

This is due to what is informally known in Hong Kong as a "high land price policy."

The mirror image of this policy is, inevitably, inequality. Hong Kong boasts some of the world's top billionaires, such as Li Ka-shing, the Kwok brothers and Lee Shau-Kee. At the same time no less than 18% of the city's seven million residents lived below the poverty line in 2011—which was measured as HK$7,000 for a three-person household per month, ac-

---

[3] 10 most expensive cities to own a home, *Overseas Property Mall*, Feb 24, 2009.
[4] *Top 10 Most Expensive Cities to Rent an Apartment in Asia*, PropGoLuxury, May 16, 2012.
[5] Photos: World's priciest places to rent retail space, *Vancouver Sun*, Jul 10, 2012.

cording to the Hong Kong Council of Social Service.[6] About 100,000 people lived in dreaded cage or cubicle homes last year.[7] This may be a sensationalist approach, but the photos do tell the story.[8]

For all the glitz and glamour that dazzle not only global tourism but also, especially, mainland Chinese tourists, the median monthly income of a local household with four members is approximately HK$14,000, according to the Hong Kong Council of Social Service.

After a lengthy battle, a new minimum wage was approved. There were rivers of speculation on what would be a decent number—from HK$30 to HK$35 an hour. The approved figure in May 2011 was a paltry HK$28.

After the 2008 global financial crisis, Hong Kong's much-vaunted economic recovery is essentially based on revenues from Chinese tourism and property investment. A trickle-down effect is not exactly in place; it's more like "rental-push" inflation, as Hong University researchers call it. Mainland Chinese gobble up at least 40% of new home sales. No wonder; property investment qualifies as the easiest path to get a much coveted Hong Kong resident card.

The land of the free

For the Heritage Foundation is a matter of routine to rank Hong Kong as the freest economy in the world—with a whopping overall score of 89.9 compared with a world average of 59.5.[9] This Milton-

---

[6] 1 in 5 live below poverty line, welfare body says, *South China Morning Post*, Sep 15, 2011.
[7] Cage homes 'worse than living on street', *South China Morning Post*, May 24, 2011.
[8] Cage dogs of Hong Kong: The tragedy of tens of thousands living in 6ft by 2ft rabbit hutches—in a city with more Louis Vuitton shops than Paris, *Daily Mail*, Jan 11, 2012
[9] *2012 Index of Economic Freedom: Hong Kong*, Heritage

Friedmanesque paradise is extolled for "small government, low taxes and light regulation."

Much is made of "business freedom" and "labor freedom." True—you can open a business in three days; you just need a Hong Kong ID, a form and US$350. But depending on the business, you will be squeezed by monopolies and oligopolies in no time. And if you are "labor," chances are in most cases you can only aspire to some sort of glorified slavery.

Heritage researchers may be excused for losing the plot between dinners at the Mandarin Oriental and partying in Lan Kwai Fong, both favored drinking and dining spots near the central business district. Behind all those luxury malls and the best bottles of Margaux, real-life Hong Kong has absolutely nothing to do with a free economy encouraging competition on a level playing field. It's more like a rigged game.

The dark secret at the heart of Hong Kong is the unmitigated collusion between the government and a property cartel—controlled by just a few tycoons; the Lis, the Kwoks, the Lees, the Chengs, the Pao and Woo duo, and the Kadoories (more about them on part 2 of this report). These tycoons and their close business associates also happen to dominate seats on the 1,200-member Election Committee that chooses Hong Kong's chief executive.

The first thing to keep in mind is that for any Chinese, land is wealth. That's sacred. And nowhere else this is more sacred than in Hong Kong.

Alice Poon is—or used to be—an insider; she was a personal assistant to Kwok Tak-seng, the legendary founder of Sun Hung Kai Properties, Hong Kong's giant developer. She also worked for the Robert Kuok group, responsible for land and property evaluation and acquisition. She now lives in Canada and blogs at the Asia Sentinel. [10]

In *Land and the Ruling Class in Hong Kong* (Enrich Professional Publishing, Singapore, 2011), Poon demonstrates how the Heritage Foundation's hard-on for government laissez faire is in fact mixed with an extremely non-competitive business environment. It all boils down to who really runs the show in Hong Kong; a group of cross-sector corporate giants controlling the property market, electricity, gas, the public buses and ferries, and the supermarkets (see them in detail in part 2 of this report).

The common denominator is that virtually all of them started with property—and then progressively gobbled up utility and public service companies.

Here are just a few examples of this cross-sector frenzy.

Cheung Kong Holdings buying Hutchison Whampoa in 1979—a monster conglomerate involved in myriad businesses, among them the Park'n Shop supermarket chain.

Sun Hung Kai Properties controlling the Kowloon Motor Bus operator.

Lee Shau-Kee accumulating shares in The Hong Kong and China Gas—the town gas monopoly—before the company was listed in 1981.

Hutchison Whampoa buying Hongkong Electric—one of the two electricity duopolies—in 1985.

New World Development being awarded the Hong Kong public bus routes franchise in 1998 and buying Hong Kong Ferry in 2000.

---

[10] An Estranged Hong Kong, *Asia Sentinel*, Jan 19, 2012.

The Pacific Century Cyberworks (PCCW) takeover of Hong Kong Telecom in 2000, masterminded by Richard Li, the younger son of Cheung Kong Holdings chairman Li Ka-shing, the wealthiest Chinese in the world.

The bottom line is that major utilities and public services are in the hands of just a few players; the Lis of the Cheung Kong/Hutchison group; the Kwoks of Sun Hung Kai Properties; the Lees of the Henderson group; the Chengs of New World Development; the Pao and Woo of the Wharf/Wheelock group; and the Kadoories of the CLP Holdings group.

Today, there are 49 constituent companies in the Hang Seng Index, which represent nearly 70% of total capitalization of the Hong Kong Stock Exchange. Taking away heavyweight Chinese state-owned enterprises such as China Mobil, China Unicom, PetroChina, Sinopec, ICBC, China Construction Bank, Bank of China, China Life, etc (which account for more than half of the total capitalization), and Britain's HSBC, the Hang Seng Index is dominated by local companies of property development tycoons such as Li Ka-shing's Cheung Kong Holdings, Hutchison Whampoa and Power Assets; the Kwok family's Sun Hung Kai Properties; Lee Shau-Kee's Henderson Land Development and Hong Kong and China Gas; as well as other property developers such as Sino Land, New World, Hang Lung Properties, and Warf (Holdings).

This amounts to roughly six families controlling virtually all of Hong Kong's economic sectors. And it will stay like this. The Chinese tradition of passing the family fortune from generation to generation amounts to what Poon derides as an "antiquated feudal system."

There's nothing "free market" about Hong Kong's major utility/public service companies. On the contrary; they are monopolies or oligopolies. The two supermarket chains—Park'n Shop and Wellcome—have no less than 70% of market share. City Super is owned by Japanese—but that's an upscale brand, with only a few locations, and out of reach for most Hongkongers.

Park'n Shop and Wellcome consolidated their dominance essentially by pricing smaller companies out of the market; they could easily afford it. Park'n Shop is the retail/food division of A S Watson, which is part of the Hutchison/Cheung Kong conglomerate. Wellcome is part of the Jardines/Hong Kong Land group. So no wonder, for instance, a Park'n Shop outlet is in or around every building developed by Hutchison or Cheung Kong.

A measure of their power is that France's Carrefour—the second-largest global supermarket chain—tried to break into the Hong Kong market in 1996. They gave up four years later.

Born to lose

We should be back again to a Chinese maxim: land is power. All the conglomerates controlled by Hong Kong tycoons are fattened on owning land. The local government is the sole supplier of land. So no wonder it keeps a vested interest in the property market—and that's a huge understatement—as it pockets fortunes from land sales and premiums on so-called "lease modifications."

As for the maxim that prevails across the city's property market cycles, it's always been the same: "Buy low and sell high."

This doesn't work for the public good—to say the least. A good example is the Guangzhou-Shenzhen-Hong Kong express rail link, which is bound to be the most expensive in the world, costing US$8.6 billion—partly because of choosing to build the terminus at West Kowloon. There was a cheaper and perhaps better alternative—to build the terminus at Kam Sheung Road on MTR's West Rail. But it was overruled because of, as some critics suspected, shady land speculation interests in West Kowloon.

The whole situation is in fact inherited from the British colonial era, when the British hongs such as Jardines, Hong Kong Land, Wheelock Marden, Swire and Hutchison controlled Hong Kong's economy—and prime urban space. This Holy Grail was beyond the reach of Chinese companies.

But then, from the late 1960s up to the mid-1970s, the hongs started to get rid of their land and property as China plunged into chaos during Mao's final years. At the same time, Cheung Kong, Sun Hung Kai, New World Development and others started using the stock market to raise funds.

But it was only by the mid-1980s that British companies were finally gobbled up by the likes of Li Ka-shing and Y K Pao. When the Sino-British Joint Declaration was signed in December 1984, sealing the 1997 handover, they finally hit the jackpot.

The champagne popped all around Paragraph 4 of Annex III of the Joint Declaration; it limited the amount of land that could be granted in Hong Kong in any one year to just 50 hectares. That also paved the way for a Land Commission, which could grant extra land when the ceiling was attained. Essentially this set up guaranteed that land in Hong Kong would always be in short supply—thus it would always be expensive. Ergo, the perennially high property prices.

The mantra of the previous two Hong Kong administrations under "one country, two systems"—by Tung Chee-Hwa and Donald Tsang—was not to deviate from a high land price policy; keep a tight land supply; and postpone the introduction of a competition law (more on this on the second part of this report). There's no evidence this would change much under new Chief Executive C Y Leung.

The absurdly high rents in Hong Kong—derived from high land prices—hurt most of all local businesses, and prevent Hong Kong from attracting more foreign investment. If Heritage Foundation researchers didn't get it, they were probably researching some island in the South China Sea.

Everything that revolves around land represents the main underlying cause for industrial and economic concentration in Hong Kong. When property prices and rents are that high, they contribute to high living and business costs. Wealth disparity gets out of control—the key popular grudge of anyone who is not a millionaire in Hong Kong.[11]

The average Hongkonger—whose median household monthly income is US$1,800, much less than our fictional Mr and Mrs Chan—not only is bound to lose in the property game but also gets to pay high prices for basic daily necessities.

Hong Kong's very simple tax structure—15% for individuals, 16.5% for corporations—may have been OK for its early stages of economic development. Now that Hong Kong is relatively wealthy in annual GDP per capita terms (over US$45,000), but with a large proportion of its population living below the poverty line, it doesn't make sense anymore.

It's enlightening to note that this average annual per capita GDP figure is double the annual household income of an average Hongkonger.

The bottom line points to a fact that should make the local ruling elite—not to mention Beijing—quite uncomfortable. Without a real democratic government, elected by Hong Kong people, there's no way

---

[11] Hong Kong Middle Class Bitter as Tycoons Choose Leaders, *Bloomberg,* Mar 23, 2012.

Hong Kong will ever reform its land and tax system. The "freest" economy in the world will continue to be a battle pitting a wealthy oligarchy against a large majority essentially struggling for survival.

The rulers of the Hong Kong game

Life is indeed sweet if you're a Hong Kong property tycoon. In what is routinely considered the "freest" economy in the world, an oligarchy of property developers sets supply and pricing (see part 1 of this report). This applies not only to residential apartments but also to shopping malls, hotels, luxury serviced apartments and industrial and office space.

Top financial muscle rules. It gobbles up Hong Kong's best locations—near mass transit systems or by the spectacular waterfront. Behind the façade of all those glitzy malls though, life is very hard. Retail tenants pay not only a base rent but also a surplus rent when business turnover reaches a certain level. You can't go wrong—if you're the owner, not the tenant.

Now let's meet the six families who essentially run the Hong Kong show.

The Li family—Li Ka-shing's family controls, among others, Cheung Kong Holdings, Hutchison Whampoa, Hong Kong Electric, Cheung Kong Infrastructure, CK Life Sciences, the popular website Tom.com and PCCW. The market capitalization of these companies—everything from property development to ports, energy, telecom, hotels, retail, manufacturing and infrastructure—is (excluding PCCW) about HK$852 billion (US$110 billion), accounting for nearly 5% of the total capitalization of HK$18.5 trillion of the Hong Kong stock exchange (as of mid-July). It's always important to remember that mainland Chinese enterprises listed in Hong Kong account for more than half of the total capitalization of the Hong Kong stock exchange.

Li Ka-shing, born in 1928 in Guangdong province, charismatic, a flawless negotiator and a renowned philanthropist, is a larger-than-life character. He's the world's 16th wealthiest individual, according to Forbes, with a net worth of US$21.3 billion. His companies are active in over 50 countries. Li's two sons, Victor and Richard, got the requisite US education. Li is the chairman of Cheung Kong Holdings and Hutchison Whampoa. Victor is the chairman of Cheung Kong Infrastructure and CK Life Sciences. Richard is the chairman of PCCW.

Cheung Kong Holdings has been a top developer in the city since the 1960s. Victor keeps a low profile, unlike Richard, who at 27 became a superstar in 1993, when he sold Star TV—very popular across Asia—to Rupert Murdoch's News Corporation for US$390 million. Needless to say, Star TV—where he previously worked—was established by Li Ka-shing.

Richard used some of his profits to set up the Pacific Century Group and later PCCW. In 1999—backed by the Hong Kong government—his group set out to build a much-ballyhooed "cyberport" for US$1.7 billion. But what was really juicy was a monster US$28.4 billion merger with Hong Kong Telecom in 2000—widely promoted in Hong Kong as a "deal of the century." Beijing totally encouraged it; after all, the competition for the deal was Singapore Telecom. Yet after the PCCW-HKT mega-merger the high-tech bubble burst—and the famous cyberport project came down to nothing.

The Kwok family—Sun Hung Kai Properties was founded by Kwok Tak-seng, another high-profile Cantonese from Guangdong province who started in business as a trader in the early 1950s and got into property development in 1958. A legendary workaholic, he died in 1990 and left three sons—Walter, Thomas and Raymond; the first two were educated in Britain, and Raymond in the UK and the United States.

The Kwok family controls Sun Hung Kai Properties, Transport International Holdings and Smartone Communications (the city's third-largest mobile phone company). These companies have a market capitalization of HK$266 billion as of July 26.

Sun Hung Kai is the largest property developer in Hong Kong—controlling over 100 companies involved in construction, property management, electrical and fire services, architecture, mechanical engineering, cement manufacturing, finance and insurance.

They're into everything from flatted factories to mega-malls and larger-than-life office towers such as the International Finance Center (IFC) at the Airport Railway Hong Kong station. Sun Hung Kai has 47.5% of IFC towers 1 and 2; Henderson Land also has 47.5%. On top of it, Sun Hung Kai holds a 100% interest in the development of Kowloon Station. Attached to it is the new International Commerce Center (ICC), another post-modern Hong Kong landmark with a Ritz Carlton on top ("the highest hotel in the world").

The three billionaire Kwok brothers used to be regarded as an iron triangle. Now a bitter family feud plus corruption charges have dissolved the dream. Brothers Thomas and Raymond have recently been charged with bribery and public misconduct—one of the highest-level corruption cases in Hong Kong's history, and a graphic illustration of what's wrong with the tycoon/government collusion model.

And yet, instead of hiring top professional managers to contain the damage, the family appointed two of the Kwoks' sons—ages 29 and 31—as alternate directors. Their business record is virtually non-existent. Back to that Chinese maxim; it all stays in the family.

The Lee family—Lee Shau-Kee, yet again from Guangdong province, started in the footsteps of his father, a gold trader and money exchanger, until getting into property development in 1958 with Kwok Tak-seng and Fung King-hey—very popular locally as "the three musketeers" (until they split in 1972).

Lee then established Wing Tai Development—whose flagship company was Henderson Land. Today his key companies are Henderson Land, Henderson Investment and The Hong Kong and China Gas Company, which have a market capitalization of HK$257 billion (as of July 26). Lee is the chairman of all three. He's the second-wealthiest of the Hong Kong tycoons, behind only Li Ka-shing, with a net worth of US$19 billion according to Forbes.

Henderson Land attacks with gusto the small and medium-sized residential apartment market. Their preferred strategy is to buy out apartments one by one in targeted old residential buildings in some of Hong Kong's top areas—such as Wan Chai, Causeway Bay and the Mid-levels.

Once again it's all in the family. Elder son Lee Ka-kit—educated in the UK—is vice chairman of two of the companies, and chairman and president of the other. He's in charge of an absolutely crucial division—the group's property development interests in mainland China, mostly in Beijing, Shanghai, Guangzhou and the Pearl River Delta. Meanwhile, younger son Lee Ka-shing and daughter Margaret are climbing their way up inside the group.

The Cheng family—The New World Development group of companies includes NWS Holdings, New World China Land and Mongolia Energy Corporation. They are controlled by Cheng Yu-tung, also from Guangdong province. The companies are involved in property, infrastructure, public services (bus and ferry services) and telecom. New World Development has a market capitalization of HK$59 billion (as of July 26).

Cheng has taken a back seat since 1989. His elder son, Henry, educated in Canada, is the managing director of New World Development and chairman of New World China Land and NWS Holdings; younger son Peter is executive director of these two. Crucially, New World China Land owns a vast land bank in—where else—mainland China.

Cheng used to be known as the "King of Jewelry" since the 1960s, when he was controlling no less than 30% of all Hong Kong diamond imports. He's always been associated with the very popular Chow Tai Fook jewelry company—until he entered the property market in the late 1960s. Some of Hong Kong's top landmarks were built by New World, such as the Regent Hotel (now Intercontinental) and the Hong Kong Exhibition and Convention Center, where the 1997 handover took place.

Y K Pao and Peter Woo—The Wharf/Wheelock Group was founded by Y K Pao—a shipping magnate born in Zhejiang province who started his career as a banker in Shanghai and moved to Hong Kong in 1949. He died in 1991. Since 1986, the chairman of both Wharf and Wheelock is Peter Woo, Pao's son-in-law, born in Shanghai and married to Pao's second daughter, Betty.

Wharf (Holdings), Wheelock and Company and i-Cable Communications have a market capitalization of HK$190 billion. They are involved in property investment, telecom, media, entertainment and container terminals.

By 1973, before the oil shock, Pao had more ships than legendary Aristoteles Onassis. When he diversified from the shipping industry and took over Wharf in 1980, with great help from HSBC, he landed some of the most valuable properties in the tourist Mecca of Tsim Sha Tsui, in Kowloon; nowadays they are occupied by Ocean City, Ocean Centre, Harbour City, the Marco Polo hotel and The Getaway. Wharf is arguably Hong Kong's king of commercial landlords.

Pao also got control of the famous Star Ferry—the most spectacular short cruise in the world, for only HK$2.30 one way across the harbor—as well as the Island tram franchise and a lot of container terminals. The companies also own Time Square, two office towers-cum-megamalls in Causeway Bay, as well as the upscale department store Lane Crawford.

Woo tried to go straight to the point and become Hong Kong's first chief executive in 1997. But he lost to Tung Chee-hwa, who got 320 out of 400 votes.

The Kadoorie family—Elly Kadoorie founded the CLP group in 1901. He's the late grandfather of the current chairman Michael Kadoorie. The family is the largest shareholder of CLP Holdings and the Hong Kong and Shanghai Hotels group—who own the luxury Peninsula chain. These two companies have a market capitalization of HK$172 billion (as of July 26). The CLP group is essentially a local electricity monopoly that then diversified to own power stations in Beijing, Tianjin and Heibei and an energy corporation in Gujarat, western India; 92% of another one in Victoria, Australia; and 50% of another one in Thailand.

They got into telecom connecting Hong Kong to China with a fiber optic cable. They also got into property—following the trail of Li Ka-shing and the Kwoks. They could only make it into this cartel because they had lots of capital and lots of cheap land in the form of power stations (some of them no longer in use); most of all, they were savvy enough to get into a joint venture with Cheung Kong Holdings.

Competition or bust

This short presentation may offer a measure of how a few monopolies and oligopolies control most of the daily life of an average Hongkonger. It suggests Hong Kong, rather than being a "free" society, is actually the domain of captive markets.

By any definition, a captive market is a market where very few actors exercise a monopoly. Captive markets—which imply scarce competition—yield immense profits, without relation to costs of production.

A way out for Hong Kong would be, of course, more competition. For two years now, the Hong Kong government has introduced a Competition Bill to the Legislative Council (Legco)—after a discussion that started in 2006. The bill went through quite a few amendments. This is more or less what it will look like. [12]

But is it what Hongkongers really want—and need?

Ronny Tong of the Civic Party, a barrister and vice-chairman of the Competition Bill panel of Legco, has been pushing for an anti-monopoly law in Hong Kong for years. The law was finally passed in mid-July, a few days before the current term of the council terminated. "After the bill is passed, if there is any evidence of price-rigging by the two major supermarket chains, the complaints will be forwarded to the competition affairs committee for investigation," Mr Tong said in a phone interview with *Asia Times Online*.

He expects the law will facilitate a "competition culture" in Hong Kong. Other legislators, however, are not so optimistic.

Albert Chan, legislative councilor (People Power), called the bill "toothless." When asked why he cast an abstain vote during the legislation of the bill, Chan explained to *Asia Times Online*, "The scope of exemption of the bill is too large to be effective. First of all, the government or statutory bodies are granted full exemption of the law. More seriously, there is no legal limitation of market share to prohibit monopolistic control of the market. On the other hand, it will be very hard to collect evi-

---

[12] The Hong Kong Competition Bill, Norton Rose, March 2012.

dence of price-rigging between oligarchic coalitions, which frequently happens in Hong Kong now."

Chan stressed the most serious monopolistic control and oligarchic coalitions can be found in sectors such as the property market, petroleum and the telecom businesses. The current competition law, he insists, is unable to deal with these problems effectively.

It may be ironic that Hong Kong, long hailed as the "freest economy" in the world, has waited for such a long time to get the law passed; and even when it is passed, it is much less effective than expected. Perhaps the answer to this question may not be found in the economic, but rather the political structure of Hong Kong itself.

August 2012

Ground Zero redux

In David Cronenberg's awesome *Cosmopolis* (France/Canada, 2012), based on the homonymous novel by Don DeLillo, young billionaire Eric Packer (Robert Pattison) slowly cruises New York in his white limo, installed in a cushy leather throne with incrusted screens.

He feels ... nothing; he essentially sucks up the world into his own inertia. Outside his moving silent chamber, it's total chaos, with activists spraying rats in posh restaurants and a tense threat of imminent apocalypse.

This is the world morphing into, or being gobbled up by, dematerialized ultra-capitalism; a world in a state of crisis, driven by violence, and with violence as the only possible horizon. As a libidinous art dealer (Juliette Binoche) tells Packer: "It's cyber-capital that creates the future."

A walk in the dead of a New York night to Ground Zero offers extra context to *Cosmopolis*. This is where our post-apocalyptic modernity began, 11 years go—and where cyber-capital still creates at least some of the future. As *Cosmopolis* shows, turbo-capitalism is not only in crisis; turbo-capitalism, in shorthand, IS crisis.

Ground Zero remains an eerie sight deep in the dead of night. There's the memorial. There's the new unfinished glass tower. And there remain holes the size of Ground Zero all over the official narrative.

This week, 11 years after 9/11, the talk of the (crisis) town is a Navy SEAL "hero" trading his anonymity for the proverbial fistful of dollars, telling it like it is—"it" being the snuffing out of "Geronimo," aka Osama bin Laden, the alleged mastermind of 9/11, the whole spectacle packaged as a celebratory "bringing him to justice."[13]

Yet the snuffing out of "Geronimo" brought no closure; what it did was to hurl a batch of inconvenient truths to the bottom of the Arabian Sea. Over three years ago, the indispensable Sibel Edmonds was certifying how Osama was "one of our bastards" right up to 9/11.[14] And Richard Behan earlier delivered a succinct deconstruction of the road to 9/11 once again exposing the fallacy of the "war on terror."[15]

When I interviewed the Lion of the Panjshir, Ahmad Shah Masoud, in late August 2001—only two weeks before his assassination on September 9, the green light for 9/11—he was convinced the US would not invade Afghanistan to snatch "Geronimo." (See Masoud: From warrior to statesman, *Asia Times Online*, September 12, 2001.)

What Masoud didn't know by then was what had taken place on August 2 in Islamabad, when US State Department negotiator Christine Rocca for the last time reiterated to Taliban ambassador to Pakistan Abdul Salam Zaeef in no uncertain terms: "Either you accept our offer of a carpet of gold, or we bury you under a carpet of bombs." The offer was all about Pipelineistan—"golden" transit rights for the Taliban for the construction by Unocal of the TAP (Turkmenistan-Afghanistan-Pakistan) pipeline.

Yet even before Rocca's final offer, the George W Bush administration—at the Group of Eight meeting in Genoa, Italy, in July—had already secretly informed the Europeans, plus Pakistan and India, that Washington would start bombing Afghanistan by October. That was several

---

[13] See CBSNews video here.
[14] See Daily Kos here.
[15] See "Masterpiece of Propaganda" here.

weeks before the neo-cons' so much cherished "Pearl Harbor" was sent by Providence in the form of 9/11.

Freedom fighter fix

Eleven years later, the proverbial stenographers of Empire are now eagerly promoting... al-Qaeda (what else is new?). The Barack Obama administration—shelving the "war on terror" terminology and Orwellianizing its methods—worked side by side with the al-Qaeda-linked Libyan Islamic Fighting Group to overthrow Muammar Gaddafi in Libya; and, side by side with the House of Saud, supports a rosary of Salafi-jihadis of the al-Qaeda variety to topple the Bashar al-Assad regime in Syria.[16]

We all remember the mujahideen in the photo side by side with Ronald Reagan; they were cherished as "freedom fighters." Blowback was inevitable in Afghanistan—as it will be in Libya and northern Africa, and Syria and the Middle East.

Meanwhile, all those myriad questions will remain unanswered. Among them:

Why "Geronimo" was never formally indicted by the FBI as responsible for 9/11? How could the alleged 19 Muslim perpetrators have been identified in less than 72 hours—without even a crime scene investigation?

Who pocketed the eight indestructible black boxes on those four 9/11 flights? How easy was it for all those elaborate Pentagon defense systems

---

[16] See Syria's eerie parallel to 1980s Afghanistan, by David Ignatius, Washington Post, September 6, 2012.

to be disabled? Why was the DC Air National Guard in Washington AWOL?

How come a huge number of reputed architects and engineers are adamant that the official narrative simply does not explain the largest structural collapse in recorded history (the Twin Towers) as well as the col- collapse of World Trade Center (WTC) building 7, which was not even hit by a jet?

Why did New York mayor Rudolph Giuliani instantly authorize the shipment of WTC rubble to China and India for recycling?

Why was metallic debris found no less than eight miles from the crash site of the plane that went down in Pennsylvania—suggesting the plane may have been shot down under Dick Cheney's orders?

Who inside the Pakistani Inter-Services Intelligence (ISI) transferred US$100,000 to Mohammed Atta in the summer of 2001—under orders of ISI head Lt Gen Ahmad himself, as Indian intelligence insists? Was it really ISI asset Omar Sheikh, Osama bin Laden's information technology specialist who later organized the slaying of journalist Daniel Pearl in Karachi? Was Pakistani intelligence directly involved in 9/11?

And was "Geronimo" admitted at the American hospital in Dubai on July 4, 2001, after flying from Quetta, Pakistan, and staying for treatment until July 11? We will never know. And "Geronimo" isn't talking. What we do know is that cyber-capital creates the future; the "war on terror" was—is—a monumental scam; and Washington elites couldn't care less about a bunch of "towel heads"; it's the Middle Kingdom that fills them with dread.

September 2012

Visions Make It All Seem So Cruel

Mona Lisa must have had the highway blues
You can tell by the way she smiles

- Bob Dylan, *Visions of Johanna*

It's 5pm on a Saturday in Shungopavi ("sand grass spring place"), established by the Bear Clan, the first to arrive on the three Hopi mesas in northeast Arizona. The whole village, plus surrounding villages, is watching a basket dance before sunset; an astonishing spectacle where Central Asia meets the American Southwest. Geology says this could easily be Afghanistan.

No photos allowed, so I was busy trying to impress in my mind the full picture of a traditional Hopi two-story adobe house as a

living organism; an old lady as a guardian angel, kids escalating the levels, an extended family in conversation. And it was all a miracle; I've stumbled into the sacred ceremony by accident, while driving by the mesas before sunset, those small villages perched on high contemplating the infinite plains.

The Hopi Nation has always lived in the Four Corners area of the Colorado Plateau. They bear one of the more sophisticated cosmologies in the world. According to it, they emerged from the underworld through a sipapu—an opening—in the Grand Canyon. Then they were thrown into the light of this—the Fourth World—with the help of a small bird, the shrike, and made a vow of righteous living to Sootukwnangwu, the Supreme Creator. The guardian spirit of the land told the Hopis they would have to serve as the Earth's steward once they had finished their mandated four migrations to the north, south, east and west in search of the center of the Earth.

Legend tells us that the Hopis traveled to the Aztec temples in Mexico, down to South America, up to the Arctic Circle and to both of the US coasts. The center of the cross formed by their four directional routes is the Hopi mesas. Every time I come back here—it has been a while—following Arizona highway 264 East, I know this is as sacred a land as it can get.

As other clans also migrated to the Hopi mesas, they contributed a different skill or ceremony dedicated to common prosperity. The Hopi ceremonial calendar is ultra-sophisticated. A holy man in each village determines the timing of each ceremony by the position of the sun.

Kachinas are the all-important spirit beings in Hopi cosmology in charge of assuring rain. They visit the Hopis and bring gifts—thus the village ladies dressed as Kachinas, with their fabulously elaborated costumes distributing baskets to the crowd and nowadays also plastic implements of daily life. At the end of a dance, prayer feathers are given to the Kachinas so that the prayers for rain and assorted auspicious events are carried in all directions.

And they vote Democrat

All archeological sites on the Hopi Reservation are protected by federal law and, most of all, Hopi tribal laws. You cannot take a photo, shoot a video or even draw a sketch of a village or a ceremony—proving once again that the most startling images in America, the land of outsized imagery, are absolutely mysterious, invisible and unpublishable.

One of the villagers even kindly requested me not to take notes on an iPhone. Alcohol and drugs are banned—although, unfortunately, bootleggers thrive, some of them Hopis, betraying their own nation's codes. Each Hopi village is autonomous—and establishes its own policies, then sanctioned by the Hopi Tribal Council.

Mitt Romney wouldn't be caught dead in a place like the Hopi Nation. For starters, the surviving Hopis are only 15,000, spread out among 12 villages. As Rhonda, my Hopi friend in Tuba City explained, this is predominantly Democrat territory in a deeply Republican state.

By American standards, these are all part of Mitt's 47%, some very poor, living in ugly cement houses, although quite a few young Hopis do enroll at the University of Arizona. Seems like the Hopi Nation is overwhelmingly voting Obama—who is invariably praised as "having done good things for our people." Yet the only Democrat president to have ever visited the Hopi Nation in person was—who else—The Great Bubba himself; Bill Clinton during his first term.

So I was blessed to watch a basket dance; got a Kachina—"Butterfly Man"—to watch my back; and a new bracelet, "bear paw," to replace the one I had and was broken. Once again I was paying my respects to what remains of the Native American dream.

But I could not find a Hopi holy man to tell me what had happened to the American Dream—the exceptionalist version. So I drove further into Navajo Nation sacred territory, following Frank Kosik's indispensable *Native Roads* (Rio Nuevo Publishers, Tucson, 2nd edition)—into the beyond-IMAX, larger-than-life Geology Spectacular of Monument Valley.

The Hopi Reservation is surrounded by the Navajo Reservation. To say they do not get along so well is quite an understatement. Not to mention the murky stories of Mormon settlers—Mitt's tribe—taking over

Navajo lands in the 19th century. Unlike Jim Morrison—who in a psychedelic haze was visited by a Navajo holy man and then saw the light—I was basically looking for a little conversation. It was not exactly uplifting to learn that Navajo President Ben Shelly is now deeply into renewing the lease for a coal-burning, high-polluting Navajo Generation Station (NGS) without even talking to the Navajos themselves.

As Marie Gladue reminded everyone in a letter published by the Navajo-Hopi Observer, "the NGS is Arizona's single biggest emitter of greenhouse gases," leading to droughts, wildfires and record temperatures, not to mention kids with asthma and older folks with bronchitis and increasingly prone to heart attacks. But it seems there's no prospect of NGS moving from coal to solar.

With no Navajo holy men in sight, I was left with an aesthetic satori that would make John Ford blush with envy. It was provided by Albert and his horse over the backdrop of Monument Valley; his daughter sells Navajo jewelry exactly at John Ford's point. Albert says it's been hard to make a living after the never-ending recession took over in 2007/'08. But he still believes in the promise of his blessed land. As in the Grey Hills Academy High School—one of the best examples of the push at the Navajo Reservation for self-determination in education.

The apparition of the Jewish cowboy

It was time to try a Hail Mary pass. I started at the Four Corners—where Utah, Colorado, Arizona and New Mexico meet. Utah and Arizona will vote Romney; New Mexico will vote Obama. Colorado is a swing state, but Obama's chances of winning stand at 63% and rising, according to Nate Silver's projections.

At the Four Corners I met Wayne, who presented me with the full Navajo cosmology drawn and painted by himself on sandstone. That was as good an omen as meeting a real-life medicine man. Still I crossed half of Colorado, through majestic pine tree forests, immaculate cafes from the American exceptionalism era, the embryonic ski season in Vail, a head-spinning cyclone of negative ads playing non-stop from both the Obama and Romney campaigns, and on to ultra-green, eco-friendly Boulder of the Naropa Institute studying Buddhism and bikers and skateboarders everywhere.

And then, finally, I saw him—in Broomfield, next to Boulder; the post-everything incarnation of an American medicine man. Make it a Jewish cowboy/rabbi telling tales with a coarse voice from beyond the grave. Of course, it was a Bob Dylan concert as part of his never-ending tour; a sort of sacred ceremony only for the initiated, or for those who know where to look for the keys to get an answer.

So here it was, this joker medicine man, always tangled up in blue, always down on highway 61, reminding everyone something's happening here and we don't know what it is, obsessed in never being other than a rolling stone, all along the watchtower and expecting rain—or the answer blowing in the wind.

At the end of my pilgrimage in search of a holy man, I did find my answer when he sang an unbelievable version of *Visions of Johanna*—the true Coloradoans by my side were also speechless. While our consciousness may explode in the search of a vanished American dream, *the harmonicas play the skeleton keys and the rain/ and these visions of Johanna are now all that remain.*

Oh yeah, exceptional America; *Ain't it just like the [Southwest] night to play tricks when you're trying to be so quiet?* It seems like we'll be sitting here stranded for quite a while—even though we all keep doing our best to deny it.

October 2012

SYRIA: A JIHADI PARADISE

So Bashar al-Assad hath martially spoken—for the first time in seven months—predictably blaming the Syrian civil war on "terrorists" and "Western puppets."

Turkish Foreign Minister Ahmet Davutoglu, he of the former "zero problems with our neighbors" policy, commented that Assad only reads the reports of his secret services. C'mon, Ahmet; Bashar may be no Stephen Hawking, but he's certainly getting his black holes right.

Assad, moreover, has a plan: a national dialogue leading to a national charter—to be submitted to a referendum—and then an enlarged government and a general amnesty. The problem is who is going to share all this bottled happiness because Assad totally dismisses the new Syria opposition coalition as well as the Free Syrian Army (FSA), describing them as foreign-recruited gangs taking orders from foreign powers to implement one supreme agenda: the partition of Syria.

Still, Assad's got a plan. First stage: all foreign powers financing the "terrorists"—as in the NATO/GCC compound—must stop doing so. That's already a major no-no. Only in a second stage would the Syrian Army cease all its operations, but still reserve the right to respond to any—inevitable—"provocation."

Assad's plan does not mention what happens to Assad himself. The only thing the multiple strands of the opposition agree on is that "the dictator must go" before any negotiations take place. Yet he wants to be a candidate to his own succession in 2014.

As if this was not a humongous "detail" torpedoing the whole construct of current UN mediator Lakhdar Brahimi, there's still the crucial nagging point of Brahimi insisting on including the Muslim Brotherhood (MB) in a Syrian transitional government. Brahimi should know better. It's as if the UN was praying for a Hail Mary pass—that is, Assad's voluntary abdication.

This ain't Tora Bora

If you want to know what's really going in Syria, look no further than Hezbollah secretary general Sheikh Nasrallah. He does tell it like it is.

Then there's what Ammar al-Musawi, Hezbollah's number 3—as in their de facto foreign minister—told my Italian colleague Ugo Tramballi. The most probable post-Assad scenario, if there is one, will be "not a unitary state, but a series of emirates near the Turkish border, and somebody proclaiming an Islamic state." Hezbollah's intelligence—the best available on Syria—is adamant: "one-third of the combatants in the opposition are religious extremists, and two-thirds of the weapons are under their control." The bottom line—this is a Western proxy war, with the GCC acting as a "vanguard" for NATO.

Asia Times Online readers have already known this for eons, as much as they know about the tectonic-plates-on-the-move fallacy of GCC autocracies promoting "democracy" in Syria. While the geologically blessed House of Saud has bribed every grain of sand in sight to be immunized against any whiff of Arab Spring, at least in Kuwait the winds of change are forcing the Al-Sabah family to accept a prime minister who is not an emir's puppet. Yes, petromonarchs; sooner or later you're all going down.

As for those who ignore Musawi, they do it at their own peril; blowback is and will remain inevitable, "like in Afghanistan." Musawi adds, "Syria is not Tora Bora; it's on the Mediterranean coast, close to Europe."

Syria in the 2010s is the 1980s Afghan remix—with exponential inbuilt blowback.

And for those who blindly follow the blind in repeating that Hezbollah is a "terrorist" organization, Hezbollah is closely cooperating with the UN—on the ground with over 10,000 blue helmets, under the command of Italian General Paolo Serra—to keep southern Lebanon free from Syrian civil war contamination.

The dictator has fallen—again

Not surprisingly, that motley crew branded as the "Syrian opposition" rejected Assad en bloc. For the Muslim Brotherhood—the self-styled power in waiting—he is a "war criminal" who should go on trial. For Georges Sabra, the vice president of that American-Qatari concoction, the National Coalition, Assad's words were a "declaration of war against the Syrian people."

Predictably, the US State Department—not yet under John Kerry—said Assad was "detached from reality." London said it was all hypocrisy and immediately launched yet another "secret" two-day conference this week at Wilton Park in West Sussex mingling coalition members with the usual gaggle of "experts," academics, GCC officials and "multilateral agencies." The spectacularly pathetic UK Foreign Secretary William Hague twitted—for the umpteenth time—that "Assad's departure from power is inevitable."

Facts on the ground though spell that Assad is not going anywhere anytime soon.

As for British claims that "the international community can provide support to a future transitional authority," that doesn't cut much slack among war-weary informed Syrians—who know this civil war has been funded, supplied and amply coordinated by the West, as in the NATO component of the NATOGCC compound.

They smell a—Western—rat in the obsessive characterization of everything in Syria as a sectarian war, as they see how loads of influent Sunnis have remained loyal to the government.

They smell a—Western—rat when they look back and see this whole thing started just as the US$10 billion Iran-Iraq-Syria gas pipeline (crucially bypassing NATO member Turkey) had a chance to be implemented. This would represent a major economic boost to an independent Syria, an absolute no-no as far as Western interests are concerned.

The Obama 2.0 administration—and Israel—would be more than comfortable with the MB in power in Syria, following the Egyptian *modus operandi*. The Brotherhood promotes the idea of a "civil state"; one just has to check the few "liberated areas" across Syria to detect rebel civility inbuilt in hardcore sharia law and assorted beheadings.

Yet what the NATOGCC compound and Israel really want is a Yemeni model for Syria; a military dictatorship without the dictator. What they're getting instead, for the foreseeable future, is Jihadi Paradise.

Off with their heads

Almost a year ago, al-Qaeda number one Ayman al-Zawahiri called on every Sunni hardcore faithful from Iraq and Jordan to Lebanon, Turkey and beyond to take a trip to Syria and merrily crush Assad.

So they've kept coming, including—just like in Afghanistan—Chechens and Uyghurs and Southeast Asians, joining everything from the FSA to Jabhat al-Nusra, the number one killing militia, now with over 5,000 jihadis.

A report published this week by the London-based counter-terrorism outfit Quilliam Foundation confirms al-Nusra's role. The lead author of the report, Noman Benotman, happens to be a former Libyan jihadi very cosy with al-Zawahiri and the late "Geronimo," aka Osama bin Laden.

Al-Nusra is in fact the Syrian branch of al-Qaeda in Iraq (AQI), the terrorist brand of late Abu Musab al-Zarqawi, also known as Islamic State of Iraq after Zarqawi was incinerated by a US missile in 2006. Even the State Department knows that AQI emir Abu Du'a runs both AQI and al-Nusra, whose own emir is Abu Muhammad al-Jawlani.

It's AQI that facilitates the back-and-forth of Iraqi commanders—with plenty of fighting experience on the ground against the Americans—to sensitive areas in Syria, while the Syrians, Iraqis and Jordanians at al-Nusra also work the phones to extract funding from Gulf sources. Al-Nusra wants—what else—an Islamic State not only in Syria but all over the Levant. Favorite tactic: car and truck suicide bombings as well as remote-controlled car bombs. For the moment, they keep a tense collaboration/competition regime with the FSA.

What happens next? The new Syrian National Coalition is a joke. Those GCC bastions of democracy are now totally spooked by the jihadi tsunami. Russia drew the red line and NATO won't dare to bomb; Russians and Americans are now discussing details. And sooner or later Ankara will see the writing on the wall—and revert to a policy of at least minimizing trouble with the neighbors.

Assad saw The Big Picture—clearly, thus his "confident" speech. It's now Assad against the jihadis. Unless, or until, the new CIA under Terminator John Brennan drones itself into the (shadow war) picture with a vengeance.

January 2013

WAR ON TERROR FOREVER

And the winner of the Oscar for Best Sequel of 2013 goes to... The Global War on Terror (GWOT), a Pentagon production. Abandon all hope those who thought the whole thing was over with the cinematographic snuffing out of "Geronimo," aka Osama bin Laden, further reduced to a fleeting cameo in the torture-enabling flick *Zero Dark Thirty*.

It's now official—coming from the mouth of the lion, Chairman of the Joint Chiefs of Staff General Martin Dempsey, and duly posted at the AFRICOM site, the Pentagon's weaponized African branch. Exit "historical" al-Qaeda, holed up somewhere in the Waziristans, in the Pakistani tribal areas; enter al-Qaeda in the Islamic Maghreb (AQIM). In Dempsey's words, AQIM "is a threat not only to the country of Mali, but the region, and if... left unaddressed, could in fact become a global threat."

With Mali now elevated to the status of a "threat" to the whole world, GWOT is proven to be really open-ended. The Pentagon doesn't do irony; when, in the early 2000s, armchair warriors coined the expression "The Long War," they really meant it.

Even under President Obama 2.0's "leading from behind" doctrine, the Pentagon is unmistakably gunning for war in Mali—and not only of the shadow variety.[17] General Carter Ham, AFRICOM's commander, already operates under the assumption Islamists in Mali will "attack American interests."

---

[17] Mali conflict exposes White House-Pentagon split, Los Angeles Times, January 18, 2013.

Thus, the first 100 US military "advisors" are being sent to Niger, Nigeria, Burkina Faso, Senegal, Togo and Ghana—the six member-nations of the Economic Community of West African States (ECOWAS) that will compose an African army tasked (by the United Nations) to reconquer (invade?) the parts of Mali under the Islamist sway of AQIM, its splinter group MUJAO and the Ansar ed-Dine militia. This African mini-army, of course, is paid for by the West.

Students of the Vietnam War will be the first to note that sending "advisors" was the first step of the subsequent quagmire. And on a definitely un-Pentagonese ironic aside, the US over these past few years did train Malian troops. A lot of them duly deserted. As for the lavishly, Fort Benning-trained Captain Amadou Haya Sanogo, not only did he lead a military coup against an elected Mali government but also created the conditions for the rise of the Islamists.

Nobody, though, is paying attention. General Carter Ham is so excited with the prospect of AFRICOM accumulating more gigs than Led Zeppelin in its heyday, and himself acquiring iconic savior status (Carter of Africa?), that he's bungling up his data.[18]

The general seems to have forgotten that AFRICOM—and then NATO—irretrievably supported (and weaponized) the NATO rebels in Libya who were the fighting vanguard in the war against Muammar Gaddafi. The general does know that AQIM has "a lot of money and they have a lot of weapons."

But he believes it was "mercenaries paid by Gaddafi" who abandoned Libya and brought their weapons, and "many of them came to northern Mali." No, general, they were not Gaddafi mercenaries; most were NATO rebels, the same ones who attacked the US consulate, actually a CIA sta-

---

[18] African nations can, must do for themselves—with US support, December 4, 2012.

tion, in Benghazi, the same ones commuting to Syria, the same ones let loose all across the Sahel.

So what is Algeria up to?

Right on cue, British Prime Minister David Cameron followed His Masters Voice, announcing the intervention in Mali will last years "or even decades."[19]

This Tuesday, the creme de la creme of Britain's intelligence establishment is meeting to plan nothing else than a pan-Sahara/Sahel war, for which they want yet another Bush-style "coalition of the willing."[20] For the moment, British involvement means yet more "advisors" in the usual "military cooperation" and "security training" categories, lots of money and, last but not least, Special Forces in shadow war mode.

The whole scenario comes complete with another providential "Geronimo"; Mokhtar Belmokhtar, aka "The Uncatchable" (at least by French intelligence), the leader of MUJAO who masterminded the raid on the In Amenas gas field in Algeria.

Haven't we seen this movie before? Of course we did. But now—it's official—Mali is the new Afghanistan (as *Asia Times Online* had already reported—Burn, burn Africa's Afghanistan, January 18, 2013). Here's Cameron: "Just as we had to deal with that in Pakistan and Afghanistan, so the world needs to come together to deal with this threat in North Africa." Right; Belmokhtar is already rehearsing for his cameo appearance in a *Zero Dark Thirty* sequel.

---

[19] David Cameron: fight against terrorism in north Africa may last decades, The Guardian, January 20, 2013.
[20] Intelligence chiefs and special forces plot Sahara mission, The Independent, January 21, 2013.

So by now it's clear where the Anglo-American Pentagon/Africom/British intelligence "special relationship" stands—with the French under President Francois Hollande, reconverted as a warlord, momentarily "leading" the way towards Operation African Quagmire. Crucially, no one in the European Union, apart from the Brits, is loony enough to follow in the footsteps of warlord Hollande.

By comparison, what is definitely not clear is where the key to this equation—Algeria—stands, from the point of view of the Western GWOT.

Number one fact is that the new "Geronimo," Belmokhtar, and his Mulathameen Brigade ("The Masked Ones"), of which the "Signed in Blood Batallion" which attacked in Algeria is a sub-group, enjoy extremely cozy links with Algerian secret intelligence. In a way, this could be seen as a remix of the relationship between the Taliban—and "historic" al-Qaeda—with the Pakistani Inter-Services Intelligence (ISI).

The Algerian military's ultra-hardcore response to the Islamist raid was predictable (this is how they did it during the 1990s in their internal war against the Islamic Salvation Front). We don't negotiate with terrorists; we kill them (along with scores of hostages). We do it by ourselves, without nosy foreigners, and we go for total information blackout.

No wonder this modus operandi raised a rosary of eyebrows across the Anglo-American "special relationship." Thus the Washington/London bottom line: we cannot trust the Algerians. Our GWOT—the Sahara/Sahel chapter—will be fought without them. Perhaps, even against them.

A serious complicating factor is that the 40 or so Islamists (including Libyans, Syrians and Egyptians) crossed at least 1,600 kilometers of high desert coming from Libya, not Mali. They had to have serious "protection"—anything from intelligence provided by a foreign power to qualified Algerian insiders. Hostages told of kidnappers "with North American accents" (including a Canadian whom Reuters has named "Chedad") and that all of them knew exactly where the foreigners were located inside the compound.[21]

Professor Jeremy Keenan of the School of Oriental and African Studies in London frames it in terms of an Algerian false-flag operation gone wrong.[22] Algiers may have wanted to signal to the West that French bombing in Mali would inevitably lead to blowback; but then Belmokhtar turned the whole thing upside down because he was furious the French were allowed to own Algerian airspace to bomb Mali. In a way, this could be seen as another remix of the Taliban revolting against the ISI.

Algerian public opinion is immensely suspicious, to say the least, of all the players' motives, including the Algerian government and especially France. Here is a fascinating sample. This perspective, by a political science professor, is worth quoting at length, as it neatly summarizes the French "lead" in the new GWOT chapter.

In an interview with the French-language daily Le Soir d'Algerie, political science professor Ahmed Adimi described the intervention as an attempt to "undermine Algeria" and a "step in a plan for the installation of foreign forces in the Sahel region." Adimi's thesis is that France has worked for years to destabilize the Sahel as a means of strengthening its geopolitical stance.

---

[21] In Amenas : les ex-otages racontent quatre jours d'angoisse, Liberation, January 20, 2013. (In French).
[22] Algeria Hostage Crisis: Terror Attack 'Inside Job' Gone Wrong, Says Professor Jeremy Keenan, The Huffington Post, January 19, 2013.

Asked whether the French operation in Mali was consistent with UN Security Council resolution 2085, Adimi states that the resolution "does not pose much of a problem in itself. Western powers have used it to intervene and adopt resolutions to justify their military operations. This has already happened in Iraq. In fact, the French operation may seem legal since it comes at the request of the Acting President of Mali. However, it is important to remember that the current government came to power in a coup. Regarding the intervention, it was certainly predictable but the French have precipitated matters. [...] These terrorist groups are being manipulated by foreign powers," continuing to argue that these groups were "allowed" to move south to Konna as means of justifying the French intervention.

Adimi argues that Algerians have "been sounding the alarm about the situation in the Sahel in general. Ahmed Barkouk and myself have organized several seminars on this topic. We discussed the role of France and its commitment to the region. It was France that was behind the creation of the movement for the Azawad, and I speak of course of the political organization and not of the people of Azawad, who have rights as a community. The French knew that their intervention in Libya would lead to a return of the pro-Qaddafi military Tuareg to Mali. They also planned the release of Libyan arms stockpiles across the Sahel band. The project is to transform the region into a new Afghanistan, the result of long-term planning."

Tariq Ramadan, in a devastating piece,[23] also unmasks Paris, drawing the connection between the dodgy Sarkozy "humanitarian" intervention in Libya and the current Hollande drive to protect a "friendly" country—

---

[23] Le Mali, la France et les extremistes, journaldumali.com, January 18, 2013. (In French).

all coupled with the hypocrisy of France for decades not giving a damn about "the people" suffering under assorted African dictatorships.

But the Oscar for Best Hypocritical Scenario certainly goes to the current French-Anglo-American concern about Mali being the new al-Qaeda playground, when the major playgrounds are actually NATO-supported northern Syria (as far as the Turkish border), north Lebanon and most parts of Libya.

Follow the gold, and follow the uranium

Even before it's possible to fully analyze the myriad ramifications—many of them unforeseen—of the expanded GWOT, there are two fronts to be carefully observed in the near future. So let's follow the gold, and let's follow the uranium.

Follow the gold. A host of nations have gold bullion deposited at the New York Federal Reserve. They include, crucially, Germany. Recently, Berlin started asking to get back its physical gold back—374 tons from the Bank of France and 300 tons out of 1,500 tons from the New York Federal Reserve.

So guess what the French and the Americans essentially said: We ain't got no gold! Well, at least right now. It will take five years for the German gold in France to be returned, and no less than seven years for the stash at the New York Federal Reserve. Bottom line: both Paris and Washington/New York have to come up with real physical gold any way they can.

That's where Mali fits in—beautifully. Mali—along with Ghana—accounts for up to 8% of global gold production. So if you're desperate for the genuine article—physical gold—you've got to control Mali. Imagine all that gold falling into the hands of... China.

Now follow the uranium. As everyone who was glued to the Niger yellowcake saga prior to the invasion of Iraq knows, Niger is the world's fourth largest producer of uranium. Its biggest customer is—surprise!—France; half of France's electricity comes from nuclear energy. The uranium mines in Niger happen to be concentrated in the northwest of the country, on the western range of the Air mountains, very close to the Mali border and one of the regions being bombed by the French.

The uranium issue is intimately connected with successive Tuareg rebellions; one must remember that, for the Tuaregs, there are no borders in the Sahel. All recent Tuareg rebellions in Niger happened in uranium country—in Agadez province, near the Mali border. So, from the point of view of French interests, imagine the possibility of the Tuaregs gaining control of those uranium mines—and starting to do deals with... China. Beijing, after all, is already present in the region.

All this crucial geostrategic power play—the "West" fighting China in Africa, with AFRICOM giving a hand to warlord Hollande while taking the Long War perspective—actually supersedes the blowback syndrome. It's unthinkable that British, French and American intelligence did not foresee the blowback ramifications from NATO's "humanitarian war" in Libya. NATO was intimately allied with Salafis and Salafi-jihadis—temporarily reconverted into "freedom fighters." They knew Mali—and the whole Sahel—would subsequently be awash in weapons.

No, the expansion of GWOT to the Sahara/Sahel happened by design. GWOT is the gift that keeps on giving; what could possibly top a new war theater to the French-Anglo-American industrial-military-security-contractor-media complex?

Oh yes, there's that "pivoting" to Asia as well. One is tempted to donate a finger—extracted Islamist-style—to know how and when will come the counterpunch from Beijing.

January 2013

ALL THAT PIVOTS IS GOLD

To quote the immortal line in Dashiell Hammett's *The Maltese Falcon*, as filmed by John Huston, "Let's talk about the black bird"—let's talk about a mysterious bird made out of gold. Oh yes, because this is a film noir worthy of Dashiell Hammett—involving the Pentagon, Beijing, shadow wars, pivoting and a lot of gold.

Let's start with Beijing's official position; "We don't have enough gold." That leads to China's current, frenetic buying spree—which particularly in Hong Kong anyone can follow live, in real time. China is already the top gold producing and the top gold importing nation in the world.

Gold accounts for roughly 70% of reserves held by the US and Germany—and more or less the same for France and Italy. Russia—also on a buying spree—is slightly over 10%. But China's percentage of gold among its whopping US$3.2 trillion reserves is only 2%.

Beijing is carefully following the current shenanigans of the New York Federal Reserve, which, asked by the German Bundesbank to return the German gold it is holding, replied it would take at least seven years.

German financial journalist Lars Schall has been following the story since the beginning, and virtually alone has made the crucial connection between gold, paper money, energy resources and the abyss facing the petrodollar.

Whenever Beijing says it needs more gold, this is justified as a hedge "against risks in foreign reserves"—aka US dollar fluctuation—but especially to "promote yuan globalization." As in, suavely, having the yuan compete with the US dollar and the euro "fairly" in the "international market."

And here's the (elusive) heart of the matter. What Beijing actually wants is to get rid of the US dollar peg. For that to happen, it needs vast gold reserves. So here's Beijing pivoting from the US dollar to the yuan—and trying to sway vast swathes of the global economy to follow the path. This golden rule is Beijing's Maltese Falcon: "The stuff dreams are made of."

Have drone, will travel

Qatar also does pivoting—but of the MENA (Middle East-Northern Africa) kind. Doha has been financing Wahhabis and Salafis—and even Salafi-jihadis—as in NATO rebels in Libya, Free Syrian Army gangs in Syria, and the pan-Islamic gang that took over northern Mali.

The State Department—and later the Pentagon—may have woken up to it, as in the arrangement brokered by Doha and Washington together to spawn a new, more palatable Syria "coalition." But still very potent are those dangerous liaisons between the francophile Emir of Qatar and the Quai d'Orsay in Paris—which gathered plenty of steam already during the reign of King Sarko, aka former French President Nicolas Sarkozy.

Every informed geopolitical observer has tracked leak after leak by former French intelligence operatives to the deliciously wicked satirical weekly Le Canard Enchaine, detailing Qatar's modus operandi. It's a no-brainer. Qatar's foreign policy reads as Muslim Brotherhood Here, There and Everywhere (but not inside the neo-feudal emirate); this is Qatar's Maltese Falcon. At the same time Doha—to the delight of French elites—is an avid practitioner of hardcore neoliberalism, and a top investor in France's economy.

So their interests may coalesce in promoting disaster capitalism—successfully—in Libya and then—still unsuccessfully—in Syria. Yet Mali is something else; classic blowback—and that's where the interests of Doha and Paris diverge (not to mention Doha and Washington; at least if one does not assume that Mali has been the perfect pretext for a renewed AFRICOM drive.)

Algerian media is awash in outrage, questioning Qatar's agenda (in French). Yet the pretext—as predicted—worked perfectly.

AFRICOM—surprise!—is on a roll, as the Pentagon gets ready to set up a drone base in Niger. That's the practical result of a visit by AFRICOM's commander, General Carter Ham, to Niger's capital Niamey only a few days ago.

Forget about those outdated PC-12 turbo props that have been spying on Mali and Western Africa for years. Now it's Predator time. Translation: chief-in-waiting John Brennan plans a CIA shadow war all across the Sahara-Sahel. With permission from Mick Jagger/Keith Richards, it's time to start humming a remixed hit: "I see a grey drone/ and I want it painted black."

AFRICOM does Niger is indeed sweeter than cherry pie. Northwest Niger is the site of all those uranium mines supplying the French nuclear industry. And it's very close to Mali's gold reserves. Imagine all that gold in an "unstable" area falling into the hands of... Chinese companies. Beijing's Maltese Falcon moment of finally having enough gold to dump the US dollar peg would be at hand.

The Pentagon even got permission for all its surveillance gear to refuel in—of all places—crucial Agadez. The French legion may have been doing the hard work on the ground in Mali, but it's AFRICOM which will ultimately reap the profits all across the Sahara-Sahel.

Don't you know about the (Asian) bird?

And that brings us to that famous pivoting to Asia—which was supposed to be the number one geopolitical theme of the Obama 2.0 administration. It may well be. But certainly alongside AFRICOM pivoting all over the Sahara/Sahel in drone mode, to Beijing's growing irritation; and Doha-Washington pivoting in their support of the former "terrorist" turned "freedom fighter," and vice-versa.

And we did not even mention the non-pivoting involved in this noir plot; the Obama 2.0 administration keeping its appalling embrace of the medieval House of Saud and "stability in the Arabian peninsula," as recommended by an usual suspect, a mediocre—yet influential—"veteran intelligence official."

Play it again, Sam. In that outstanding *Maltese Falcon* scene at the start of our plot between Humphrey Bogart (let's say he plays the Pentagon) and Sydney Greenstreet (let's say he plays Beijing), the official is the goon, the third guy in the picture. The pivoting to Asia is essentially a product of Andrew Marshall, an allegedly Yoda-like totem of US national security.

Marshall has been behind the Revolution in Military Affairs (RMA)—all of you Donald Rumsfeld freaks know about it; failed Shock and Awe (which only served to destroy Iraq almost beyond repair, even with disaster capitalism involved); and now the concept called Air Sea Battle.

Air Sea Battle's premise is that Beijing will attack US forces in the Pacific, which is, frankly, ridiculous (even with help from a monster false-flag operation). The US would then retaliate via a "blinding campaign"—the naval equivalent of Shock and Awe. Both the US Air Force and the US Navy loved the concept because it implies a lot of hardware spending to be stationed in plenty of sophisticated Pacific bases, and in the high seas.

So even as David Petraeus-style counter-insurgency has pivoted to John Brennan's CIA shadow wars, the real deal is the pivoting to Asia; a pseudo-strategy, concocted to keep the Pentagon budget at exorbitant levels, promoting a new Cold War with China. "They will never amass enough gold to impose their evil plans," one could hear Marshall say about China (without Bogart or Greenstreet's aplomb, of course). Hammett would be appalled; Marshall's Maltese Falcon is the stuff (war) dreams are made of.

February 2013

THE FALL OF THE HOUSE OF EUROPE

The Enchanters came / Cold and old,
Making day gray / And the age of gold
Passed away, / For men fell
Under their spell, / Were doomed to gloom.
Joy fled, / There came instead,
Grief, unbelief, / Lies, sighs,
Lust, mistrust, / Guile, bile,
Hearts grew unkind, / Minds blind,
Glum and numb, / Without hope or scope.
There was hate between states,
A life of strife, / Gaols and wails,
Dont's, wont's, / Chants, shants,
No face with grace, / None glad, all sad.

—W H Auden, *The Golden Age*

We have, unfortunately, no post-modern version of Dante guided by Virgil to tell a startled world what is really happening in Europe in the wake of the recent Italian general election.

On the surface, Italians voted an overwhelming "No"—against austerity (imposed the German way); against more taxes; against budget cuts in theory designed to save the euro. In the words of the center-left mayor of Florence, Matteo Renzi, "Our citizens have spoken loud and clear but maybe their message has not been fully grasped." In fact it was.

There are four main characters in this morality/existential play worthy of the wackiest tradition of *commedia dell'arte*.

The Pyrrhic winner is Pier Luigi Bersani, the leader of the center-left coalition; yet he is unable to form a government. The undisputed loser is former Goldman Sachs technocrat and caretaker Prime Minister Mario Monti.

And then there are the actual winners; "two clowns"—at least from a German point of view and also the City of London's, via The Economist. The "clowns" are maverick comedian Beppe Grillo's 5 Star movement; and notorious billionaire and former Prime Minister Silvio "Bunga Bunga" Berlusconi.

To muddle things even further, Berlusconi was sentenced to one year in prison last Thursday by a Milan court over a wiretapping scandal. He will appeal; and as he was charged and convicted before, once again he will walk. His mantra remains the same: "I'm 'persecuted' by the Italian judiciary."

There's more, much more. These four characters—Bersani, Monti, Grillo, Berlusconi—happen to be at the heart of a larger-than-life Shakespearean tragedy: the political failure of the troika (European Commission, European Central Bank and IMF), which translates into the politics of the European Union being smashed to pieces.

That's what happens when the EU project was never about a political "union"—but essentially about the euro as a common currency. No wonder the most important mechanism of European unification is the European Central Bank. Yet abandon all hope of European politicians asking their disgruntled citizens about a real European union. Does anybody still want it? And exactly under what format?

Meet Absurdistan

Why things happened in Italy the way they did? There is scarcely a better explanation than Marco Cattaneo's, expressed in this blog where he tries to understand "Absurdistan."

It all started with an electoral law that even in Italy was defined as *ulna porcata* (a load of rubbish), validating a "disproportional" system (political scientists, take note) that could only lead to an ungovernable situation.

In Cattaneo's matchless depiction, in the Senate the One for All, All For One coalition (Bersani's) got 31.6% of the votes. The Everyone for Himself coalition (Berlusconi's) got 30.7%. And the brand new One Equals One All the Others Equal No One movement (Grillo's) got a surprising 23.8%.

And yet, defying all logic, in the end Everyone for Himself got 116 seats, One for All, All for One got 113 seats, and One Equals One All the Others Equal No One got only 54—less than half.

At street level, from Naples to Turin and from Rome to Palermo, there's a parallel explanation. No less than 45% of Italians, from retired civil servants living on 1,000 euros (US$1,300) a month to bankers making 10 million euros a year, don't want any change at all. Another 45%— the unemployed, the underpaid—want radical change. And 10% don't care—ever. Add that to the ungovernability lasagna.

And extract from it a nugget of cappuccino-at-the-counter wisdom. Absurdistan's finances will soon be in a state as dire as Hellenistan— those neighborly descendants of Plato and Aristotle. And then Absurdistan will become a model to Europe and the world—where 1% of the population will control 99% of the national wealth. From Lorenzo de Medici to Berlusconi; talk about Decline and Fall.

Bunga Bunga me baby

Tried to death (including being convicted for tax fraud in October 2012; he walked); beneficiary of dodgy laws explicitly designed to protect himself and his enormous businesses empire; the Rabelaisian Bunga Bunga saga. He beat them all (so far). Silvio Berlusconi may be the ultimate comeback kid. How did he pull it off this time?

It's easy when you mix a billionaire's media wattage (and corporate control) with outlandish promises—such as scrapping a much-detested property tax. How to make up for the shortfall? Simple: Silvio promised new taxes on gambling, and a shady deal to recover some of the funds held by Italians in Swiss banks.

Does it matter that Switzerland made it clear it would take years for this scheme to work? Of course not. Even Silvio's vast opposition was forced to admit the idea was a "stroke of genius." Nearly 25% of Italians voted for Silvio's party. Nearly a third backed his right-wing coalition. In Lombardy—informally known as the Italian Texas—the coalition smashed the center-left to pieces; Tuscany on the other hand voted traditionally left, while Rome is a quintessential swing city.

Silvio's voters are essentially owners of small and medium-sized businesses; the northern Italy that drives the economy. They are all tax-crazy; that ranges from legions of tax evaders to those who are being asphyxiated by the burden. Obviously, they couldn't care less about Rome's budget deficits. And they all think German Chancellor Angela Merkel should rot in Dante's ninth circle of hell.

Frau Merkel, for her part, had been entertaining the idea of quietly cruising the euro zone waters towards her third term in the coming September elections. Fat chance—now thanks to Silvio's and Beppe Grillo's voters. Talk about a North-South abyss in Europe. The EU summit this month is going to be—literally—a riot.

Those sexy polit-clowns

All hell is breaking loose in the EU. Le Monde insists Europe is not in agony. Oh yes, it is; in a coma.

And yet Brussels (the bureaucrat-infested European Commission) and Berlin (the German government) simply don't care about a Plan B; it's austerity or bust. Predictably, Dutch Finance Minister Jeroen Dijsselbloem—the new head of the spectacularly non-transparent political committee that runs the euro—said that what Monti was doing (and was roundly rejected by Italians) is "crucial for the entire euro zone."

In 2012, Italy's economy shrank 2.2%, more than 100,000 small businesses went bust (yes, they all voted for Silvio), and unemployment is above 10% (in reality, over 15%). Italy may have the highest national debt in the euro zone after Greece. But here Absurdistan manifests itself once again via austerity; Italy's fiscal deficit is much lower than France's and Holland's.

Pop up the champagne; France is in vertical decadence. It's not only the industrial decline but also the perennial recession, social turbulence and public debt beyond 90% of GDP. France, the second-largest euro zone economy, asked the European Commission for an extra year to lower its deficit below 3% of GDP. Jens Weidman, president of the Bundesbank, roared "Forget it."

Portugal is also asking the troika for some room. Portugal's economy is shrinking (by 2%) for the third year running, with unemployment at over 17%.

Spain is mired in a horrendous recession, also under a monster debt crisis. GDP fell 0.7% in 2012 and according to Citibank will fall a further 2.2% this year. Unemployment is at an overwhelming 26%, with youth unemployment over 50%. Not everyone can hit the lottery playing for Barcelona or Real Madrid. Ireland has the euro zone's highest deficit, at 8%, and has just restructured the debt of its banks.

Greece is in its fifth recession year in a row, with unemployment over 30%—and this after two austerity packages. Athens is running around in circles trying to fend off its creditors while at least trying to alleviate some of the draconian cuts. Greeks are adamant; the situation is worse than Argentina in 2001. And remember, Argentina defaulted.

Even Holland is under a serious banking crisis. And to top it off, David Cameron has thrown Britain's future in Europe in turmoil.

So once again it was Silvio's turn—who else?—to spice it all up. Only the *Cavaliere* could boom out that the famous spread—the difference between how much Italy and Germany pay to borrow on the bond markets—had been "invented" in 2011 by Berlin (the German government) and Frankfurt (the European Central Bank), so they could get rid of himself, Silvio, and "elect" the technocrat Monti.

German media, also predictably, has been taking no prisoners with relish. Italy and Italians are being routinely derided as "childlike", "ungovernable", "a major risk to the euro zone." (See, for example, Der Spiegel.)

The ultra-popular tabloid Bild even came up with a new pizza; not a Quattro Stagioni (Four Seasons) but a Quattro Stagnazioni (Four Stagnations).

The verdict is of an Italy "in the hands of polit-clowns that may shatter the euro or force the country to exit." Even the liberal-progressive Der Tagesspiegel in Berlin defines Italy as "a danger to Europe."

Peer Steinbruck, Germany's former finance minister and the Social Democratic candidate against Merkel next September, summed it all up: "To a certain degree, I am horrified that two clowns won the election."

So whatever government emerges in Italy, the message from Brussels, Berlin and Frankfurt remains the same: if you don't cut, cut and cut, you're on your own.

Germany, for its part, has only a plan A. It spells out "Forget the Club Med." This means closer integration with Eastern Europe (and further on down the road, Turkey). A free trade deal with the US. And more business with Russia—energy is key—and the BRICS in general. Whatever the public spin, the fact is German think-tanks are already gaming a dual-track euro zone.

The people want quantitative easing

This aptly titled movie, Girlfriend in a Coma, directed by Annalisa Piras and co-written by former editor of The Economist Bill Emmett, did try to make sense of Italy's vices and virtues.

And still, not only via Prada or Maserati, Parma ham or Brunello wines, Italy keeps delivering flashes of brilliance; the best app in the world—Atom, which allows the personalization of functions on a mobile phone even if one is not a computer programmer—was created by four 20-somethings in Rome, as La Repubblica reported.

Philosopher Franco Berardi—who way back in the 1970s was part of the Italian autonomous movements—correctly evaluates that what Europe is living today is a direct consequence of the 1990s, when financial capital hijacked the European model and calcified it under neoliberalism.

Subsequently, a detailed case can be made that the financial Masters of the Universe used the aftermath of the 2008 financial crisis to turbocharge the political disintegration of the EU via a tsunami of salary cuts, job precariousness for the young, the flattening of pensions and hardcore privatization of everything. No wonder roughly 75% of Italians ended up saying "No" to Monti and Merkel.

The bottom line is that Europeans—from Club Med countries to some northern economies—are fed up of having to pay the debt accumulated by the financial system.

Grillo's movement per se—even capturing 8.7 million votes—is obviously not capable of governing Italy. Some of its (vague) ideas have enormous appeal among the younger generations, especially an unilateral default on public debt (look at the examples of Argentina, Iceland and Russia), the nationalization of banks, and a certified, guaranteed "citizenship" income for everyone of 1,000 euros a month. And then there would be referendum after referendum on free-trade agreements, NATO membership and, of course, to stay or not stay within the euro zone.

What Grillo's movement has already done is to show how ungovernable Europe is under the Monti-Merkel austerity mantra. Now the ball is in the European financial elite's court. Most wouldn't mind letting Italy become the new Greece.

So we go back full circle. The only way out would be a political reformulation of the EU. As it is, most of Europe is watching, impotently, the death of the welfare state, sacrificed in the altar of Recession. And that runs parallel to Europe slouching towards global irrelevance—Real Madrid and Bayern Munich notwithstanding.

The Fall of the House of Europe might turn into a horror story beyond anything imagined by Poe—displaying elements of (already visible) fascism, neo-Dickensian worker exploitation and a wide-ranging social, civil war. In this context, the slow reconstruction of a socially based Europe may become no more than a pipe dream.

What would Dante make of it? The great Roberto Benigni, a native of Tuscany, is currently reading and commenting on in depth 12 cantos—from the XI to the XXII—in Dante's *Inferno*, a highlight of the *Divine Comedy*. Spellbound, I watched it on RAI—the square in front of the fabulous Santa Croce church in Florence packed to the rafters, the cosmic perfection of the Maestro's words making sense of it all.

If only his spirit would enlighten Inferno dwellers from Monti to Merkel, from Silvio to European Central bankers—aligning Man once again with the stars and showing troubled Europe the way.

March 2013

SEARCH AND DESTROY: THE RAPE OF IRAQ

First thing we do, let's kill all mythographers (lawyerly or not): the rape of Iraq is the biggest, man-made humanitarian disaster of our times. It's essential to keep in mind this was a direct consequence of Washington smashing international law to pieces; after Iraq, any freak anywhere can unleash pre-emptive war, and quote Bush/Cheney 2003 as precedent.

And yet, 10 years after Shock and Awe, even so-called "liberals" have been trying to legitimize something, anything, out of the "Iraq project." There was never a "project"; only a dizzying maze of lies—including a posteriori justifications of bombing the Greater Middle East into "democracy."

I've been thinking about The Catalyst lately. The Catalyst was the tank I had to negotiate every time in and out of my cramped digs on the way to the red zone, in the first weeks of the US occupation of Baghdad. The marines were mainly from Texas and New Mexico. We used to talk. They were convinced they hit Baghdad because "the terrorists attacked us on 9/11."

Years later, most Americans still believed The Outstanding Lie. Which proves that the cosmically arrogant and ignorant neo-cons at least got one thing right. The Saddam Hussein-al-Qaeda connection may not have been the prime piece of the puzzle in their "project" of invading and remaking Iraq from Year Zero (there were also the non-existing WMDs); but it was immensely effective as a brainwashing technique for rallying the galleries.

When the torture porn spectacle of Abu Ghraib was revealed in the spring of 2004 (I was driving through Texas on an assignment, and virtually everybody deemed the whole show "normal") The Outstanding Lie still ruled. Ten years on, after Abu Ghraib, the destruction of Fallujah, the widespread "dead-checking" (killing wounded Iraqis), "360-degree rotational fire" (target-practice on scores of Iraqi civilians), calling air strikes on civilian areas, not to mention "killing all military-age men"; after US$3 trillion, and counting, spent (remember the neo-cons promised a short, easy war costing no more than $60 billion); after over 1 million Iraqis killed directly or indirectly by the invasion and occupation, the maze of lies still engulf us all like a giant Medusa.

Oh yes, and the Oscar-winning CIA—true to character—continues to cover it all up.

Faster, counter-insurgent, kill, kill

Iraq Year Zero lasted roughly 10 days. I watched the official birth of the resistance; a mass rally in Baghdad, starting in Adhamiya, uniting Sunnis and Shi'ites. Then came the exploits of that Stooge Central called the Coalition Provisional Authority (CPA), "led" by the ghastly Paul Bremer, unfailingly displaying interplanetary ignorance of Mesopotamian culture. And then a sort of larger-than-life search and destroy offensive, deployed as a "tactic," masquerading as counter-insurgency. No wonder this quickly turned into a sandy Vietnam.

The Sunni resistance drove the Pentagon literally crazy. This is how the "triangle of death" looked like in the summer of 2004. And this is the Pentagon's response four months later, applying what I called "precision-strike democracy."

In the end, the triangle of death won—sort of. Fast forward to Dubya's "surge." Gullible millions in the US still believe Horny General David

Petraeus's narrative of the surge. I was there at the beginning of the surge, in the spring of 2007. The horrendous US-engineered civil war—remember, it's always about divide and rule—was only subsidizing because Shi'ite commandos—Badr Corps and Madhi Army—had managed to conduct a devastating ethnic cleansing of Sunnis in what used to be mixed neighborhoods. Baghdad, once a slightly predominantly Sunni city, had turned predominantly Shi'ite. This had nothing to do with Petraeus.

As for the Awakening Councils, they were essentially Sunni militias (numbering over 80,000), organized by clans, who became fed up with al-Qaeda in Iraq's gory tactics, mostly in the very same triangle of death, including Fallujah and Ramadi. Petraeus paid them with suitcases full of cash. Before that—when, for instance, they were defending Fallujah in November 2004—they were branded as "terrorists." Now they were duly reconverted into Ronald Reagan-style "freedom fighters."

I had met some of those sheikhs. Their wily plan was long-term; instead of fighting the Americans, we take their money, lay low for a while, get rid of those al-Qaeda fanatics, and later attack our real enemy; the Shi'ites in power in Baghdad.

That's exactly the next step in Iraq, where yet another civil war is slowly brewing. And by the way, some of these former "terrorists"—with ample battleground experience—are now the key commanders in that alphabet soup of Syrian "rebel" units fighting against the Assad regime in Syria. And yes, they remain "freedom fighters."

Balkanize or bust

Americans obviously don't remember that Joe Biden, when still in the Senate, eagerly campaigned for the balkanization of Iraq into three sectarian parts. Considering that he is now one of the Obama 2.0 administration's point men for Syria, he may even end up having it both ways.

True, Iraq is the first Arab nation ruled by a Shi'ite government since fabled Saladin got rid of the Fatimids in Egypt way back in 1171. But this is a nation on the way to total fragmentation.

The Green Zone, once an American town, may now be Shi'ite. But even Grand Ayatollah Sistani—the top Shi'ite religious leader, who actually broke the back of the neo-cons and the CPA in Najaf in 2004—is disgusted with the mess orchestrated by Prime Minister Nouri al-Maliki. And even Tehran is caught in a bind. Contrary to think-tank belief in the Beltway—do these people ever get anything right?—Iran does not manipulate Iraq's politics. Above all, what Tehran really fears in Iraq is a civil war not quite dissimilar to what's happening in Syria.

Patrick Cockburn's coverage of Iraq for these past 10 years as a foreign correspondent is unrivalled. This is his current evaluation.

Important facts are that kingmaker Muqtada al-Sadr—remember when he was the most dangerous man in Iraq, on the cover of every American magazine?—may have criticized Maliki for his Shi'ite hegemony bias, but he does not want regime change. Shi'ites have the numbers, so in a still unified Iraq there's bound to be a Shi'ite majority government anyway.

The overwhelmingly Shi'ite south of Iraq remains very poor. The only possible source of employment is government jobs. Infrastructure, all over, remains in tatters—direct consequence of UN and US sanctions, then the invasion and occupation.

But then there's the shining city on a hill; Iraqi Kurdistan, a somewhat warped development of Pipelineistan.

Big Oil never had a chance to fulfill its 2003 dream of lowering the price of a barrel back to $20—in line with Rupert Murdoch's wishful thinking. But there's a lot of action all over the place. Greg Muttitt has been unmatched following the new Iraq oil boom.

Yet nowhere else the action is more convoluted than in the Kurdistan Regional Government (KRG), where up to 60 oil companies—from ExxonMobil to Chevron, Total and Gazprom—are in play.

The holy of the holies is a new pipeline linking Iraqi Kurdistan to Turkey, the theoretical Kurdish passport to export oil bypassing Baghdad. No one knows whether that will be the straw to break the Iraqi camel's back—as Iraqi Kurds are getting closer and closer to Ankara and drifting away from Baghdad. The ball is definitely in Turkish Prime Minister Recep Tayyip Erdogan's court—just as Kurds have a once in many lifetimes chance of juggling between Ankara, Baghdad and Tehran's interests and finally ending up with an independent, and economically self-sufficient Kurdistan.

So yes, there are plenty of balkanization signs on the horizon. But what about lessons learned by the US out of one of the biggest foreign policy blunders in history? Nothing. Nada. We will have to wait for Nick Turse to come up, in a few years, with an Iraqi equivalent of his masterful book on Vietnam, Kill Anything That Moves. Even more than Vietnam, Iraq's catalogue of horrors was the inevitable result of not only official Pentagon policy, but also official White House policy.

Will this harrowing spiral of Iraqi suffering ever be fully acknowledged? We could always start here, with the case stated by former UN Humanitarian Coordinator for Iraq, Hans Sponeck.

Or, in a pop vein, a non-Hollywood/CIA producer could invest in a made in Iraq movie, distributed worldwide, where in the final act Dubya,

Dick, Rummy, Wolfie and assorted hoodlums of the Douglas Feith mould are all sent on a one-way ticket to a Guantanamo faithfully recreated in the triangle of death—to the sound of Bob Dylan's *Masters of War*. Now that would be some global catharsis to die for.

March 2013

THE SOUTH ALSO RISES

The Poorer Nations: A Possible History of the Global South

by Vijay Prashad

It is not so far-fetched to imagine Walter Benjamin's Angel of History succumbing to the temptation, and stressing that the time of the Global South has finally come.

Oh yes, it will be a long, arduous and winding road. But would the Google/Facebook generation need only one textbook detailing the stuff of dreams, trials and tribulations of the developing world in the early 21st century, this would be it, Vijay Prashad's just published The Poorer Nations.

Call it the post-modern, digital follow-up to Frantz Fanon's classic *The Wretched of the Earth*.

This is an absolutely essential book to be read alongside another delight written by a global Asian, Pankaj Mishra's *From the Ruins of Empire: The Revolt Against the West and the Remaking of Asia*, which uses key figures such as Jamal al-Din al-Afghani, Liang Qichao and Rabindranath Tagore to tell an extraordinary story.

Prashad, director of international studies at Trinity College, Connecticut, and author of the splendid *The Darker Nations*, which should be read as a preamble to this book, sets the scene right from the start—using the requisite Fanon quote; by 1961, what was configured was a fight between the Third World Project ("for peace, for bread and for justice") and the Atlantic Project. Key actors: the Non-Aligned Movement

(NAM), the de facto secretariat of the Third World Project, and the Group of 77 developing nations, created in 1964 to act on behalf of NAM in the United Nations.

The founders of the NAM enjoyed iconic status in the post-colonial world; Jawaharlal Nehru in India, Gamal Abdel Nasser in Egypt, Sukarno in Indonesia, Josip Broz Tito in Yugoslavia. Yet they knew this was an uphill battle. As Prashad notes, "the UN had been hijacked by the five permanent members of the Security Council. The IMF and the World Bank had been captured by the Atlantic powers, and the GATT [General Agreement on Tariffs and Trade, precursor to the World Trade Organization] was designed to undermine any attempt by the new nations to revise the international economic order."

As for the Atlantic Project, a 1969 quote from Henry Kissinger—co-destructor of Cambodia, Pinochet enabler, disgusted Saudi ally (the "most feckless and gutless of the Arabs") and praiser-in-chief of the Iranian Shah ("a tough, mean guy")—would suffice: "Nothing important can come from the South. The axis of history starts in Moscow, goes to Bonn, crosses over to Washington, and then goes to Tokyo. What happens in the South is of no importance."

Atlanticists were fiercely against the "no importance" Third World Project, but also against social democracy and communism. Their Holy Grail was to wallow in easy profits provided by a new global geography of production, "technological shifts that enabled firms to take advantage of differential wage rates"—most of all, those very low wages paid all across East Asia.

So the stage was set for the emergence of neoliberalism. Here Prashad moves in parallel with the indispensable David Harvey, detailing how the Global South became ripe to be fully (re)exploited; bye-bye national liberation ideas of collective good.

Keep the barbarians out

With the IMF currently part of the troika dictating austerity to most of Western Europe (alongside the European Commission and the European Central Bank), it's easy to forget that in 1944 things were already pretty warped. The developing world had no say whatsoever in Bretton Woods, not to mention any sort of control over the UN's five-member Security Council. It was the silence of the lambs; the wolves prevailed, and inequality was set in stone.

Prashad proceeds with the indispensable details of how the US dollar became the effective world currency, with the US swinging the price of the dollar globally, regardless of any consequences; the formation of the Group of Seven as essentially an anti-developing world mechanism (and not anti-Soviet); and of course the much-dreaded Trilateral Commission, set up by Chase Manhattan's David Rockefeller to impose the will of the North against the South.

And guess who was the Trilateral's intellectual architect? The ineffable Zbigniew Brzezinski, later president Jimmy Carter's consigliere. Dr. Zbig wanted to "contain the "contagious threat of global anarchy." Divide and rule, once again; the periphery needed to be put in its place.

By the way, one should always remember that in his 1997 epic *The Grand Chessboard*, Dr. Zbig, who became the foreign policy advisor to Barack Obama in 2008, wrote, "The three grand imperatives of imperial geo-strategy are to prevent collusion and maintain security dependence among the vassals, to keep tributaries pliant and protected, and to keep the barbarians from coming together." For a long while the "vassals" were easily contained; but Dr. Zbig, one step ahead of Kissinger, was already planning how to contain the two key "barbarians," ascending Eurasian powers Russia and China.

The Group of Seven anyway was a roaring success, pushing its "theory of governance" everywhere, implemented by—who else—the Bretton Woods mafia. Prashad neatly defines it: "What went by the name of neoliberalism was less a coherent economic doctrine than a fairly straightforward campaign by the propertied classes to maintain or restore their position of dominance," via the David Harvey-coined "accumulation by dispossession," now also known by millions of Europeans under the codename "austerity."

The numbers tell the story. In 1981, the net flow of capital to the Third World was $35.2 billion. In 1987, $30.7 billion left the Third World for Western banks. Praise the Lord and his law set in stone, also known as Structural Adjustment, based on "conditionality" (savage privatization, deregulation, destruction of social services, financial "liberalization").

Paraphrasing Dylan, when you got nothing, you still got this nothing to lose. There was never any political strategy by the North to deal with the debt crisis of the 1980s. The Global South lambs were only allowed in a sorry procession to receive their Structural Adjustment consecrated host one by one.

But still that was not enough. With the fall of the USSR, Washington was free to develop Full Spectrum Dominance. Those who did not fully abide were branded "rogue states"—as in Cuba, Iran, Iraq, Libya, North Korea and even, for a while, Malaysia (because it would not bow to the IMF).

But then, slowly but surely, the Global South began to rise. Prashad details the reasons—the commodity boom driven by China; commodity profits improving Latin American finances; more foreign direct investment roaming the world. The Global South started trading more within itself.

Then, in June 2003, at the margins of the Group of Eight gathering in Evian, France, emerged something called IBSA (the India-Brazil-South Africa Dialogue). IBSA was keen to "maximize the benefits of globalization" and promote sustained economic growth. Brazilian Foreign Minister Celso Amorim defined it at the time as "an ideology in the best sense of the word—an ideology of democracy, diversity, tolerance, a search for cooperation."

In parallel, China was—what else—booming. It's essential to remind anyone at this point of that fateful November 1978 trip by Deng Xiaoping to Singapore, where he was hosted by Lee Kuan Yew; Prashad could have built a whole chapter around it. This was the clincher. Deng knew right away that he would milk the *guanxi* ("connections") of the Chinese diaspora for all it's worth. I'll never forget my very own first visit to Shenzhen only one month after Deng's fabled Southern Tour of January 1992. That's when the boom really started. At the time, I felt I was mostly neck-deep in Maoist China.

Fast forward to China now helping to develop Africa. Vast swathes of the developing world would not consider blindly adopting a *zhongguo moshi*—the Chinese Model. It's more like Prashad introducing this wonderful quote from Donald Kaberuka, a former minister of finance in Rwanda and now president of the African Development Bank: "We can learn from [the Chinese] how to organize our trade policy, to move from low to middle income status, to educate our children in skills and areas that pay off in just a couple of years."

BRIC by BRIC

Which brings us to the BRICS, created as a group in 2009 out of the BRIC-IBSA union—and now the top locomotive of the Global South.

By then, inevitably, Blame China had already become an established fine art in Washington; the Chinese must imperatively become consumers. They are, and they will—but in their own rhythm, and following their own political model.

Even the IMF already admits that by 2016 the US may cease to be the world's largest economy. So the great Fernand Braudel was already right when he wrote *The Perspective of the World: Civilization and Capitalism, Fifteenth- Eighteenth Century*, stressing this would be the "sign of autumn" for Atlantic hegemony.

Of course there are huge problems with the BRICS, as Prashad details. Their domestic policies can indeed be interpreted as a sort of "neoliberalism with Southern characteristics." They are far from being an ideological alternative to neoliberalism. They have been helpless to counteract the overwhelming military hegemony of the US and NATO (see, for instance, the Libya fiasco). And they are not the embryo of a revolutionary shift in the world order.

But at least they are "allowing a breath of fresh air to oxygenate the stagnant world of neoliberal imperialism."

The fresh air will circulate in the form of a new development bank, a BRICS Bank of the South version of the South American Banco del Sur, founded in 2009 (here's Prashad's critical take.) China and Brazil have set up a $30 billion currency swap deal to pay for trade, bypassing the US dollar. Beijing and Moscow are deepening their strategic partnership. (See BRICS go over the wall, *Asia Times Online*, March 26, 2013.)

The BRICS as they stand—three major commodities producers plus two major commodities consumers trying to find a way out of a Western-conducted disaster—are just a start. They are already evolving as a powerful geopolitical actor stressing multipolarity. They are bound to be joined by the next BRICS—the MIST (Mexico, Indonesia, South Korea and Turkey). And don't forget Iran. Time for BRICS MIIST?

What's graphically obvious is that the Global South has had enough—from the ravages of casino turbo-capitalism to NATO playing Robocop from North Africa to Southwest Asia, not to mention Eurasia being encircled by that Dr. Strangelove chimera—a missile shield.

The Global South remains fraught with absurdities; one just has to think of the oil and gas GCC petro-monarchies—those paragons of "democracy"—now configured as an annex to NATO. Few developments lately have been so appalling as the Arab League licking their NATO master's boots, breaking international law to install dodgy Syrian "rebels" in the chair of a sovereign state, one of its very own founding members.

Weird scenes inside the goldmine

The fall of neoliberalism will be bloody—and it will take time. Prashad attempts an objective analysis in terms of the unity of the Global South, drawing on the work of Indian Marxist Prabhat Patnaik.

Patnaik is a sound fellow. He knows that "a coordinated global resistance is not on the horizon." Instead, "he emphasizes the centrality of building resistance within the nation-state, and his analysis can easily be extended to regions (he writes mainly of India, but the analysis he provides is equally applicable to the Bolivarian experiments in Latin America)."

So the road map spells tackling the "peasant question," which is essentially about land and rights; and to concentrate on the immediate struggles of improving people's living and working conditions. Inevitably Prashad has to refer to Bolivian vice president Alvaro Garcia Linera, one of Latin America's top contemporary intellectuals.

In many aspects, where the emancipation of the Global South is more advanced is in parts of South America; I was hugely impressed when I was in Bolivia in early 2008. Prashad neatly summarizes Linera's analysis of how the process develops:

It begins with a crisis of the state that enables a "dissident social bloc" to mobilize the people into a political project. A "catastrophic stand-off" develops between the bloc of power and the bloc of the people, which in the case of Latin America was able to be resolved for the moment on the side of the people. The new government must then "convert opposition demands into acts of state," and build a deeper and broader hegemony by "combining the ideas of mobilized society with material resources provided by or via the state." The turning point ("point of bifurcation"), for Garcia Linera, comes through a "series of confrontations" between the blocs that are resolved in unexpected ways, with either the consolidation of the new situation or the reconstitution of the old. We are at or near the point of bifurcation. What will come next cannot be predicted.

What is definitely known by now by the best minds in Asia, Africa and Latin America, is that there was never an end of history, as parroted by pathetic orphans of Hegel; and there was never an end of geography, as parroted by "world is flat" globalization dancing fools. The Global South's intellectual liberation from the North is finally on. And it's irreversible. There's no turning back to the old order. If this was a movie, it would be 1968 replayed all over again—full time, all the time; let's be realists, and demand, and implement, the impossible.

The Poorer Nations: A Possible History of the Global South by Vijay Prashad. Verso, March 2013. ISBN-10: 1844679527. Price US$26. 300 pages.

April 2013

THE ISLAMIC EMIRATE OF SYRIASTAN

And now some breaking news coming from the Islamic Emirate of Syriastan. This program is brought to you by the NATOGCC corporation. Please also tune in for a word from our individual sponsors, the United States government, Britain, France, Turkey, the House of Saud and the Emir of Qatar.

It all started early this week, with a proclamation by the elusive leader of al-Qaeda Central, Ayman "The Doctor" al-Zawahiri, hidden somewhere in the Pakistani tribal areas; how come Double O Bama with his license to kill (list) and prime drone fleet cannot find him?

Al-Zawahiri called for all the Islamist brigades in the Jihad Inc business fighting the government of Syrian President Bashar al-Assad to found an Islamic emirate, the passport du jour leading to an Islamic Caliphate.

Two days later, the Islamic State of Iraq—for all practical purposes al-Qaeda in Iraq—announced, via a video starring its leader Abu Bakr al-Husseini al-Qurashi al-Baghdadi, a mergers and acquisition spectacular; from now on, it would be united with the Syrian jihadist group Jabhat al-Nusra, and be referred to as the Islamic State of Iraq and the Levant.

But then, the next day, the head of Jabhat al-Nusra, the shady Abu Muhammad al-Joulani, said that yes, we do pledge our allegiance to al-Qaeda Sheikh, Doctor al-Zawahiri; but there has been no M&A business whatsoever with al-Qaeda in Iraq.

Puzzled infidels from Washington to Beijing may be entitled to believe this is straight from Monty Python—but it's actually deadly serious; especially as the House of Saud, the Emir of Qatar, the neo-Ottoman Erdogan in Turkey and King Playstation from Jordan—vastly supported by Washington—continue to weaponize the Syrian "rebels" to Kingdom Come. And one of the top beneficiaries of this weaponizing orgy has been—who else—the M&A gang now known as the Islamic State of the Iraq and Levant.

Let's hit them with our option

Every grain of sand in the Syrian-Iraqi desert knows that the "rebels" who really matter in fighting terms in Syria are from Jabhat al-Nusra—hundreds of transnationals fond of beheading and suicide bombings.

They control, for instance, a few important suburbs of Aleppo. They've perpetrated scores of kidnappings, torture and summary executions. Crucially, they killed a lot of civilians. And they want to impose no-compromise, hardcore sharia law. No wonder middle-class, educated Syrians fear them more than anything lethal the government might resort to.

Al-Baghdadi admitted the obvious: Syrian jihadis are an annex to Iraqi jihadis, from whom, crucially, they have been receiving on-the-ground battle experience. After all, it was these hardcore Iraqis who fought the Americans, especially from 2004 to 2007. The plum tomato in the kebab is that al-Nusra itself was founded by Sunni Syrians fighting alongside Sunni Iraqis in Iraq.

Then there's what the House of Saud is up to. The Saudis are competing in a regional marathon against al-Qaeda to see who enrolls more Sunni fanatics to fight those apostate Iranians, both in Iraq and the northern Levant. The House of Saud loves any jihadi, local or transnational, as long as he does not raise hell inside Saudi Arabia.

The alphabet soup of US intel agencies should know all that by now; otherwise suspicion that they spent all this time watching Monty Python reruns will be proven correct. Reason seemed to have prevailed when a puzzled State Department, via Secretary John Kerry, reversed Hillary Clinton's Artemis syndrome and last month called for the Assad regime and the "rebels" to negotiate—anything—although he also had the temerity to proclaim there are "moderates" among the jihadis.

But then, earlier this week in Jerusalem, just as the jihadi merger and acquisition was about to be announced in Syria/Iraq, Kerry insisted that for the Obama administration "no option is off the table" in terms of a US attack on—Iran.

Abandon all hope all you geopolitical dwellers in this valley of tears. The State Department does remain as puzzled as ever, as no rational adults seem to be able to distinguish between hardcore Sunni jihadis—of the 9/11 kind—and "axis of evil" Iranians.

The Europeans at least seem to be having second thoughts. The French announced this week they want to convince the European Union and the UN Security Council to brand Jabhat al-Nusra as a "terrorist organization." Yet everybody runs for cover when the question of what happens to the weaponizing of the Syrian "rebels" arises; it's obvious that Jabhat al-Nusra is having a ball with the status quo.

And still, next week, they will meet again—the main producers of this ghastly Z-movie, *Regime Change Special Ops*, plus some marginal players. It will be the US, the Brits and the French, Turkey, Germany, Italy, Jordan, the UAE, Qatar and Saudi Arabia. They will agree to keep the weaponizing going—and actually turbo-charge it.

So what is the CIA doing in all this mess? Well, hoping it gets messier, by supporting Baghdad-approved Shi'ite Iraqi militias to go after the jihadi superstars of the Islamic State of Iraq and the Levant. Iraqi Prime Minister al-Maliki even asked for CIA drones to bomb them to paradise. No luck—for now.

Baghdad has seen the writing on the wall—a direct consequence of the divide and rule, Sunni-against-Shi'ite games the Americans have been encouraging for 10 years now; the next stage is set for a civil war, Syria-style, in Iraq. Iraqi intelligence is seriously infiltrated by Islamic State of Iraq jihadis. There are no desert borders to speak of; Anbar province is watching what's unfolding in Syria as a dress rehearsal for what will happen in Iraq.

It's as if the brand new Islamic State of Iraq and the Levant cannot wait for Iraq to be back to that sinister, gruesome period between 2004 and 2008, when the body count could make Bruce Willis cringe. So what's a Pentagon in retreat to do? Shock and awe them all over again? Oh, no; this option is not for Iraq or the Islamic Emirate of Syriastan; it's only on the table for Iran.

April 2013

How Bowiemania buries Thatcherism

She'll come, she'll go
She'll lay belief on you
But she won't stake her life on you
How can life become her point of view?

- David Bowie, *Lady Grinning Soul*

When the tone of the music changes
The walls of the city shake.

- Plato, *The Republic*

There's a brand new dance but I don't know its name/that people from bad homes do again and again/It's big and it's bland full of tension and fear/They do it over there but we don't do it here. Tension and fear; oh, that's so Europe 2013. But people from bad homes, you bet they do it over here; it's the Ziggy plays Maggie dance.

The Roving Eye landed in London a few days ago smack in the middle of Thatcherism hysteria. Digital Fleet Street is agog; Baroness Thatcher's funeral today will be "beamed to millions." The BBC—caught in yet another scandal, this time over an "undercover" trip to North Korea risking the lives of London School of Economics students—provides the only live, no commercial breaks coverage on that relic of the past, terrestrial TV. No match for phone hacking enabler Rupert Murdoch's swirling Skycopter shots. Or even crypto-glamorous Pentagon/State Department stenographer Christiane Amanpour anchoring CNN's coverage from New York.

The royal family doesn't like it one bit; this whole affair is way over the top. Big Ben and the Great Clock at Westminster will be silenced. The last time that happened was for Winston Churchill's funeral in 1965. This funeral though, contrary to rumors, won't be privatized. And Prime Minister David of Arabia Cameron is getting no bounce; only 16% of Britons believe he is Thatcher's heir. Iraq war enabler Tony Blair fared a hefty 17%. Elsewhere, no Starman is waiting in the sky. He wouldn't like to come and meet us. Even though he'd blow our minds.

And all the fat-skinny people, and all the tall-short people/and all the no-bo-dy people, and all the somebody people, all yearning to be crammed inside St Paul's Cathedral. With only 50 spots assigned for reporters, The Roving Eye decided to watch it from the red zone, also known as London's police- and CCTV-saturated streets, which after Boston are under an even thicker cloud of paranoia.

All across town, *under the moonlight, the serious moonlight,* lies an Orwellian spidery web of censorship; concentric circles of media silencing; thundering propaganda. Antidote, in preparation for the funeral; a mock funeral—what else?

One more weekend/ of lights and evening faces/ fast food, living nostalgia. Trafalgar Square, a miserable Saturday evening. Over 3,000 people from all corners of the UK. Ding Dong, The Witch is Dead—they celebrated. Just like supporters of Liverpool football club have been doing for quite a while.

Police in the thousands. A virtual media blackout. Georgie Sutcliffe, actress and serious candidate for Queen of Soho, knocks on the door of a satellite truck and asks, "Who you're with?" Someone mutters "Sky" in horror, as if a Murdoch outfit was caught in an act of sabotage. After all, the British ruling class must be protected at all costs.

Look out you rock'n rollers/pretty soon you're gonna get older. So what's an older rock'n roller to do? The Roving Eye, a former London resident and a former music writer, meets his roving son—born in the early years of Thatcherism—and the destination had to be the venerable Victoria and Albert, one of the world's foremost museums, for the David Bowie Is exhibition. Watch out. It's Ziggy against Maggie. *We are the goon squad and we're coming to town. Beep-Beep.*

Your circuit's dead, there's something wrong

Margaret Thatcher was in power from May 4, 1979 to November 28, 1990. London pub lore rules that after leaving Somerville College in Oxford, she was a bit lost, on a T S Eliot-style "I have measured my life with coffee spoons" daze, clutching a dog-eared copy of an Ayn Rand book, when she was spotted by a visiting Chicago academic superstar by the name of Milton Friedman. He fell in love with her ankles—and the rest is (neoliberal) history, with the crucial footnote that her path to 10 Downing Street was mostly paved by millions of pounds courtesy of businessman hubby Denis.

She may not have been your average bag lady of Brit street mythology. She was certainly imprinted with the cosmology of the ultimate shopkeeper—courtesy of Dad's little grocery store in nondescript Grantham. But most of all she was the ultimate frugal housewife responsible for creating a nation of homeowners. Well, at least quite a few; 13.4 million by the end of the 1980s, compared to 10.2 million early in the decade.

If you were in a council tenancy you could—for the first time ever—buy your home at a huge discount, and run straight into mortgage hell. It was this housing boom—debt boom, actually—that along with financial liberalization turbocharged the consumer boom of the early 2000s. Then all went bust. The Sex Pistols, only four years after *Ziggy played guitar* had already prophesied it way back in 1976, in *Anarchy in the UK*; your future dream is a shopping scheme. *I thought it was the UK/ or just another country/another council tenancy.*

And even before that, in 1974, post-Spiders from Mars reconverted Diamond Dogs Bowie had already seen it: In the year of the scavenger, the season of the bitch/ sashay on the boardwalk, scurry to the ditch/ just another future song, lonely little kitsch/ (There's gonna be sorrow), try and wake up tomorrow. Talk about a preview of an inevitable social collapse.

During the Thatcher 1980s (the season of Queen bitch?), median household income grew by 26%. But for families at the bottom 10%, it grew by only 4.6%. The top 10% did way better. Child poverty almost doubled—reaching 3.3 million. Thatcher even privatized milk for children. The number of poor pensioners exploded to 4.1 million. Public spending was 44.6% of GDP in 1979. By 1990, it had been reduced to 39.1%. Now it's up again at 46.2%. *Oh don't lean on me, man,/ Cause you can't afford the ticket.*

The key legacy of all this is deindustrialization; including manufacturing, industry in Britain was 40% of GDP in 1979; it had fallen to 34% in 1990. Now it's at less than a paltry 22%. And to think that pints and pints of neoliberalism and extreme social conservatism, plus extra vodka shots of "traditional moral values," ended up generating masses of unemployed. *Oh you pretty things/Don't you know you're driving your/Mamas and papas insane?*

Ground control to Major Maggie

David Bowie is Byronesque, Baudelairean, Oscar Wildean, a man of theater, lover of masks, master of artifice and a dandy supreme. He is everything a cut-up can carve up—out of random words or random programming—as shown in the V&A exhibition. Compared to Thatcher, he *is* indeed a Spider from Mars.

The cut-up—fast, asymmetrical jump cuts in the fabric of time—are the essence of Bowie's creativity, his eternal legacy. As a post-Dada experiment that William Burroughs brilliantly summarized as "a new dimension into writing enabling the writer to turn images in cinematic variations," cut-up techniques perfectly suited, as Bowie himself admitted, his fragmented consciousness (and the minds of millions around the world).

So there I was at the V&A, looking for a Ziggy playing Maggie crossover. It had to be the video for *Boys Keep Swinging*, a song on *Lodger* (1979), the final album in Bowie and Eno's Berlin Trilogy, which came out just as Maggie was coming to power. Here is Bowie as icy Valkyrie, Lauren Bacall, Bette Davis, Katharine Hepburn, Marlene Dietrich, and the ultimate Queen Bitch; as the inimitable Camille Paglia puts it in her catalogue essay, it's Bowie penetrating "the cold masculine soul and monstrous lust for power of the great female stars." Ziggy playing Maggie—and she didn't even know it.

And then there's Bowie as Pierrot—the classic 17th century *commedia dell'arte* character—in the still mesmerizing video for *Ashes to Ashes* (a phrase straight from the classic Anglican funeral.)

And then there's the Lady Grinning Soul; a mix of Circe, Calypso, Carmen, Judith (the Klimt version) and Lulu. Maggie may have been no *femme fatale*. But socially, "she will be your living end."

Not for Young Americans (*I got a suite and you got defeat*)—and older Americans as well. Vast swathes of the US—where the Iron Lady is hailed as some Brit Statue of Liberty, a beacon of "freedom and democracy"—have now been taken over by Thatcher's children, ruthlessly using good ol' class struggle against state, and even private sector, working families.

Affable Barry, the US president, also known as Double O Bama with a license to kill (list), has sung the Iron Lady's praises as if she was Dame Judi Dench on a James Bond franchise. The rest of the world, as usual, knows better. She was an enthusiastic supporter of apartheid; branded Nelson Mandela as a "terrorist"; detested "alien cultures,"[24] supported the Khmer Rouge in Cambodia; and was so cozy with Chilean mass murderer Augusto Pinochet that she hosted him when he was trying to flee his heavy load. All across Latin America, her *Fame, what's your name?* may barely be hinted at here.[25] The custard in the rhubarb pie was a nasty, military coup-loving son.[26]

A Thatcherism (and its side effects) roadmap would have to include Stephen Frears's *My Beautiful Launderette* (1985), Ken Loach's *Riff-Raff* (1991), and endless reruns of the cocaine-turbocharged *The Tube* on Channel 4. On pop music, if the Spice Girls later configured themselves as Thatcherism's spitting image, the aversion is best expressed by Elvis Costello in *Tramp the Dirt Down*. The Cure played Buenos Aires last Friday. Look at Robert Smith's guitar; the aversion is perennial. And packaging the whole zeitgeist, as a narrative still nothing beats *Money* by Martin Amis (1985).

But the film is a saddening bore/ cause I wrote it ten times or more/it's about to be writ again./ And I ask you to focus on this piece by Will Hutton, former editor of the Observer. Post-Thatcherism is all here; the seeds of the current despair—provoked by a monstrous 3D bubble of credit,

---

[24] Thatcher and the Inner City Riots, Huffington Post, April 16, 2013.
[25] Why Thatcher's shadow still lingers over Latin America, Al Jazeera, April 15, 2013.
[26] Margaret Thatcher 'gave her approval' to her son Mark's failed coup attempt in Equatorial Guinea, The Guardian, April 14, 2013.

banking and property—were planted in 1979. Financial greed up, investment/innovation down.

So much for "labor market flexibility"; inequality—exacerbated by the Big Bang of 1986, which consolidated the City of London as the center of a global financial boom—is now spelled as Doom and Gloom. Worse, actually, than in 1990. *Perhaps you're smiling now, smiling through this darkness/ But all I have to give is guilt for dreaming.*

Anger? Not really. *Waiting so long, I've been waiting so, waiting so/Look back in anger, driven by the night.* There was hardly any anger, for instance, in 1997; everyone was looking back towards Swingin' London, to be re-enacted by a Tony Blair winning by a landslide; but he lost the plot right away, and later would shrink to the sad, one-trick pony legacy of a vacuous warmonger.

I thought you died alone, a long, long time ago/Oh no, not me, I never lost control./ You're face to face/ With the man who sold the world.

It's time to leave the capsule if you dare

Europe 2013, full of tension and fear. *All the young dudes/ carry the news.* Civil rights are melting down, melting down. Thatcherism's trademark class struggle—Divide and Rule the disparate tribes—ended up fragmenting Britain's social tissue beyond repair. There may be the odd *brother back at home with his Beatles and his Stones/we never got it off on that revolution stuff/what a drag, too many snags.* But across the fence, *one still may find these children that you spit on/as they try to change their worlds/ they're quite aware of what they're going through.*

In a fabulous PR coup—a single coming out of nowhere on his 66th birthday this past January, after 10 years of silence—Bowie tried to answer the question *Where Are We Now?*. He looks back on his 1970s Berlin days—which yielded the fabulous trilogy of *Low*, *Heroes* and *Lodger*. By itself, in terms of shaping the Western zeitgeist, the trilogy has been as influential as the fall of the Berlin Wall. *Sometimes you get so lonely/sometimes you get nowhere/I've lived all over the world/I've lived every place.*

In a curioser and curioser way, Bowie had been silent all through the Global War on Terror (GWOT) years. But *boys keep swinging, boys always work it out*—even as terror, including shadow and drone wars, has become the new normal.

> *How to break out? Still, in this valley of unequal tears,*
> *O no love! You're not alone*
> *No matter what or who you've been*
> *No matter when or where you've seen*
> *All the knives seem to lacerate your brain*
> *I've had my share, I'll help you with the pain*
> *You're not alone.*

Knives now lacerate the Facebook/Google generation's brains—from orphans of the true Arab Spring to legions of unemployed-for-life Europeans. There's hardly any evidence that *we can beat them/ for ever and ever*. After all, *We're nothing, and nothing will help us.* But the old order won't get away with it. *Cause we can be heroes/ just for one day.*

April 2013

Post-History Strip Tease

How cozy it would be to summon the retro-spirit of Burt Bacharach to define our geopolitical future and start singing, "What the world needs now / is love, sweet love."

Sorry to scratch the vinyl. We interrupt this lovey-dovey to bring you breaking news. You have been catapulted to the age of the new Hobbesian "hero"—digital and virtual as well as physical.

Casino capitalism—aka turbocharged neoliberalism—is ruthlessly destroying the last vestiges of the welfare state and the egalitarian consensus in the industrialized West, possibly with the odd Scandinavian exception. It has established a "New Normal" consensus, intruding into private lives, dominating the political debate and institutionalizing for good the marketization of life itself—the final act of fierce corporate exploitation of natural resources, land and cheap labor.

Integration, socialization and multiculturalism are being corroded by disintegration, segregation, and widespread de-socialization—a direct consequence of the David Harvey-coined notion of "dis-accumulation" (society devouring its own).

This state of things is what Flemish philosopher and art historian Lieven De Cauter, in his book *Entropic Empire*, calls "the Mad Max phase of globalization."

It is a Hobbesian world, a latent global civil war, a war of all against all; the economic haves against the have-nots; intolerant Wahhabis against "apostate" Shi'ites; the children of the Enlightenment against all manner of fundamentalists; the Pentagon militarization of Africa against Chinese mercantilism.

The disintegration and balkanization of Iraq, detonated by the Pentagon's Shock and Awe 10 years ago, was a sort of prelude for this Brave New Disorder. The neocon worldview, from 2001 to 2008, advanced the project with its ideology of Let's Finish Off The State, everywhere; once again Iraq was the best example. But from bombing a sovereign nation back to the Stone Age, the project moved to civil war engineering—as in Libya and, hopefully for the engineers, Syria.

When we have armchair analysts, influential or otherwise, paid by flush foundations—usually in the US but also in Western Europe—pontificating about "chaos and anarchy," they are just reinforcing a self-fulfilling prophecy. If "chaos and anarchy" turns them on, it's because they are just reflecting the predominant libidinal economy, from reality TV to all sorts of what De Cauter describes as "psychotic games"—inside a room, inside an octagon, inside an island or virtually inside a digital box.

So welcome to the geopolitics of the young 21st century: an age of non-stop war (virtualized or not), sharp polarization and a pile-up of catastrophies.

After Hegel, Marx and that mediocre functionary of Empire, Fukuyama; but also after brilliant deconstructions by Gianni Vattimo, Baudrillard or Giorgio Agamben, this is what we get.

For Marx the end of history was a classless society. How romantic. Instead, in the second half of the 20th century, capitalism married Western liberal democracy till death do them part. Well, death is now upon them both. The Red Dragon, as in China, has joined the party and came up with a new toy; single-party neoliberalism.

An individualistic, self-indulgent, passive, easily controllable consumer drowned in a warped form of democracy that basically favors insiders—and very wealthy players; how could that be a humanist ideal? Yet the PR was so good that this is what legions in Asia, Africa, the Middle East and South America aspire to. But it's still not enough for the geoeconomic Masters of the Universe.

Thus post-history as the ultimate reality show. And war neoliberalism as its favorite weapon.

Choose your camp

We are now familiar with Giorgio Agamben's paradigm of the state of emergency—or state of exception. The ultimate example, until the mid-20th century, was the concentration camp. But post-history is more creative.

We have the Muslim-only concentration camp—as in Guantanamo. We have the simulacrum of a concentration camp—as in Palestine, which is virtually walled and under 24/7 surveillance, and where "the law" is dictated by an occupying power. And we have what happened—as a dry run—last week in Boston; the euphemistic "lockdown," which is a suspension of the law to the benefit of martial law; no freedom of movement, no cell phone network, and you if you go the corner shop to buy a soft drink you may be shot. A whole city in the industrialized North turned into a high-tech concentration camp.

Agamben talked about the state of exception as a top-down excess of sovereignty, and the state of nature—as in Hobbes—as a bottom-up absence of sovereignty. After the Global War on Terror (GWOT), which, despite whatever the Pentagon says, is indeed eternal (or The Long War, as defined in 2002, and part of the Pentagon doctrine of Full Spectrum Dominance), we can talk about a merger.

The war on terror, seductively normalized by the Obama administration, was and remains a global state of exception, even though trappings come and go; the Patriot Act; shadowy executive orders; torture—a recent US bipartisan panel accused all top officials of the George W Bush administration of torture; extraordinary rendition, with which secular then allies of the West such as Libya and Syria collaborated, not to mention Eastern European nations and the usual Arab puppets, Egypt under Mubarak included; and the sprawling apparatus of homeland security.

As for a real concentration camp, once again we don't need to look further than Guantanamo—which, contrary to Obama's campaign promise, will remain open indefinitely, as well as some among the vast number of Bush-era CIA "secret" prisons.

In all these cases whatever happens to social life—suspension, dissolution, balkanization, implosion, a state of emergency—what happens to normal citizens is that citizenship (*bios*) evaporates. But ruling elites—political, economic, financial—don't care about citizenship. They're only interested in passive consumers.

Pick your dystopia

The dystopias of the New Global Disorder are all being normalized. We're familiar with state terrorism—as in the CIA's "secret" drone war over tribal areas in Pakistan, in Yemen, Somalia and soon in other African latitudes. And we're also familiar with non-state terrorism, as applied by that nebula that we in the West describe as "al-Qaeda," with its myriad franchises and copycats.

We have a bunch of hyper-states—such as the US, China and Russia and the EU as whole—and myriad infra-states or failed states, some by design (Libya, and Syria is on the way), as well as satellite states, some essential to the Western-controlled system such as the Gulf Counter-Revolution Club (GCC—Gulf Cooperation Council).

It's always enlightening to look back at how the Pentagon interprets this world. Here we find an "integrating core" opposed to a "non-integrated gap." The "core" is what matters, in this case North America and most, but not all, of the EU. Sheepish, passive populations, with a consumer elite—the fast, mobile elites of liquid modernity, described by Bauman—and a vast mass of surviving toilers, a great deal of them expendable (as the millions of European victims of troika austerity policies who will never find a decent job again).

For the non-integrated gap, it's Hobbes all the way. In the case of Africa—until virtually yesterday derided as a black hole—there's an added geopolitical power play; how to counter-attack the extraordinary penetration of Chinese mercantilism over the last decade. The Pentagon's response is to deploy AFRICOM everywhere; to subdue nations that are too independent, such as Libya; and in the case of the French elite, also on the bandwagon, to try to regain some imperial muscle in Mali, profiting exactly from the implosion and balkanization of Libya.

The look of post-history, its aesthetic ideal, is the city as theme park. Los Angeles may have been the archetype but the best examples are Las Vegas, Dubai and Macao. In the absence of Umberto Eco and Baudrillard, who reveled in the mirror images of simulacra, we may follow master architect Rem Koolhaas—a keen observer of the urban dementia in southern China—to learn what junk space is all about.

Then there's the security obsession—from cities like London turning into a sprawling version of Bentham's Panopticon to the pathetic strip tease ritual at every airport, not to mention the gated condo or "community," more like gated atoms, as the emblem of capsular civilization. Guerrilla counter-attacks, though, may be as lethal as Sunni Iraqis fighting the Americans in the "triangle of death" in the mid-2000s. In Sao Paulo, Brazil—the ultimate violent megalopolis—gangs "clone" cars and license plates, fool security at the door of gated condos, drive to the garage, and proceed to systematically rob each apartment in every floor.

You're history

Conceptually, post-history cuts all corners. The flow of history is degraded as fake. Simulacrum trumps reality. We see history repeating not as tragedy and farce but as a double farce; an overlapping example is jihadis in Syria weaponized just like the former "freedom fighters" in Afghanistan in the 1980s anti-Soviet jihad conflating with the Western gang in the UN Security Council trying to apply to Syria what they got away with in Libya; regime change.

We also have history repeating itself as cloning; neoliberalism with Chinese characteristics beating the West in its industrialization game—in terms of speed—while at the same time repeating the same mistakes, from the mindless excesses of an acquisition mentality to no respect for the environment.

It goes without saying that post-history buries the Enlightenment—as favoring the emergence of all sorts of fundamentalisms. So it had also to bury international law; from bypassing the UN to launch a war on Iraq in 2003 to using a UN resolution to launch a war on Libya in 2011. And now Britain and France are taking no prisoners trying to bypass the UN or even NATO itself and weaponize the "rebels" in Syria.

So we have a New Medievalism that cannot but fit wealthy neo-theocracy—as in Saudi Arabia and Qatar; because they are Western allies, or puppets, internally they may remain medieval. Superimposed, we have the politics of fear—which essentially rules Fortress America and Fortress

Europe; fear of The Other, which can be occasionally Asian but most of the time Islamic.

What we don't have is a political/philosophical vision of the future. Or a historical political program; political parties are only worried about winning the next election.

How would a post-state system look like? Independent minds don't trust mammoth, asymmetrical, wobbly blocs like the EU, or the G-20, or even aspiring multipolars such as the BRICS (Brazil, Russia, India, China, South Africa—which still do not represent a real alternative to the Western-controlled system). No one is thinking in terms of a structural mutation of the system. Marx was beyond right on this: what determines history are objective, concrete, palpable processes—some of them very complex—affecting the economic and technological infrastructure.

What is possible to infer is that the real historical subject from now on is technology—as Jean-Francois Lyotard and Paul Virilio were already conceptualizing in the 1980s and 1990s. Technology will keep advancing way beyond the capitalist system. Techno-science is on the driving seat of history. But that also means war.

War and technology are Siamese twins; virtually all technology gets going as military technology. The best example is how the Internet completely changed our lives, with immense geoeconomic and political ramifications; Beijing, in a 2010 white paper, may have hailed the Internet as a "crystallization of human wisdom," but no state filters more information on the Internet than China. Pushing the scenario to a dystopian limit, Google's Eric Schmidt argues, correctly, that with a flip of a switch, soon an entire country could even disappear from the Internet.

So, essentially, we may forget about a utopian regression to the state of the tribal nomad—as much as we may be fascinated by them, be they in Africa or in the Wakhan corridor in Tajikistan. If we survey the geopolitical landscape from Ground Zero to Boston, the only "models" are declinations of entropy.

Meet the neoliberal Adam

Now for post-history's favorite weapon: war neoliberalism. The best analysis these past few years by far is to be found in French geostrategist Alain Joxe's book Les Guerres de L'Empire Global.

Joxe mixes it all up, because it is all interconnected—the eurocrisis, the European debt crisis, occupations and wars, restriction of civil liberties, totally corrupted elites—to unmask the project of Neoliberalism's Global Empire, which goes way beyond the American Empire.

Financialization's ultimate goal is unlimited accumulation of profit—a system where the wealthy get much wealthier and the poor get literally nothing (or, at best austerity). The real-life Masters of the Universe are a denationalized rentier class—cannot even call them noblesse, because mostly their absence of taste and critical sense is appalling, as in purveyors of unabashed bling bling. What they do is to the benefit of corporations, instead of the protecting functions of states. In this state of things military adventures become police doctrine. And a new information technology—from drones to "special" munitions—can be used against popular movements, not only in the South but also the North.

Joxe is able to show how a technological revolution led at the same time to the IT management of that goddess, The Market, as well as the robotization of war. So here we have a mix of economic, military and technological mutations, in parallel, leading to an acceleration of decisions that totally pulverize the long span of politics, generating a system incapable of regulating either finance or violence. Between the dictatorship of the "markets" and social democracy, guess who's winning hands down.

In fact, Slavoj Zizek had already posed the key question, at least in terms of the Decline of the West. The (closet) winner is in fact "capitalism with Asian values'—which, of course, has nothing to do with Asian people and everything to do with the clear and present tendency of contemporary capitalism to limit or even suspend democracy." (See here.)

French philosopher Jean Claude Michea takes the political analysis further. He argues that post-modern politics has become in fact a negative art—defining the least bad society possible. That's how liberalism—which shaped modern Western civilization—became, as neoliberalism, the "politics of lesser evil." Well, "lesser evil" for who's in control, of course, and damn the rest.

In another crucial book, Michea comes up with the delightful metaphor of the neoliberal Adam as the new Orpheus, condemned to escalate the path of Progress with no authorization to look back.

Not many contemporary thinkers are equipped to thrash Left and Right in equally devastating measure. Michea tells us that both Left and Right have submitted to the original myth of capitalist thinking; this "noir anthropology" that makes Man an egoist by nature. And he asks how could the institutionalized Left have abandoned the ambition of a just, decent society—or how the neoliberal wolf has wreaked havoc among the socialist sheep.

Beyond neoliberalism and/or a desire for social democracy, what the reality show tells us is that an internecine global civil war is at hand—the hypothesis I explored in my 2007 book *Globalistan*. When we mix Washington's pivoting to Asia; the obsession with regime change in Iran; the fear of Western elites with the ascension of China; the real Arab Spring, which has not even started, via young generations who want political participation but without being constrained by religious fundamentalism; Muslim resentment against what is perceived as a New Crusade against them; the growth of neo-fascism in Europe; and the advanced pauperization of the Western middle class, it's hard to think about love.

And still—Burt Bacharach to the rescue—that's exactly what the world needs now.

April 2013

Catfight—and it's US vs EU

Lovers of turbo-neoliberalism, rejoice—and take your bottles of Moet to a prime ringside seat; there won't be a nastier catfight this summer than the opening rounds opposing two Western giants. Forget about the Pentagon "pivoting" to Asia without ever abandoning the Middle East; nothing compares with this voyage in the entrails of turbo-capitalism, worthy of a neo-Balzac.

We're talking about a new Holy Grail—a free-market deal between the United States and the European Union; the advent of a giant, internal transatlantic market (25% of global exports, 31% of global imports, 57% of foreign investment), where goods and services (but not people) will "freely" circulate, something that in theory will lead Europe out of its current funk.

The problem is that to reach this Brave New World presided by the Market Goddess, Europe will have to renounce some of its quite complex juridical, environmental, cultural and health norms.

In that Kafkaesque/Orwellian bureaucratic paradise also known as Brussels, hordes of faceless equivalents of the bowler hat men in a Magritte painting openly complain about this "adventure"; there's a growing consensus Europe has everything to lose and little to gain out of it, in contrast with the much-derided enemies of the European integration, as in the fanatics of an "pro-American" and "ultra-liberal" Europe.

That yellow peril again

It gets curioser and curioser when one observes that the great majority of European nations actually have wanted a free-market deal for quite a while, unlike the much more protectionist US. By now, at least officially, not a single EU nation is opposed to the deal. Here's the non-official reason; none can afford to be blamed an enemy of the United States.

The European Commission (EC) estimates that the gross national product growth of the EU as a whole will grow by 0.5%—not exactly a Chinese target. The Americans, on the other hand, are way more excited; the US Senate estimates that without custom duties, US exports to Europe will grow by almost 20%.

The meat of the matter in clinching the deal will be harmonizing rules that are blamed for blocking the much-vaunted totally free circulation of goods. "Harmonizing" means diluting European rules. And there's the rub; Washington does not want just a transatlantic deal. The final countdown is to set in stone a global free-for-all that would later be imposed everywhere; that's code for totally opening the Chinese market, with absolutely no restrictions, for Western corporations.

The German Marshall Fund of the United States goes straight to the point; Western capitalism must remain the universal norm, against the "threat" of state-managed Chinese capitalism. Reduced to ashes is the irony that Chinese capitalism has been—and will continue to be—the savior in the massive ongoing crisis of Western capitalism.

The US-EU deal is also supposed to be the icing on a cake of deals already being struck by the US with individual nations in Asia. There's absolutely no question about who the stronger side is. US President Barack Obama is already engaged in high-stakes PR, spinning on every possible occasion that Europe has been in trouble trying to find a recipe for growth. And the US may count on fifth column elements such as the European Commissioner for Commerce, Karel De Gucht, for whom the French—who defend a lot of exceptions—are already isolated.

Make no mistake; Washington will go for broke, *Iron Man 3*-style—as in smashing European norms of sanitation and phyto-sanitation, and "liberalizing" food, everything genetically modified from meat enhanced with hormones to chlorine chicken. The pesky rules established by the faceless men in Brussels have been routinely derided in Washington as "non-scientific," unlike the American non-rules.

The ultimate bowler hat man

Startled European citizens are only now coming to grips with the fact that the EU proposed the deal to the US—and not the other way around. EU here means the European Commission. And that's where the juice hits the throat; it's all about the ambition of one man (a Portuguese) against the pride of a whole country (France).

Compounded to the fact that the negotiation was personally greenlighted by Obama, and with the US Congress interfering at every level, the bottom line is that for the Americans, "everything is on the table"—code for we want it all, and we're willing to give no ground.

France—already supported by the ministers of culture of 12 nations—wants the audiovisual industry to be excluded from all negotiations, in the name of its much-prized "cultural exception." This is one of the few countries in the world—China is a different matter altogether—not totally swamped by Hollywood products.

If that's not the case, Paris will veto everything—even if, off the record, French officials admit they don't have the power to veto anything; the French corporate world also badly wants the deal.

Still, Paris will battle for everything ranging from the "cultural exception" to the most crucial sanitary/environmental norms. It will be joined by Italy on many fronts; there's already open revolt in sublimely artisanal Italy about a bleak future where people all over the world will be consuming Made-in-USA Parmesan cheese, Parma ham and Brunello wines.

On a different front, it's certain that Washington will not open the US market to European financial services or maritime transportation. That's just one example of how much Europe has to lose and practically nothing to gain.

In the end it all amounts to the blind ambition of an astonishing mediocre European career functionary—the Portuguese EC head, Jose Manuel Barroso. Barroso expects to get a mandate to negotiate in the name of all member-states on June 14. And he expects the negotiations to finish before the end of his current mandate, on November 2014.

Some audibly furious EU diplomats confirmed off the record to *Asia Times Online* that Barroso mounted this formidable operation virtually by himself, eyeing a handsome future reward from his masters—in Brussels? Forget it; Washington. Barroso wants either to become the secretary general of either the UN or NATO. Neither of these posts can be had without Washington's green light.

That would explain Barroso's chief of cabinet being nominated EU ambassador in Washington, furiously lobbying the Americans alongside Portugal's ambassador to the US and Portugal's ambassador to the EU.

All bets are off on the winner of this monstrous catfight. EU member-states may vote against their own interests; but another thing entirely would be an overwhelming eruption of anger by already beleaguered Eu ropean citizens. This new saga of Western turbo-capitalism has all the elements to be, well, quite revolutionary.

May 2013

Pipelineistan and the New Silk Road(s)

Ask Western elites; oh, those were the days, in the 17th century, when the rise of European sea powers led to the collapse of the caravan trade and the end of the Silk Road as Europe found a cheaper—and safer—way of trading between East and West.

Now, centuries after Tang armies establishing nodes all over Central Asia as far as Khorasan in northeast Iran, the 21st century Silk Road(s) are back. The camels now wear iPads, with the Persian Gulf as a high-tech caravanserai.

Si chou zhi lu ("Silk Road" in Mandarin). What's in a name? Trouble. A lot of trouble. At least if you ask the Pentagon, which places most of these roads—from the Persian Gulf to Central Asia and even the South China Sea—smack in the middle of its famous "arc of instability." In parallel, in rising Eastern latitudes, it's Dream Team time: and the name of the game is Eurasian integration.

Who's the real Iron Man in this picture? It has to be Beijing Man, expanding his economy at a dizzying pace, securing all the resources he needs—not only oil and gas but by being the world's largest consumer of aluminum, copper, lead, nickel, zinc, tin, iron ore—and breathlessly moving global power tectonic plates.

So no wonder Beijing is appalled by the carnage/civil war forced upon Syria by foreign actors; that's bad for business. The PRC has historically viewed Syria as a *ning jiu li*—a cohesive force in the Arab world—in many aspects the epicenter of the Arab world, and much more progressive, socially, than the Persian Gulf. And while Beijing always praised

Syria's stability, the Syrian establishment had been in thrall to China's economic miracle.

When the saints go marchin' in

What we are experiencing now could be described as The Long March West (from the point of view of Beijing) versus The Short March East, as in Pivoting to Asia (from the point of view of Washington).

But it's not pivoting in the sense of the best the US has to offer—the university-based research system absorbing talent from all over; the drive to dare, to risk, to take a second chance; that vortex of invention—new companies, new industries, new products.

In this vast chessboard where the complex, intertwined geoeconomic competition known as the New Great Game in Eurasia is being played, both kings are easy to identify: Pipelineistan, and the multiple intersections of the 21st century Silk Road. Call them the new iron and steel Silk Roads.

Across this immense Eurasian grid, speed trumps institutional politics. Nobody—from the European Union to the Shanghai Cooperation Organization (SCO)—is on top of all that's going on; we would need a 4D version of the pipeline map room at Gazprom's headquarters in Moscow, a Star Wars version of the London Underground map.

What we can do is set out on a lightning quick road trip. Starting with Turkey, a NATO and Group of 20 member—keen to bill itself as the energy crossroads for Caspian oil, Iraqi oil, and now Kurdistan oil in northern Iraq.

Turkey has gone totally New Silk Road. Last month, it officially became a dialogue partner of the SCO. Why dream of entering a sinking

EU? No. Better reinforce a political and trading partnership with Moscow and Beijing—not to mention the Central Asian "stans."

Now that's certainly a more sound application of Foreign Minister Davotuglu's "strategic depth" than that muddled "logistical support" for regime change in Syria.

Then there's the Southeast Anatolia Project, and the Ataturk Dam—not very far, by the way, from the Syrian border. The Euphrates river dam system—planned in the 1970s—is also propelling Turkey as a great power in the Arab Middle East. Inescapable, when you can divert as much as 90% of Iraq's and 40% of Syria's water power.

But only Iran can enable Turkey to fulfill its core strategic goal—as in the prime energy crossroads from East to West—because that would mean Turkey as the prime mover of oil and gas from Iran to Europe. If or when that happens, Turkey will be way more important than just a land bridge. Turkey and Iran may be competitors but more than ever they need to be allies.

Most of all what happens in Iran and to Iran will determine which way the wind will blow in Eurasia. Iran strategically straddles Mesopotamia, Anatolia, the Caucasus, the Caspian Sea, Central and South Asia, the Persian Gulf, and the Arabian Sea. Iran dominates the Persian Gulf—from the Shatt al Arab to the Strait of Hormuz. Location, population, energy wealth: the absolute key to Southwest Asia. Ask Dick Cheney; no wonder for Washington this has always been the Great Prize.

Pipelineistan—from a Western point of view—has always carried an obsessive theme; how to bypass both Russia and Iran. So inevitably Pipelineistan explains a great deal about why Syria is being destroyed. Take the agreement for the US$10 billion Iran-Iraq-Syria gas pipeline that was signed in July 2012. This crucial Pipelineistan node will export gas from the South Pars field in Iran (the largest in the world, shared with Qatar), through Iraq, towards Syria, with a possible extension to Lebanon, with certified customers in Western Europe. It's what our friends in Beijing describe as a "win-win" situation.

But not for—guess who?—Turkey and Qatar. Qatar wants a rival pipeline from its North field (contiguous with Iran's South Pars field), through Saudi Arabia, Jordan, Syria and finally Turkey. Final destination: once again, Western Europe.

In terms of bypassing both Iran and Russia, the Qatari pipeline totally fits the bill, while with the Iran-Iraq-Syria pipeline, the export route may originate nowhere else than in Tartus, the Syrian port in the Eastern Mediterranean that hosts the Russian Navy. And Gazprom would certainly be part of the whole picture, from investment to distribution.

Go West, young Han

Non-stop movement in Pipelineistan, a railway frenzy, a network of underground fiber optic cables. As far as Beijing is concerned, does it need to behave as a neo-colonial power, like Europe in the past? Of course not. And unlike the US, Beijing sports no ideology. No Western liberal democracy as Promised Land. No "moral progress" in geopolitics. No missionary drive. They just buy their way in.

Thus those Himalayas of new geopolitical "facts on the ground" all across Eurasia—from deep-water ports in Myanmar to special economic zones in North Korea.

We may already glimpse the contours of a new Eurasian land bridge—including, for instance, the integration of Central Asia with Xinjiang as well as a southern Silk Road branching through Indochina, linking China to Thailand. Thus the emergence of Kunming as a crack

Chinese hub for an immense sub-region of Eurasia. We may interpret some of it as China Going West—a much more refined expansion of the original 1999 Go West campaign, which centered on Xinjiang. And we're not even talking about a Chinese trade-fueled economic renaissance of the Russian Far East.

China will be involved in the building of a high-speed railway line in Iran. And then there's China's AfPak vision: a maze of roads and pipelines connected to Indian Ocean ports linked with Central Asian roads connecting Xinjiang with Kyrgyzstan, Tajikistan and Afghanistan.

Afghanistan, India and Iran also plan to build a new Southern Silk Road, centered on Chabahar port in southeast Iran.

Eventually, Pakistan is bound to become a node of Greater China. The crucial game will be played in the Arabian Sea port of Gwadar. Beijing bets on Gwadar as a key transshipment hub linking it to Central Asia and the Gulf. Both ports—Chabahar and Gwadar—are key pawns in the New Great Game in Eurasia and also happen to be at the heart of Pipelineistan.

The Iran-Pakistan (IP) pipeline will go through Gwadar—with the distinct possibility of a Chinese-built extension all the way to Xinjiang. Gwadar might also become a terminal in case the ultimate Pipelineistan soap opera—the Turkmenistan-Afghanistan-Pakistan-India (TAPI) pipeline—is ever built. We all know it won't.

Then there's the Russia-China strategic partnership. Finally Beijing and Moscow agreed on the delivery of 38 billion cubic meters of Russian natural gas per year to China starting in 2015. That's Moscow helping Beijing to accomplish a key national security goal; the simultaneous escape from Hormuz and Malacca—not to mention a big help for China to develop its landlocked provinces.

Obviously China needs a powerful navy; 85% of Chinese imports arrive by the Indian Ocean and the South China Sea. Then there's all that oil and gas to be exploited across the South China Sea—which could become a sort of mini-Persian Gulf.

So the first step towards a Greater China would be to—peacefully—engage the whole of the South China Sea and Southeast Asia. Then to adequately protect the sea routes to the Middle East across the Indian Ocean, through which China receives oil from Angola, Sudan and Nigeria, iron ore from mines in Zambia and Gabon, copper and cobalt from mines in Democratic Republic of Congo. But more than anything China will privilege a steady network of energy supply from Myanmar, Russia, Central Asia and Iran.

Hillary's 3 am nightmare

Faced with this Eurasian integration frenzy, the US does appear like an island on the other side of the world. The US counter-strategy to all the action in Eurasia has been to designate the Indian Ocean as the new, global strategic center of gravity; that's the essence of the Obama administration's "pivoting to Asia." For the White House/Pentagon, who controls this strategic center, in theory, controls Eurasia; but if you read the fine print, rather controls Chinese energy imports from the Persian Gulf and Africa—as well as the developing South-South economic axis between China and Africa, not to mention interferes in the free-trade area between China and the Association of Southeast Asian Nations (ASEAN).

Here we find the Obama administration's Trans-Pacific Partnership (TPP) drive—that collection of shady free trade agreements shaped by 600 "secret" US corporate advisors currently being negotiated with the

Pacific Rim, including Australia, New Zealand and ASEAN members Malaysia, Singapore and Vietnam.

That may be a cool deal, for instance, to Big Pharma—smashing access to cheap generic medications in the developing world. It will be a wet dream for Wall Street finance capital gangsters—because it will allow a derivative funfest and an orgy of currency speculation. It will be a sort of financial Shock and Awe over Asia—once more with US big businesses telling governments it's our way or the highway. We may also call it the economic arm of the Obama administration's pivoting.

For a time, it seemed that Hillary Clinton had brushed up on Ancient Persia, Alexander the Great, the Mongols, Mughals, and Sikhs, and "saw the light" in Afghanistan; that's when she came up with a Washington vision of a New Silk Road (road, rail, pipelines) running through Afghanistan.

Maybe Hillary had a 3 am nightmare about the Iranian Eastern Corridor—built by India in 2008, from Chabahar to the Afghan border, roughly 200 km, and then connecting with the Zaranj-Delaram highway (also built by India) in Nimruz, in western Afghanistan, and further with the Afghan Ring Road. New Delhi, Tehran, and Kabul have planned a railway line along the entire route to facilitate trade—especially Afghan mineral wealth—to and from Central Asia.

So here we have India getting huge strategic leverage, not to mention exploring part of that $3 trillion in Afghan mineral wealth alongside China; and Afghanistan finding an access to the sea, bypassing the Pakistani grip, and once again configuring Iran as the privileged Silk Road in and out of Central Asia.

Add to Pipelineistan the Economic Cooperation Organization freight railway Istanbul-Tehran-Islamabad, already carrying $20 billion in goods a year—and counting.

The lesson here? No matter Washington's obsession in isolating Iran, India—as well as Turkey—not to mention China and Russia, would always be betting on Asian integration.

Washington's obsession with isolating Iran led, for instance, to the Bill Clinton administration embracing the Taliban in the 1990s in the hope of building TAPI. Instead of that chimera—TAPI—or that other expensive soap opera, Nabucco—gas from the Caspian shipped through the Caucasus to Turkey—Iran is the real deal to carry Turkmenistan's gas to Europe.

Talk about the Asian Energy Security Grid; all exports from gas republic Turkmenistan already go to Iran, China and Russia. And Iran and Kazakhstan are also linked by rail and pipeline—meaning Kazakhstan has a direct access to the Persian Gulf.

We all know by now how the "pivoting" follows what has been the US's strategic target in Central Asia since the first Clinton administration; to interfere in Pipelineistan not as much in terms of diversifying sources of energy for the West, but in preventing strategic victories for Russia, China and Iran.

Washington has had its own New Silk Road ideas, Hillary-style, linking Central to South Asia. None of them incorporate Iran. The only US Silk Road so far has been the Northern Distribution Network (NDN)—that logistical/military marathon snaking across Central Asia with—what else—a narrow military purpose, so the US and NATO could resupply their spectacular failure in Afghanistan bypassing "unreliable" Pakistan.

So the Big Picture, long term, indicates relentless Chinese expansion westwards—based on trade—versus a US strategy that is essentially military. What is certain is that a great escape from the Atlanticist-dominated routes of trade, commerce and finance has been on for quite some time. And the New Silk Road(s) will be built by emerging Asia—and not by a fearful, declining West.

May 2013

SEE YOU ON THE DARK SIDE

The lunatic is in my head / The lunatic is in my head
You raise the blade / you make the change
You re-arrange me 'til I'm sane.
You lock the door / And throw away the key
There's someone in my head but it's not me

- Pink Floyd, *Brain Damage*

Let's talk about PRISM. And let's see some implications of the Edward Snowden-leaked National Security Agency (NSA) Power Point presentation for Total Cyber-Domination.

What's in a name? A prism breaks light into a spectrum of color. PRISM, as expressed in its Dark-Side-of-the-Moon-ish logo, is no less than a graphic expression of the ultimate Pentagon/neocon wet dream; the Full Spectrum Dominance doctrine.

The NSA—also known as No Such Agency—is part of the Pentagon.

Full Spectrum Dominance was conceptualized in the Pentagon's 2002 Joint Vision 2020.[27] It's the Pentagon/NSA blueprint for the foreseeable future; in trademark Pentagonese, it identifies "four capabilities—"dominant maneuver, precision engagement, focused logistics and full-dimensional protection." In sum: Total Information Awareness (TIA).

Care for a drive to Utah?

---

[27] Joint Vision 2020 Emphasizes Full-spectrum Dominance, American Forces Press Service, June 2, 2000.

The new, US$2 billion NSA Utah Data Center was uncovered by *Wired* way back in March 2012.[28] Call it the Matrix—rather a key node of the Matrix. It will be up and running in September.

The Utah Matrix node is the Total Information Awareness dream come true. TIA, if anyone remembers, was a Bush 1.0 invention concocted by Defense Advanced Research Projects Agency (DARPA) that was killed by the US Congress in 2003, allegedly because it would destroy the privacy of American citizens.

Well, *iiiiit's back*—as the Utah Matrix node. And fully privatized—operated by the usual legions of contractors with top-secret clearances.

Enter—again—the privatized racket. In March, Director of National Intelligence (DNI) James Clapper flatly denied the NSA collects "any type of data at all on millions or hundreds of millions of Americans." That was a flat out lie. And Senator Dianne Feinstein let it pass.

Former NSA and DNI director Mike McConnell now happens to be vice chairman of Booz Allen Hamilton—Snowden's employer up to this week. Talk about revolving door; from the NSA to Booz Allen to DNI and back to Booz Allen. Only this year McConnell has already raked in US$1.8 million by selling Booz Allen shares and options.[29] Clapper, the current DNI, is a former Booz Allen executive.

The US government spin feels like the dark monolith in Kubrick's *2001*. PRISM is benign. PRISM is legal. It only targets non-US citizens outside of the US. Well, it "may" sweep US citizens' digital information; that's also legal but we can't tell you how.

---

[28] The NSA Is Building the Country's Biggest Spy Center (Watch What You Say), Wired, March, 2012.
[29] Booz Allen Vice Chairman McConnell, Former Government Official, Nets $1.8 Million on Stock Sales, The Daily Beast, June 11, 2013.

But then there's the mantra PRISM has been essential to foil major terrorist plots; that has been thoroughly debunked.[30] What is never acknowledged is that PRISM is TIA in action. Anyone—with the right clearance—may use TIA to amass serious inside financial information and make staggering profits. So yes, follow the money.

Snowden goes TIA

Google is adamant there is a "serious misperception" concerning PRISM, according to its chief legal officer David Drummond. Google insists "there's no lockbox, there's no backdoor" for NSA's direct access to its servers. But "legal restrictions" won't allow Google to explain how.

Unbounded by "legal restrictions," Snowden was certainly smart enough to smell a rat, major rats. After the Clapper denial, he could not possibly trust Congress. Not to mention the parroting US mainstream media. He did contact the Washington Post—but eventually settled on Glenn Greenwald, who's definitely not mainstream. The UK Guardian's position is more dubious; it badly wants to crack the American market, but at the same time solemnly ditched, even smeared, Julian Assange after it got what it wanted from him.

Snowden is surfing the PR tsunami as a master—and controlling it all the way. Yes, you do learn a thing or two at the CIA. The timing of the disclosure was a beauty; it handed Beijing the ultimate gift just as President Obama was corralling President Xi Jinping in the California summit about cyber war. As David Lindorff nailed it, [31] now Beijing simply cannot let Snowden hang dry. It's culture; it's a matter of not losing face.

---

[30] NSA surveillance played little role in foiling terror plots, experts say, The Guardian, June 12, 2013.
[31] Why is Edward Snowden in Hong Kong?, Counterpunch, June 12, 2013.

And then Snowden even doubled down—revealing the obvious; as much as Beijing, if not more, Washington hacks as hell.[32]

Following the money, the security privatization racket and Snowden's moves—all at the same time—allows for a wealth of savory scenarios... starting with selected players embedded in the NSA-centric Matrix node making a financial killing with inside information.

Snowden did not expose anything that was not already known—or at least suspected—since 2002. So it's business as usual for those running the game. The only difference is the (Digital Blackwater) Big Brother is Watching You ethos is now in the open. TIA, a bunch of wealthy investors and a sound business plan—privatized Full Spectrum Dominance—all remain in play. From now on, it's just a matter of carefully, gradually guiding US public opinion to fully "normalize" TIA. After all, we're making all these sacrifices to protect you.

June 2013

---

[32] Edward Snowden: US government has been hacking Hong Kong and China for years, South China Morning Post, June 12, 2013

THE CHIMERICA DREAM

Sun Tzu, the ancient author of The Art of War, must be throwing a rice wine party in his heavenly tomb in the wake of the shirtsleeves California love-in between President Obama and President Xi Jinping. "Know your enemy" was, it seems, the theme of the meeting. Beijing was very much aware of—and had furiously protested—Washington's deep plunge into China's computer networks over the past 15 years via a secretive NSA unit, the Office of Tailored Access Operations (with the apt acronym TAO). Yet Xi merrily allowed Obama to pontificate on hacking and cyber-theft as if China were alone on such a stage.

Enter—with perfect timing—Edward Snowden, the spy who came in from Hawaii and who has been holed up in Hong Kong since May 20th. And cut to the wickedly straight-faced, no-commentary-needed take on Obama's hacker army by Xinhua, the Chinese Communist Party's official press service. With America's dark-side-of-the-moon surveillance programs like PRISM suddenly in the global spotlight, the Chinese, long blistered by Washington's charges about hacking American corporate and military websites, were polite enough. They didn't even bother to mention that PRISM was just another node in the Pentagon's Joint Vision 2020 dream of Full Spectrum Dominance.

By revealing the existence of PRISM (and other related surveillance programs), Snowden handed Beijing a roast duck banquet of a motive for sticking with cyber-surveillance. Especially after Snowden, a few days later, doubled down by unveiling what Xi, of course, already knew—that the NSA had for years been relentlessly hacking both Hong Kong and mainland Chinese computer networks.

But the ultimate shark fin's soup on China's recent banquet card was an editorial in the Communist Party-controlled Global Times. "Snowden," it acknowledged, "is a 'card' that China never expected," adding that "China is neither adept at nor used to playing it." Its recommendation: use the recent leaks "as evidence to negotiate with the U.S." It also offered a warning that "public opinion will turn against China's central government and the Hong Kong SAR [Special Administrative Region] government if they choose to send [Snowden] back."

With a set of cyber-campaigns—from cyber-enabled economic theft and espionage to the possibility of future state-sanctioned cyber-attacks—evolving in the shadows, it's hard to spin the sunny "new type of great power relationship" President Xi suggested for the US and China at the recent summit.

It's the (State) Economy, Stupid

The unfolding Snowden cyber-saga effectively drowned out the Obama administration's interest in learning more about Xi's immensely ambitious plans for reconfiguring the Chinese economy—and how to capture a piece of that future economic pie for American business. Essential to those plans is an astonishing investment of $6.4 trillion by China's leadership in a drive to "urbanize" the economy yet further by 2020.

That will be the dragon's share of a reconfigured development model emphasizing heightened productivity, moving the country up the international manufacturing quality ladder and digital pecking order, and encouraging ever more domestic consumption by an ever-expanding middle class. This will be joined to a massive ongoing investment in scientific and technological research. China has adopted the US model of public-private sector academic integration with the aim of producing dual-use technologies and so boosting not only the military but also the civilian economy.

Beijing may, in the end, spend up to 30% of its budget on defense-related research and development. This has certainly been a key vector in the country's recent breakneck expansion of information technology, microelectronics, telecommunications, nuclear energy, biotechnology, and the aerospace industry. Crucially, none of this has happened thanks to the good graces of the Goddess of the Market.

The pace in China remains frantic—from the building of supercomputers and an explosion of innovation to massive urban development. This would include, for example, the development of the southwestern hinterland city of Chongqin into arguably the biggest urban conglomeration in the world, with an estimated population of more than 33 million and still growing. A typical savory side story in the China boom of recent years would be the way that energy-gobbling country "won" the war in Iraq. The *New York Times* recently reported that it is now buying nearly 50% of all the oil Iraq produces. (If that doesn't hit Dick Cheney right in the heart, what will?)

Dreaming of What?

As soon as he was confirmed as general secretary at the Chinese Communist Party's 18th Party Congress in November 2012, Xi Jinping started to weave a "China dream" (zhongguo meng) for public consumption. Think of his new game plan as a Roy Orbison song with Chinese characteristics. It boils down to what Xi has termed "fulfilling the great renaissance of the Chinese race." And the dreaming isn't supposed to stop until the 20th Party Congress convenes in 2022, if then.

The $6.4 trillion question is whether any dream competition involving the Chinese and American ruling elites could yield a "win-win" relationship between the planet's "sole superpower" and the emerging power in Asia. What's certain is that to increase the dream's appeal to distinctly standoffish, if not hostile neighbors, China's diplomats would have to embark on a blockbuster soft-power charm offensive.

Xi's two predecessors could not come up with anything better than the vague concept of a "harmonious society" (Hu Jintao) or an abstruse "theory of the Three Represents" (Jiang Zemin), as corruption ran wild among the Chinese elite, the country's economy began to slow, and environmental conditions went over a cliff.

Xi's dream comes with a roadmap for what a powerful future China would be like. In the shorthand language of the moment, it goes like this: strong China (economically, politically, diplomatically, scientifically, militarily), civilized China (equity and fairness, rich culture, high morals), harmonious China (among social classes), and finally beautiful China (healthy environment, low pollution).

The Holy Grail of the moment is the "Two 100s"—the achievement of a "moderately prosperous society" by the Chinese Communist Party's 100th birthday in 2021, one year before Xi's retirement; and a "rich, strong, democratic, civilized, and harmonious socialist modern country" by 2049, the 100th birthday of the founding of the People's Republic.

Wang Yiming, senior economist at the National Development and Reform Commission, has asserted that China's gross domestic product (GDP) will reach 90 trillion yuan ($14.6 trillion) by 2020, when annual per capita GDP will, theoretically at least, hit the psychologically groundbreaking level of $10,000. By 2050, according to him, the country's GDP could reach 350 trillion yuan ($56.6 trillion), and annual per capita GDP could pass the 260,000 yuan ($42,000) mark.

Built into such projections is a powerful belief in the economic motor that a relentless urbanization drive will provide—the goal being to put 70% of China's population, or a staggering one billion people, in its cities by 2030.

Chinese academics are already enthusing about Xi's dreamscape. For Xin Ming from the Central Party School (CPS)—an establishment pillar—what's being promised is "a sufficient level of democracy, well-developed rule of law, sacrosanct human rights, and the free and full development of every citizen."

Don't confuse "democracy," however, with the Western multiparty system or imagine this having anything to do with political "westernization." Renmin University political scientist Wang Yiwei typically describes it as "the Sinocization of Marxism… opening up the path of socialism with Chinese characteristics."

Hail the Model Urban Citizen (aka Migrant Worker)

Of course, the real question isn't how sweet China's party supporters and rhapsodists can make Xi's dream sound, but how such plans will fare when facing an increasingly complex and anxiety-producing reality.

Just take a stroll through Hong Kong's mega-malls like the IFC or Harbour City and you don't need to be Li Chunling, from the Chinese Academy of Social Sciences, to observe that China's middle class is definitely dreaming about achieving one kind of westernization—living the full consumer life of their (now embattled) American middle-class counterparts.

The real question remains: On a planet at the edge and in a country with plenty of looming problems, how can such a dream possibly be sustainable?

A number of Chinese academics are, in fact, worrying about what an emphasis on building up the country's urban environment at a breakneck pace might actually mean. Peking University economist Li Yining, a mentor of Premier Li Keqiang, has, for instance, pointed out that when "everyone swarmed like bees" to invest in urban projects, the result was a near bubble-bursting financial crisis. "The biggest risk for China is in the financial sector. If growth comes without efficiency, how can debt be repaid after a boom in credit supply?" he asks.

Chen Xiwen, director of the Party's Central Rural Work Leading Group, prefers to stress the obvious ills of hardcore urbanization: the possible depletion of energy, resources, and water supplies, the occupation of striking amounts of land that previously produced crops, massive environmental pollution, and overwhelming traffic congestion.

Among the most pressing questions raised by Xi's dream is what it will take to turn yet more millions of rural workers into urban citizens, which often turns out to mean migrant workers living in shanty towns at the edge of a monster city. In 2011 alone, a staggering 253 million workers left the countryside for the big city. Rural per capita income is three times less than urban disposable income, which is still only an annual 21,800 yuan, or a little over $3,500 (a reminder that "middle-class China" is still a somewhat limited reality).

A 2012 report by the National Population and Family Planning Commission revealed that 25.8% of the population is "self-employed," which is a fancy way of describing the degraded state of migrant workers in a booming informal economy. Three-quarters of them are employed by private or family-owned businesses in an off-the-books fashion. Fewer than 40% of business owners sign labor contracts. In turn, only 51% of all migrant workers sign fixed-term labor contracts, and only 24% have medical insurance.

As working citizens, they should—in theory—have access to local health care. But plenty of local governments deny them because their *hukou*—household registrations—are from other cities. In this way, slums swell everywhere and urban "citizens" drown in debt and misery. In the meantime, top urban management in Beijing, Shanghai, Shenzhen, and Chongqin is working to eliminate such slums in order to clear the way for the wildest kinds of financial speculation and real-estate madness. Something, of course, will have to give.

When former World Bank chief economist Justin Lin Yifu warned that China should avoid "over-urbanization," he nailed it. On the ground, President Xi's big dream looks suspiciously like a formula for meltdown. If too many migrants flood the big cities and the country fails to upgrade productivity, China will be stuck in the dreaded middle-income trap.

If, however, it succeeds in such a crash way, it can only do so by further devastating the national environment with long-term consequences that are hard to calculate but potentially devastating.

We Don't Want No Historical Nihilism

Xi, the dreamer, may simply be a master modernist PR tactician hiding an old school outlook. Hong Kong-based political analyst Willy Lam, for instance, is convinced that "ideologically Xi is a Maoist" who wants to maintain "tight control over the party and the military."

Consider the political landscape. Xi must act as the ideological guide for 80 million Communist Party members. The first thing he did after becoming general secretary was to launch an "inspection tour" of the major southern city of Shenzhen, which in the early 1980s was made China's initial "special economic zone." In this, he was emulating China's first "capitalist roader," the Little Helmsman Deng Xiaoping's landmark 1992 turbo-reform tour of the same area. It was undoubtedly his way of promising to lead the next capitalist surge in the country.

However, a fascinating academic and Internet debate in China now revolves around Xi's push to restore the authority and legitimacy of the ur-Communist leader Mao Zedong. Otherwise, the president claims, there would be nothing left but "historical nihilism." As his example of the road not to take, Xi points to the Soviet Union; that is, he is signaling that whatever he will be, it won't be the Chinese equivalent of the USSR's last leader, Mikhail Gorbachev, nor by implication will he lose control over China's military.

Xi is indeed meticulous in his interactions with the People's Liberation Army (PLA), always stressing "the dream of a strong China" and "the dream of a strong military." At the same time, his attitude perfectly embodies the Communist Party's grand narrative about its own grandness. Only the Party, they claim, is capable of ensuring that living standards continue to improve and the country's ever-widening inequality gap is kept in check. Only it can ensure a stable, unified country and a "happy," "harmonious" society. Only it can guarantee the continuing "rejuvenation of the Chinese nation," defend "core interests" (especially what it refers to as "territorial sovereignty"), and ensure China, kicked around by other great powers in much of the nineteenth and twentieth centuries, global respect.

A Sinophile Western cynic would be excused for thinking that this is just a more elaborate way of stressing, as the Chinese do, that the might of the pen (*bi gan zi*) and the barrel of a gun (*qiang gan zi*) are the two pillars of the People's Republic.

All of this was essentially sketched out by senior PLA colonel Liu Mingfu in his recently republished 2010 book, *China Dream: Great Power Thinking and Strategic Posture in the Post-American Era*. On one thing

Liu and Xi (along with all China's recent leaders and PLA commanders) agree: China is "back as the most powerful nation where it's been for a thousand years before the 'century of humiliation.'" The bottom line: when the problems start, Xi's dream will feed on nationalism. And nationalism—that ultimate social glue—will be the essential precondition for any reforms to come.

In April, one month after the National People's Congress, Xi repeated that his dream would be fulfilled by 2050, while the Party's propaganda chief Liu Yunshan ordered that the dream be written into all school textbooks. But repeating something hardly makes it so.

Xi's father, former vice-premier Xi Zhongxun, was a man who thought outside the box. In many ways, Xi is clearly trying to do the same, already promising to tackle everything from massive corruption ("fighting tigers and flies at the same time") to government rackets. (Forget lavish banquets; from now on, it's only supposed to be "four dishes and a soup.")

But one thing is certain: Xi won't even make a gesture towards changing the essential model. He'll basically only tweak it.

Fear and Loathing in the South China Sea

Everyone wants to know how Xi's dream will translate into foreign policy. Three months ago, talking to journalists from the emerging BRICS group (Brazil, Russia, India, China, and South Africa), the Chinese president emphasized that "the China Dream also will bring opportunities to the world."

Enter the charm offensive: in Xi's new world, "peaceful development" is always in and "the China threat" is always out. In Beijing's terms, it's called "all-dimensional diplomacy" and has been reflected in the incessant global travel schedule of Xi and Prime Minister Li Keqiang in their first months in office.

Still, as with the dream at home, so abroad. Facts on the ground—or more specifically in the waters of the South China Sea—once again threaten to turn Xi's dream into a future nightmare. Nationalism has unsurprisingly proven a crucial factor and there's been nothing dreamy about the continuing clash of claims to various energy-rich islands and waters in the region.

Warships have recently been maneuvering as China faces off against, among other countries, Japan, Vietnam, and the Philippines. This unsettling development has played well in Washington as the Obama administration announced a "pivot" to or "rebalancing" in Asia and a new strategy that visibly involves playing China's neighbors off against the Middle Kingdom in what could only be considered a twenty-first century containment policy.

From Washington's point of view, there have, however, been more ominous aspects to China's new moves in the world. In bilateral trade with Japan, Russia, Iran, India, and Brazil, China has been working to bypass the US dollar. Similarly, China and Britain have established a currency swap line, linking the yuan to the pound, and France plans to do the same thing with regard to the euro in an attempt to turn Paris into a major offshore trading hub for the yuan.

Nor was it an accident that Xi's first trip abroad took him to Moscow. There is no more crucial economic and strategic relationship for the Chinese leadership. As much as Moscow won't accept NATO's infinite eastward expansion, Beijing won't accept the US pivot strategy in the Pacific, and Moscow will back it in that.

I was in Singapore recently when Secretary of Defense Chuck Hagel dropped in at the Shangri-La Dialogue, an Asian defense and security forum, to sell the new US focus on creating what would essentially be an anti-Chinese alliance in South and Southeast Asia, as well as the Pacific. Major-General Qi Jianguo, deputy chief of the general staff of the PLA, was there as well listening attentively to Hagel, ready to outline a Chinese counter-strategy that would highlight Beijing's respect for international law, its interest in turbo-charging trade with Southeast Asia, but most of all its unwillingness to yield on any of the escalating territorial disputes in the region. As he said, "The reason China constantly patrols the South China Sea and East Sea is because China considers this to be sovereign territory."

In this way, the dream and nationalism are proving uncomfortable bedfellows abroad as well as at home. Beijing sees the US pivot as a not-so-veiled declaration of the coming of a new Cold War in the Asia-Pacific region, and a dangerous add-on to the Pentagon's Air-Sea Battle concept, a militarized approach to China's Pacific ambitions as the (presumed) next rising power on the planet.

At the Shangri-La, Hagel did call for "a positive and constructive relationship with China" as an "essential part of America's rebalance to Asia." That's where the new U.S.-driven Trans-Pacific Partnership (TPP)—essentially the economic arm of the pivot—would fit in. China's Ministry of Commerce is reportedly even studying the possibility of being part of it.

There is, however, no way a resurgent Beijing would accept unfettered US economic control across the region, nor is there any guarantee that TPP will become the dominant trading group in the Asia-Pacific. After all, with its economic muscle China is already leading the Regional Comprehensive Economic Partnership that includes all ten members of ASEAN plus Australia, India, Japan, New Zealand, and South Korea.

In April, after visiting Beijing, Secretary of State John Kerry began spinning his own "Pacific dream" during a stopover in Tokyo. Yet Beijing will remain wary of Washington's dreaming, as the Chinese leadership inevitably equates any dream that involves moves everywhere in Asia as synonymous with a desire to maintain perpetual American dominance in the region and so stunt China's rise.

However nationalism comes into play in the disputed, energy-rich islands of the South China Sea, the notion that China wants to rule even the Asian world, no less the world, is nonsense. At the same time, the roadmap promoted at the recent Obama-Xi summit remains at best a fragile dream, especially given the American pivot and Edward Snowden's recent revelations about the way Washington has been hacking Chinese computer systems. Perhaps the question in the region is simply whose dream will vanish first when faced with economic and military realities.

At least theoretically, a strategic adjustment by both sides could ensure that the dream of cooperation, of Chimerica, might prove less them chimerical. That, however, would imply that Washington was capable of acknowledging "core" Chinese national interests—on this Xi's dream is explicit indeed. Whatever the confusions and difficulties the Chinese leadership faces, Beijing seems to understand the realities behind Washington's strategic intentions. One wonders whether the reverse applies.

June 2013. Originally at TomDispatch.com

Magic Carpet Ride

I've got to confess that Anna Badkhen beat me to it. Sometimes I have the feeling the world is a carpet. She went one up, writing a marvelously evocative book with the same title, centered on a village in Northern Afghanistan so remote that Google Maps cannot find it.

This is a book for those who love the Silk Road; who love Afghanistan; who love carpets; and all of the above. The Roving Eye fits all these descriptions; no wonder Badkhen's delicate tale projected me on a magic carpet ride down memory lane, as I retraced my own steps over the years in bits and pieces of the Silk Road, from Balkh to Bukhara, from Herat to Hamadan; and all these roads, of course, were paved with carpets.

Historic Khorasan—which includes Northern Afghanistan—is quite special. Around Balkh, Turkomen have been spinning wool for 7,000 years. People are born on carpets. They pray on carpets. They sleep on carpets. They even adorn their tombs with carpets.

When Alexander the Great conquered Khorasan in 327 BC he sent his mum, Olympias, a carpet as a souvenir of his victory in Balkh. Balkh is the fabled feudal capital, now in ruins (blame the Mongols) about 36 kilometers southwest of Oqa—the beyond-the-reach-of-the-NSA village in the salt-frosted Afghan desert where Badkhen chose to follow one year in the life of Thawra's mud-and-dung loom room as she weaves a *yusufi*, a magnificent carpet.

I have always been a Balkh freak; after all, for 1,500 years Balkh ruled over Central Asia. It was "the ornament of Ariana," according to the fifth-century Greek historian Strabo. His Roman contemporary Quintus

Curtius Rufus wrote about a "rich soil" but also "a large area of the country engulfed by desert sands." Oqa is a dot in this "desolate and arid region."

Badkhen, a Russian-born, American resident, no stranger to Iraq, Somalia and Chechnya, did not exactly live in the village for one year; she was commuting from a rented room in Mazar-e-Sharif. The locals adopted her—but remained slightly puzzled. After all she was a foreign woman; she just took notes and sketched; she did no hard work; she had to be protected; and her breasts were "too small." "She's no good to us," thundered an elder. What she did was to immortalize their dwindling way of life.

Badkhen could go further because she speaks Farsi—to which the villagers switched from Turkoman, for her benefit. There are riotous dialogues—such as a discussion on where America is located. Turkmenistan is "four days by donkey." But they can't get to America by donkey—and they don't know what is an ocean. "So how do their [America's] soldiers get to Afghanistan?" The notion of a long plane ride elicits wonder. Then a village elder finds the solution: "The world is not round. It is rectangular! There is Pakistan on one end. Turkmenistan and Uzbekistan on the other end. Iran over there. The world has four corners." Well, he's certainly better informed than many at the Pentagon and the State Department.

There's opium, of course—coming in brown-black disks "weighing about a fifth of an ounce, with a quarter-size gobbet worth a quarter of a dollar" locally. Only 40 km to the northeast, smugglers carry opium across the Amu Darya river to Uzbekistan, and get hundreds of times more bucks for their bang. At $4 billion a year, opium trade remains the second-largest source of revenue of NATO-in-retreat Afghanistan after international aid—making up roughly half the Taliban's budget. Opium, by the way, was brought to Afghanistan by Alexander's troops.

And then there's the Taliban—after all perpetual war is one of the weavers of Khorasan. Not to mention those B-52s weaving the skies overhead—like creatures from another planet. There's the place where the Taliban hanged a young man. The site of a bloody fight between the Taliban and other mujahideen. The crater where a Taliban on a bicycle blew up. The memories of the Taliban mutilating, shooting and slitting the throats of 6,000 Hazaras in Balkh in 1998. But in Oqa itself, nothing. It's too remote—and thus of no value for the Taliban.

The mystery of the loom room

The money quote comes from a carpet merchant in Mazar; "Look at this. The women who weave are illiterate and very poor. But they make this unbelievable beauty." That was always on my mind whenever I stumbled over spectacular rugs along the Silk Road. One day in the scorching summer of 2000, in Taliban-controlled Afghanistan, I had spent a whole afternoon in the crowded Herat carpet bazaar looking for a miracle. And then it happened, just as I was leaving; an elder peasant was barging in, carrying it over his shoulder. It just took one look. The weaver was probably his wife, a Turkoman woman like Thawra. No wonder this is one of my cat's favorite rugs. He certainly smells those 7,000 years of history.

Badkhen puts it beautifully; "Study your carpet. The hands of three generations of illiterate women created it. It is soiled by chicken droppings and stained yellow where the weaver threw her tea dregs at the loom. Its knots fasten wedding songs and women's murmurs. The metronome of a silk blade and the buzzing of noon flies. The whistle of a gale in the grass roof. An old woman's breath as she, at last, sat down on the floor to rest."

Whenever we fall in love with a carpet we try to imagine its own road trip. Badkhen details it. From the loom room in Oqa, Thawra's carpet would be sold to a dealer in the larger village of Dawlatabad. The dealer will call one of the Carpet Row merchants in Mazar-e-Sharif, beside the Blue Mosque. In Mazar, the carpet will be washed, carefully scrutinized—"a journal of her months at the loom"—and then a decision will be made about destination.

It could go by truck south to Kabul, and then be flown to Dubai, and onward to London and New York; by truck east on the Great Trunk Road, across the border to Pakistan and the Peshawar bazaar; or west to Turkmenistan, across the Karakum desert and onwards to Istanbul's Grand Bazaar. Most probably it will get into the cargo hold of a dilapidated bus "with a fancy English name such as Bazarak Panjshir International." And for less than $25 per bundle—about $5 per rug—this carpet, along with others, will abandon Bactria and enter the world at large. And land one day on eBay as a $,1000 bargain.

As I was finishing the book, I got into a long conversation with a carpet merchant in Hong Kong on how the art is fast disappearing in Afghanistan. It takes too long—up to a year—to weave a masterpiece. Opium is more profitable. There's the Invasion of the Cheap Chinese Rug. He told me that some Afghan merchants are even re-importing carpets back into Afghanistan. Yet as Badkhen reminds us, "on the edge of a sand-dune sea, on the edge of a war zone, in their crepuscular loom room on the edge of the world," there will always be one last solitary woman keeping the flame of 7,000 years of beauty.

July 2013

China: The Bo Factor

The larger-than-life geopolitical-economic question of our time, arguably, is not Syria, Iran, or even NSA spying. It's all about China; how on Earth the Chinese Communist Party (CCP) will be successful in tweaking Beijing's economic growth model, and how China will manage its now slowed-down ascension.

But first there's no less than a "trial of the century" to get rid of.

Disgraced former Politburo superstar Bo Xilai—of the "Chongqing model" fame—was finally indicted this week, accused of relatively minor charges of accepting bribes of US$3.2 million and embezzling roughly $800,000.

The fascinating screenplay opens with how Chinese media reacted to it. Three minutes before Xinhua announced it, the People's Daily was already meticulously drawing a distinction between "Bo Xilai's personal issues" and "the successes in the economic and social development" of Chongqing.

Fifteen minutes later, Xinhua followed with a commentary essentially warning that Bo had fallen because a local "tiger" had become too powerful; and thus "the nation's long-term stability can only be secured by protecting the authority of the central leadership."

Also 15 minutes after, the Global Times sealed the deal, stressing that corrupt Party bigwigs like Bo were "a cancer" and should be dealt with by the letter of the law.

The problem is all this heavy artillery does not even begin to tell the story.

The Ferrari vs the Hondas

Tall, energetic, charismatic, a fluent English speaker (learned when he was still in junior high, before the Cultural Revolution) and a princeling to boot—the prodigal son of Bo Yibo, one of the "Eight Immortals," the group of Mao Zedong's close pals led by Deng Xiaoping, who later opened China to the world—Bo Xilai is the stuff "rise and fall" epics are made of.

A princeling—as defined by the Hong Kong-based media way back in the 1980s—was one of the hundreds of children of CCP leaders who danced to the mojo of unlimited money, power and privilege. Bo—who inherited all the priceless *guanxi* woven by his illustrious father—preferred the term "red successor."

It's absolutely impossible to understand what's happening to Bo without following his complex family interactions with current Chinese President Xi Jinping, former President Hu Jintao and former premier Wen Jiabao. It's like comparing a Ferrari with a trio of Honda Civics.

Bo, the maverick, dashing Ferrari, is communist aristocracy by birth. Hu and Wen are hard workers who came from practically nothing. Wen's family, in Tianjin, was persecuted by the princeling Red Guards during the Cultural Revolution. But later, in 1966, it was the poor Red Guards from his university who ended up arresting Bo's father.

Hu Jintao's father was a tea merchant. He was persecuted during the Cultural Revolution—and never "rehabilitated." Later, during the 1980s, Bo's father, duly rehabilitated, went all-out against Hu Yaobang—who happened to be the mentor of both Hu and Wen.

The key point is that bad blood between these families was the name of the game for at least one generation.

By the end of 2007, Bo had lost his internal fight at the 17th Party Congress to become a vice-premier. He got into the Politburo—but was "exiled" to Chongqing, in Sichuan—some 1,500 kilometers away from Beijing. Chongqing has been a provincial-level municipality since 1997. The sprawling city has a population of 7 million, but the wider metropolis in the Yangtze valley holds no fewer than 33 million—and counting. Chongqing was one of the nodes of the late 1990s' "Go West" policy—the push to industrialize the Chinese hinterland at breakneck speed.

Bo arrived in Chongqing ready to roll. 2008 was the crucial year when the CCP unveiled a new narrative of a confident China finally overcoming "a century of humiliation" under foreign colonial powers. Beijing's answer to the Wall Street-provoked financial crisis was a nearly $600 billion stimulus package—the largest in history—to turbo-charge the Chinese economy. But after that yet another narrative was needed to justify the CCP's power monopoly.

Bo smelled a winner. He capitalized on a widespread popular sense of alienation, resentment against inequality, and nostalgia for those egalitarian early days of socialism. Simultaneously he capitalized on Hu and Wen's campaign to fight inequality, as well as their ambivalence towards the role of private capital, and turned left, big time.

His masterful channeling of public resentment led to a reawakening of "the masses"; Bo was talking again about the bogeyman—the bourgeoisie—complete with nostalgic production values of the revolutionary era (as in Mao songs and quotations, which he knew by heart because he had spent five years in prison during the Cultural Revolution).

That was the "Sing Red" campaign. Couple that with sending 200,000 officials "down to the countryside," Mao-style, to "learn from the people" and a so-called "Red GDP" economic program—as in socialist equality, an orgy of affordable housing, sleek new highways, seducing global corporations (Hewlett-Packard, Foxconn, Samsung, Ford) to be based in Chongqing, and we had the municipality's annual GDP growing at an astonishing 16%.

The problem is that much of that was financed by loans from other parts of China. In four years, Chongqing's banking debts ballooned. Yet impressed on the masses was the idea of a mobilization of China for a higher purpose—even as Bo followed the official mantra of "harmonious society" preached by Hu and Wen. The difference was these were real facts on the ground—not just rhetoric.

The tiger is trapped

By then, The Fall loomed. The day would come when Wen's vague calls for "democracy" and the rule of law would collide with Bo's neo-Maoism. In 2010 and 2011 it was practically war in the Politburo between Wen and Bo. And here another subplot is crucial.

Bo was very close to former president Jiang Zemin. And Jiang was always very protective of Bo. Jiang was supporting every Bo move against Wen—including his push for China's top security position, which happened to be occupied by another Jiang protege, Zhou Yongkang, who would be retiring from the Politburo Standing Committee at the 18th Party Congress.

So far, Xi Jinping—another "red successor" and placed to succeed Hu Jintao as president—was at least in theory supporting Bo, both of them faithful to Jiang Zemin. Bo would always be a Ferrari compared to Xi's Honda Civic. After all, Bo's father, for no less than seven decades, had

455

always been one step ahead and above Xi's father. And when directly compared, Bo was—hands down—smarter, bolder and infinitely more charismatic than Xi. The unspoken wisdom in Beijing was that Xi would never be able to keep Bo under control if they were both in action in the rarified Politburo Standing Committee.

All tensions came to a head in March 2012, at the National People's Congress. It started with Wen referring to "the mistakes of the Cultural Revolution and feudalism" that still remained, just to depict Bo as a man of the past, who wanted to block the necessary reform of China's economy, its opening to the world, and its full modernization. Wen implied that Bo had to go so the Maoist past would be finally buried. With Bo, said Wen, "a historical tragedy like the Cultural Revolution may happen again." The (posthumous) winner would have to be Hu Yaobang—not by accident Wen's mentor and a very close friend to Xi's father.

That was major hardball. The next day Bo was unceremoniously fired from his position of Party boss of Chongqing. And if that was not enough, murder had to creep into the screenplay—part of a cascade of sleaze which has been in full flow since Bo's police chief Wang Lijun had defected to the US consulate in Chengdu earlier in the year.

Bo's lawyer wife Gu Kailai became the central character in the plot of a small-time but dashing English man of mystery (Neil Heywood) poisoned by the wife of a Politburo heavy. All hell broke loose. Soon it was public knowledge that Bo had tapped Hu Jintao's phone; that Gu Kilai's siblings had assets of nearly $130 million; that future president Xi Jinping's siblings had family assets of over $1 billion; and that "democracy" crusader Wen's family assets were at over $2.7 billion. The Politburo as a larger-than-life kleptocracy was fully exposed.

Bo was suspended from the Politburo and the Central Committee for "serious" violations of Party "discipline." Everybody stopped talking about the "Chinese model." Bo spent months in the custody of the sinister Central Commission for Discipline Inspection—which translates as being incommunicado and under hardcore interrogation (that would not break someone who withstood five years in jail during the Culture Revolution). Meanwhile, the CCP leadership was debating what to do about him.

Now we know. What we still don't know is what sort of trial of the century it will be. China's "trial of the 20th century"—starring the Gang of Four—was on TV. Imagine Bo's on 24/7 saturation coverage on all imaginable formats. Not likely; probably it will be something meticulously choreographed—and speedy—as in Gu Kailai's trial, although the script would be a writers' dream if Bo would take no prisoners, deviate from the micro-managed CCP-imposed script, and really spill the beans.

It seems that in the upcoming Beidaihe summer retreat the CCP heavyweights will finally decide Bo's fate. This whole fascinating saga can be seen as a deadly, scorpions in a cage, internal Politburo war with a definite winner—Xi; two relative winners—Hu and Wen; and a definite loser—Bo. It gets curioser and curioser when Jiang Zemin himself imperially breaks his silence, as he did this week, and hands out his verdict, last-word style—announcing his public support for Xi.

And so the fractious Politburo, after a hasty trial, may finally become "harmonious" again—and ready to tackle the Earth-shattering question of tweaking the Chinese model.

But the specter of Bo will not go away. He did turn Chinese politics upside down, while revealing a lot about its extremely shady practices. What's not to like? As no Chinese filmmaker would be allowed to touch such sensitive material, Hollywood might be tempted to have a go—with Chow Yun-Fat playing Bo. *Fallen Tiger, Cruel Dragon*, anyone?

July 2013

Bandar Bush, "Liberator" of Syria

Talk about The Comeback Spy. Prince Bandar bin Sultan, aka Bandar Bush (for Dubya he was like family), spectacularly resurfaced after one year in speculation-drenched limbo (was he or was he not dead, following an assassination attempt in July 2012). And he was back in the limelight no less than in a face-to-face with Russian President Vladimir Putin.

Saudi King Abdullah, to quote Bob Dylan, "is not busy being born, he's busy dying." At least he was able to pick up a pen and recently appoint Bandar as head of the Saudi General Intelligence Directorate; thus in charge of the joint US-Saudi master plan for Syria.

The four-hour meeting between Bandar Bush and Vlad the Hammer by now has acquired mythic status. Essentially, according to diplomatic leaks, Bandar asked Vlad to drop Syrian President Bashar al-Assad and forget about blocking a possible UN Security Council resolution on a no-fly zone (as if Moscow would ever allow a replay of UN resolution 1973 against Libya). In return the House of Saud would buy loads of Russian weapons.

Vlad, predictably, was not impressed. Not even when Bandar brazenly insisted that whatever form a post-Assad situation would take, the Saudis will be "completely" in control. Vlad—and Russian intelligence—already knew it. But then Bandar went over the top, promising that Saudi Arabia would not allow any GCC member country—as in Qatar—to invest in Pipelineistan across Syria to sell natural gas to Europe and thus damage Russian—as in Gazprom's—interests.

When Bandar saw he was going nowhere, he reverted to his fallback position; the only way out in Syria is war—and Moscow should forget about the perennially postponed Geneva II peace conference because the "rebels" will be a no show.

Once again, Vlad did not need a reminder that the Saudis—in "cooperation" with Washington—have now taken over the "rebel" galaxy. Qatar has been confined to a (expensive) dustbin, as Vijay Prashad alludes to here. This is part of Washington's plan—if there is one—to isolate the Syrian Muslim Brotherhood and its shady jihadi ramifications/connections.

Wily Bandar, for his part, is not a fool to believe his own propaganda; he knows Moscow has more complex geostrategic interests other than just keeping Syria as a weapons client. And he might have suspected that Moscow simply does not bother with Gulf competition in Pipelineistan targeting European markets.

It's instructive to remember that in 2009, Damascus did not sign an agreement with Qatar for a pipeline via Syria; but they did sign the memorandum of understanding last year for the US$10 billion Iran-Iraq-Syria pipeline. So the point is for Damascus, the deal with Iran was much better; and if the pipeline is ever built Gazprom may even be part of it, in infrastructure and distribution. What Moscow has concluded is that Gazprom won't lose its energy grip over Europe to the benefit of Qatari natural gas. A case can be made that Gazprom holds more power over the distressed, decaying, virtually insolvent euro zone than the European Central Bank (ECB).

What Vlad does fear is a potential post-Assad utter chaos, to be fully exploited by Salafi-jihadis. It's never enough to remember that from Aleppo to Grozny it's roughly 900 kilometers. The next stop for the Global Jihad in Syria would be the Caucasus. And that's where Bandar

Bush and Vlad the Hammer might converge; their mutual strategic interest is to reign in jihadis—although Bandar, in fact, is also weaponizing them.

The new Afghanistan

Moscow won't drop Damascus. Period. At the same time, as Bandar threatened, Geneva II seems more unlikely to happen than the Obama administration ceasing to drone Yemen to death.

As *Asia Times Online* has extensively reported, the name of the game, in practice, remains Syria as the new Afghanistan, with the House of Saud in control of all aspects of jihad (with Washington "leading from behind"). Deadly historic irony also applies; instead of clashing with the Soviet Union, now the Saudis clash with the Russian federation. Bandar is simultaneously the new Weaponizer-in-Chief, as well as Liberator-in-Chief of Syria. The Comeback Spy is not accounting for future, inevitable, ghastly blowback; what's alarming is that the Obama administration is right behind him.

Bandar Bush's visit to Moscow simply could not have happened without a green light from Washington. So what's the (muddled) master plan? The Obama administration seems to believe in a remixed Sykes-Picot—almost a century after the original. The problem is they are clueless on how to configure the new zones of influence. Meanwhile, they're letting the Saudis do the heavy lifting. The first step was to eliminate Qatar from the picture. It's astonishing how fast the emirate, up to two months ago a prospective mini-superpower, now has been reduced to less than an afterthought.

Yet Bandar by now may have seen the writing on the (bloody) wall; Bashar al-Assad will be in power until the 2014 elections in Syria, and may even win those elections. The Saudis might accept a form of compensation in Lebanon, with their protege, the cosmically incompetent Saad al-Hariri, back in power in a coalition government including the political branch of Hezbollah—not the other one which the European poodles branded "terrorist." This also seems unlikely.

So what is Bandar the Liberator to do? Well, he can always direct his private jet to Dallas and liberate his sorrows in a sea of single malt, provided by the House of Dubya.

August 2013

OPERATION TOMAHAWK WITH CHEESE

This deafeningly hysterical show of Syria as Iraq 2.0 is only happening because a president of the United States (POTUS) created a "credibility" problem when, recklessly, he pronounced the use of chemical weapons in Syria a "red line."

Thus the US government urgently needs to punish the transgressor—to hell with evidence—to maintain its "credibility." But this time it will be "limited." "Tailored." Only "a few days." A "shot across the bow"—as POTUS qualified it. Still, some—but not all—"high-value targets", including command and control facilities and delivery systems, in Syria will have to welcome a barrage of Tomahawk cruise missiles (384 are already positioned in the eastern Mediterranean).

We all know how the Pentagon loves to christen its assorted humanitarian liberations across the globe with names like Desert Fox, Invincible Vulture or some other product of brainstorming idiocy. So now it's time to call Operation Tomahawk With Cheese.

It's like ordering a pizza delivery. "Hello, I'd like a Tomahawk with cheese." "Of course, it will be ready in 20 minutes." "Hold on, wait! I need to fool the UN first. Can I pick it up next week? With extra cheese?"

In 1998, Operation Desert Fox—launched by Bill "I did not have sex with that woman" Clinton—was designed to "degrade", but not destroy, Saddam Hussein's capacity to manufacture non-existent weapons of mass destruction. Now, the deployment of those deeply moral Tomahawks is also designed to "degrade" the Bashar al-Assad's government capacity to unleash unproven chemical weapons attacks.

Yet there's always that pesky problem of perennially ungrateful Arabs who, according to the *New York Times*, "are emotionally opposed to any Western military action in the region no matter how humanitarian the cause".

The deeply humanitarian Operation Tomahawk With Cheese is running into all sorts of problems with the calendar. POTUS leaves next Tuesday to Sweden—and from there he will go to St. Petersburg for the Group of 20 summit, on Thursday and Friday next week. The proverbial horde of "unnamed White House officials" has been spinning like mad centrifuges, emphasizing that POTUS must wrap up Tomahawk With Cheese before he musters the courage to face Russian President Vladimir Putin and other leaders of emerging powers.

Surveying his impossibilities—with one eye to the calendar and another to the resistance to enlarge his mini-coalition of the willing—now POTUS seems to be looking for an exit strategy that in fact would all but abandon Operation Tomahawk With Cheese.

Others are way more resilient. A predictable bunch of 66 former "government officials" and "foreign policy experts"—all of them Ziocons under the umbrella of the Foreign Policy Initiative—has published a letter urging POTUS to go way beyond Operation Tomahawk With Cheese, arguing for a pizza sparing no lethal ingredients. This would be a true humanitarian mission, able to support "moderate" Syrian "rebels" and on top of it "dissuade Iran from developing nuclear weapons."

A rebel, but not a jerk

Let's see what a "moderate" Syrian "rebel" thinks about all this. Haytahm Manna, in exile for 35 years, is a key member of the non-armed Syrian opposition (yes, they do exist). But he's not following the script;

he's resolutely against Operation Tomahawk, with cheese or with extra cheese. (See here (in French).

Worse; he debunks the US government's "evidence" of a chemical weapons attack as "propaganda" and "psychological war." He stresses the chemicals were launched with "artisanal weapons"; that ties up with Russian intelligence, which is sure the gas was delivered by a homemade missile fired from a base under opposition control (extensive details compiled here; scroll down to "Qaboun rocket launches").

Manna also points to "videos and photos on the Internet before the attacks"; to al-Qaeda's previous use of chemical weapons; and to the Russians as "seriously working for the Geneva II negotiations", unlike the Americans.

Ooops. This is not exactly what the designers of Operation Tomahawk With Cheese were expecting. If a Syrian exile draws these conclusions, the same applies to Syria civilians who are about to be greeted by those deeply moral Tomahawks.

The Pentagon could always go for Plan B. A single Tomahawk costs at least US$1.5 million. Multiply that for 384. That's not a great bang for your buck—because even if they all go humanitarian, the Bashar al-Assad government would still remain in place.

So why not drop planeloads of sexy, Pininfarina-designed Ferrari Californias? They retail for around $200.000. Imagine the frenzy among Assad elite forces struggling to seize the Big Prize, one among 2,000 Californias. With their eyes off the ball, the "rebels" could easily sneak in everywhere and take over Damascus. And perhaps even stage the victory parade on a fleet of photogenic Ferraris. Call that an improvement over Libya.

Operation Tomahawk With Cheese may still happen; even with the calendar pressing; even bypassing the UN; even with a mini-coalition of the willing; even making a total mockery of international law. The White House has made it clear that "diplomatic paralysis" cannot infringe on its "credibility."

As for what is happening 10 years after the invasion and occupation of Iraq, it's about the US government, parts of NATO (Britain and France) and parts of the GCC (Saudi Arabia and the UAE) burying the previous, much-lauded Euro-Arab "dialogue" and turning into a shady Atlanticist-Islamist cabal bent on smashing yet another secular Arab republic. Talk about rotten cheese.

August 2013

US: THE INDISPENSABLE (BOMBING) NATION

Yes We Scan. Yes We Drone. And Yes We Bomb. The White House's propaganda blitzkrieg to sell the Tomahawking of Syria to the US Congress is already reaching pre-bombing maximum spin—gleefully reproduced by US corporate media.

And yes, all parallels to Iraq 2.0 duly came to fruition when US Secretary of State John Kerry pontificated that Bashar al-Assad "now joins the list of Adolf Hitler and Saddam Hussein" as an evil monster. Why is Cambodia's Pol Pot never mentioned? Oh yes, because the US supported him.

Every single tumbleweed in the Nevada desert knows who's itching for war on Syria; vast sectors of the industrial-military complex; Israel; the House of Saud; the "socialist" Francois Hollande in France, who has wet dreams with Sykes-Picot. Virtually nobody is lobbying Congress NOT to go to war.

And all the frantic war lobbying may even be superfluous; Nobel Peace Prize winner and prospective bomber Barack Obama has already implied—via hardcore hedging of the "I have decided that the United States should take military action" kind—that he's bent on attacking Syria no matter what Congress says.

Obama's self-inflicted "red line" is a mutant virus; from "a shot across the bow" it morphed into a "slap on the wrist" and now seems to be "I'm the Bomb Decider." Speculation about his real motives is idle. His Hail Mary pass of resorting to an extremely unpopular Congress packed with certified morons may be a cry for help (save me from my stupid "red line"); or—considering the humanitarian imperialists of the Susan Rice kind who surround him—he's hell bent on entering another war for the American Israel Public Affairs Committee (AIPAC) and the House of Saud lobby under the cover of "moral high ground." Part of the spin is that "Israel must be protected." But the fact is Israel is already over-protected by an AIPAC remote-controlled United States Congress.[33]

What about the evidence?

The former "cheese-eating surrender monkeys" are doing their part, enthusiastically supporting the White House "evidence" with a dodgy report of their own, largely based on YouTube intel.[34]

Even Fox News admitted that the US electronic intel essentially came from the 8200 unit of the Israeli Defense Forces (IDF)—their version of the NSA.[35] Here, former UK ambassador Craig Murray convincingly debunks the Israeli intercepted intel scam.

The most startling counterpunch to the White House spin remains the Mint Press News report by Associated Press (AP) correspondent Dale Gavlak on the spot, in Ghouta, Damascus, with anti-Assad residents stressing that "certain rebels received chemical weapons via the Saudi intelligence chief, Prince Bandar bin Sultan, and were responsible for carrying out the gas attack."

I had a jolt when I first read it—as I have been stressing the role of Bandar Bush as the dark arts mastermind behind the new Syria war strat-

---

[33] White House to Congress: Help protect Israel, Politico, September 2, 2013.
[34] Le document des services de renseignement sur l'attaque chimique syrienne, Liberation, September 2, 2013.
[35] Israeli intelligence first confirmed Assad regime behind alleged chemical attack, Fox News, August 28, 2013.

egy (See Bandar Bush, 'liberator' of Syria, *Asia Times Online*, August 13, 2013).

Then there's the fact that Syrian Army commandos, on August 24, raiding "rebel" tunnels in the Damascus suburb of Jobar, seized a warehouse crammed with chemicals required for mixing "kitchen sarin." The commando was hit by some form of nerve agent and sent samples for analysis in Russia. This evidence certainly is part of President Vladimir Putin's assessment of the White House claims as totally unconvincing.

On August 27, Saleh Muslim, head of the Kurdish Democratic Union Party (PYD), told Reuters the attack was "aimed at framing Assad." And in case the UN inspectors found the "rebels" did it, "everybody would forget it." The clincher; "Are they are going to punish the Emir of Qatar or the King of Saudi Arabia, or Mr Erdogan of Turkey?"

So, in a nutshell, no matter how it happened, the locals in Ghouta said Jabhat al-Nusra did it; and Syrian Kurds believe this was a false flag to frame Damascus.

By now, any decent lawyer would be asking *cui bono*? What would be Assad's motive—to cross the "red line" and launch a chemical weapons attack on the day UN inspectors arrive in Damascus, just 15 kilometers away from their hotel?

This is the same US government who sold the world the narrative of a bunch of unskilled Arabs armed with box cutters hijacking passenger jets and turning them into missiles smack in the middle of the most protected airspace on the planet, on behalf of an evil transnational organization.

So now this same evil organization is incapable of launching a rudimentary chemical weapons attack with DIY rockets—a scenario I first outlined even before Gavlak's report.[36] Here is a good round-up of the "rebels" dabbling with chemical weapons. Additionally, in late May, Turkish security forces had already found sarin gas held by hardcore Jabhat al-Nusra jihadis.

So why not ask Bandar Bush?

We need to keep coming back over and over again to that fateful meeting in Moscow barely four weeks ago between Putin and Bandar Bush.[37]

Bandar was brazen enough to tell Putin he would "protect" the 2014 Winter Olympics in Sochi. He was brazen enough to say he controls all Chechens jihadis from the Caucasus to Syria. All they needed was a Saudi green light to go crazy in Russia's underbelly.

He even telegraphed his next move; "There is no escape from the military option, because it is the only currently available choice given that the political settlement ended in stalemate. We believe that the Geneva II Conference will be very difficult in light of this raging situation."

That's a monster understatement—because the Saudis never wanted Geneva II in the first place. Under the House of Saud's ultra-sectarian agenda of fomenting the Sunni-Shi'ite divide everywhere, the only thing that matters is to break the alliance between Iran, Syria and Hezbollah by all means necessary.

---

[36] 'War on chemical weapons': Obama traps himself into Syrian combat, Russia Today, August 28, 2013.
[37] Russian President, Saudi Spy Chief Discussed Syria, Egypt, Al Monitor, August 21, 2013.

The House of Saud's spin *du jour* is that the world must "prevent aggression against the Syrian people." But if "the Syrian people" agrees to be bombed by the US, the House of Saud also agrees.[38]

Compared to this absurdity, Muqtada al-Sadr's reaction in Iraq stands as the voice of reason. Muqtada supports the "rebels" in Syria—unlike most Shi'ites in Iraq; in fact he supports the non-armed opposition, stressing the best solution is free and fair elections. He rejects sectarianism—as fomented by the House of Saud. And as he knows what an American military occupation is all about, he also totally rejects any US bombing.

The Bandar Bush-AIPAC strategic alliance will take no prisoners to get its war. In Israel, Obama is predictably being scorned for his "betrayal and cowardice" in the face of "evil." The Israeli PR avalanche on Congress centers on the threat of a unilateral strike on Iran if the US government does not attack Syria. As a matter of fact Congress would gleefully vote for both. Their collective IQ may be sub-moronic, but some may be led to conclude that the only way to "punish" the Assad government is to have the US doing the heavy work as the Air Force for the myriad "rebels" and of course jihadis—in the way the Northern Alliance in Afghanistan, the Kurdish peshmerga in Iraq and the anti-Gaddafi mercenaries in Libya duly profited.

So here, in a nutshell, we have the indispensable nation that drenched North Vietnam with napalm and agent orange, showered Fallujah with white phosphorus and large swathes of Iraq with depleted uranium getting ready to unleash a "limited," "kinetic" whatever against a country that has not attacked it, or any US allies, and everything based on extremely dodgy evidence and taking the "moral high ground."

---

[38] Arab states urge action against Syrian government, Reuters, September 2, 2013.

Anyone who believes the White House spin that this will be just about a few Tomahawks landing on some deserted military barracks should rent a condo in Alice in Wonderland. The draft already circulating in Capitol Hill is positively scary.[39]

And even if this turns out to be a "limited," "kinetic" whatever, it will only perpetuate the chaos. Russian Foreign Minister Sergei Lavrov has referred to it as "controlled chaos." Not really; the Empire of Chaos is now totally out of control.

September 2013

---

[39] President Obama's draft legislation regarding the Syrian conflict, Washington Post, September 1, 2013.

Dogs of War Versus the Emerging Caravan

The dogs of war bark and the emerging powers caravan... keeps on trucking. That's the Group of 20 meeting in St. Petersburg in a nutshell. Count on the indispensable (bombing) nation—via US President Barack "Red Line" Obama—to disrupt a summit whose original agenda was to tackle the immense problems afflicting the global economy.

Economy is for suckers. Get me to my Tomahawk on time. The Obama doctrine—Yes We Scan, Yes We Drone—reached a new low with its Yes We Bomb "solution" to the chemical weapons attack in Ghouta, Syria, presenting world public opinion in the run-up towards the G-20 with the illusionist spectacle of a "debate" in the US Senate about the merits of a new bout of humanitarian bombing.

What in fact was served was the appalling spectacle of serial wacko Republicans of the John McCain and Lindsey Graham mould squeezing the desperate Obama administration like little lemons. Their Orwellian gambit—"reverse the battlefield momentum"—pushed by the senile McCain, was duly approved by the Senate Foreign Relations Committee. This means bombing the hell out of Damascus during a "window of opportunity" of three months, with a possibility of extension. Red Line Obama is on board, assuring, before leaving to Sweden and the G-20, that his former "slap on the wrist" would "fit in" with regime change.

Not even the ghost of Machiavelli would come up with an adjective to describe the whole planet waiting in disbelief to see whether the almost universally despised House of Representatives (15% approval rating, according to RealClearPolitics) decides, Roman Empire style, to give the thumbs down and authorize the bombing of one of the oldest cities in humanity (well, they have an illustrious precedent of applauding Shock and Awe over Baghdad, which topped the Mongols going medieval in the 13th century).

And all this against the will of the "American people" who, according to a Reuters/Ipsos poll support this folly by an overwhelming 9%.

Yes We Bomb. But what for? The following exchange might have come straight from Monty Python. Unfortunately, it's real.

Chairman of the Joint Chiefs of Staff General Martin Dempsey: "The answer to whether I support additional support for the moderate opposition is yes."

Senator Bob Corker (R, Tennessee): "And this authorization will support those activities in addition to responding to the weapons of mass destruction."

Dempsey: "I don't know how the resolution will evolve, but I support—"

Corker: "What you're seeking. What is it you're seeking?"

Dempsey: "I can't answer that, what we're seeking... "

The Pentagon may be clueless—rather, playing clueless. But Bandar Bush, AIPAC/Israel and vast sectors of the industrial-military complex know exactly what they are seeking. And Secretary of State John Kerry knows not only what they are seeking but also who's footing the bill, as in "if the United States is prepared to go do the whole thing the way we've done it previously in other places, they'll carry that cost. That's how dedicated they are to this."

Free bombing. For three months. With inbuilt free upgrading. Operation Tomahawk With Cheese but also bacon, onions, chilies, mayo, guacamole, the works. All courtesy of Saudi Arabia's Prince Bandar bin Sultan—aka Bandar Bush—plus minions Emirates and Qatar. What's not to like? The inestimable Vijay Prashad, author of *The Poorer Nations*, has been using his calculator:

Exhibit A: Saudis have put "on the table" their offer to pay for the entire US assault on Syria. Exhibit B: in case of an attack on Syria, the price of oil is slated to go from $109 to $125 per barrel (base case scenario), with an upside scenario of $150 per barrel. Saudi Arabia will produce 9.8 million barrels of oil a day. Which means if the spike is only the base case scenario, Saudi will gross a super-profit of $156.8 million per day. If it is the upside scenario, then the Saudi super-profits will be $401.8 million per day. Not a bad arbitrage game from Mr Bandar and his gang of Saudi "democrats."

Addendum: each Tomahawk costs only US$1.5 million. With a prospective free flow of Bandar Bush's cash, no wonder there's a compatible free flow of Krug at Raytheon's HQ.

Confronted with the sumptuous marriage of the industrial-military complex and the House of Saud producing lethal cruise offspring duly employed as al-Qaeda's Air Force, a pesky detail like hardcore Chechen jihadis forming their own militia, The Mujahedin of the Caucasus and the Levant, is, well, irrelevant. As irrelevant as the fact that these jihadis are run by none other than Bandar Bush, who bragged to President Vladimir Putin he can turn them on and off at will.

So if these Chechens are Bandar's minions, they are also Friends of Obama/Kerry/Rice/Power. Just like the jihadis who are fighting to take over the "crusader" village of Maloula—where people still speak Aramaic, the language of Jesus—so they can proceed to gleefully behead a few Christian infidels.

What would Zbig say?

Red Line Obama anyway has already telegraphed that he's bombing—whatever Congress decides. Obama of course is just a cipher—he couldn't point to Maloula on a map (not to mention his "security advisors" of the Ben Rhodes mould). Syria is a peach—and it has to be devoured. Too independent. Allied with Iran and Russia. Those river sources in the Golan coveted by Israel. The chance to further provoke Russia in the Caucasus. The chance, in the long run, to destabilize China in Xinjiang. The chance to isolate Hezbollah, allow a new Israeli invasion of southern Lebanon, open the (lethal) road to Tehran.

Yet the agendas will keep diverging. Prime Minister Recep Tayyip Erdogan in Turkey would bless regime change, but he's terrified of Syrian Kurds becoming totally independent and further giving toxic ideas to Turkish Kurds. The House of Saud wants all-out regime change, so it may be able, in one swoop, to wound Iran, Iraq and Hezbollah. So what if those Allahu Akbar Friends of Kerry and company run amok? They are not on Saudi Arabian soil threatening the petromonarchy; let them fight those "apostate" Shi'ites in assorted latitudes.

Let's see what the man who in theory instilled little nuggets of international relations realities into Red Line Obama's brain think about all this. Zbigniew "Grand Chessboard" Brzezinski is in favor of "some symbolic military action." Well, a cost-effective version would be to parachute Kerry in Maloula.

Dr. Zbig also wants to "involve the oriental powers," as "they have to be very worried as to where this is headed." Correct; that's what Chinese President Xi Jinping told Putin, he worries about oil at $150 a barrel. The Russians, according to Dr. Zbig, are using "aggressive and insulting language." Ridiculous—when Putin dubbed Kerry a liar that was the understatement of the year. Dr. Zbig is in fact terrified that "the Russians may use this conflict, if it explodes, to undermine overall our position in the Middle East." Memo: your "position" is already undermined all over the planet, not only the Middle East.

And when Dr. Zbig says that the Russians are "fearful of stability in the Caucuses," and "Putin has a stake in the Winter Olympics," and "there is leverage here that we can use intelligently," he sounds eerily like Bandar Bush threatening Putin to unleash "his" Chechens in Sochi in 2014.

More enlightening, and with no double talk, is what the manipulated "opposition" wants. It's all about Iran—and "terrorist ally" Hezbollah (scroll down to page 6 here.)

The Xi-Putin show

Even immersed in all this hysteria, the BRICS caravan managed to engage in serious business at the G-20. They held a mini-summit to coordinate their common position—which, as far as Syria is concerned, is totally anti-war (you won't see this reported in Western corporate media). They did say, *en bloc*, that Obama's war will have "an extremely negative effect on the global economy."

So they discussed, as a group, how to increase their trade using their own currencies; how to develop their markets (that's part of the original Russian agenda for this G-20); and how to improve trade relations. Common strategy: multiple escape routes against US dollar hegemony.

They advanced on negotiations relative to the capital structure, shareholding and governance of the BRICS development bank; initial capital of $50 billion and an emergency fund of $100 billion, a sort of emerging powers IMF. The bank should have a head start in the next BRICS summit in 2014 in Brazil.

And as far as Russia and China are concerned, there's the annual meeting of the Shanghai Cooperation Organization (SCO) next week. Before that, already contemplating the prospect of $200 billion in bilateral trade by 2020, Xi and Putin discussed a rash of mega-projects—not only revolving around Pipelineistan—and the proverbial "further strategic international coordination." The official Chinese version to their strategic partnership is a beauty: "Sowing in spring and harvesting in autumn."

It's like sleeping in one of those fabulous beds at a Four Seasons resort. No hysteria. No "red lines." No Tomahawks. No "credibility on the line."

This is what Obama said in August 2012:

We have been very clear to the Assad regime, but also to other players on the ground, that a red line for us is we start seeing a whole bunch of chemical weapons moving around or being utilized. That would change my calculus. That would change my equation.

Note the "my" and then again another "my" invoking responsibility, not "the world."

So while the Xi and Putin caravan reenacts the spirit of the Silk Road, the dogs of war keep barking; and informed public opinion everywhere starts to consider the possibility that Obama, by not assuming full responsibility for what he said, and blaming "the world," may also be a coward.

September 2013

AL-QAEDA'S AIR FORCE STILL ON STAND-BY

It was 12 years ago today. Historians will register that, according to the official narrative, 19 Arabs armed with box cutters and minimal flying skills pledged to a transnational Terror Inc turned jets into missiles to attack the US homeland, fooling the most elaborate defense system on Earth.

Fast forward to 2013. Here's a 15-second version of the President of the United States (POTUS) address on Syria, one day before the 12th anniversary of 9/11:

> *Our ideals and principles, as well as our national security, are at stake. The United States is "the anchor of global security." Although the United States military "doesn't do pin pricks," we still carry the burden to punish regimes that would flout long-held conventions banning the use of biological, chemical and nuclear weapons.*
>
> *That's why I have decided to pursue an unlimited, targeted military strike against Washington DC.*

For countless global citizens, this alternative version predictably sounds as far-fetched as the official version of what happened 12 years ago. The fog of war obscures in mysterious ways. But the fact remains that the current, "reluctant" (farcical) Emperor continues to stake his—and his nation's—"credibility" on a "limited," "kinetic" operation to reinforce his self-defined red line against chemical weapons.

Lose face, will travel

In theory, the Russian plan of having Damascus surrender its chemical weapons arsenal works because of its inbuilt Chinese wisdom; nobody loses face—from Obama and the US Congress to the European Union, the UN and the even more farcical "Arab" League, which is essentially a Saudi Arabian colony.

Although Obama is on a media blitzkrieg stealing the credit for it, *Asia Times Online* has confirmed that the plan was elaborated by Damascus, Tehran and Moscow last week—after a visit to Damascus by the head of the national security committee of the Iranian Majlis (parliament), Alaeddin Boroujerdi. US Secretary of State John Kerry's now famous "slip" provided the opening.

So, essentially, it's this "axis"—Damascus, Tehran and Moscow—that is helping Obama to crawl out of his self-inflicted abyss. Needless to say, that is absolutely unbearable for the plutocrats in charge of unleashing the new Syria (lethal) production. A brand new propaganda/manufactured hysteria campaign must be unfurled to justify war. And that's exactly what the Anglo-French-American axis is working on.

No wonder the French proposal for a new UN Security Council resolution falls under the UN's Chapter 7—which would explicitly allow the use of force against Damascus in case of non-compliance. As it is, this resolution will inevitably be vetoed by Russia and China. And that will be the new pretext for war. The (farcical) emperor may easily invoke plausible deniability, stress he made "every effort" to avoid a military conflict, and then convince skeptics in the US Congress this is the only way to go.

And to think that a perfectly sound development of the Damascus-Tehran-Moscow plan is at hand. Syria's chemical weapons may be transferred to Russian—or European—supervision. Syria joins the Organization for the Prohibition of Chemical Weapons (OPCW) and ratifies the Chemical Weapon Convention (CWC). OPCW inspectors start working in coordination with the UN. Every expert knows the whole process will take years.

Damascus has already declared it's ready to join the OPCW and abide by the CWC. So Damascus does not need a UN Security Council resolution forcing it to do what it wants to do. Any serious, comprehensive UN resolution on chemical weapons across the Middle East would have to include Israel's chemical weapons. Note that nobody, absolutely nobody, is talking about Israel's vast arsenal of chemical, not to mention nuclear weapons.

The sound path, though, will not be followed—because Washington and its barking poodles afflicted with Sykes-Picot wet dreams, London and Paris, are already blocking it.

Fly me to the (war) moon

There are no signs that the Obama administration is prepared to even reconsider the yo-yo "Obama doctrine" all across the Middle East. This would imply dumping the Saudi-Israeli axis and making a concerted effort for the success of the Geneva II conference, the only possible diplomatic solution for the Syrian tragedy.

I have argued before that the (farcical) emperor is just a paperboy—a docile employee. Those who are paying for the upcoming lethal production, as in the House of Saud, or cheering in the sidelines, as in the Israel lobby, simply won't give up.

The House of Saud wants regime change, now. The Israel lobby/AIPAC (American Israel Public Affairs Committee) and its masters in Tel Aviv want a massive spillover of the Syria war into Lebanon to entangle Hezbollah. Financial Masters of the Universe, significant sectors of the industrial-military-security Orwellian/Panopticon complex, and Western-propped petro-monarchies want an independent, secular Arab republic profitably integrated in their monopoly.

The problem is the unilateral "kinetic" whatever may be too "limited" to satisfy the Saudi-Israeli axis and most of all the financial Masters of the Universe, and illegal enough to qualify as a war crime.

At least there is a counter-power. *Asia Times Online* has confirmed that an outstanding meeting will take place later this week in Kyrgyzstan, during the annual summit of the Shanghai Cooperation Organization (SCO). Picture Chinese President Xi Jinping, Russian President Vladimir Putin and new Iranian President Hassan Rouhani together, in the same room, discussing their common position on Syria. Iran is an SCO observer—and may soon be admitted as a full member. This is what the Anglo-French-American axis is up against.

And that brings us back to 12 years ago—and the myth that aluminum jets are able to penetrate the thick steel perimeters of the Twin Towers and kerosene is capable of instantaneously melting steel perimeters and steel cores into fluffy steel dust.

As for that "evil," transnational Terror Inc, it didn't even have a name when Jihad International hopefuls were being recruited in the early 1980s by assorted Islamic charities, and then trained and funded by the CIA and Saudi Arabia. One day the database was finally named—by the US—as "al-Qaeda." Or, more appropriately, "al-CIAeda." They were elevated to Ultimate Evil status. They did 9/11. They reproduced like rabbits from Mali to Indonesia. Now the CIA works side by side with them—as it did in Libya. And eagerly they await the US Air Force to clear their road to Damascus. Hey, it's just (war) business. Allahu Akbar.

September 2013

CHINA STITCHES UP (SCO) SILK RD

While the whole world was terrified by the prospect of the Obama administration bombing Syria, Chinese President Xi Jinping was busy doing the Silk Road.

One has to love that famous Deng Xiaoping dictum; "Always maintain a low profile." This being the second-largest economy in the world, "low profile" always packs a mighty punch. Cue to September 7, in Astana, Kazakhstan's capital, when Xi officially proposed no less than a New Silk Road in co-production with Central Asia.

Xi's official "economic belt along the Silk Road" is a supremely ambitious, Chinese-fueled trans-Eurasian integration mega-project, from the Pacific to the Baltic Sea; a sort of mega free-trade zone. Xi's rationale seems to be unimpeachable; the belt is the home of "close to 3 billion people and represents the biggest market in the world with unparalleled potential."

Talk about a "wow" factor. But does that mean that China is taking over all of the Central Asian "stans"? It's not that simple.

A roomful of mirrors

On Xi's Silk Road trip, the final destination was Bishkek, Kyrgyzstan's capital, for the 13th summit of the Shanghai Cooperation Organization (SCO). And to cap it all off, nothing less than a graphic reminder of the stakes involved in the New Great Game in Eurasia; a joint meeting on the sidelines of the SCO, featuring Xi, Russian President Vladimir Putin, and new Iranian President Hassan Rouhani.

This is Rouhani's first foreign trip since he took office on August 4. Not an epic like Xi's; only two days in Bishkek. In a preliminary meeting face-to-face with Xi, Rouhani even started speaking "diplomatic Chinese"—as in the upcoming negotiations over the Iranian nuclear dossier leading, hopefully, to a "win-win" situation. Xi emphatically supported Iran's right to a peaceful nuclear program under the Non-Proliferation Treaty, while Rouhani stressed the Iran-China relationship "bears vital significance for Asia and the sensitive Middle East issue."

And that leads to the common Iran-China-Russia front in relation to Syria. Even before meeting with Putin, Rouhani had agreed with the Russian four-part plan for Syria, which, as *Asia Times Online* had reported, was brokered between Damascus, Tehran and Moscow (See Al-Qaeda's air force still on stand-by, September 11, 2013). According to the plan, Damascus joins the Organization for the Prohibition of Chemical Weapons (OPCW); discloses the location of chemical stockpiles; allows OPCW inspectors access to the sites; and then comes the long process of destroying the stockpiles.

In the nuclear front, Tehran and Moscow remain open for business. Russia will hand operation of Unit 1 of the Bushehr nuclear power plant over to Iran in less than two weeks. And there will be more "cooperation" ahead.

The importance of this triangulation cannot be overstated. Oh, to be a fly on the wall in that Xi-Putin-Rouhani Kyrgyz room. Tehran, Moscow and Beijing are more than ever united on bringing about a new multipolar international order. They share the vision that a victory for the axis of warmongers on Syria will be the prelude for a future war on Iran—and further harassment of both Russia and China.

The God of the market, it's us

Meanwhile, monster business—and strategic—opportunities beckon in the Eurasian corridor. Xi's Silk Road Economic Belt, with trademark Chinese pragmatism, is all about free trade, connectivity and currency circulation (mostly, of course, in yuan). It's ready to go because there are no more border problems between Russia and Central Asia. It ties up perfectly with China's push to develop its Far West—as in Xinjiang; consider the extra strategic Central Asian support for the development of China's Far West.

Here's an example. At a China-Eurasia Expo in Urumqi, Xinjiang's capital, earlier this week, China Telecom and two Hong Kong telecom companies signed seven deals with the governments and companies from Kazakhstan, Tajikistan, Russia and Mongolia. Not many people know that Urumqi boasts more than 230 Internet companies; nearly half are connected with neighboring countries. Xinjiang is not only about Han Chinese encroaching on Uyghurs; it's no less than the communications base for the Eurasian corridor—a hub for broadband and cloud computing.

Beijing is already massively investing in new roads and bridges along the Eurasian Land Bridge—another denomination of the New Silk Road. As *Asia Times Online* has reported, the New Silk Road is all about highways, railways, fiber optics and pipelines—with now the added Chinese push for logistics centers, manufacturing hubs and, inevitably, new townships.

There are plenty of Pipelineistan gambits to implement, and a lot of mineral resources to be exploited. And, crucially—considering the original Silk Road traversed Afghanistan—there's also the prospect of an Afghan revival as a privileged bridge between Central, East and South Asia.

Not to mention speeding up China's land access to both Europe and the Middle East.

In China, no major decisions such as this are "spontaneous," but there's a neat softening PR behind it. In Astana, Xi said, "my home, Shaanxi province, is the start of the ancient Silk Road"; and he was "moved" as he reviewed Silk Road history during the trip.

He indulged in sightseeing in Samarkand's fabulous Registan square, flanked by Uzbek President Islam Karimov, and even waxed "poetic," telling Karimov, "this gives us a special feeling. We are far away in distance, but we are also so near to each other in our soul. It is just like time travel." Well, the Timurid empire has finally met its match. It's not that China hadn't done it before; during the Western Han dynasty (206 BC—AD 24), imperial envoy Zhang Qian was dispatched to Central Asia twice to open up China to global trade.

"Poetic" or not, Xi was always on message. All along his Silk Road trip, he left no doubts this is a foreign policy priority for China. China has now established strategic partnerships with all five Central Asian "stans."

The Pipelineistan angle

Kashagan is your usual Pipelineistan nightmare. Significantly, on 9/11 this week, the North Caspian Operating Co, which runs Kashagan—one of the largest oil fields discovered in the past 40 years, with 35 billion barrels in reserves—said the first oil was finally in sight.

Kashagan is in the northern Caspian Sea. I've been there. Technically, oil extraction is immensely complex; that is certainly the case here. Production should have started in 2005. No less than US$46 billion has been spent by a consortium featuring Italy's ENI, France's Total, Royal

Dutch/Shell, ExxonMobil and ConocoPhillips. Nasty bickering has been the norm. A week ago, Astana finally signed an agreement for China's CNPC to buy the former ConocoPhillips' 8.4% share.

With China stepping in, major hard cash will flow. Beijing is determined to become a major player in the Kazakh energy market. Ideally, Kashagan should be producing 370,000 barrels a day in 2014 and 1.6 million barrels by 2016.

China's strategy in Kazakhstan is basically about oil. But China also badly needs a lot of natural gas. Russia's Gazprom is betting on Beijing's non-stop thirst for gas to facilitate its shift from exporting mainly to Europe. But competition is stiff. And Turkmenistan is a key part of China's equation.

China is already planning expansions for the Central Asia-China pipeline—which it built and paid for. Exports should be up by 2015. In his Silk Road trip, Xi naturally hit Turkmenistan, inaugurating no less than one of the largest gas fields in the world, massive Galkynysh, which began production only three months ago. Most of the gas will flow through—where else—the pipeline to China. China is paying the bill, $8 billion so far, and counting.

Turkmenistan's economy now virtually depends on natural gas exports to China (at 60% of GDP). Beijing's ultimate strategy is to use its Turkmenistan leverage to extract better gas deals from Gazprom.

Kyrgyzstan also features in China's Pipelineistan strategy. Beijing will finance and operate the proposed Kyrgyzstan-China gas pipeline—which will be a key part of the fourth Turkmenistan-China pipeline. Beijing is also building a railroad linking it to with Kyrgyzstan and Uzbekistan.

Observing all this frenzy, we have to come back to the ultimate adage of the times; while the (Washington) dogs of war bark, the (Chinese) caravan does deals.

Those three evils

The SCO is also involved in boosting this major transportation route connecting East Asia, West Asia and South Asia, and ultimately the Pacific to the Baltic Sea.

Yet Stalin's legacy lives—as in the demented way he partitioned Central Asia. China will need to shell out a fortune in transportation. Chinese trains are always in trouble traveling on Soviet-era railways. Airline service is dodgy. For instance, there's only one flight every two days between Uzbekistan and Kyrgyzstan (I took it; always crowded, the usual delays, stranded luggage...)

The SCO was founded 12 years ago, when Uzbekistan joined the members of the original Shanghai Five; China, Russia, Kazakhstan, Kyrgyzstan and Tajikistan. Turkmenistan preferred its splendid isolation.

The original emphasis was on mutual security. But now the SCO encompasses politics and economics as well. Yet the obsession remains on what the Chinese define as "the three evil forces" of terrorism, separatism and extremism. That's code for the Taliban and its offshoots, the Islamic Movement of Uzbekistan (IMU) and the Uyghurs in Xinjiang. The SCO also tries to fight drug trafficking and arms smuggling.

Again in classic Chinese style, the SCO is spun as fostering "mutual trust, mutual benefit, equality, consultation, respect for diverse civilizations and seeking common development," in an atmosphere of "non-alliance, non-confrontation and not being directed against any third party."

It may go a long way before becoming a sort of Eastern NATO. But it's increasingly carving its territory as a direct counterpunch to NATO—not to mention Washington's Central/South Asian chapter of the Global War on Terror (GWOT) and the push for "color revolutions." The SCO is actively discussing its regional options after Washington's withdrawal from Afghanistan in 2014. China and Russia will be deeply involved. Same for Iran—for the moment a SCO observer.

Xi's Silk Road belt, in principle, is not detonating alarm bells in the Kremlin. The Kremlin spin is that Russia and China's economies are complementary—as in China's "sizable financial resources" matching Russia's "technologies, industrial skills and historical relations with the region."

One wonders what the adults in assorted rooms in the Beltway think about all this (assuming they know it's happening). Former US Secretary of State Hillary Clinton used to wax lyrical about an American-propped New Silk Road. Well, after Xi's trip that sounds like yet another Barack Obama campaign promise.

September 2013

Breaking American exceptionalism

Never underestimate American soft power.

What if the US government actually shut down to mourn the passing of *Breaking Bad*, arguably the most astonishing show in the history of television? It would be nothing short of poetic justice—as *Breaking Bad* is infinitely more pertinent for the American psyche than predictable cheap shots at Capitol Hill.

Walter White, aka Heisenberg, may have become the ultimate, larger-than-life hero of the Google/YouTube/Facebook era. In an arc of tragedy spanning five seasons, *Breaking Bad* essentially chronicled what it takes for a man to accept who he really is, while in the process ending up paying the unbearable price of losing everything he holds dear and what is assumed to be his ultimate treasure; the love of his wife and son.

Along the way, *Breaking Bad* was also an entomologist study on American turbo-capitalism—with the 1% haves depicted as either cheats or gangsters and the almost-haves or have-nots barely surviving, as in public school teachers degraded to second-class citizen status.

Walter White was dying of cancer at the beginning of *Breaking Bad*, in 2008. Progressively, he gets rid of Mr Hyde—a placid chemistry teacher—for the benefit of Dr. Jekyll—undisputed crystal meth kingpin Heisenberg. It's not a Faustian pact. It's a descent into the dark night of his own soul. And in the end he even "wins," under his own terms, burning out with a beatific smile.

His secret is that it was never only about the transgressive high of producing the purest crystal meth. It was about the ultimate Outsider act, as in a Dostoevsky or Camus novel; a man confronting his fears, crossing the threshold, taking full control of his life, and finally facing the consequences, with no turning back.

And then, as in all things *Breaking Bad*, the music told a crucial part of the story. In this case, no less than the closing with Badfinger's My Baby Blue, the bleakest of love songs:

> *Guess I got what I deserve*
> *Kept you waiting there, too long my love*
> *All that time, without a word*
> *Didn't know you'd think, that I'd forget, or I'd regret*
> *The special love I have for you*
> *My baby blue*

So—as Walter White finally admits, fittingly, in the last episode—he did it all, Sinatra's *My Way*, not for the sake of his family, but for him. And here we have the purest crystal meth as a reflection of this purest revelation in this purest of TV shows, blessed with unmatched writing (you can almost palpably feel the exhilaration in the writers' room), direction, sterling cast, outstanding cinematography quoting everything from *Scarface* to *Taxi Driver* via *The Godfather*, meticulous character development and gobsmacking plot twists.

But then again, that spectral song *My Baby Blue* is not only about crystal meth—just like Tommy James and the Shondell's *Crystal Blue Persuasion*, used in a spectacular montage in season four.

It's about Jesse Pinkman, Walter White's repeatedly used and abused young business associate. It's as if it was written by Walt as a tribute to

Jesse; Jesse is the "baby" always evoking Walt's "special love" in the form of usually spectacularly misfiring paternal feelings.

I'm in the Empire business

Walt/Heisenberg is a scientist. His scientific genius was appropriated by unscrupulous partners in the past, who enriched themselves in a tech company. As Heisenberg, finally the scientific/mechanical genius comes to full fruition—from a wheelchair bomb to a raid based on magnets and even a remix of the 1963 Great Train Robbery in the UK, not to mention the perfectly cooked meth.

Here's one the writers' take on cooking *Breaking Bad*. Yet that does not explain why Walter White touched such a nerve and became a larger-than-life global pop phenomenon from Albuquerque to Abu Dhabi.

A classic underdog narrative explains only part of the story. In the slow burn of five seasons, what was crystallized was Walter White as Everyman fighting The Establishment—which included everyone from demented criminals (a Mexico drug cartel, brain-dead neo-nazis) to vulture lawyers ("Better Call Saul"), cheating former associates and, last but not least, the US government (via the Drug Enforcement Agency).

Nihilism—of a sub-Nietzschean variety—also explains only part of the story. One can feel the joy of the *Breaking Bad* writers tomahawking the Judeo-Christian concept of guilt. But this has nothing to do with a world without a moral code.

One glance at James Frazer's *The Golden Bough* is enough to perceive how Walter White, in his mind, does hark back to family-based tribal society. So is he essentially rejecting the Enlightenment?

We're getting closer when we see *Breaking Bad* as a meditation on the myth of the American Dream—and its extrapolation as American exceptionalism. As Walter White admits to Jesse, he's deep into "the Empire business." In real life, Walter White might have been a mastermind of the Orwellian-Panopticon complex.

So with *My Baby Blue* ringin' in my head, I ended up finding my answer in a book I always take with me while on the road in America: D H Lawrence's *Studies in Classic American Literature*. Not by accident Lawrence was a deep lover of New Mexico—where *Breaking Bad*'s geopolitics is played out. And Walter White is indeed there, as Lawrence dissects James Fenimore Cooper's *The Deerslayer*. (Here's a digital version of the essay.)

Walter White, once again, embodies "the myth of the essential white America. All the other stuff, the love, the democracy, the floundering into lust, is a sort of by-play. The essential American soul is hard, isolate, stoic, and a killer. It has never yet melted."

When Walter White turns into Heisenberg he morphs into Deerslayer:

A man who turns his back on white society. A man who keeps his moral integrity hard and intact. An isolate, almost selfless, stoic, enduring man, who lives by death, by killing, but who is pure white.

This is the very intrinsic—most American. He is at the core of all the other flux and fluff. And when this man breaks from his static isolation, and makes a new move, then look out, something will be happening.

The genius of the *Breaking Bad* writers' room—with creator Vince Gilligan at the core—was to depict Walter White's descent into the maelstrom as primeval, intrinsically "most American." No wonder Gilligan defined *Breaking Bad* essentially as "a western." Clint Eastwood was fond of saying that the western and jazz were the only true American art forms (well, he forgot film noir and blues, rock'n roll, soul and funk, but we get the drift).

So call this warped western a masterful depiction of American exceptionalism. And mirror it with the soft pull of a dying, lone superpower which is still capable of turning the whole planet into junkies, addicted to the cinematically sumptuous spectacle of its own demise.

October 2013

FEAR AND LOATHING IN HOUSE OF SAUD

Every sentient being with a functional brain perceives the possibility of ending the 34-year Wall of Mistrust between Washington and Tehran as a win-win situation.

Here are some of the benefits:

- The price of oil and gas from the Persian Gulf would go down;

- Washington and Tehran could enter a partnership to fight Salafi-jihadis (they already did, by the way, immediately after 9/11) as well as coordinate their policies in Afghanistan to keep the Taliban in check post-2014;

- Iran and the US share the same interests in Syria; both want no anarchy and no prospect of Islamic radicals having a shot at power. An ideal outcome would balance Iranian influence with a power-sharing agreement between the Bashar al-Assad establishment and the sensible non-weaponized opposition (it does exist, but is at present marginalized);

- With no more regime change rhetoric and no more sanctions, the sky is the limit for more trade, investment and energy options for the West, especially Europe (Iran is the best possible way for Europeans to soften their dependence on Russia's Gazprom);

- A solution for the nuclear dossier would allow Iran to manage civilian use of nuclear energy as an alternative source for its industry, releasing more oil and gas for export;

- Geopolitically, with Iran recognized for what it is—the key actor in Southwest Asia—the US could be released from its self-imposed strategic dogma of depending on the Israeli-Saudi axis. And Washington could even start pivoting to Asia for real—not exclusively via military means.

Ay, there's the rub. Everybody knows why the Israeli right will fight an US-Iran agreement like the plague—as Iran as an "existential threat" is the ideal pretext to change the debate from the real issue; the occupation/apartheid regime imposed on Palestine.

As for the House of Saud, such an agreement would be nothing short of Apocalypse Now.

I'm just a moderate killer

It starts with Syria. Everybody now knows that shadow master Bandar bin Sultan, aka Bandar Bush, has been fully in charge of the war on Syria since he was appointed Director of National Intelligence by his uncle, Saudi King Abdullah.

Bandar is taking no prisoners. First he eliminated Qatar—the major financier of the so-called Free Syrian Army (FSA)—from the picture, after having a helping hand in Qatar's emir, Sheikh Hamad, deposing himself to the benefit of his son, Sheikh Tamin, in late June.

Then, in late July, Bandar spectacularly resurfaced in public during his now famous "secret" trip to Moscow to try to extort/bribe Russian President Vladimir Putin into abandoning Syria.

Notoriously, the House of Saud's "policy" on Syria is regime change, period. This is non-negotiable in terms of dealing a blow to those "apostates" in Tehran and imprinting Saudi will on Syria, Iraq, in fact the whole, mostly Sunni Levant.

In late September, the Jaish al-Islam ("Army of Islam") entered the picture. This is a "rebel" combo of up to 50 brigades, from supposedly "moderates" to hardcore Salafis, controlled by Liwa al-Islam, which used to be part of the FSA. The warlord in charge of Jaish al-Islam is Zahran Alloush—whose father, Abdullah, is a hardcore Salafi cleric in Saudi Arabia. And the petrodollars to support him are Saudi—via Bandar Bush and his brother Prince Salman, the Saudi deputy defense minister.

If this looks like a revamp of the David Petraeus-concocted "Sunni Awakening" in Iraq in 2007 that's because it is; the difference is this Saudi-financed "awakening" is geared not to fight al-Qaeda but towards regime change.

This (in Arabic) is what Alloush wants; a resurrection of the Umayyad Caliphate (whose capital was Damascus), and to "cleanse" Damascus of Iranians, Shi'ites and Alawites. These are all considered *kafir* ("unbelievers"); either they submit to Salafist Islam or they must die. Anybody who interprets this stance as "moderate" has got to be a lunatic.

Incredibly as it may seem, even Ayman al-Zawahiri—as in al-Qaeda central—has issued a proclamation banning the killing of Shi'ites.

Yet this "moderate" tag is exactly at the core of the present, Bandar Bush-concocted PR campaign; sectarian warlords of the Alloush kind are being "softened," so they are palatable to a maximum range of Gulf sources of funds and, inevitably, gullible Westerners. But the heart of the matter is that Jaish al-Islam, essentially, sports just a slight chromatic difference with the Islamic State of Iraq and al-Sham (ISIS)—the al-Qaeda-linked umbrella which is the prime fighting force in Syria; as in a bunch of weaponized fanatics on varying degrees of (religious) crystal meth addiction.

Paranoia paradise

To complicate matters, the House of Saud is in disarray because of the succession battle. Crown Prince Salman is the last son of King Abdul Aziz, the founder of the Saud dynasty, to have a shot at power gradually by age.

Now all bets are off—with hordes of princes engulfed in the battle for the great prize. And here we find none other than Bandar Bush—who is now, for all practical purposes, the most powerful entity in Saudi Arabia after Khalid Twijri, the chief of King Abdullah's office. The nonagenarian Abdullah is about to meet his Maker. Twijri is not part of the royal family. So Bandar is running against the clock. He needs a "win" in Syria as his ticket to ultimate glory.

That's when the Russia-US agreement on Syria's chemical weapons intervened. The House of Saud as a whole freaked out—blaming not only the usual suspects, UN Security Council members Russia and China, but also Washington. No wonder the perpetual foreign minister, Prince Saud al-Faisal, snubbed his annual address to the UN General Assembly last week. To say he was not missed is an understatement.

The House of Saud's nightmare is amplified by paranoia. After all those warnings by King Abdullah for Washington to cut "the head of the snake" (Iran), as immortalized on WikiLeaks cables; after all those supplications for the US to bomb Syria, install a no-fly zone and/or weaponize the "rebels" to kingdom come, this is what the House of Saud gets: Washington and Tehran on their way to reaching a deal at the expense of Riyadh.

So no wonder fear, loathing and acute paranoia reign supreme. The House of Saud is and will continue to do all it can to bomb the emergence of Lebanon as a gas producer. It will continue to relentlessly fan the flames of sectarianism all across the spectrum, as Toby Matthiesen documented in an excellent book.

And the Israeli-Saudi axis will keep blossoming. Few in the Middle East know that an Israeli company—with experience in repressing Palestinians—is in charge of the security in Mecca. (See here and here (in French)). If they knew—with the House of Saud's hypocrisy once more revealed—the Arab street in many a latitude would riot en masse.

One thing is certain; Bandar Bush, as well as the Saudi-Israeli axis, will pull no punches to derail any rapprochement between Washington and Tehran. As for the Bigger Picture, the real "international community" may always dream that one day Washington elites will finally see the light and figure out that the US-Saudi strategic alliance sealed in 1945 between Franklin D Roosevelt and King Abdul Aziz ibn Saud makes absolutely no sense.

October 2013

THE BIRTH OF THE "DE-AMERICANIZED" WORLD

This is it. China has had enough. The (diplomatic) gloves are off. It's time to build a "de-Americanized" world. It's time for a "new international reserve currency" to replace the US dollar.

It's all here, in a Xinhua editorial, straight from the dragon's mouth. And the year is only 2013. Fasten your seat belts—and that applies especially to the Washington elites. It's gonna be a bumpy ride.

Long gone are the Deng Xiaoping days of "keeping a low profile." The Xinhua editorial summarizes the straw that broke the dragon's back—the current US shutdown. After the Wall Street-provoked financial crisis, after the war on Iraq, a "befuddled world," and not only China, wants change.

This paragraph couldn't be more graphic:

> Instead of honoring its duties as a responsible leading power, a self-serving Washington has abused its superpower status and introduced even more chaos into the world by shifting financial risks overseas, instigating regional tensions amid territorial disputes, and fighting unwarranted wars under the cover of outright lies.

The solution, for Beijing, is to "de-Americanize" the current geopolitical equation—starting with more say in the IMF and World Bank for emerging economies and the developing world, leading to a "new international reserve currency that is to be created to replace the dominant US dollar."

Note that Beijing is not advocating completely smashing the Bretton Woods system—at least for now, but it is for having more deciding power. Sounds reasonable, considering that China holds slightly more weight inside the IMF than Italy. IMF "reform"—sort of—has been going on since 2010, but Washington, unsurprisingly, has vetoed anything substantial.

As for the move away from the US dollar, it's also already on, in varying degrees of speed, especially concerning trade amongst the BRICS group of emerging powers (Brazil, Russia, India, China and South Africa), which is now overwhelmingly in their respective currencies. The US dollar is slowly but surely being replaced by a basket of currencies.

"De-Americanization" is also already on. Take last week's Chinese trade charm offensive across Southeast Asia, which is incisively leaning towards even more action with their top commercial partner, China. Chinese President Xi Jinping clinched an array of deals with Indonesia, Malaysia and also Australia, only a few weeks after clinching another array of deals with the Central Asian "stans."

Chinese commitment to improve the Iron Silk Road reached fever pitch, with shares of Chinese rail companies going through the roof amid the prospect of a high-speed rail link with and through Thailand actually materializing. In Vietnam, Chinese Premier Li Keqiang sealed an understanding that the two country's territorial quarrels in the South China Sea would not interfere with even more business. Take that, "pivoting" to Asia.

All aboard the petroyuan

Everyone knows Beijing holds Himalayas of US Treasury bonds—courtesy of those massive trade surpluses accumulated over the past three decades plus an official policy of keeping the yuan appreciating very slowly, yet surely.

At the same time, Beijing has been acting. The yuan is also slowly but surely becoming more convertible in international markets. (Just last week, the European Central Bank and the People's Bank of China agreed to set up a US$45-$57 billion currency swap line that will add to the yuan's international strength and improve access to trade finance in the euro area.)

The unofficial date for full yuan convertibility could fall anywhere between 2017 and 2020. The target is clear; move away from piling up US debt, which implies, in the long run, Beijing removing itself from this market—and thus making it way more costly for the US to borrow. The collective leadership in Beijing has already made up its mind about it, and is acting accordingly.

The move towards a full convertible yuan is as inexorable as the BRICS move towards a basket of currencies progressively replacing the US dollar as a reserve currency. Until, further on down the road, the real cataclysmic event materializes; the advent of the petroyuan—destined to surpass the petrodollar once the Gulf petro-monarchies see which way the historical winds are blowing. Then we will enter a completely different geopolitical ball game.

We may be a long way away, but what is certain is that Deng Xiaoping's famous set of instructions is being progressively discarded; "Observe calmly; secure our position; cope with affairs calmly; hide our capacities and bide our time; be good at maintaining a low profile; and never claim leadership."

A mix of caution and deception, grounded on China's historical confidence and taking into consideration serious long-term ambition, this was classic Sun Tzu. So far, Beijing was laying low; letting the adversary commit fatal mistakes (and what a collection of multi-trillion-dollar mistakes...); and accumulating "capital."

The time to capitalize has now arrived. By 2009, after the Wall Street-provoked financial crisis, there were already Chinese rumblings about the "malfunctioning of the Western model" and ultimately the "malfunctioning of Western culture."

Beijing has listened to Dylan (with Mandarin subtitles?) and concluded yes, the times they-are-a-changing. With no foreseeable social, economic and political progress—the shutdown is just another graphic illustration, if any was needed—the US slide is as inexorable as China, bit by bit, spreading its wings to master 21st century post-modernity.

Make no mistake; the Washington elites will fight it like the ultimate plague. Still, Antonio Gramsci's intuition must now be upgraded; the old order has died, and the new one is one step closer to being born.

October 2013

TURKEY PUSHES CROSSROADS POLITICS

While everyone is concentrated on the possibility of a tectonic shift in US-Iran relations, and while a solution may be found for the Syrian tragedy in another upcoming set of negotiations in Geneva, Turkey is silently toiling in the background. Let's see what these sultans of swing are up to.

We start on the internal front. Abdul Mejid I, the 31st Ottoman sultan (in power from 1839 to 1861) always dreamed of a submerged tunnel under the Bosphorus linking Europe to Asia.

It took "Sultan" Erdogan, as in Prime Minister Recep Tayyip Erdogan, to make it happen, when last month he inaugurated—on the 90th anniversary of the founding of Ataturk's Republic—the US$3 billion, 76-kilometer Marmaray rail system which, in the hardly hyperbolic words of Mustafa Kara, mayor of Istanbul's Uskudar district (where the tunnel comes out), will "eventually link London to Beijing, creating unimagined global connections."[40]

It certainly helps that this technological marvel fits right into China's extremely ambitious New Silk Road(s) strategy which, just like the original Silk Road, starts in Xian, and aims to cross to Europe via, where else, Istanbul.[41]

So the fact remains that "Sultan" Erdogan simply has not been downed by the Gezi Park protests last June. All the ruling party AKP's

---

[40] Asia and Europe to get Bosphorus rail link as Marmaray opens, Hurriyet Daily News, October 28, 2013.
[41] New Silk Road starts with Xian, South China Morning Post, October 29, 2013.

mega-projects—supported by millions in rural Anatolia, ignored for decades by the secular elites in Istanbul—are alive and kicking.

By 2025, more than a million commuters will be using the Marmaray. The third Bosphorus bridge, close to the Black Sea, is being built—despite Alevi fury that it will be named after Selim The Grim, a sultan who ordered the slaughter of thousands of Alevis. Same for the new six-runway airport northwest of Istanbul. And then there's the 50 km "crazy canal" (Erdogan's own definition), linking the Sea of Marmara to the Black Sea, so monstrous tanker traffic may be diverted away from the Bosphorus. The Turkish green movement insists this could destroy whole aquatic ecosystems, but Erdogan is unfazed.

That oily Kurdish factor

In the wider world, Turkish foreign policy is now on overdrive. And inevitably, it's all related to energy.

Foreign Minister Ahmet Davutoglu earlier this month hosted Iranian Foreign Minister Javad Zarif in Ankara. Then he went to Baghdad and met Iraqi Prime Minister Nouri al-Maliki.

Davutoglu also visited Washington; he wrote an editorial published by *Foreign Policy* praising the US-Turkish "strategic partnership," now facing "an increasingly chaotic geopolitical environment"; and he made sure to support US-Iran negotiations.

Earlier this week, Davutoglu teamed up with Erdogan for a high-level meeting with Russian President Vladimir Putin and Foreign Minister Sergei Lavrov in St. Petersburg. Next week he'll be in Tehran.

The question is what does Ankara want from Washington for so eagerly supporting a US-Iran normalization?

The key is Iraqi Kurdistan. Ankara wants Washington's blessing for the now famously fractious 250,000 barrel-a-day oil pipeline from northern Iraq, bypassing Baghdad. This pipeline would add to the perennially troubled Kirkuk-Ceyhan, controlled (sort of) by Baghdad; currently operating at best at one-fifth of its official capacity of 1.6 million barrels a day, bombed virtually every week, and with zero maintenance.

It's not as much about the oil (which Turkey badly needs) as a political/economic alliance that ideally translates into more Kurdish votes for the ruling AKP party in the 2014 Turkish elections.

The (insurmountable) problem is the Obama administration has no intention—at the present negotiation junction—to provoke Tehran by allowing a Turkish project that most of all provokes Iran's ally Baghdad. That's just another instance that everything of consequence happening in Southwest Asia nowadays involves Iran.[42]

So it all depends on how far the US-Iran rapprochement will go—leaving Ankara unable to alienate Baghdad and Tehran at the same time. Ankara, though, is also aware of huge potential benefits down the line. That would mean much more oil and gas flowing from Iran than the current long-term annual contract for natural gas via the Tabriz-Ankara pipeline if—and when—Western investment start pumping again into Iran's energy industry.

That Wahhabi-Likudnik axis

President Obama gets along very well with Turkish Prime Minister Erdogan. But while Obama has nothing but praise for Erdogan, for the House of Saud the name "Obama" is now worse than any plague. And Erdogan is not exactly that much popular.

---

[42] Deal or No Deal, Iran's Stock Keeps Rising, Al-Akhbar English, November 20, 2013.

Erdogan enthusiastically supported Morsi and the Muslim Brotherhood in Egypt, while the House of Saud's hero is coup plotter General Sisi. In Syria, Erdogan once again supports the Muslim Brotherhood-linked "rebels," while the Saudis, with Bandar Bush ahead of the pack, de facto finance and weaponize all sorts of nasties including the al-Qaeda offshoot Islamic State of Iraq and the Levant (ISIL). Erdogan has evolved an extremely fractious relationship with Israel, while the Wahhabi-Likudnik anti-Iran/Syria axis has never been stronger.[43]

It's easy to forget an Ankara-Damascus-Tehran alliance was in place before the foreign-imposed Syrian civil war. That was part of Davutoglu's "zero problems with our neighbors" doctrine, then morphed into "all kinds of problems." The House of Saud obviously did what it could to undermine the former alliance with the carrot of more trade and investment in Turkey. It worked for a while, when the myth of an "Arab Spring" still held sway, and Turkey and the Saudis were even coordinating their support for assorted Syrian "rebels."

Now it's a totally different configuration. Only in Turkey we find assorted Islamists, secularists, the left and assorted liberals all in agreement that the House of Saud is a pretty nasty bunch. And not by accident "Sultan Erdogan"—who allegedly wants the return of the Caliphate—has been derided non-stop all over pan-Arab media, which for all practical purposes is 90%-controlled by Saudis.

Ankara seems to have finally realized it must be very careful regarding its Syria position. Not very far from its borders, Syrian Kurds are fighting Saudi-supported jihadis.

---

[43] The Wahhabi-Likudnik war of terror, *Asia Times Online*, November 20, 2013.

Worse; scores of al-Qaeda-linked jihadis-to-be—a Mujahideen International—are congregating in a network of safe houses in southern Turkey, including Antakya, the capital of Hatay province, before being smuggled over the border to mostly join the Islamic State of Iraq and the Levant (ISIL). Predictably, NATO is not amused.[44]

It's all about Pipelineistan

Turkey's number one foreign policy aim is to position itself as a critical energy crossroads for any oil and natural gas coming from Russia, the Caspian, Central Asia and even the Middle East to Europe.

Yet Turkey has been squeezed by two conflicting Pipelineistan narratives. One is the never-ending soap opera Nabucco, which basically means delivering natural gas to Europe from just about anywhere (Azerbaijan, Turkmenistan, Iran, Iraq, even Egypt) except Russia. And the other is the South Stream pipeline, proposed by Russia and crossing the Black Sea.

Insisting in its role as a neutral bridge between East and West, Ankara hedged its bets. But after the European financial crisis took over, Nabucco was, for all practical purposes, doomed. What's left now is the so-called Nabucco West—a shorter, 1,300 km pipeline from Turkey to Central Europe—and the much cheaper Trans-Adriatic Pipeline (TAP), just 500 km from Turkey across the Balkans to Italy.

The consortium (including BP, Total and Azerbaijan's SOCAR) developing the huge Shah Deniz II field in Azerbaijan ended up choosing TAP. So Nabucco is now virtually six feet under.

---

[44] The secret jihadi smuggling route through Turkey, CNN, November 5, 2013.

To say that's been a nifty deal for Moscow is a huge understatement. TAP does not threaten Gazprom's hold on the European market. And besides, Moscow got closer to Baku. Dick Cheney must adjust his pacemaker for another heart attack; after all his elaborate energy plans, Moscow and Baku are nothing less than discussing transporting Russian oil through the notorious Baku-Tbilisi-Ceyhan (BTC) pipeline, which Dr. Zbig Brzezinski dreamed up to exactly bypass Russia. On top of it, they are also bound to reverse the Baku-Novorossiysk pipeline to pump Russian oil into Azerbaijan.

Additionally, that's the end of Turkish (and European) pipe dreams of having wacky "gas republic" Turkmenistan supplying energy across the Caspian through the Caucasus and Turkey to Europe. For Moscow, this is non-negotiable; we control the transit of Central Asian energy to Europe. Moreover, Turkmenistan already has better sturgeon to fry—via its ultra-profitable gas pipeline to China.

The bottom line: Russia getting even more ascendant in the Caucasus equals Turkey—which imports nearly all of its oil, coal and natural gas—becoming even more energy dependent on Russia. Russia supplies nearly 60% of Turkey's natural gas—and rising. Iran supplies 20%. Moscow is sure Turkey will soon overtake Germany as its biggest energy client.

That's certainly what Erdogan was discussing in detail this past Wednesday in Moscow. And then there is Turkey's ambitious plan to build 23 nuclear power plants by 2023. Guess who's ahead? Moscow, of course. Not only as builder but also as primary supplier of nuclear fuel. No package of Western sanctions seems to be on the horizon.

So Ankara seems to be (silently) hectic on all fronts. Erdogan is carefully cultivating his friend Obama—positioning himself as a privileged sort of messenger. Erdogan supports Iran's civilian nuclear program—which instantaneously placed him as highly suspicious in the eyes of the

Wahhabi-Likudnik axis of fear and loathing. That's the key reason for the widening estrangement between Ankara and Riyadh.

Ankara's desire to be a key actor in an eventual US-Iran rapprochement springs out of a simple calculation. Faced with tremendous political, economic and security barriers, Turkey may only fulfill its wish of becoming the privileged East-West energy transit corridor with Iran by its side.

November 2013

CHINA VS US "SEA-TO-SHINING-SEA"

It happened now and it will happen again: a near-collision between an American and a Chinese naval vessel in the South China Sea.

The USS *Cowpens*, a 10,000-ton guided-missile cruiser, got "too close" to a drill involving the *Liaoning*, China's first aircraft carrier, and its carrier task force, according to the *Global Times*.

The US Pacific Fleet stressed that the cruiser had to take emergency measures to avoid a collision. Yet the Global Times accused the cruiser of "harassing" the *Liaoning* formation by taking "offensive actions."

The paper spelt it loudly; "If the American navy and air force always encroach near China's doorstep, confrontation is bound to take place."

Finally, China's Defense Ministry intervened to clarify that the vessels had "met" each other in the South China Sea but the worst was avoided via "effective and normal communication."

Communication had better be damned "effective" from now on as China asserts itself as a rising sea power and it's obviously unclear who can really do what in the South as well as the East China Sea, not to mention the oceans beyond.

It's a fact that China's still booming economy is directly dependent on its complex maritime lines of supply (and demand)—mostly over the Indian Ocean and the Western Pacific. But that does not mean that China is trying to control its surrounding seas by imposing a sino-version of the 19th century Monroe Doctrine, which was essentially a continental strategy of hemispheric domination (ask any informed Latin American about it).

Beijing is indeed increasing maritime patrols in the South and East China Sea. There have been some scuffles, mostly rhetorical, with, for instance, the Philippines. And as Beijing decided to create its new air defense identification zone (ADIZ), commercial airlines—not inclined to jeopardize their insurance arrangements—are all filing their flight plans with Beijing, which means they acknowledge China's right and authority.

Let's say China is now in the stage of creating facts on the sea. For the moment, a kind of uneasy accommodation seems to prevail involving the Americans and also the Japanese. Beijing knows that the US Navy and the Japanese Navy have better training—and more experience—than the Chinese navy. Once again, for now.

Slouching across the Rimland

This is a pretty decent summary in the *South China Morning Post* of the recent growth of China's naval power in the context of a speech given by then-President Hu Jintao last November "against the backdrop of US President Barack Obama's 'pivot to Asia'."

It does connect a few dots between the new mantra coined by President Xi Jinping—the "Chinese dream"—and the rise of China as a maritime power.

But there's way much more to it. There's no question Chinese strategists have stripped Obama's "pivot" upside down, and that means furiously brushing up on their Mahan, as in US Navy captain Alfred Mahan, and specifically The Influence of Sea Power Upon History, 1660-1783, published in 1890.

Yes, it's always about a "pivot." Mahan believed that the geographical pivot of empires was not the Heartland of Eurasia—as with Mackinder—but the Indian and Pacific oceans. For Mahan, whoever controlled these oceans would be able to project power all around the Eurasian Rimland, and also affect the "Heartland," deep in Central Asia. The Chinese know how this has translated into the US Navy being able to become a factor in Eurasia—part of that "sea-to-shining-sea" domination enshrined in Manifest Destiny.

Our strategists in Beijing are very much aware of how China—as a state and even more as a civilization—extends from the Heartland to the warm waters of the Pacific Rim. They are also aware of an absolutely crucial text, A Cooperative Strategy for 21st Century Sea Power, published by the US Navy in 2007. This is essentially the blueprint for Obama's pivot, based—in theory—on cooperation with local navies (Australia, Singapore, Philippines) rather than dominance. (Incidentally, the Navy advertises to whomever is concerned that "sea power protects the American way of life.")

Inevitably, our Chinese strategists also brushed up on their Spykman, as in Dutchman Nicholas Spykman, who founded the Institute of International Studies at Yale in 1935. It was Spykman who conceptualized South Asia, Southeast Asia, China and Japan, as well as the Middle East, as part of the Rimland, which for him was the key to world power (not the Heartland).

And it's also here that we see how what a sea power like the US calls "containment" is interpreted by a Heartland power like China (not to mention Russia) as "encirclement."

It's also easy for Westerners to forget how China was once a formidable sea power, at the apex in the 15th century, via the exceptionally gifted

Admiral Zheng He, commanding an extensive fleet of often remarkably large ships under the Ming emperors.

Now the sea power has re-awakened. No more *taoguang yanghui*—as in "keeping a low profile," the notorious Deng Xiaoping motto.

And it's as if Spykman had also somewhat seen the future. Just check this passage of America's Strategy in World Politics: the United States and the Balance of Power, published in 1942:

> *A modern, vitalized, and militarized China... is going to be a threat not only to Japan, but also to the position of the Western Powers in the Asiatic Mediterranean. China will be a continental power of huge dimensions in control of a large section of the littoral of that middle sea. Her geographic position will be similar to that of the United States in regard to the American Mediterranean. When China becomes strong, her present economic penetration in that region will undoubtedly take on political overtones. It is quite possible to envisage the day when this body of water will be controlled not by British, American, or Japanese sea power but by Chinese air power.*

It's happening now, only seven decades later, as Obama's Mahanian "pivot" slouches towards ever more containment of rising China. May we live in "effective and normal communication" times.

December 2013

ALL IN PLAY IN THE NEW GREAT GAME

The big story of 2014 will be Iran. Of course, the big story of the early 21st century will never stop being US-China, but it's in 2014 that we will know whether a comprehensive accord transcending the Iranian nuclear program is attainable; and in this case the myriad ramifications will affect all that's in play in the New Great Game in Eurasia, including US-China.

As it stands, we have an interim deal of the P5+1 (the UN Security Council's five permanent members plus Germany) with Iran, and no deal between the US and Afghanistan. So, once again, we have Afghanistan configured as a battleground between Iran and the House of Saud, part of a geopolitical game played out in overdrive since the US invasion of Iraq in 2003 along the northern rim of the Middle East all the way to Khorasan and South Asia.

Then there's the element of Saudi paranoia, extrapolating from the future of Afghanistan to the prospect of a fully "rehabilitated" Iran becoming accepted by Western political/financial elites. This, by the way, has nothing to do with that fiction, the "international community"; after all, Iran was never banished by the BRICS, (ie Brazil, Russia, India, China and South Africa), the Non-Aligned Movement and the bulk of the developing world.

Those damned jihadis

Every major player in the Barack Obama administration has warned Afghan President Hamid Karzai that either he signs a bilateral "security agreement" authorizing some ersatz of the US occupation or Washington will withdraw all of its troops by the end of 2014.

Wily puppet Karzai will milk this for all it's worth—as in extracting hardcore concessions. Yet, whatever happens, Iran will maintain if not enlarge its sphere of influence in Afghanistan. This intersection of Central and South Asia is geopolitically crucial for Iranian to project power, second only to Southwest Asia (what we call the "Middle East").

We should certainly expect the House of Saud to keep using every nasty trick available to the imagination of Saudi Arabia's Bandar bin Sultan, aka Bandar Bush, to manipulate Sunnis all across AfPak with a target of, essentially, preventing Iran from projecting power.

But Iran can count on a key ally, India. As Delhi accelerates its security cooperation with Kabul, we reach the icing on the Hindu Kush; India, Iran and Afghanistan developing their southern branch of the New Silk Road, with a special niche for the highway connecting Afghanistan to the Iranian port of Chabahar (Afghanistan meets the Indian Ocean).

So watch out for all sorts of interpolations of an Iran-India alliance pitted against a Saudi-Pakistani axis. This axis has been supporting assorted Islamists in Syria—with nefarious results; but because Pakistan has also been engulfed in appalling violence against Shi'ites, Islamabad won't be too keen to be too closely aligned with the House of Saud in AfPak.

Washington and Tehran for their part happen to be once more aligned (remember 2001?) in Afghanistan; neither one wants hardcore jihadis roaming around. Even Islamabad—which for all practical purposes has lost all its leverage with the Taliban in AfPak—would like jihadis to go up in smoke.

All these players know that any number of remaining US forces and swarms of contractors will not fill the power vacuum in Kabul. The whole thing is bound to remain murky, but essentially the scenario points to the Central-South Asia crossroads as the second-largest geopolitical—and sectarian—battleground in Eurasia after the Levantine-Mesopotamian combo.

Zero energy from our neighbor?

As much as India, Iraq is also in favor of a comprehensive deal with Iran. And to think that Iran and Iraq might have been engaged in a silent nuclear arms race with one another at the end of the last century, just for Baghdad now to fiercely defend Tehran's right to enrich uranium. Not to mention that Baghdad depends on Iran for trade, electricity and material help in that no-holds-barred war against Islamists/Salafi-jihadis.

Turkey also welcomes a comprehensive agreement with Iran. Turkey's trade with Iran has nowhere to go but up. The target is US$30 billion by 2015. More than 2,500 Iranian companies have invested in Turkey. Ankara cannot possibly support Western sanctions; it makes no business sense. Sanctions go against its policy of expanding trade. Moreover, Turkey depends on inexpensive natural gas imported from Iran.

After deviating wildly from its previous policy of "zero problems with our neighbors," Ankara is now waking up to the business prospect of Syrian reconstruction. Iraq may help, drawing from its oil wealth. Energy-deprived Turkey can't afford to be marginalized. A re-stabilized Syria will mean the go-ahead for the $10 billion Iran-Iraq-Syria pipeline. If Ankara plays the game, an extension could be in the cards—fitting its self-proclaimed positioning as a privileged Pipelineistan crossroads from East to West.

The bottom line is that the Turkish-Iranian conflict over the future of Syria pales when compared with the energy game and booming trade.

This points to Ankara and Tehran increasingly converging into finding a peaceful solution in Syria.

But there's a huge problem. The Geneva II conference on January 22 may represent the nail in the coffin of the House of Saud's push to inflict regime change on Bashar al-Assad. Once again, this implies that Bandar Bush is ready to go absolutely medieval—plowing the whole spectrum of summary executions, beheadings, suicide and car bombings and all-out sectarianism all along the Iraqi-Syrian-Lebanese front.

At least there will be a serious counterpunch; as Sharmine Narwani outlines here, the former "Shi'ite crescent"—or "axis of resistance"—is now reconstituting itself as a "security arc" against Salafi-jihadis. Pentagon conceptualizers of the "arc of instability" kind never thought about that.

Missile nonsense, anyone?

Adults in Washington—not exactly a majority—may have already visualized the fabulous derivatives of a Western deal with Iran by examining China's approval and the possibility of future Iranian help to stabilize Afghanistan.

For China, Iran is a matter of national security—as a top source of energy (plus all those myriad cultural affinities between Persians and Chinese since Silk Road times). Threatening a country to which the US owes over $1 trillion with third-party, Department of the Treasury sanctions for buying Iranian oil seems to be off the cards, at least for now.

As for Moscow, by coming with a diplomatic resolution to the chemical weapons crisis in Syria, Vladimir Putin no less than saved the Obama administration from itself, as it was about to plunge into a new Middle Eastern war of potentially cataclysmic consequences. Immediately afterwards, the door was opened for the first breach since 1979 of the US-Iran Wall of Mistrust.

Crucially, after the Iranian nuclear interim deal was signed, Russian Foreign Minister Sergei Lavrov went for the jugular; the deal cancels the need for NATO's ballistic missile-defense in Central Europe—with interceptor bases in Romania and Poland set to become operational in 2015 and 2018, respectively. Washington has always insisted on the fiction that this was designed to counter missile "threats" from Iran.

Without the Iranian pretext, the justification for ballistic missile defense is unsustainable.

The real negotiation starts more or less now, in early 2014. Logically the endgame by mid-2014 would be no more sanctions in exchange for close supervision of Iran's nuclear program. Yet this is a game of superimposed obfuscations. Washington sells itself the myth that this is about somewhat controlling the Iranian nuclear program, an alternative plan to an ultra high-risk Shock and Awe strike to annihilate vast swathes of Iranian infrastructure.

No one is talking, but it's easy to picture BRICS heavyweights Russia and China casually informing Washington what kind of weaponry and material support they would offer Iran in case of an American attack.

Tehran, for its part, would like to interpret the tentative rapprochement as the US renouncing regime change, with Supreme Leader Ayatollah Khamenei paying the price of trading elements of a nuclear program for the end of sanctions.

Assuming Tehran and Washington are able to isolate their respective confrontational lobbies—a titanic task—the benefits are self-evident. Tehran wants—and badly needs—investment in its energy industry (at least $200 billion) and other sectors of the economy. Western Big Oil is dying to invest in Iran. The economic opening will inevitably be part of the final agreement—and for Western turbo-capitalism this is a must; a market of 80 million largely well-educated people, with fabulous location, and swimming in oil and gas.[45] What's not to like?

Peacemaker or just a trickster?

Tehran supports Assad in large part to combat the jihadi virus—incubated by wealthy sponsors in Saudi Arabia and the Gulf. So whatever the spin in Washington, there's no possibility of a serious solution for Syria without involving Iran. The Obama administration now seems to realize that Assad is the least bad among unanimously bad options. Who would have bet on it only three months ago?

The interim deal with Iran is the first tangible evidence that Barack Obama is actually considering leaving his foreign policy mark in Southwest Asia/Middle East. It helps that the 0.00001% who run the show may have realized that a US president globally perceived as a dancing fool engenders massive instability in the Empire and all its satrapies.

The bottom line is that Obama needs to respect his partner Hassan Rouhani—who has made clear to the Americans he must secure non-stop political backing by Khamenei; that's the only way to sideline the very powerful religious/ideological lobby in Tehran/Qom against any deal with the former "Great Satan." So "Great Satan" needs to negotiate in good faith.

A realpolitik old hand (with a soft heart) would say that the Obama administration is aiming at a balance of power between Iran, Saudi Arabia and Israel.

---

[45] Iran Deal Opens Door for Businesses, Wall Street Journal, December 1, 2013.

A more Machiavellian realpolitik old hand would say this is about pitting Sunni versus Shi'ite, Arabs versus Persians, to keep them paralyzed.

Perhaps a more prosaic reading is that the US as a mob protector is no more. As much as everyone is aware of a powerful Israel lobby and an almost as powerful Wahhabi petrodollar lobby in Washington, it's never discussed that neither Israel nor the House of Saud have a "protector" other than the US.

So from now on, if the House of Saud sees Iran as a threat, it will have to come up with its own strategy. And if Israel insists on seeing Iran as an "existential threat"—which is a joke—it will have to deal with it as a strategic problem. If a real consequence of the current shift is that Washington will not fight wars for Saudi or Israeli sake anymore, that's already a monumental game changer.

Xi Jinping and Vladimir Putin see it is in their interest to "protect" peacemaker Obama. And yet everyone remains on slippery territory; Obama as peacemaker—this time really honoring his Nobel Prize—may be just a mirror image. And Washington could always march towards regime change in Tehran led by the next White House tenant after 2016.

For 2014 though, plenty of signs point to a tectonic shift in the geopolitical map of Eurasia, with Iran finally emerging as the real superpower in Southwest Asia over the designs of both Israel and the House of Saud. Now that's (geopolitical) entertainment. Happy New Year.

December 2013

Reliving Machiavelli in Florence

2014 has barely dawned, and I'm standing in a cold, rainy evening at the Piazza della Signoria in Florence, staring at the round plaque on the floor—ignored by the throngs of Chinese tourists—celebrating the hanging and burning of the monk Savonarola in May 23, 1498, accused of conspiring against the Florentine Republic.

Yet I'm thinking—how could I not—of Machiavelli. He was only 29 on that fateful day. He was standing only a few feet away from where I am. What was he thinking?

He had seen how Savonarola, a popular Dominican preacher, had been hailed as the savior of the republic. Savonarola rewrote the constitution to empower the lower middle class; talk about a risky (populist) move. He allied Florence with France. But he had no counterpunch when the pro-Spanish pope Alexander VI imposed harsh economic sanctions that badly hurt Florence's merchant class (a centuries-old anticipation of US sanctions on Iranian bazaaris).

Savonarola had also conducted the original bonfire of the vanities, whose flaming pyramid included wigs, pots of rouge, perfumes, books with poems by Ovid, Boccaccio and Petrarch, busts and paintings of "profane" subjects (even—horror of horrors—some by Botticelli), lutes, violas, flutes, sculptures of naked women, figures of Greek gods and on top of it all, a hideous effigy of Satan.

In the end, Florentines were fed up with Savonarola's hardcore puritan antics—and a murky papal Inquisition sentence sealed the deal. I could picture Machiavelli exhibiting his famous wry smile—as the bonfire had burned exactly one year before at the very same place where Savonarola was now in flames. The verdict: realpolitik had no place for a "democracy" directed by God. God, for that matter, didn't even care. It was only human nature that is able to condition which way the wind blows; towards freedom or towards servitude.

So this is what happened in that day at the Piazza della Signoria in 1498—in the same year Lorenzo the Magnificent died and Christopher Columbus crossed the Atlantic on his third voyage to "discover" the New World; no less than the birth of Western political theory in the mind of young Niccolo.

Study humanity, young man

Florence is the first modern state in the world, as Jacob Burckhardt makes it clear in his magisterial *The Civilization of the Renaissance in Italy*, in awe about "the wondrous Florentine spirit, at once keenly critical and artistically creative."

Florentines spent a long time weaving the proud, patriotic tradition of a self-governing republic; a very Aristotelian set up according to which "the end of the state is not mere life, it is rather a good quality of life." Very cooperative, with everyone involved, completely different from Plato's Republic, whose rules were imposed from above.

At the dawn of the 15th century, Aristotle-reading Florentines eager to celebrate their civic and political freedom were busy on their way to carve—alongside their fabulous traditions of pictorial realism and fondness for classical architecture—no less than what became known as the Renaissance.

Why did Florence invent the Renaissance? Vasari's answer was as good as any: "The air of Florence making minds naturally free, and not content with mediocrity." It helped that education focused on the *studia humanitatis*—the "study of humanity" (on the way to oblivion now in the early 21st century), featuring history (to understand the greatness of ancient Greece and Rome); rhetoric; Greek and Roman literature (to improve eloquence); and moral philosophy, which boiled down to Aristotle's *Ethics*.

Machiavelli, born in 1469, the same year young Lorenzo de' Medici, or Lorenzo the Magnificent, his grandfather Cosimo's favorite, ascended to power after the death of his father Piero, lived for the most part in a Florence under the Medici. So he understood the nature of the (rigged) game; as crack historian Francesco Guicciardini put it, Lorenzo was a "benevolent tyrant in a constitutional republic."

Machiavelli's family was not wealthy—but totally committed to the ideal of civic humanism. Unlike Lorenzo, he may not have received the finest humanist education available, but Machiavelli studied Latin and read ancient philosophers and especially historians—Thucydides, Plutarch, Tacitus, and Livius, whose works were found in Florence's bookshops. In the ancient Greek and Roman heroes he saw examples of great virtue, courage and wisdom; what a sorry contrast with the corruption and stupidity of his contemporaries (we could say the same thing half a millennium later).

While Machiavelli was an Aristotelian, Lorenzo was somewhat a Platonist. Yet it was Cosimo's protege, the philosopher Marsilio Ficino, the coordinator of the Platonic Academy, who best explained it; Lorenzo did not believe in Plato, he used him. And on top of it he knew how to show off—as in installing Donatello's spectacularly ambisexual *David* on its pedestal in the cortile of the Palazzo Medici, and avidly promoting the leading philosopher among his circle of friends, the dashing Pico della Mirandola, known as the "man who knew everything"—or at least the entire range of human knowledge available in the Renaissance since the fall of Constantinople in 1453.

And then, only one month after Savonarola's burning, the slender, beady black-eyed and black-haired man with a small head and aquiline nose, described by his biographer Pasquale Villari as "a very acute observer with a sharp mind" got a job; and for 14 years he was a loyal servant of the restored Florentine republic, always on horseback on sensitive missions, negotiating, among others, with Pope Julius II, the King of France Louis XII, the Holy Roman Emperor Maximilian I, and the unpredictable, larger-than-life Cesare Borgia, the illegitimate second son of the man who would become pope Alexander VI. Machiavelli was in charge of Florence's foreign policy; definitely not your usual Beltway think-tank armchair "expert."

While Machiavelli was hanging out with Cesare Borgia, he became friends with Borgia's chief military engineer, none other than Leonardo da Vinci. One would need a Dante to imagine the dialogue between the man crafting the new science of politics and the most accomplished scientific mind of the Renaissance; the bifurcation of the humanist spirit, from art, poetry and philosophy into reality—politics and science.

A satire or a living book?

As I sat down in my favorite *enoteca* in front of the Pitti palace to re-read *The Prince*, I also delved on other sources; there has been a deluge of books on Machiavelli celebrating the 500th anniversary of the writing of *The Prince*, which was concluded after roughly four months in late 1513. The best happened to be *Il sorriso di Niccolo* (Editori Laterza), by Princeton's Maurizio Viroli. Viroli established for good that Machiavelli was never a Medici puppet.

Before he became secretary of the Second Chancery, in June 1498, Machiavelli was admittedly very close to Lorenzo the Magnificent. Soon after the Medicis returned to power in Venice after a period of exile, he had to endure the *strappado*—the Florentine torture of hands tied behind the back, body lifted to the ceiling by rope and pulley, and dropped straight down—no less than six times (is the CIA aware of it?). Yet he didn't become a rat: he was left to rot; and after 22 days was set free from his cell at the Bargello tower in early 1513 by the intervention of two Medici supporters.

In the final years of his life, Machiavelli was under various guises at the service of pope Clemente VII, none other than Giulio de Giuliano de Medici. But the bottom line is that Machiavelli was not a Medici follower; he wanted above all for the Medici to follow his advice.

So he left jail, impoverished but not broken, retreated to his small farmhouse, and set out to write. *The Prince* came out as history—not political theory. Rousseau actually branded it a "satire." Gramsci called it "a living book"—a celebration of a utopian Prince "via so many passionate, mythical elements that come alive in the conclusion, in the invocation of a really existing prince." So Machiavelli in fact designed the myth of the founder and the redeemer of a free republic—imagining that the redemption of the state would be at the same time his own redemption after he was stripped of his job of secretary by a laconic communique and later accused of being a conspirator.

It has been a blessing to re-read *The Prince* alongside *The Discourses*—which, in time, became the intellectual and political guide of all who cherished the ideal of republican freedom in Europe and the Americas. *The Discourses* is Machiavelli's fusion of Polybius and Aristotle. The Romans had found out that a great empire was doomed if it did not keep Aristotle's balance of monarchy, aristocracy and democracy. Machiavelli went one step ahead; every real republic is actually doomed. In a free republic like in Ancient Greece and Rome, or Florence before the Medici, too much prosperity, success, greed—and over-extension—distorts men's drive towards self-enrichment (or dissolves it into complacency) rather than keep it at the service of the state.

The real rot comes from within—not from an external power. Think of the late Soviet Union. Think of the current decline of the American Empire. But then again, mediocre exceptionalists never got the picture; Leo Strauss, at the University of Chicago in the 1950s, taught that Machiavelli was "a teacher of evil."

As the rot from within grows, that's where the Prince steps in. He's like the Last Man Standing—very far from the idealized figure of a philosopher-king or a Platonic teacher. He's the ruler who pulls a corrupt society out of its devious, self-destructive ways and hurls it back towards sound political life—and preeminence. (Machiavelli was specifically thinking of someone to save Italy from foreign invaders and its own deaf, blind and dumb rulers).

And if the Prince must resort to violence to defend the republic, it must never be gratuitous, but always subordinated to a well-argued *ragion di stato* (the 2003 bombing and occupation of Iraq obviously does not qualify). The Prince anyway is not a political messiah; rather a mix of the fox ("in order to recognize traps") and the lion ("to frighten off wolves"). The most apt contemporary version would be Vladimir Putin.

In that fateful day in May 1498, Machiavelli saw in Savonarola's burning how religious fundamentalism is incompatible with a successfully commercial and politically viable society (House of Saud princes never read *The Prince*). And then he displayed to us the wall of mistrust between ethics and the science of government—as if drawing an abridged road map for the future global hegemony of Western civilization.

It's curioser and curioser how the Medici dynasty rejected *The Prince* at the time; after all, that was the ultimate handbook on how to become a (political) Godfather, in the post-Renaissance and beyond. In parallel, I always wondered what wise Ming dynasty courtiers would have made of *The Prince*. Probably, imperially, ignore it.

So this is how I celebrated the half-a-millennium anniversary of *The Prince*; sharing a few glasses of Brunello, as if we were in a Florentine *osteria* in the early 16th century, with the spirit of a very distinguished senior civil servant of the Florentine Republic who was thrown out of office exactly as he was admitted; poor, incorruptible and with his dignity intact. I could not but admire his wry smile dying in his lips and barely hiding his pain—but then again, he knew we're nothing but playing a small part in this whole human, all too human, comedy.

January 2014

WE ARE ALL LIVING PASOLINI'S THEOREM

In the early morning of November 2, 1975, in Idroscalo, a terminally dreadful shanty town in Ostia, outside Rome, the body of Pier Paolo Pasolini, then 53, an intellectual powerhouse and one of the greatest filmmakers of the 1960s and 1970s, was found badly beaten and run over by his own Alfa Romeo.

It was hard to conceive a more stunning, heartbreaking, modern mix of Greek tragedy with Renaissance iconography; in a bleak setting straight out of a Pasolini film, the author himself was immolated just like his main character in *Mamma Roma* (1962) lying in prison in the manner of the Dead Christ, aka the Lamentation of Christ, by Andrea Mantegna.

This might have been a gay tryst gone terribly wrong; a 17-year-old low life was charged with murder, but the young man was also linked with the Italian neo-fascists. The true story has never emerged. What did emerge is that "the new Italy"—or the aftereffects of a new capitalist revolution—killed Pasolini.

"Those destined to be dead"

Pasolini could only reach for the stars after graduating in literature from Bologna University—the oldest in the world—in 1943. Today, a Pasolini is utterly unthinkable. He would be something like an UFIO (unidentified flying intellectual object); the total intellectual—poet, dramatist, painter, musician, fiction writer, literary theorist, filmmaker and political analyst.

For educated Italians, he was essentially a poet (what a huge compliment that meant, decades ago...) In his masterpiece *The Ashes of Gramsci* (1952), Pasolini draws a striking parallel, in terms of striving for a heroic ideal, between Gramsci and Shelley—who happen to be buried in the same cemetery in Rome. Talk about poetic justice.

Then he effortlessly switched from word to image. The young Martin Scorsese was absolutely gobsmacked when he first saw *Accattone* (1961); not to mention the young Bernardo Bertolucci, who happened to be learning the facts on the ground as Pasolini's cameraman. At a minimum, there would be no Scorsese, Bertolucci, or for that matter Fassbinder, Abel Ferrara and countless others without Pasolini.

And especially today, as we wallow in our tawdry 24/7 *Vanity Fair*, it's impossible not to sympathize with Pasolini's method—which veers from sulphuric acid critique of the bourgeosie (as in *Teorema* and *Porcile*) to seeking refuge into the classics (his Greek tragedy phase) and the fascinating medieval "Trilogy of Life"—the adaptations of the *Decameron* (1971), *The Canterbury Tales* (1972) and *Arabian Nights* (1974).

It's also no wonder Pasolini decided to flee corrupt, decadent Italy and film in the developing world—from Cappadocia in Turkey for *Medea* to Yemen for *Arabian Nights*. Bertolucci later would do the same, shooting in Morocco (*The Sheltering Sky*), Nepal (his Buddha epic) and China (*The Last Emperor*, his formidable Hollywood triumph).

And then there was the unclassifiable *Salo, or The 120 Days of Sodom*, Pasolini's last tortured, devastating film, released only a few months after his assassination, banned for years in dozens of countries, and unforgiving in extrapolating way beyond Italy's (and Western culture's) flirt with fascism.

From 1973 to 1975, Pasolini wrote a series of columns for the Milan-based Corriere della Sera, published as *Scritti Corsari* in 1975 and then as *Lutheran Letters*, posthumously, in 1976. Their overarching theme was the "anthropological mutation" of modern Italy, which can also be read as a microcosm for most of the West.

I belong to a generation where many were absolutely transfixed by Pasolini on screen and on paper. At the time, it was clear these columns were the intellectual RPGs of an extremely sharp—but utterly alone—intellectual. Re-reading them today, they sound no less than prophetical.

When examining the dichotomy between bourgeois boys and proletarian boys—as in Northern Italy vs Southern Italy—Pasolini stumbled into no less than a new category, "difficult to describe (because no one had done it before)" and for which he had "no linguistic and terminological precedents." They were "those destined to be dead." One of them in fact, may have become his killer at Idroscalo.

As Pasolini argued, the new specimens were those who until the mid-1950s would have been victims of infant mortality. Science intervened and saved them from physical death. So they are survivors, "and in their life there's something of *contro natura*." Thus, Pasolini argued, as sons that are born today are not, a priori, "blessed," those that are born "in excess" are definitely "unblessed."

In short, for Pasolini, sporting a sentiment of not being really welcomed, and even being guilty about it, the new generation was "infinitely more fragile, brutish, sad, pallid, and ill than all preceding generations." They are depressed or aggressive. And "nothing may cancel the shadow that an unknown abnormality projects over their life." Nowadays, this interpretation can easily explain the alienated, cross-border Islamic youth who joins a jihad in desperation.

At the same time, according to Pasolini, this unconscious feeling of being fundamentally expendable just feeds "those destined to be dead" in their yearning for normality, "the total, unreserved adherence to the horde, the will not to look distinct or diverse." So they "show how to live conformism aggressively." They teach "renunciation," a "tendency towards unhappiness," the "rhetoric of ugliness," and brutishness. And the brutish become the champions of fashion and behavior (here Pasolini was already prefiguring punk in England in 1976).

The self-described "rationalist, idealist old bourgeois" went way beyond these reflections about the "no future for you" generation. Pasolini piled up, among other disasters, the urban destruction of Italy, the responsibility for the "anthropological degradation" of Italians, the terrible condition of hospitals, schools and public infrastructure, the savage explosion of mass culture and mass media, and the "delinquent stupidity" of television, on the "moral burden" of those who have governed Italy from 1945 to 1975, that is, the US-supported Christian Democrats.

He deftly configured the "cynicism of the new capitalist revolution—the first real rightist revolution." Such a revolution, he argued, "from an anthropological point of view—in terms of the foundation of a new 'culture'—implies men with no link to the past, living in 'imponderability'. So the only existential expectation possible is consumerism and satisfying his hedonistic impulses." This is Guy Debord's scathing 1960s "society of the spectacle" critique expanded to the dark, "dream is over" cultural horizon of the 1970s.

At the time, this was radioactive stuff. Pasolini took no prisoners; if consumerism had lifted Italy out of poverty "to gratify it with a wellbeing" and a certain non-popular culture, the humiliating result was obtained "through miming the petite bourgeoisie, stupid obligatory school and delinquent television." Pasolini used to deride the Italian bourgeoisie as "the most ignorant in all of Europe" (well, on this he was wrong; the Spanish bourgeoisie really takes the cake).

Thus arose a new mode of production of culture—built over the "genocide of precedent cultures"—as well as a new bourgeois species. If only Pasolini had survived to see it acting in full regalia, as *Homo Berlusconis*.

The Great Beauty is no more

Now, the consumerist heart of darkness—"the horror, the horror"—prophesized and detailed by Pasolini already in the mid-1970s has been depicted in all its glitzy tawdriness by an Italian filmmaker from Naples, Paolo Sorrentino, born when Pasolini, not to mention Fellini, were already at the peak of their powers. *La Grande Bellezza* ("The Great Beauty")—which has just won the Golden Globes as Best Foreign Film and will probably win an Oscar as well—would be inconceivable without Fellini's *La Dolce Vita* (of which it is an unacknowledged coda) and Pasolini's critique of "the new Italy."

Pasolini and Fellini, by the way, both hailed from a fabulous intellectual tradition in Emilia-Romagna (Pasolini from Bologna, Fellini from Rimini, as well as Bertolucci from Parma). In the early 1960s, Fellini used to quip with friend and still apprentice Pasolini that he was not equipped for criticism. Fellini was always pure emotion, while Pasolini—and Bertolucci—were emotion modulated by the intellect.

Sorrentino's astonishing film—a wild ride on the ramifications of Berlusconian Italy—is *La Dolce Vita* gone horribly sour. How not to empathize with Marcello (Mastroianni) now reaching 65 (and played by the amazing Toni Servillo), suffering from writer's block in parallel to surfing his reputation of king of Rome's nightlife. As the great Ezra Pound—who loved Italy deeply—also prophesized, a tawdry cheapness ended up outlasting our days into a Berlusconian vapidity where—according to a character—everyone "forgot about culture and art" and the former apex of civilization ended up being known only for "fashion and pizza."

This is exactly what Pasolini was telling us almost four decades ago—before an eerie, gory manifestation of this very tawdriness silenced him. His death, in the end, proved—*avant-la-lettre*—his theorem; he had always been, unfortunately, dead right.

January 2014

Asia will not "isolate" Russia

Any (bureaucratic) doubts the New Cold War is on have been dispelled by the Group of Seven issuing a pompous, self-described Hague Declaration. Abandon all hope those who expected The Hague to become the seat of a tribunal judging the war crimes of the Cheney regime.

The G-7 also cancelled its upcoming summer summit in Sochi as a means of "punishing" Moscow over Crimea. As if this carried any practical value. Russian Foreign Minister Sergei Lavrov responded with class; if you don't want us, we have better things to do.[46] Everyone knows the G-7 is an innocuous, self-important talk shop. It's in the G-20—much more representative of the real world—where crucial geopolitical and geo-economic issues gain traction.

The Hague Declaration comes complete with the kiss of death, as in, "The IMF has a central role leading the international effort to support Ukrainian reform, lessening Ukraine's economic vulnerabilities, and better integrating the country as a market economy in the multilateral system." That's code for "wait till structural adjustment starts biting."

And then there will be "measures to enhance trade and strengthen energy security"—code for "we will destroy your industry" but "are not very keen on paying your humongous Gazprom bill."

All this in the sidelines of a supposed summit on nuclear security in the Netherlands, where US President Barack Obama, at the Rijksmuse-

---

[46] Russia not clinging to G8 if West does not want it—Russian FM, Russia Today, March 24, 2014.

um, in front of Rembrandt's *The Night Watch*, extolled Washington's "support of the Ukrainian government and Ukrainian people." Rembrandt's watchers have never seen anything like it in their glorious lifespan. It pays to be a Nazi after all; you just need to be in the right government, against the right enemy, and fully approved by the hyperpower.

King Willem-Alexander hosted a lavish dinner for the members of the nuclear security summit at the Royal Palace Huis ten Bosch in The Hague—after Obama met with Chinese President Xi Jinping in a (failed) bid to "isolate" Russia. The White House would later add that, as long as Russia continues "flagrantly" to violate international law, "there is no need for it to engage with the G7." Unless, of course, it starts conducting a drone war in Ukrainian badlands—with kill list attached.

All about NATO

The US Senate—always enjoying superb popularity ratings—laboriously laid the groundwork for debating a bill backing a US$1 billion loan guarantee for the regime changers in Kiev, plus $150 million in aid also including "neighboring countries." These figures are enough to pay Ukraine's bills for maybe two weeks.

Meanwhile, in the facts on the ground department, Crimea will be booming soon—tourism included—and may even become a "special economic zone."[47] Subjects of the upcoming IMF/agrobusiness-plundered Khaganate of Nulands will see the results for themselves.

Hysteria within NATO that Russia is about to invade everyone and his neighbor literally tomorrow—remember *The Russians Are Coming!*—

---

[47] Crimea to become Russian special economic zone-Medvedev, Russia Today, March 24, 2014.

persists unabated. Independent observers, The Roving Eye included, always insisted this is all about NATO, and not the European Union.[48]

Since the go-go days of the Bill Clinton era, NATO has been expanding to the doorstep of Russia. The process graphically represents US hegemony over Europe; NATO "annexed" Eastern Europe even before the EU. And even those certified US Cold Warriors such as Paul Nitze always thought this was a needless, dangerous provocation of Russia.

Very few remember how "Bubba" Clinton, to make sure terminal alcoholic Boris Yeltsin was re-elected in 1996, postponed NATO's expansion for a year. Afterwards, the expansion turbocharged into NATO as global Robocop—from the Balkans to the intersection of Central and South Asia, and to Northern Africa.

NATO's humanitarian bombing of Yugoslavia—36,000 combat missions, 23,000 bombs and missiles—whose 15th anniversary is "celebrated" this week, codified the new realities. NATO had nothing to do with defense; it was a multi-lethal (transformer) attack dog. It was the epitome of clean war; aerial *blitzkrieg*, and no casualties. And it was totally legitimized by "human rights" over national sovereignty; that was humanitarian imperialism in the making, opening the way to "responsibility to protect" and the destruction of Libya.

Moscow knows very well the lineaments of the neo-barbarian behemoth at its gates, in the form of NATO bases in Ukraine, assuming the regime changers in Kiev remain in power. And their response has absolutely nothing to do with "Putin's aggression." Or the so-called "Medvedev Doctrine" of Russia theoretically extending military protection to Russians everywhere. As if Russia was about to "threaten" its

---

[48] Why the EU won't annex Ukraine, Russia Today, March 24, 2014.

business interests in Kazakhstan, Kyrgyzstan, Turkmenistan, Tajikistan or Mongolia.

What the White House calls "the international community"—roughly the "Hague Declaration" G-7 plus a few European minions—could not possibly admit that. Asia, on the other hand, clearly identifies it. China, Japan and South Korea, for starters, identify Russia with a steady supply of oil and gas and further business deals. Even considering that Japan and South Korea are essentially US protectorates, nothing could be more anachronistic in their calculations than a Western-provoked New Cold War.

Asia will not "isolate" Russia—and Asians and Russians know it, as much as The White House is in denial. Beijing's abstention in "condemning" Moscow—talk about the American angry-schoolmaster brand of politics—is classic Deng Xiaoping-style "keep a low profile," as China is Russia's strategic partner and both are busy working for the emergence of a multipolar world. Not to mention Beijing's utmost rejection of US-style color-coded "revolutions" and regime change ops—as well as that "pivoting to Asia" encirclement ops.

Oh, to have been a EU-regulated fly on the wall in that Hague room where Obama and Xi were talking; cool Xi meets Obama pivoting around himself.

March 2014

BREAKING BAD IN SOUTHERN NATOSTAN

To quote Lenin, what is to be done? Back to Brussels and Berlin? A close encounter with dreary Northern NATOstan, consumed by its paranoid anti-Russia obsession and enslaved by the infinitely expandable Pentagon euro-scam? Perhaps a jaunt to Syria war junkie Erdogastan?

Talk about a no contest. *Joie de vivre* settled it; thus The Roving Eye hooked up with Nick, The Roving Son, in Catalonia, and armed with La Piccolina—Nick's vintage, go-go '80s Peugeot caravan powered by a Citroen engine—we hit the road in Provence, prime southern NATOstan real estate. Instead of breaking crystal meth, non-stop breaking of fine infidel liquids and choice Provencal gastronomy.

Call it a subterranean, non-homesick, non-bluesy investigation into the economic malaise of Club Med nations; the pauperization of the European middle class; the advance of the extreme right; and the looming prospect of an economic NATO. All within the framework of exceedingly cool family quality time. And subversively enough, with both laptop and mobile turned off.

Does God drink Bandol?

We were fortunate enough to catch the inaugural week of the Van Gogh Foundation in Arles—with its remarkable entrance portal inscribed with Van Gogh's enlarged signature; its suspended garden of colored mirrors; and a crack exhibition on the master's chromatic evolution up to the frenetic 15 months he lived in Arles. A few minutes contemplating *La Maison Jaune* (1888) is an intimation of immortality, revealing what exceptionalism is really all about.

Aesthetic illuminations were a given—from Baux castle at sunset to sipping a Perrier mint on a terrace overlooking the countryside around hilltop Gordes; from a starry night in the open at the Colorado Provencal (intriguingly trespassed by a military helicopter flying low, Baghdad surge-style) to debating the merits of each variation of *chevre de Banon*—that Epicurean "cheese of exception" wrapped up in chestnut leaves.

And then the crossing to the Grand Canyon of Verdon—the most American of European canyons, attacked on different angles from both the north and south rim, including a trek along the old Roman trail and a close encounter with the jagged, chaotic, ghostly rock silhouettes of Les Cadieres (chairs, in Provencal)—the Verdon's answer to the Twin Towers. Call it a quirky Provencal take on Osama and al-Zawahiri trekking the Hindu Kush.

As we descended from the Col de Leques, the owner of a mountainside cafe told us he had just opened for the whole season, lasting until mid-September. But here, in early April, the Verdon was bathed in silent glory, except for the occasional badass biker.

Then—as in Godard's *Pierrot Le Fou*—a dash towards La Mediterranee. First stop in Front National-controlled Toulon—so proper, so regimented, so fearful even of non-immigrant skateboarders, yet displaying a monster NATO cargo ship in full regalia.

It's impossible to have a *plateau de moules* in mid-afternoon at the port, but at the Ah-Ha Chinese restaurant there are Verdon canyons of food available around the clock, which once again goes to show how Asia's entrepreneurial drive has left Europe in the dust.

Cue to a Platonic banquet at the venerable Auberge Du Port in Bandol—orgiastic bouillabaisse paired with the best local wine, which would be a close match between Bastide de la Ciselette and Domaine de Terrebrune. None of these infidel liquid marvels, by the way, have been touched by globalization.

There's hardly a single millimeter of free land space in the coast around Marseille—that's part of a well-known dossier, the environmental destruction of southern NATOstan. Still we managed to find a relatively secluded grove for the appropriate Paul Valery mood (*la mer, la mer, toujours recommence*).

Then the dreaded moment reared its ugly head—at Sanary-sur-Mer, where Huxley wrote *Brave New World* at his Villa Huley and Thomas Mann held court in the Chemin de la Colline. Brecht in fact might have sung anti-Hitler songs out of a table at Le Nautique; so after debating with Nick the comparative merits of Beneteau sailing boats, I finally decided to stop with all that Brechtian distancing and walked to the nearby kiosk to buy the papers, order a cafe au lait, and turn on the mobile.

Not impressed is an understatement. One week off the grid, and the same sarabande of paranoia, frenetic pivoting and monochromatic exceptionalism. Yet, there it was, like a pearl at the bottom of the turquoise Mediterranean, buried in the info-avalanche: the definitive news of the week, perhaps the year, perhaps the decade.

Gazprom CEO Alexey Miller had met with China National Petroleum Corporation chairman Zhou Jiping in Beijing on Wednesday. They were on their way to sign the 30-year, mega-contract deal to supply China with Siberian natural gas "as soon as possible." Probably on May 20, when Putin goes to Beijing.

Now this is the genuine article. Pipelineistan meets the strategic partnership Russia-China, as solidified in the BRICS and the SCO, with the tantalizing prospect of pricing/payment bypassing the petrodollar, otherwise known as the "thermonuclear option." Ukraine, compared to this, is a mere sideshow.

Welcome to the Brussels rat-o-drome

It was on the road from the Mediterranean back to Arles via Aix-en-Provence that it hit me like an Obama drone. This whole trip was after all about the sublime *chevre* wrapped up in chestnut leaves in Banon, those "rose petal" bottles of wine in Bandol; artisan producers and season mountain folks spelling out their fears in village markets and unpretentious chateaux. This was all about economic NATO.

The Trans-Atlantic Free Trade Agreement is a top priority of the Obama administration. Tariffs are already almost negligible across most products between the US and the European Union. So a deal is essentially about a power grab over continental markets by Big American Agro-Business (as in an invasion of genetically modified products), as well as American media giants. Call it a nice add-on to the Trans-Pacific Partnership (TPP)—which in a nutshell means an American takeover of the heavily protected Japanese economy.

Southern NATOstan does offer glimpses of a European post-historical paradise—a Kantian rose garden protected from a nasty Hobbesian world by the "benign" Empire (the new denomination of choice, coined by—who else—neo-cons of the Robert Kagan variety). Yet the main emotion enveloping southern NATOstan, as I witnessed since the start of 2014 successively in Italy, Spain and France, is fear. Fear of The Other—as in the poor interloper, black or brown; fear of perennial unemployment; fear for the end of middle-class privileges until recently taken for granted; and fear of economic NATO—as virtually no average European trusts those hordes of Brussels bureaucrats.

For nine months now, the European Commission has been negotiating a so-called Trade and Investment Partnership. The "transparency" surrounding what will be the largest free-trade agreement ever, encompassing more than 800 million consumers, would put North Korea's King Jong-eun to shame.

The whole secret blah blah blah revolves around the euphemistic "non-tariff obstacles"—as in a web of ethical, environmental, juridical and sanitary norms that protect consumers, not giant multinationals. What the behemoths aim for, on the other hand, is a very profitable free-for-all—implying, just as an example, the indiscriminate use of ractopamine, an energy-booster for pork that is even outlawed in Russia and China.

So why is the Obama administration suddenly so enamored of a free-trade agreement with Europe? Because US Big Business has finally found out that the Holy Grail of an economic pivoting to China won't be so holy after all; the whole thing will be conducted under Chinese terms, as in major Chinese brands progressively upgrading to control most of the Chinese market.

Thus Plan B as a transatlantic market submitting 40% of international trade to the same big business-friendly norms. Obama has been heavily spinning the agreement will create "millions of well-paid American jobs." That's highly debatable, to say the least. But make no mistake about the American drive; Obama himself is personally implicated.

As for the Europeans, it's more like rats scurrying in a secret casino. As much as the NSA monitors every phone call in Brussels, average Europeans remain clueless about what they will be slapped with. Public debate over the agreement is for all practical purposes verboten for European civil society.

European Commission negotiators meet only with lobbyists and multinational CEOs. In case of "price volatility" down the road, European farmers will be the big losers, not Americans, now protected by a new Farm Bill. No wonder the direct and indirect message I received from virtually everyone in the Provencal countryside is that "Brussels is selling us out"; in the end, what will disappear, in a death by a thousand cuts manner, is top-quality agriculture, scores of artisan producers with a *savoir-faire* accumulated over centuries.

So long live hormones, antibiotics, chlorine and genetically modified organisms (GMOs). And off with their heads in the *terroir*! NATO issuing threats to Russia is such a lame, convenient diversionary tactic. As La Piccolina left Provence carrying its share of sublime artisan goods, I could not but understand why the locals see an economic NATO future with such Van Goghian apprehension.

April 2014

Ukraine and the Grand Chessboard

The US State Department, via spokeswoman Jennifer Psaki, said that reports of CIA Director John Brennan telling regime changers in Kiev to "conduct tactical operations"—or an "anti-terrorist" offensive—in Eastern Ukraine are "completely false." This means Brennan did issue his marching orders. And by now the "anti-terrorist" campaign—with its nice little Dubya rhetorical touch—has degenerated into farce.

Now couple that with NATO secretary general, Danish retriever Anders Fogh Rasmussen, yapping about the strengthening of military footprint along NATO's eastern border: "We will have more planes in the air, mores ships on the water and more readiness on the land."

Welcome to the Two Stooges doctrine of post-modern warfare.

Pay up or freeze to death

Ukraine is for all practical purposes broke. The Kremlin's consistent position for the past three months has been to encourage the European Union to find a solution to Ukraine's dire economic mess. Brussels did nothing. It was betting on regime change to the benefit of Germany's heavyweight puppet Vladimir Klitschko, aka Klitsch The Boxer.

Regime change did happen, but orchestrated by the Khaganate of Nulands—a neocon cell of the State Department and its assistant secretary of state for European and Eurasian Affairs Victoria Nuland. And now the presidential option is between—what else—two US puppets, choco-billionaire Petro Poroshenko and "Saint Yulia" Timoshenko, Ukraine's former prime minister, ex-convict and prospective president. The EU is left to pick up the (unpayable) bill. Enter the IMF—via a nasty, upcoming "structural adjustment" that will send Ukrainians to a hellhole even grimmer than the one they are already familiar with.

Once again, for all the hysteria propagated by the US Ministry of Truth and its franchises across the Western corporate media, the Kremlin does not need to "invade" anything. If Gazprom does not get paid all it needs to do is to shut down the Ukrainian stretch of Pipelineistan. Kiev will then have no option but to use part of the gas supply destined for some EU countries so Ukrainians won't run out of fuel to keep themselves and the country's industries alive. And the EU—whose "energy policy" overall is already a joke—will find itself with yet another self-inflicted problem.

The EU will be mired in a perennial lose-lose situation if Brussels does not talk seriously with Moscow. There's only one explanation for the refusal: hardcore Washington pressure, mounted via NATO.

Again, to counterpunch the current hysteria—the EU remains Gazprom's top client, with 61% of its overall exports. It's a complex relationship based on interdependence. The capitalization of Nord Stream, Blue Stream and the to-be-completed South Stream includes German, Dutch, French and Italian companies.

So yes, Gazprom does need the EU market. But up to a point, considering the mega-deal of Siberian gas delivery to China which most probably will be signed next month in Beijing when Russian President Vladimir Putin visits President Xi Jinping.

The crucial spanner in the works

Last month, while the tortuous Ukraine sideshow was in progress, President Xi was in Europe clinching deals and promoting yet another branch of the New Silk Road all the way to Germany.

In a sane, non-Hobbesian environment, a neutral Ukraine would only have to gain by positioning itself as a privileged crossroads between the EU and the proposed Eurasian Union—as well as becoming a key node of the Chinese New Silk Road offensive. Instead, the Kiev regime changers are betting on acceptance into the EU (it simply won't happen) and becoming a NATO forward base (the key Pentagon aim).

As for the possibility of a common market from Lisbon to Vladivostok—which both Moscow and Beijing are aiming at, and would be also a boon for the EU—the Ukraine disaster is a real spanner in the works.

And a spanner in the works that, crucially, suits only one player: the US government.

The Obama administration may—and "may" is the operative word here—have realized the US government has lost the battle to control Pipelineistan from Asia to Europe, despite all the efforts of the Dick Cheney regime. What energy experts call the Asian Energy Security Grid is progressively evolving—as well as its myriad links to Europe.

So what's left for the Obama administration is this spanner in the works—still trying to scotch the full economic integration of Eurasia.

The Obama administration is predictably obsessed with the EU's increasing dependency on Russian gas. Thus its grandiose plan to position US shale gas for the EU as an alternative to Gazprom. Even assuming this might happen, it would take at least a decade—with no guarantee of success. In fact, the real alternative would be Iranian gas—after a comprehensive nuclear deal and the end of Western sanctions (the whole package, not surprisingly, being sabotaged en masse by various Beltway factions.)

Just to start with, the US cannot export shale gas to countries with which it has not signed a free trade agreement. That's a "problem" which might be solved to a great extent by the secretly negotiated Trans-Atlantic Partnership between Washington and Brussels (see Breaking bad in southern NATOstan, *Asia Times Online*, April 15, 2014.)

In parallel, the Obama administration keeps applying instances of "divide and rule" to scare minor players, as in spinning to the max the specter of an evil, militaristic China to reinforce the still crawling "pivoting to Asia." The whole game harks back to what Dr. Zbig Brzezinski conceptualized way back in his 1997 opus *The Grand Chessboard*—and fine-tuned for his disciple Obama: the US ruling over Eurasia.

Still the Kremlin won't be dragged into a military quagmire. It's fair to argue Putin has identified the Big Picture in the whole chessboard, which spells out an increasing Russia-China strategic partnership as crucial as an energy-manufacturing synergy with Europe; and most of all the titanic fear of US financial elites of the inevitable, ongoing process centered on the BRICS-conducted (and spreading to key Group of 20 members) drive to bypass the petrodollar.

Ultimately, this all spells out the progressive demise of the petrodollar in parallel to the ascent of a basket to currencies as the reserve currency in the international system. The BRICS are already at work on their alternative to the IMF and the World Bank, investing in a currency reserve pool and the BRICS development bank. While a tentative new world or der slouches towards all points Global South to be born, Robocop NATO dreams of war.

April 2014

THE BIRTH OF A EURASIAN CENTURY

A specter is haunting Washington, an unnerving vision of a Sino-Russian alliance wedded to an expansive symbiosis of trade and commerce across much of the Eurasian land mass—at the expense of the United States.

And no wonder Washington is anxious. That alliance is already a done deal in a variety of ways: through the BRICS group of emerging powers (Brazil, Russia, India, China, and South Africa); at the SCO, the Asian counterweight to NATO; inside the G20; and via the 120-member-nation Non-Aligned Movement. Trade and commerce are just part of the future bargain. Synergies in the development of new military technologies beckon as well. After Russia's Star Wars-style, ultra-sophisticated S-500 air defense anti-missile system comes online in 2018, Beijing is sure to want a version of it. Meanwhile, Russia is about to sell dozens of state-of-the-art Sukhoi Su-35 jet fighters to the Chinese as Beijing and Moscow move to seal an aviation-industrial partnership.

This week should provide the first real fireworks in the celebration of a new Eurasian century-in-the-making when Russian President Vladimir Putin drops in on Chinese President Xi Jinping in Beijing. You remember "Pipelineistan," all those crucial oil and gas pipelines crisscrossing Eurasia that make up the true circulatory system for the life of the region. Now, it looks like the ultimate Pipelineistan deal, worth $1 trillion and 10 years in the making, will be inked as well. In it, the giant, state-controlled Russian energy giant Gazprom will agree to supply the giant state-controlled China National Petroleum Corporation (CNPC) with 3.75

billion cubic feet of LNG a day for no less than 30 years, starting in 2018. That's the equivalent of a quarter of Russia's massive gas exports to all of Europe. China's current daily gas demand is around 16 billion cubic feet a day, and imports account for 31.6% of total consumption.

Gazprom may still collect the bulk of its profits from Europe, but Asia could turn out to be its Everest. The company will use this mega-deal to boost investment in Eastern Siberia and the whole region will be reconfigured as a privileged gas hub for Japan and South Korea as well. If you want to know why no key country in Asia has been willing to "isolate" Russia in the midst of the Ukrainian crisis—and in defiance of the Obama administration—look no further than Pipelineistan.

Exit the Petrodollar, Enter the Gas-o-Yuan

And then, talking about anxiety in Washington, there's the fate of the petrodollar to consider, or rather the "thermonuclear" possibility that Moscow and Beijing will agree on payment for the Gazprom-CNPC deal not in petrodollars but in Chinese yuan. One can hardly imagine a more tectonic shift, with Pipelineistan intersecting with a growing Sino-Russian political-economic-energy partnership. Along with it goes the future possibility of a push, led again by China and Russia, towards a new international reserve currency—actually a basket of currencies—that would supersede the dollar (at least in the optimistic dreams of BRICS members).

Right after the potentially game-changing Sino-Russian summit comes a BRICS summit in Brazil in July. That's when a $100 billion BRICS development bank, announced in 2012, will officially be born as a potential alternative to the IMF and the World Bank as a source of project financing for the developing world.

More BRICS cooperation meant to bypass the dollar is reflected in the "Gas-o-yuan," as in natural gas bought and paid for in Chinese currency. Gazprom is even considering marketing bonds in yuan as part of the financial planning for its expansion. Yuan-backed bonds are already trading in Hong Kong, Singapore, London, and most recently Frankfurt.

Nothing could be more sensible for the new Pipelineistan deal than to have it settled in yuan. Beijing would pay Gazprom in that currency (convertible into rubles); Gazprom would accumulate the yuan; and Russia would then buy myriad made-in-China goods and services in yuan convertible into rubles.

It's common knowledge that banks in Hong Kong, from Standard Chartered to HSBC—as well as others closely linked to China via trade deals—have been diversifying into the yuan, which implies that it could become one of the de facto global reserve currencies even before it's fully convertible. (Beijing is unofficially working for a fully convertible yuan by 2018.)

The Russia-China gas deal is inextricably tied up with the energy relationship between the European Union (EU) and Russia. After all, the bulk of Russia's GDP comes from oil and gas sales, as does much of its leverage in the Ukraine crisis. In turn, Germany depends on Russia for a hefty 30% of its natural gas supplies. Yet Washington's geopolitical imperatives—spiced up with Polish hysteria—have meant pushing Brussels to find ways to "punish" Moscow in the future energy sphere (while not imperiling present day energy relationships).

There's a consistent rumble in Brussels these days about the possible cancellation of the projected 16 billion euro South Stream pipeline, whose construction is to start in June. On completion, it would pump yet more Russian natural gas to Europe—in this case, underneath the Black

Sea (bypassing Ukraine) to Bulgaria, Hungary, Slovenia, Serbia, Croatia, Greece, Italy, and Austria.

Bulgaria, Hungary, and the Czech Republic have already made it clear that they are firmly opposed to any cancellation. And cancellation is probably not in the cards. After all, the only obvious alternative is Caspian Sea gas from Azerbaijan, and that isn't likely to happen unless the EU can suddenly muster the will and funds for a crash schedule similar to the construction of the fabled Baku-Tblisi-Ceyhan (BTC) oil pipeline, conceived during the Clinton years expressly to bypass Russia and Iran.

In any case, Azerbaijan doesn't have enough capacity to supply the levels of natural gas needed, and other actors like Kazakhstan, plagued with infrastructure problems, or unreliable Turkmenistan, which prefers to sell its gas to China, are already largely out of the picture. And don't forget that South Stream, coupled with subsidiary energy projects, will create a lot of jobs and investment in many of the most economically devastated EU nations.

Nonetheless, such EU threats, however unrealistic, only serve to accelerate Russia's increasing symbiosis with Asian markets. For Beijing especially, it's a win-win situation. After all, between energy supplied across seas policed and controlled by the US Navy and steady, stable land routes out of Siberia, it's no contest.

Pick Your Own Silk Road

Of course, the US dollar remains the top global reserve currency, involving 33% of global foreign exchange holdings at the end of 2013, according to the IMF. It was, however, at 55% in 2000. Nobody knows the percentage in yuan (and Beijing isn't talking), but the IMF notes that reserves in "other currencies" in emerging markets have been up 400% since 2003.

The Fed is arguably monetizing 70% of the US government debt in an attempt to keep interest rates from heading skywards. Pentagon advisor Jim Rickards, as well as every Hong Kong-based banker, tends to believe that the Fed is bust (though they won't say it on the record). No one can even imagine the extent of the possible future deluge the US dollar might experience amid a $1.4 quadrillion Mount Ararat of financial derivatives. Don't think that this is the death knell of Western capitalism, however, just the faltering of that reigning economic faith, neoliberalism, still the official ideology of the United States, the overwhelming majority of the European Union, and parts of Asia and South America.

As far as what might be called the "authoritarian neoliberalism" of the Middle Kingdom, what's not to like at the moment? China has proven that there is a result-oriented alternative to the Western "democratic" capitalist model for nations aiming to be successful. It's building not one, but myriad new Silk Roads, massive webs of high-speed railways, highways, pipelines, ports, and fiber optic networks across huge parts of Eurasia. These include a Southeast Asian road, a Central Asian road, an Indian Ocean "maritime highway" and even a high-speed rail line through Iran and Turkey reaching all the way to Germany.

In April, when President Xi Jinping visited the city of Duisburg on the Rhine River, with the largest inland harbor in the world and right in the heartland of Germany's Ruhr steel industry, he made an audacious proposal: a new "economic Silk Road" should be built between China and Europe, on the basis of the Chongqing-Xinjiang-Europe railway, which already runs from China to Kazakhstan, then through Russia, Belarus, Poland, and finally Germany. That's 15 days by train, 20 less than for cargo ships sailing from China's eastern seaboard. Now that would represent the ultimate geopolitical earthquake in terms of integrating economic growth across Eurasia.

Keep in mind that, if no bubbles burst, China is about to become—and remain—the number one global economic power, a position it enjoyed for 18 of the past 20 centuries. But don't tell London hagiographers; they still believe that US hegemony will last, well, forever.

Take Me to Cold War 2.0

Despite recent serious financial struggles, the BRICS countries have been consciously working to become a counterforce to the original and—having tossed Russia out in March—once again Group of 7, or G7. They are eager to create a new global architecture to replace the one first imposed in the wake of World War II, and they see themselves as a potential challenge to the exceptionalist and unipolar world that Washington imagines for our future (with itself as the global Robocop and NATO as its robo-police force). Historian and imperialist cheerleader Ian Morris, in his book War! What is it Good For?, defines the US as the ultimate "globocop" and "the last best hope of Earth." If that globocop "wearies of its role," he writes, "there is no plan B."

Well, there is a plan BRICS—or so the BRICS nations would like to think, at least. And when the BRICS do act in this spirit on the global stage, they quickly conjure up a curious mix of fear, hysteria, and pugnaciousness in the Washington establishment. Take Christopher Hill as an example. The former assistant secretary of state for East Asia and US ambassador to Iraq is now an advisor with the Albright Stonebridge Group, a consulting firm deeply connected to the White House and the State Department. When Russia was down and out, Hill used to dream of a hegemonic American "new world order." Now that the ungrateful Russians have spurned what "the West has been offering"—that is, "special status with NATO, a privileged relationship with the European Union, and partnership in international diplomatic endeavors"—they are, in his view, busy trying to revive the Soviet empire. Translation: if you're not our vassals, you're against us. Welcome to Cold War 2.0.

The Pentagon has its own version of this directed not so much at Russia as at China, which, its think-tank on future warfare claims, is already at war with Washington in a number of ways. So if it's not apocalypse now, it's Armageddon tomorrow. And it goes without saying that whatever's going wrong, as the Obama administration very publicly "pivots" to Asia and the American media fills with talk about a revival of Cold War-era "containment policy" in the Pacific, it's all China's fault.

Embedded in the mad dash towards Cold War 2.0 are some ludicrous facts on the ground: the US government, with $17.5 trillion in national debt and counting, is contemplating a financial showdown with Russia, the largest global energy producer and a major nuclear power, just as it's also promoting an economically unsustainable military encirclement of its largest creditor, China.

Russia runs a sizeable trade surplus. Humongous Chinese banks will have no trouble helping Russian banks out if Western funds dry up. In terms of inter-BRICS cooperation, few projects beat a $30 billion oil pipeline in the planning stages that will stretch from Russia to India via Northwest China. Chinese companies are already eagerly discussing the possibility of taking part in the creation of a transport corridor from Russia into Crimea, as well as an airport, shipyard, and liquid natural gas terminal there. And there's another "thermonuclear" gambit in the making: the birth of a natural gas equivalent to the Organization of the Petroleum Exporting Countries that would include Russia, Iran, and reportedly disgruntled US ally Qatar.

The (unstated) BRICS long-term plan involves the creation of an alternative economic system featuring a basket of gold-backed currencies that would bypass the present America-centric global financial system.

(No wonder Russia and China are amassing as much gold as they can.) The euro—a sound currency backed by large liquid bond markets and huge gold reserves—would be welcomed in as well.

It's no secret in Hong Kong that the Bank of China has been using a parallel Society for Worldwide Interbank Financial Telecommunication (SWIFT) network to conduct every kind of trade with Tehran, which is under a heavy US sanctions regime. With Washington wielding Visa and Mastercard as weapons in a growing Cold War-style economic campaign against Russia, Moscow is about to implement an alternative payment and credit card system not controlled by Western finance. An even easier route would be to adopt the Chinese Union Pay system, whose operations have already overtaken American Express in global volume.

I'm Just Pivoting With Myself

No amount of Obama administration "pivoting" to Asia to contain China (and threaten it with U.S. Navy control of the energy sea lanes to that country) is likely to push Beijing far from its Deng Xiaoping-inspired, self-described "peaceful development" strategy meant to turn it into a global powerhouse of trade. Nor are the forward deployment of US or NATO troops in Eastern Europe or other such Cold-War-ish acts likely to deter Moscow from a careful balancing act: ensuring that Russia's sphere of influence in Ukraine remains strong without compromising trade and commercial, as well as political, ties with the European Union—above all, with strategic partner Germany. This is Moscow's Holy Grail; a free-trade zone from Lisbon to Vladivostok, which (not by accident) is mirrored in China's dream of a new Silk Road to Germany.

Increasingly wary of Washington, Berlin for its part abhors the notion of Europe being caught in the grips of a Cold War 2.0. German leaders have more important fish to fry, including trying to stabilize a wobbly EU while warding off an economic collapse in southern and central Europe and the advance of ever more extreme right-wing parties.

On the other side of the Atlantic, President Obama and his top officials show every sign of becoming entangled in their own pivoting—to Iran, to China, to Russia's eastern borderlands, and (under the radar) to Africa. The irony of all these military-first maneuvers is that they are actually helping Moscow, Tehran, and Beijing build up their own strategic depth in Eurasia and elsewhere, as reflected in Syria, or crucially in ever more energy deals. They are also helping cement the growing strategic partnership between China and Iran. The unrelenting Ministry of Truth narrative out of Washington about all these developments now carefully ignores the fact that, without Moscow, the "West" would never have sat down to discuss a final nuclear deal with Iran or gotten a chemical disarmament agreement out of Damascus.

When the disputes between China and its neighbors in the South China Sea and between that country and Japan over the Senkaku/Diaoyou islands meet the Ukraine crisis, the inevitable conclusion will be that both Russia and China consider their borderlands and sea lanes private property and aren't going to take challenges quietly—be it via NATO expansion, US military encirclement, or missile shields. Neither Beijing nor Moscow is bent on the usual form of imperialist expansion, despite the version of events now being fed to Western publics. Their "red lines" remain essentially defensive in nature, no matter the bluster sometimes involved in securing them.

Whatever Washington may want or fear or try to prevent, the facts on the ground suggest that, in the years ahead, Beijing, Moscow, and Tehran will only grow closer, slowly but surely creating a new geopolitical axis in Eurasia. Meanwhile, a discombobulated America seems to be aiding and abetting the deconstruction of its own unipolar world order, while offering the BRICS a genuine window of opportunity to try to change the rules of the game.

Russia and China in Pivot Mode

In Washington's think-tank land, the conviction that the Obama administration should be focused on replaying the Cold War via a new version of containment policy to "limit the development of Russia as a hegemonic power" has taken hold. The recipe: weaponize the neighbors from the Baltic states to Azerbaijan to "contain" Russia. Cold War 2.0 is on because, from the point of view of Washington's elites, the first one never really left town.

Yet as much as the US may fight the emergence of a multipolar, multi-powered world, economic facts on the ground regularly point to such developments. The question remains: Will the decline of the hegemon be slow and reasonably dignified, or will the whole world be dragged down with it in what has been called "the Samson option"?

While we watch the spectacle unfold, with no end game in sight, keep in mind that a new force is growing in Eurasia, with the Sino-Russian strategic alliance threatening to dominate its heartland along with great stretches of its inner rim. Now, that's a nightmare of Mackinderesque proportions from Washington's point of view. Think, for instance, of how Zbigniew Brzezinski, the former national security advisor who became a mentor on global politics to President Obama, would see it.

In his 1997 book *The Grand Chessboard*, Brzezinski argued that "the struggle for global primacy [would] continue to be played" on the Eurasian "chessboard," of which "Ukraine was a geopolitical pivot." "If Moscow regains control over Ukraine," he wrote at the time, Russia would "automatically regain the wherewithal to become a powerful imperial state, spanning Europe and Asia."

That remains most of the rationale behind the American imperial containment policy—from Russia's European "near abroad" to the South China Sea. Still, with no endgame in sight, keep your eye on Russia pivoting to Asia, China pivoting across the world, and the BRICS hard at work trying to bring about the new Eurasian Century.

May 2014. Originally at TomDispatch.com

THE FUTURE VISIBLE IN ST. PETERSBURG

The unipolar model of the world order has failed.

- Vladimir Putin, *St. Petersburg, May 22*

In more ways than one, last week heralded the birth of a Eurasian century. Of course, the US$400 billion Russia-China gas deal was clinched only at the last minute in Shanghai, on Wednesday (a complement to the June 2013, 25-year, $270 billion oil deal between Rosneft and China's CNPC.)

Then, on Thursday, most of the main players were at the St. Petersburg International Economic Forum—the Russian answer to Davos. And on Friday, Russian President Vladimir Putin, fresh from his Shanghai triumph, addressed the participants and brought the house down.

It will take time to appraise last week's whirlwind in all its complex implications. Here are some of the St. Petersburg highlights, in some detail. Were there fewer Western CEOs in town because the Obama administration pressured them—as part of the "isolate Russia" policy? Not many less; Goldman Sachs and Morgan Stanley may have snubbed it, but Europeans who matter came, saw, talked and pledged to keep doing business.

And most of all, Asians were ubiquitous. Consider this as yet another chapter of China's counterpunch to US President Barack Obama's Asian tour in April, which was widely described as the "China containment tour."[49]

On the first day at the St. Petersburg forum I attended this crucial session on Russia-China strategic economic partnership. Pay close attention: the roadmap is all there. As Chinese Vice President Li Yuanchao describes it: "We plan to combine the program for the development of Russia's Far East and the strategy for the development of Northeast China into an integrated concept."

That was just one instance of the fast-emerging Eurasia coalition bound to challenge the "indispensable" exceptionalists to the core. Comparisons to the Sino-Soviet pact are infantile. The putsch in Ukraine—part of Washington's pivot to "contain" Russia—just served to accelerate Russia's pivot to Asia, which sooner or late would become inevitable.

It all starts in Sichuan

In St. Petersburg, from session to session and in selected conversations, what I saw were some crucial building blocks of the Chinese New Silk Road(s), whose ultimate aim is to unite, via trade and commerce, no less than China, Russia and Germany.

For Washington, this is beyond anathema. The response has been to peddle a couple of deals which, in thesis, would guarantee American monopoly of two-thirds of global commerce; the Trans-Pacific Partnership (TPP)—which was essentially rebuked by key Asians such as Japan and Malaysia during Obama's trip—and the even more problematic Trans-Atlantic Partnership with the EU, which average Europeans absolutely

---

[49] China Thwarts U.S. 'Containment' With Vietnam Oil Rig Standoff, Forbes, May 8, 2014.

abhor (see Breaking bad in southern NATOstan, *Asia Times Online*, April 15, 2014). Both deals are being negotiated in secret and are profitable essentially for US multinational corporations.

For Asia, China instead proposes a Free Trade Area of Asia-Pacific; after all, it is already the largest trading partner of the 10-member Association of Southeast Asian Nations (ASEAN).

And for Europe, Beijing proposes an extension of the railway that in only 12 days links Chengdu, the capital of Sichuan, to Lodz in Poland, crossing Kazakhstan, Russia and Belarus. The total deal is the Chongqing-Xinjiang-Europe network, with a final stop in Duisburg, Germany. No wonder this is bound to become the most important commercial route in the world.[50]

There's more. One day before the clinching of the Russia-China gas deal, President Xi Jinping called for no less than a new Asian security cooperation architecture, including of course Russia and Iran and excluding the US.[51] Somehow echoing Putin, Xi described NATO as a Cold War relic.

And guess who was at the announcement in Shanghai, apart from the Central Asian "stans": Iraqi Prime Minister Nouri al-Maliki, Afghan President Hamid Karzai and crucially, Iranian President Hassan Rouhani.

The facts on the ground speak for themselves. China is buying at least half of Iraq's oil production—and is investing heavily in its energy infrastructure. China has invested heavily in Afghanistan's mining industry—

---

[50] Le president chinois appelle la Chine et l'Allemagne—construire la ceinture economique de la Route de la Soie (in French), Xinhua, March 30, 2014.
[51] China calls for new Asian security structure, Washington Post, May 21, 2014.

especially lithium and cobalt. And obviously both China and Russia keep doing business in Iran.[52]

So this is what Washington gets for over a decade of wars, incessant bullying, nasty sanctions and trillions of misspent dollars.

No wonder the most fascinating session I attended in St. Petersburg was on the commercial and economic possibilities around the expansion of the Shanghai Cooperation Organization (SCO), whose guest of honor was none other than Li Yuanchao. I was arguably the only Westerner in the room, surrounded by a sea of Chinese and Central Asians.

The SCO is gearing up to become something way beyond a sort of counterpart to NATO, focusing mostly on terrorism and fighting drug trafficking. It wants to do major business. Iran, India, Pakistan, Afghanistan and Mongolia are observers, and sooner rather than later will be accepted as full members.

Once again that's Eurasian integration in action. The branching out of the New Silk Road(s) is inevitable; and that spells out, in practice, closer integration with Afghanistan (minerals) and Iran (energy).

The new Crimea boom

St. Petersburg also made it clear how China wants to finance an array of projects in Crimea, whose waters, by the way, boasting untold, still unexplored, energy wealth, are now Russian property. Projects include a crucial bridge across the Kerch Strait to connect Crimea to mainland Russia; expansion of Crimean ports; solar power plants; and even manu-

---

[52] Russia plans to build up to eight new nuclear reactors in Iran, Reuters, May 22, 2014.

facturing special economic zones (SEZs). Moscow could not but interpret it as Beijing's endorsement of the annexation of Crimea.

As for Ukraine, it might as well, as Putin remarked in St. Petersburg, pay its bills.[53] And as for the European Union, at least outgoing president of the European Commission Jose Manuel Barroso understood the obvious: antagonizing Russia is not exactly a winning strategy.

Dmitry Trenin, director of the Carnegie Moscow Center, has been one of those informed few advising the West about it, to no avail: "Russia and China are likely to cooperate even more closely… Such an outcome would certainly benefit China, but it will give Russia a chance to withstand US geopolitical pressure, compensate for the EU's coming energy re-orientation, develop Siberia and the Far East, and link itself to the Asia-Pacific region."[54]

On the (silk) road again

The now symbiotic China-Russia strategic alliance—with the possibility of extending towards Iran[55]—is *the* fundamental fact on the ground in the young 21st century. It will extrapolate across the BRICS, the SCO, the Collective Security Treaty Organization and the Non-Aligned Movement.

Of course the usual shills will keep peddling that the only possible future is one led by a "benign" empire.[56] As if billions of people across the real world—even informed Atlanticists—would be gullible enough to buy

---

[53] Naftogaz Debt to Gazprom Stands at $4 Bln—EU Energy Commissioner, Ria Novosti, May 28, 2014.

[54] See here.

[55] China, Iran and Russia: Restructuring the global order, Al Jazeera, May 20, 2014.

[56] In Defense of Empire, The Atlantic, March 19, 2014.

it. Still, unipolarity may be dead, but the world, sadly, is encumbered with its corpse. The corpse, according to the new Obama doctrine, is now "empowering partners."

To paraphrase Dylan ("I left Rome and landed in Brussels"), I left St. Petersburg and landed in Rome, to follow yet another episode in the slow decadence of Europe—the parliamentary elections. But before that, I was fortunate to experience an aesthetic illumination. I visited a virtually deserted Institute of Oriental Manuscripts of the Russian Academy of Sciences, where two dedicated, extremely knowledgeable researchers gave me a private tour of some pieces belonging to arguably the most outstanding collection of Asian manuscripts on the planet. As a serial Silk Road traveler fanatic, I had heard about many of those documents, but I had never actually seen them. So there I was, on the banks of the Neva, a kid in a (historical) candy store, immersed in all those marvels from Dunhuang to Mongolia, in Vedic or Sanskrit, dreaming of Silk Roads past and future. I could stay there forever.

May 2014

Return of the living (neocon) dead

Amid much hysteria, the notion has been widely peddled in the United States that President Obama's "new" foreign policy doctrine, announced last week at West Point, rejects neo-cons and neo-liberals and is, essentially, post-imperialist and a demonstration of realpolitik.

Not so fast. Although stepping back from the excesses of the Cheney regime—as in bombing whole nations into "democracy"—the "desire to lead" still crystallizes might is right.

Moreover, "exceptionalism" remains the norm. Now not so blatant, but still implemented via a nasty set of tools, from financial warfare to cyber war, from National Endowment for Democracy-style promotion of "democracy" to Joint Special Operations Command-driven counter-terrorism, drone war and all shades of shadow wars.

In the early 2000s, the model was the physical destruction and occupation of Iraq. In the 2010s the model is the slow-mo destruction, by proxy, of Syria.

And still, those who "conceptualized" the destruction of Iraq keep rearing their *Alien*-like slimy head. Their icon is of course Robert Kagan—one of the founders of the apocalyptically funereal Project for a New American Century (PNAC) and husband of crypto-Ukrainian hell raiser Victoria "F**k the EU" Nuland (thus their dream of Ukraine as the Khaganate of Nulands, or simply Nulandistan.)

Kagan has been devastatingly misguided on everything, as in his 2003 best-seller *Of Paradise and Power: America and Europe in the New World*

Order, an eulogy of "benign" Americans standing guard against the "threats" (as in Muslim fundamentalism) emanating from a Hobbesian world way beyond the cozy Kantian precinct inhabited by Europe.

Then, in *The Return of History and the End of Dreams* (2008), the "evil" was not Muslim fundamentalism anymore (too shabby), but the emerging of those vast autocracies, Russia and China, antithetical to Western democracies. But with *The World America Made* (2012), the paradisiacal shining city on the hill would once again triumph, more than capable to see those autocracies off; after all, the only reliable guarantee of global peace is American exceptionalism.

Kagan still commands the attention even of the otherwise aloof Commander-in-Chief, who avidly consumed *The World America Made* before his 2012 State of the Union Address, in which he proclaimed "America is back."

It's enlightening to flash back to Kagan writing in the Weekly Standard in March 2011, sounding like an awestruck schoolboy praising Obama; "He thoroughly rejected the so-called realist approach, extolled American exceptionalism, spoke of universal values and insisted that American power should be used, when appropriate, on behalf of those values."

Any similarity with Obama's "new" foreign policy doctrine is, indeed, intentional.

Catfight at the Singapore corral

Now comes Kagan's latest opus, "Superpowers Don't Get to Retire: What our tired country still owes the world," with a sorry mess already inbuilt in the title (he's never read Paul Kennedy after all). History tells us that superpowers do retire because of overextension—not only military but mostly economic and fiscal, as in facing bankruptcy.

Yet it's hopeless to expect from Kagan and the neocon nebula anything other than blindness to the lessons of history—with a special, tragic mention of Shock and Awe, trampling of Geneva Conventions, and institutionalized torture. Their parochial dichotomy is either eternal American global hegemony or outright chaos.

Progressives in the US still try to save the day, frantically calling for a core "restoration" of American economic and democratic health; a rather impossible undertaking when casino capitalism rules and the US is now for all practical purposes an oligarchy. These dreamers actually believe this "restoration" is what Obama has done or is trying to do; and that would project the US once again as a global model—and thus "encourage" democracy everywhere. Sorry to break the news, but for the overwhelming majority of the genuine, fact on the ground "international community," the notion of the US promoting democracy is now D.O.A.

So under the banner of exceptionalism—versus the competing birth of a Eurasian century—it's been a fascinating exercise to witness the catfight at the Shangri-La Dialogue in Singapore, which I described last year as the Spielbergs and Clooneys of the military sphere all locked up in a Star Wars room (actually a ballroom with chandeliers at the Shangri-La Hotel.)

It all started with Shinzo Abe, the militaristic prime minister of that American protectorate, Japan, denouncing "unilateral efforts" to alter the strategic status quo in Asia. General Martin Dempsey, chairman of the Joint Chiefs of Staff, piled up, saying Asia-Pacific was becoming less stable because of "coercion and provocation" by China. And Pentagon supremo Chuck Hagel also blasted Beijing, accusing it of "destabilizing, unilateral actions" in the South China Sea.

But then Lt Gen Wang Guanzhong, the deputy chief of general staff of the PLA, counterpunched in kind, saying Hagel's talk was "full of hegemony, full of words of threat and intimidation" and part of "a provocative challenge against China."

Major-General Zhu Chenghu even allowed himself to be condescending (oh, those barbarians...); "The Americans are making very, very important strategic mistakes right now... If you take China as an enemy, China will absolutely become the enemy of the US."

Major-General Zhu also accused Hagel of hypocrisy; "Whatever the Chinese do is illegal, and whatever the Americans do is right." Zhu was quick to register Hagel's own threat, as in "the US will not look the other way when fundamental principles of the international order are being challenged." Translation: Don't mess with the exceptionalist. WE are the international order.

It's as if everyone was reading from Kagan's playbook. The difference is that Beijing is not Baghdad, and will not respond to threats by lying down. Instead, it is deploying selective, savvy, tactical moves all across the Western Pacific chessboard. Washington's Asian network of vassals/clients/protectorates is and will be slowly but surely undermined. And on top of it, Beijing clearly sees that both Hagel and Kerry—who know next to nothing about the complexities of Asia—are clearly panicking.

Those Deng Xiaoping dictum days—from "crossing the river by feeling the stones" to "carry a low profile"—are in the past. Now we're talking about the imminent number one economic power, already the world's top trading nation and America's top creditor.

Highway to Hillary

Russia—and not the US—is now the key partner or broker in negotiating hardcore international conflicts. The recent flurry of China-Russia energy and trade agreements, an essential part of their strategic partnership; the progressive integration and concerted economic/financial strategy of the BRICS; and even the slow moving process of Latin American integration all point towards a multipolar world.

Which bring us back to Obama's "new" foreign policy doctrine. Let's quickly survey the recent record.

Obama only refrained from pursuing his reckless, self-imposed red line and bombing Syria because he was saved (from himself) at the eleventh hour by Russian diplomacy.

The Iran dossier remains vulnerable to relentless pressure by neocons/Israel lobby/sectors of the weaponizing industry, with the Obama administration introducing extraneous factors bound to sidestep the negotiation.

Obama's sanctions on Russia because of Ukraine were not only unlawful; they are peripheral, as astute European Union business leaders quickly recognized.

A simulacrum of withdrawal is being pushed in Afghanistan—to be replaced by all-out shadow war.

And the Obama administration—covertly and not so covertly—has been supporting neo-nazis in Ukraine and jihadists in Syria.

All this is still not enough for the Kagan bunch—the "conceptual" architects of the 9/11 wars, who always wanted Obama to bomb Syria; bomb Iran; start a war with Russia over Crimea; and even, sooner rather than later, bomb China to prevent it from getting back to number one.

Hobbesians gone mad—wallowing in their psychotic sense of perennial entitlement—will stop at nothing to prevent the emergence of a multipolar world. It's Exceptionalist Empire with NATO as global Robocop, or hell.

Moscow and Beijing, to say the least, are not exactly impressed; rather, they detect desperation. Yet things could—and should—get much nastier, irrespective of imploding Khaganates. Just wait for the Hillary doctrine.

June 2014

Burn, Men in Black, burn

Let's cut to the chase. As in chasing that Zara outdoor summer collection, complete with state-of-the-art assault rifles, brand new white Nike sneakers and brand new, unlimited mileage white Toyotas crossing the Syrian-Iraqi desert; the Badass Jihadis in Black.

Once upon a (very recent) time, the US government used to help only "good terrorists" (in Syria), instead of "bad terrorists." That was an echo of a (less recent) time when it was supporting only "good Taliban" and not "bad Taliban."

So what happens when Brookings Institution so-called "experts" start blabbering that the Islamic State of Iraq and Sham (ISIS) is really the baddest jihadi outfit on the planet (after all they were cast out of al-Qaeda)? Are they so badass that by warped newspeak logic they're now the new normal?

Since late last year, according to US government newspeak, the "good terrorists" in Syria are the al-Qaeda spin-off gang of Jabhat al-Nusra and (disgraced) Prince Bandar bin Sultan, aka Bandar Bush, the Islamic Front (essentially a Jabhat al-Nusra multiple outlet). And yet both Jabhat and ISIS had pledged allegiance to Ayman "the doctor" al-Zawahiri, the perennial gift that keeps on giving al-Qaeda capo.

That still leaves the question of what Men in Black ISIS, the catwalk-conscious beheading stormtroopers for a basket of hardcore tribal Sunnis and Ba'ath party "remnants" (remember Rummy in 2003?) are really up to.

We interrupt this desert catwalk to announce they will NOT invade Baghdad. On the other hand, they are busy accelerating the balkanization—and eventual partition—of both Syria and Iraq. They are NOT a CIA brainchild (how come Langley never thought about it?); they are in fact the bastard children of (disgraced) Bandar Bush's credit card largesse.

The fact that ISIS is NOT directly in Langley's payroll does not imply their strategic agenda essentially differs from that of the Empire of Chaos. The Obama administration may be sending a few marines to protect the swimming pools of the largest, Vatican-sized embassy on Planet Earth, plus a few "military advisors" to "retrain" the dissolving Iraqi Army. But that's a drop of Coke Zero in the Western Iraqi desert. There's no evidence Obama is about to authorize "kinetic support" against ISIS, even though Baghdad has already green-lighted it.

Even if Obama went ballistic ("targeted military action"), and/or manufactured a new kill list to be itemized by his drones, that would amount to no more than a little diversion. What matters is that the confluent ISIS/Beltway agenda remains the same; get rid of Iraqi Prime Minister al-Maliki (not by accident the new meme in US corporate media); curb Iran's political/economic influence over Iraq; fundamentally erase Sykes-Picot; and promote the "birth pangs" (remember Condi?) of vast wastelands bypassing centralized power and run by hardcore tribal Sunnis.

For the Empire of Chaos, ISIS is the agent provocateur that fell from (Allah's?) Heaven; the perfect ski mask-clad tool to keep the Global War on Terror (GWOT) in Enduring Freedom Forever mode.

The icing in the (melted) cake is that the House of Saud has officially denied support of ISIS. So this means it's true, even over Bandar Bush's carcass. Cue to the official House of Saud and House of Thani narrative about ISIS: they are not in charge of what's happening in Iraq. It's all organized by the Ba'athist "remnants."

Bring on more regime change

Now for the all-encompassing Iranian angle, because the whole drama, as usual, is mostly about "containment" of Iran. We just need to endure this to confirm it; the same old regurgitation about "evidence" that "Iran and its Syrian allies" have "cooperated" with ISIS and that Bashar al-Assad in Syria has a "business partnership" with ISIS. And don't forget the scaremongering; what's ahead is a "nuclear Iran" against a "Sunni Arab world" in which the great bogeymen remains al-Qaeda.

Neocon propaganda denouncing the US government for being in bed with Tehran against ISIS is, once again, disinformation.

Commander of Iran's Basij, General Mohammad Reza Naqudi, was very close to the mark when he said, "Takfiri and Salafi groups in different regional states, especially in Syria and Iraq, are supported by the US," and that "the US is manipulating the Takfiri terrorists to tarnish the image of Islam and Muslims." The same applies to Speaker of the Majlis Ali Larijani; "It is obvious that the Americans and the countries around it have made such moves... Terrorism has grown into an instrument for the big powers to advance their goals."

What this all implies is that Tehran has identified the ISIS catwalk parade for what it is; a trap. Moreover, they are also convinced Washington won't break with its vassals at the House of Saud. Translation: Washington remains committed to old school GWOT. What Tehran is already, practically, supporting—also with "advisors" on the ground—is a myriad of Shi'ite militias who are being deployed to secure Baghdad and especially the Shi'ite holy cities, Najaf and Karbala.

US Return of the Living Neocon Dead, meanwhile, insist on regurgitating their favorite theme; Maliki Maliki Maliki. Nothing of what's goin' on in Iraq has anything to do with Shock and Awe, the invasion, occupation and destruction of most of the country, Abu Ghraib, or the vicious, totally Washington-instigated sectarian war (Divide and Rule, all over again). It's all Maliki's fault. So he must be booted out. When everything fails—to the tune of trillions of dollars—the neocon playbook always resets to default; regime change.

Slouching towards Hardcore Sunnistan

It's all extremely fishy about ISIS leader Abu Bakr al-Baghdadi, aka Abu Dua, born in Samarra in 1971, a Saddam "remnant" but—crucially—a former prisoner of the US government in Camp Bocca from 2005 to 2009, as well as a former leader of al-Qaeda in Iraq. It's no secret in the Levant that ISIS Men in Black were trained in 2012 by US instructors at a secret base in Safawi, in the northern desert of that fiction disguised as a country, Jordan, so they would later fight as Western-approved "rebels" in Syria.

It was al-Baghdadi who sent a batch of Men in Black to set up Jabhat al-Nusra ("good terrorists," remember?) in Syria. He may have split from Jabhat in late 2013, but still remains in charge of a vast desert wasteland from northern Syria to Western Iraq. He's the new Osama bin Laden (the gift that keeps on giving, again), the all but certain Emir of an Islamically correct desert Caliphate in the heart of the Levant.

Forget about Osama in the Hindu Kush; this is so much sexier.

A hardcore Sunnistan between Iraq's Kurdish north and the Shi'te south, swimming in oil, extending all the way to Aleppo, Rakka and Deir ez-Zor in Syria, between the two rivers—the Tiger and the Euphrates—

with Mosul as capital, back to its ancestral role of pivot between the twin rivers and the Mediterranean. Sykes-Picot, eat your heart out.

Obviously, al-Baghdadi could not have pulled that awesome feat off all by himself. Enter his top Saddam "remnant" sidekick, Ba'ath party theorist extraordinaire Izzaat Ibrahim al-Douri, who happens to be from strategic Mosul. And most of all, enter the General Military Council for Iraqi Revolutionaries—an awesomely "secret" organization which has had the guile to dribble, like an infernal composite of Lionel Messi and Luiz Suarez, the whole Western intel apparatus, Orwellian-Panopticon NSA included.

Well, not really, because this ISIS-Ba'athist coalition of the willing was brokered by none other than Bandar Bush—while he was still in action, with crucial, lateral input from Turkey's Prime Minister Erdogan. No way to trace it all back to the Beltway.

What the General Military Council managed to assemble was no less than all the "remnants" of the good old early 2000s Iraqi resistance, top tribal sheiks, merge it with ISIS, and create what might be dubbed a "Resistance Army"—those Badass Jihadis in Black in their white Toyotas, now the stuff of legend, performing the miracle of being untrackable by the NSA's satellite maze. They're so hip they even have their own Facebook page, with over 33,000 "likes."

Balkanize or bust

Meanwhile, the agenda of the Empire of Chaos proceed unabated. Balkanization is already a fact. Iraqi Foreign Minister Hoshyar Zebari, crucially a Kurd, pledged Kurdish Peshmerga "cooperation" with the Iraq army to keep oil-rich Kirkuk away from ISIS. Like clockwork, the Peshmergas for all practical purposes annexed Kirkuk. Grand Kurdistan beckons.

Grand Ayatollah Sistani, also for all practical purposes, launched a Shi'ite jihad against ISIS. For his part, the leader of the Islamic Supreme Council of Iraq, Sayyid Ammar al-Hakim, all but resurrected their formidable paramilitary, the Badr Corps—very close to the Iranian Revolutionary Guards Corps. These are real badasses, against which ISIS does not stand a chance. And Muqtada al-Sadr is launching "Peace Brigades" to protect the Shi'te holy cities and also Christian churches. Civil war rules.

Meanwhile, in the Land of Oz, the Pentagon will certainly be able to extract extra funds for its perennial crusade to save Western civilization from Islamist terror. After all, there's a (ski masked) neo-Osama bin Laden in da hood.

Although the majority of Iraqis reject balkanization, Sunnis will keep accusing Shi'ites of being Iranian pawns, and Shi'ites will keep accusing Sunnis of being the House of Saud's fifth column. ISIS will keep getting loads of cash from wealthy Saudi "donors." The US government will keep weaponizing Sunnis in Syria against Shi'ites and (perhaps) conducting soft "targeted military strikes" for Shi'ites against Sunnis in Iraq. Welcome to Divide and Rule run amok.

June 2014

BRICS AGAINST WASHINGTON CONSENSUS

The headline news is that this Tuesday in Fortaleza, northeast Brazil, the BRICS group of emerging powers (Brazil, Russia, India, China, South Africa) fights the (Neoliberal) World (Dis)Order via a new development bank and a reserve fund set up to offset financial crises.

The devil, of course, is in the details of how they'll do it.

It's been a long and winding road since Yekaterinburg in 2009, at their first summit, up to the BRICS's long-awaited counterpunch against the Bretton Woods consensus—the IMF and the World Bank—as well as the Japan-dominated (but largely responding to US priorities) Asian Development Bank (ADB).

The BRICS Development Bank—with an initial US$50 billion in capital—will be not only BRICS-oriented, but invest in infrastructure projects and sustainable development on a global scale. The model is the Brazilian BNDES, which supports Brazilian companies investing across Latin America. In a few years, it will reach a financing capacity of up to $350 billion. With extra funding especially from Beijing and Moscow, the new institution could leave the World Bank in the dust. Compare access to real capital savings to US government's printed green paper with no collateral.

And then there's the agreement establishing a $100 billion pool of reserve currencies—the Contingent Reserve Arrangement (CRA), described by Russian Finance Minister Anton Siluanov as "a kind of mini-IMF." That's a non-Washington Consensus mechanism to counterpunch capital flight. For the pool, China will contribute with $41 billion, Brazil, India and Russia with $18 billion each, and South Africa with $5 billion.

The development bank should be headquartered in Shanghai—although Mumbai has forcefully tried to make its case (for an Indian take on the BRICS strategy, see here)

Way beyond economy and finance, this is essentially about geopolitics—as in emerging powers offering an alternative to the failed Washington Consensus. Or, as consensus apologists say, the BRICS may be able to "alleviate challenges" they face from the "international financial system." The strategy also happens to be one of the key nodes of the progressively solidified China-Russia alliance, recently featured via the gas "deal of the century" and at the St. Petersburg economic forum.

7 Let's play geopolitical ball

Just as Brazil managed, against plenty of odds, to stage an unforgettable World Cup—the melting of the national team notwithstanding—Vladimir Putin and Xi Xinping now come to the neighborhood to play top class geopolitical ball.

The Kremlin views the bilateral relation with Brasilia as highly strategic. Putin not only watched the World Cup final in Rio; apart from Brazilian President Dilma Rousseff, he also met German Chancellor Angela Merkel (they discussed Ukraine in detail). Yet arguably the key member of Putin's traveling party is Elvira Nabiulin, president of Russia's Central Bank; she is pressing in South America the concept that all negotiations with the BRICS should bypass the US dollar.

Putin's extremely powerful, symbolic meeting with Fidel Castro in Havana, as well as writing off $36 billion in Cuban debt could not have had a more meaningful impact all across Latin America. Compare it with the perennial embargo imposed by a vengeful Empire of Chaos.

In South America, Putin is meeting not only with Uruguay's President Pepe Mujica—discussing, among other items, the construction of a deep-water port—but also with Venezuela's Nicolas Maduro and Bolivia's Evo Morales.

Xi Jinping is also on tour, visiting, apart from Brazil, Argentina, Cuba and Venezuela. What Beijing is saying (and doing) complements Moscow; Latin America is viewed as highly strategic. That should translate into more Chinese investment and increased South-South integration.

This Russia-China commercial/diplomatic offensive fits the concerted push towards a multipolar world—side by side with political/economic South American leaders. Argentina is a sterling example. While Buenos Aires, already mired in recession, fights American vulture funds—the epitome of financial speculation—in New York courthouses, Putin and Xi come offering investment in everything from railways to the energy industry.

Russia's energy industry of course needs investment and technology from private Western multinationals, just as Made-in-China developed out of Western investment profiting from a cheap workforce. What the BRICS are trying to present to the Global South now is a choice; on one side, financial speculation, vulture funds and the hegemony of the Masters of the Universe; on the other side, productive capitalism—an alternative strategy of capitalist development compared to the Triad (US, EU, Japan).

Still, it will be a long way for the BRICS to project a productive model independent of the casino capitalism speculation "model," by the way still recovering from the massive 2007/2008 crisis (the financial bubble has not burst for good.)

One might view the BRICS's strategy as a sort of running, constructive critique of capitalism; how to purge the system from perennially financing the US fiscal deficit as well as a global militarization syndrome—related to the Orwellian/Panopticon complex—subordinated to Washington. As Argentine economist Julio Gambina put it, the key question is not being emergent, but independent.

In this piece, La Stampa's Claudio Gallo introduces what could be the defining issue of the times: how neoliberalism—ruling directly or indirectly most of the world—is producing a disastrous anthropological mutation that is plunging us all into global totalitarianism (while everyone swears by their "freedoms").

It's always instructive to come back to Argentina. Argentina is imprisoned by a chronic foreign debt crisis essentially unleashed by the IMF over 40 years ago—and now perpetuated by vulture funds. The BRICS bank and the reserve pool as an alternative to the IMF and World Bank offer the possibility for dozens of other nations to escape the Argentine plight. Not to mention the possibility that other emerging nations such as Indonesia, Malaysia, Iran and Turkey may soon contribute to both institutions.

No wonder the hegemonic Masters of the Universe gang is uneasy in their leather chairs. This Financial Times piece neatly summarizes the view from the City of London—a notorious casino capitalism paradise.

These are heady days in South America in more ways than one. Atlanticist hegemony will remain part of the picture, of course, but it's the

BRICS's strategy that is pointing the way further on down the road. And still the multipolar wheel keeps rolling along.

July 2014

A CHESSBOARD DRENCHED IN BLOOD

"The intelligence and facts were being fixed around the policy." Everyone remembers the Downing Street Memo, which unveiled the Bush/Blair "policy" in the run-up to the 2003 bombing/invasion/occupation of Iraq. The "policy" was to get rid of Saddam Hussein via a lightning war. The justification was "terrorism" and (nonexistent) weapons of mass destruction (WMD), which had "disappeared," mounted in trucks, deep into Syria. Forget about intelligence and facts.

The tragedy of MH17—turned, incidentally, into a WMD—might be seen as a warped rerun of imperial policy in Iraq. No need for a memo this time. The "policy" of the Empire of Chaos is clear, and multi-pronged; diversify the "pivot to Asia" by establishing a beachhead in Ukraine to sabotage trade between Europe and Russia; expand NATO to Ukraine; break the Russia-China strategic partnership; prevent by all means the trade/economic integration of Eurasia, from the Russia-Germany partnership to the New Silk Roads converging from China to the Ruhr; keep Europe under US hegemony.

The key reason why Russian President Vladimir Putin did not "invade" Eastern Ukraine—as much as he's been enticed to by Washington/NATO—to stop a US military advisor-facilitated running slaughter of civilians is that he does not want to antagonize the European Union, Russia's top trading partner.

Crucially, Washington's intervention in Kosovo invoking R2P—Responsibility to Protect—was justified at the time for exactly the same reasons a Russian intervention in Donetsk and Luhansk could be totally justified now. Except that Moscow won't do it—because the Kremlin is playing a very long game.

The MH17 tragedy may have been a horrendous mistake. But it may also have been a desperate gambit by the Kiev minions of the Empire of Chaos. By now, Russian intel may have already mastered the key facts. Washington's predictable modus operandi was to shoot from the hip, igniting and in theory winning the spin war, and doubling down by releasing the proverbial army of "top officials" brimming with social media evidence. Moscow will take time to build a meticulous case, and only then lay it out in detail.

Hegemony lost

The Big Picture spells out the Empire of Chaos elites as extremely uneasy. Take Dr. Zbigniew "The Grand Chessboard" Brzezinski, who as a former foreign policy mentor has the ears of the increasingly dejected White House paperboy. Dr. Zbig was on CNN this Sunday challenging Europe's leaders to "stand up to Putin." He wonders if "Europe wants to become a satellite" and worries about "a moment of decisive significance for the future of the system—of the world system."

And it's all Putin's fault, of course: "We're not starting the Cold War. He [Putin] has started it. But he has gotten himself into a horrendous jam. I strongly suspect that a lot of people in Russia, even not far away from him who are worried that Russia's status in the world is dramatically being undermined, that Russia's economically beginning to fail, that Russia's threatened by the prospect of becoming a satellite to China, that Russia's becoming self-isolated and discredited."

Obviously Dr. Zbig is blissfully unaware of the finer points of the Russia-China strategic partnership, as well as their concerted voice inside the

BRICS, the G-20 and myriad other mechanisms. His trademark Russophobia in the end always gets the better of him. And to think that in his latest book, *Strategic Vision* (2012), Dr. Zbig was in favor of an enlarged "West" annexing Turkey and Russia, with the Empire of Chaos posing as "promoter" and "guarantor" of broader unity in the West, and a "balancer" and "conciliator" between the major powers in the East. A quick look at the record since 2012—Libya, Syria, Ukraine, encirclement of China—reveals the Empire of Chaos only as fomenter of, what else, chaos.

Now compare a fearful Dr. Zbig with Immanuel Wallerstein—who was a huge influence in my 2007 warped geopolitical travel book Globalistan. In this piece (in Spanish) Wallerstein argues that the Empire of Chaos simply can't accept its geopolitical decadence—and that's why it has become so dangerous. Restoring its hegemony in the world-system has become the supreme obsession; and that's where the whole "policy" that is an essential background to the MH17 tragedy reveals Ukraine as the definitive do or die battleground.

In Europe, everything hinges on Germany. Especially after the NSA scandal and its ramifications, the key debate raging in Berlin is how to position itself geopolitically bypassing the US. And the answer, as pressed by large swathes of German big business, lies in a strategic partnership with Russia.

Show me the missile

Slowly, with no hype and no spin, the Russian military are starting to deliver the goods. Here, courtesy of the Vineyard of The Saker blog, is their key presentation so far. As The Saker put it, Russia had—and has—a "20/20 radar vision," or full spectrum surveillance, on everything going on in Ukraine. And so, arguably, does NATO. What the Russian Ministry of Defense is saying is as important as the clues it is laying out for experts to follow.

The damaged MH17 starboard jet engine suggests a shape charge from an air-to-air missile—and not a Buk; that's consistent with the Russian Ministry of Defense presentation graphically highlighting an Ukrainian Su-25 shadowing MH17. Increasingly, the Buk scenario—hysterically peddled by the Empire of Chaos—is being discarded. Not to mention, again, that not a single eyewitness saw the very graphic, thick missile trace that would have been clearly visible had a Buk been used.

Way beyond the established fact of a Ukrainian Su-25 trailing MH17, plenty of unanswered questions remain, some involving a murky security procedure at Amsterdam's Schiphol airport—where security is operated by ICTS, an Israeli company based in The Netherlands and founded by former officers from the Israeli Shin Bet intel agency. And then there is the unexplained presence of "foreign" advisors in Kiev's control tower.

As much as Bashar al-Assad in Syria had absolutely no motive to "gas his own people"—as the hysterical narrative went at the time—the Eastern Ukraine federalists have no motive to down a civilian airliner. And as much as Washington doesn't give a damn about the current civilian slaughter in Gaza, it doesn't give a damn about the MH17 civilian deaths; the one and only obsession is to force Europeans to sanction Russia to death. Translation: break up Europe-Russia commercial and geopolitical integration.

One week before the MH17 tragedy, the Russian Institute of Strategic Studies was already sounding the alarm concerning the Empire of Chaos's "policy" and its refusal to "adhere to the principles and norms of international law and the rules and spirit of the existing system of international relations."

Moscow, in building its case on the MH17 tragedy, will bide its time to debunk Kiev's claims and maximize its own credibility. The game now moves to the black boxes and the cockpit voice recorder. Still Ukraine will remain the do or die battlefield—a chessboard drenched in blood.

July 2014

Operation Tomahawk The Caliph

The Tomahawks are finally flying again—propelled by newspeak. 42 Tomahawks fired from a Sixth Fleet destroyer parked in Mare Nostrum, plus F-22s raising hell and Hellfires spouted by drones, that's a neat mini-Shock and Awe to honor Caliph Ibrahim, aka Abu Bakr al-Baghdadi, self-declared leader of Islamic State.

It's all so surgical. All targets—from "suspected" weapons depots to the mayor's mansion in Raqqah (the HQ of The Caliph's goons) and assorted checkpoints—were duly obliterated, along with "dozens of", perhaps 120, jihadis.

And praise those "over 40" (Samantha Power) or "over 50" (John Kerry) international allies in the coalition of the unwilling; America is never alone, although in this case mightily escorted, *de facto*, only by the usual Gulf petrodollar dictatorships and the realm of King Playstation, Jordan, all none too keen to engage in "kinetic activities".

Aseptic newspeak aside, no one has seen or heard a mighty Gulf Cooperation Council air force deployed to bomb Syria. After all the vassals are scared as hell to tell their own populations they are—once again—bombing a fellow Arab nation. As for Damascus, it meekly said it was "notified" by the Pentagon its own territory would be bombed. Nobody really knows what the Pentagon is exactly telling Damascus.

The Pentagon calls it just the beginning of a "sustained campaign"—code for Long War, which is one of the original denominations of the Global War on Terror (GWOT) anyway. And yes, for all practical purposes this is a coalition of one. Let's call it Operation Tomahawk The Caliph.

I am Khorasan

Hold your F-22s. Not really. The tomahawking had barely begun when an Israeli, made in USA Patriot missile shot a Syrian Su-24 which had allegedly "violated" Israeli air space over the Golan Heights. How about that in terms of sending a graphic message in close coordination with the Pentagon?

So this is not only about bombing The Caliph. It is a back-door preamble to bombing Bashar al-Assad and his forces. And also about bombing—with eight strikes west of Aleppo—a ghost; an al-Qaeda cell of the mysterious Khorasan group.

No wonder global fans of the Marvel Comics school of geopolitics are puzzled. Two simultaneous villains? Yep. And the other bad guy is even more evil than The Caliph.

Astonishing mediocrity Ben Rhodes, Obama's deputy national security adviser, has defined Khorasan as "a group of extremists that is comprised of a number of individuals who we've been tracking for a long time."

The Obama administration's unison newspeak is that Khorasan includes former al-Qaeda assets not only from across the Middle East—including al-Qaeda in Iraq and Jabhat al-Nusra—but also Pakistan, as in an ultra-hardcore extension of the Pakistani Taliban.

What a mess. Al-Qaeda in Iraq is the embryo of ISIS, which turned into IS. Jabhat al-Nusra is the al-Qaeda franchise in Syria, approved by CEO Ayman al-Zawahiri. Both despise each other, and yet Khorasan holds the merit of bundling Caliph's goons and al-Qaeda goons together.

Additionally, for Washington Jabhat al-Nusra tend to qualify as "moderate" jihadis—almost like "our bastards". Too messy? No problem; when in doubt, bomb everybody.

The Caliph, then, is old news. Those ghostly Khorasan goons are the real deal—so evil that the Pentagon is convinced their "plotting was imminent" leading to a new 9/11.

The ghost in the GWOT machine

Khorasan is the perfect ghost in the GWOT machine; the target of a war within a war. Because Obama in fact launched two wars—as he sent two different notifications to Congress under the War Powers Resolution to cover both The Caliph and Khorasan.

And what's in a name? Well, a thinly disguised extra demonization of Iran, why not—as historic Khorasan, the previous Parthia, stretched from mainly Iran towards Afghanistan.

Khorasan is theoretically led by The Joker, sorry, al-Qaeda honcho Muhsin al-Fadhli, born in Kuwait in 1981, a "senior facilitator and financier" to Abu Musab al-Zarqawi in Iraq, in the priceless assessment of the State Department. Although Ayman al-Zawahiri, ever PR-conscious, has not claimed the credit, the Pentagon is convinced he sent al-Fadhli to the Syrian part of the Caliphate to attract Western jihadis with EU passports capable of evading airport security and plant bombs on commercial jets.

The Treasury Department is convinced al-Fadhli even led an al-Qaeda cell in Iran—demonization habits die hard -, "facilitating" jihadi travel to Afghanistan or Iraq.

And what a neat contrast to the Society of the Spectacle-addicted Caliph. Khorasan is pure darkness. Nobody knows how many; how long they've existed; what do they really want.

By contrast, there are about 190,000 live human beings left in bombed out Raqqa. Nobody is talking about collateral damage—although the body count is already on, and The Caliph's slick PR operation will be certainly advertising them on YouTube. As for The Caliph's goons, they will predictably use Mao tactics and dissolve like fish in the sea. The Pentagon will soon be bombing vast tracts of desert for nothing—if that's not the case already.

There is no "Free Syrian Army"—that Qatari myth—anymore. There are no "moderate" jihadis left in Syria. They are all fighting for The Caliph or for al-Zawahiri. And still the Obama administration extracted a Congressional OK to train and weaponize "moderate rebels".

US ambassador to the UN Samantha Power—Undisputed Queen of Batshit Craziness—at least got one thing right. Their "training" will "service these troops in the same struggle that they've been in since the beginning of this conflict against the Assad regime." So yes—this "sustained campaign" is the back door to "Assad must go" remixed.

People who are really capable of defeating The Caliph's goons don't tomahawk. They are the Syrian Arab Army (roughly 35,000 dead so far killed in action against ISIS/ISIL/IS and/or al-Qaeda); Hezbollah; Iranian Revolutionary Guards advisers/operatives; and Kurdish militias. It won't happen. This season's blockbuster is the Empire of Chaos bombing The Caliph and the ghost in the GWOT machine. Two tickets for the price of one. Because we protect you even from "unknown unknown" evil.

September 2014

WILL NATO LIBERATE JIHADISTAN?

*Drive your cart and your plow
Over the bones of the dead ...*

- William Blake, *The Marriage of Heaven and Hell*

Caliph Ibrahim, aka Abu Bakr al-Baghdadi, self-declared leader of Islamic State, formerly the Islamic State of Iraq and Syria, really sports a mean PR vein. When the show seemed scheduled for the NATO to save Ukraine and Western Civilization—at least rhetorically—from that Evil Empire remixed, Russia, The Caliph, accessing his expensive watch wisdom, intervened with—what else—yet another "off with their heads" special.

Eyebrows were properly raised until the United States' intel alphabet soup solemnly concluded that Islamic State (IS) really beheaded yet another American journalist on video (US President Barack Obama: "An horrific act of violence").

And then, out of the blue, The Caliph doubled down, proclaiming to the whole world his next target is none other than Russian President Vladimir Putin. Was he channeling the recently ostracized Saudi Prince Bandar bin Sultan, aka Bandar Bush?

In thesis, everything would be settled. The Caliph becomes a contractor to NATO (well, he's been on to it, sort of). The Caliph beheads Putin. The Caliph liberates Chechnya—fast; not the usual, deeply embarrassing NATO quagmire in Afghanistan. The Caliph, on a roll, attacks the BRICS—Brazil, Russia, India, China and South Africa. The Caliph becomes NATO's shadow secretary-general. And Obama finally stops complaining that his calls to Putin always end up on voicemail.

Ah, if geopolitics was as simple as a Marvel Comics blockbuster.

Instead, The Caliph should know—even as he is largely a Made-in-the-West product, with substantial input from Gulf Cooperation Council petrodollar cash—that NATO never promised him a rose garden.

So, predictably, those ungrateful Obama and David Cameron, the British Prime Minister—oh yes, because the "special relationship" is all that matters in NATO, the others are mere extras—have vowed to go after him with a broad (well, not that broad) "coalition of the willing" with the usual GCC suspects plus Turkey and Jordan, bombing Iraqi Kurdistan, parts of Sunni Iraq and even Syria.

After all, Syrian President "Assad must go", rather "Assad brutality" in Cameron's formulation, is the real culprit for The Caliph's actions.

And all in the name of the Enduring Freedom Forever-style Global War on Terror (GWOT).

Now get me that Slavic Caliph

NATO's outgoing secretary-general Anders "Fogh of War" Rasmussen was somehow rattled. After all, this was supposed to be the "crucial moment", at the NATO summit in Wales, when NATO would be at its Cold War 2.0 best, rescuing "the allies", all 28 of them, from the dark gloom of insecurity.

One just had to look at the replica of a glorious Eurofighter Typhoon deployed in front of the NATO summit hotel in the southern Welsh town of Newport.

To round it all off, that evil Slavic Caliph, Vlad Putin himself, designed a seven-point peace plan to solve the Ukrainian quagmire—just as Kiev's appalling army has been reduced to strogonoff by the federalists and/or separatists in the Donbass. Ukrainian President Petro Poroshenko—who until virtually yesterday was screaming "Invasion!" at the top of his lungs—breathed long sighs of relief. And as an aside, he disclosed Kiev was receiving high-precision weapons from an unnamed country that could only be the US, the UK or Poland.

The whole thing posed a problem, though. What is NATO to defend Western Civilization from when all that threat embodied by "Russian aggression" dissolves into a road map to peace?

No wonder the 60 heads of state and government with their Ministers of Defense and Foreign Relations who performed a soft invasion/breaching of the "ring of steel" protecting Newport from protesting hordes were also somehow dazed an confused.

Over 11 years after Shock and Awe, we are still living in a Rumsfeldian world. It was the former Pentagon head Donald Rumsfeld under George "Dubya" Bush who conceptualized "Old Europe" and "New Europe". "Old" were Venusian sissies; "New" were vigorous Martians.

"New" totally supported Shock and Awe, and the subsequent invasion/occupation of Iraq. Now they support, in fact beg, for NATO to stare down Russia.

"Old", for its part, was trying at least to save a negotiating space with Putin. And in the end dear prudence, especially by Berlin, was rewarded with the Putin peace plan.

Just in case, not to rattle the Empire of Chaos too much, Paris announced it won't deliver the first of two Mistral helicopter carrier battleships to Moscow according to schedule. And of course NATO strongly condemned Russia on Ukraine, and the European Union followed up with yet more sanctions.

As for Fogh of War, predictably, he kept juggling his "Mars Attacks!" rhetoric (see Asia Times Online, September 3, 2014). It was all Moscow's fault. NATO is nothing but an innocent force of appeasement—powerful and solid. At the same time, NATO would not be foolish to start depicting Russia as an enemy outright.

So, as Asia Times Online reported, NATO at best will help train Kiev's forces; the Donbass performance showed they badly need it. But there will be no Ukraine "integration"—for all the hysteria deployed by Kiev as well as Poland and the Baltic states calling for permanent bases. The new element will be the remixed NATO Response Force (NRF) which, by the way, was never used before.

NRF even comes with a catchy slogan: "Travel light and strike hard". An 800-strong battalion will be able to strike in two days, and a 5,000-strong brigade between five and seven days. Well, by those "travel light" standards it would hardly be enough to prevent The Caliph from annexing larger parts of Jihadistan with his gleaming white Toyota combo. As for "strike hard", ask Pashtuns in the Hindu Kush for an informed opinion.

So Wales yielded NRF; permanent "rotation" and permanent forward bases to "protect" Central and Eastern Europe; and everybody shelling out more cash (no less than 2% of their GDP each, for all 28 members, from here to 2025). All this in the middle of the third European recession in five years.

Now compare the astonishing combined NATO military budget of US$900 billion (75% of all expenses monopolized by the US) with only $80 billion for Russia. Yet Moscow is the "threat".

Needless to add, even under so much sound and fury, Wales did not yield NATO sitting on a Freudian divan—analyzing in an endless monologue its abject failure in both Afghanistan and Libya.

In Afghanistan, the Taliban basically run rings around NATO's bases and "strike hard" movements, demoralizing them to oblivion. That was NATO in GWOT mode.

And in Libya, NATO created a failed state ravaged by militias and called it "peace". That was NATO in "Responsibility To Protect" (R2P) mode.

NATO liberating Jihadistan? The Pentagon couldn't care less. The Pentagon wants eternal GWOT. US Think Tankland is ecstatic at NATO finding a "renewed purpose" and its long-term survival now assured by a "unifying threat". Translation: Russia.

So The Caliph is not exactly quaking in his Made-in-USA desert boots. He's even dreaming of taking on the Slavic Caliph himself. How come Marvel Comics never thought about that?

September 2014

CAN CHINA AND RUSSIA SQUEEZE WASHINGTON OUT OF EURASIA?

A specter haunts the fast-aging "New American Century": the possibility of a future Beijing-Moscow-Berlin strategic trade and commercial alliance. Let's call it the BMB.

Its likelihood is being seriously discussed at the highest levels in Beijing and Moscow, and viewed with interest in Berlin, New Delhi, and Tehran. But don't mention it inside Washington's Beltway or at NATO headquarters in Brussels. There, the star of the show today and tomorrow is the new Osama bin Laden: Caliph Ibrahim, aka Abu Bakr al-Baghdadi, the elusive, self-appointed beheading prophet of a new mini-state and movement that has provided an acronym feast—ISIS/ISIL/IS—for hysterics in Washington and elsewhere.

No matter how often Washington remixes its Global War on Terror, however, the tectonic plates of Eurasian geopolitics continue to shift, and they're not going to stop just because American elites refuse to accept that their historically brief "unipolar moment" is on the wane. For them, the closing of the era of "full spectrum dominance," as the Pentagon likes to call it, is inconceivable. After all, the necessity for the indispensable nation to control all space—military, economic, cultural, cyber, and outer—is little short of a religious doctrine. Exceptionalist missionaries don't do equality. At best, they do "coalitions of the willing" like the one crammed with "over 40 countries" assembled to fight ISIS/ISIL/IS and either applauding (and plotting) from the sidelines or sending the odd plane or two toward Iraq or Syria.

NATO, which unlike some of its members won't officially fight Jihadistan, remains a top-down outfit controlled by Washington. It's never fully bothered to take in the European Union (EU) or considered allowing Russia to "feel" European. As for the Caliph, he's just a minor diversion. A postmodern cynic might even contend that he was an emissary sent onto the global playing field by China and Russia to take the eye of the planet's hyperpower off the ball.

Divide and Isolate

So how does full spectrum dominance apply when two actual competitor powers, Russia and China, begin to make their presences felt? Washington's approach to each—in Ukraine and in Asian waters—might be thought of as divide and isolate.

In order to keep the Pacific Ocean as a classic "American lake," the Obama administration has been "pivoting" back to Asia for several years now. This has involved only modest military moves, but an immodest attempt to pit Chinese nationalism against the Japanese variety, while strengthening alliances and relations across Southeast Asia with a focus on South China Sea energy disputes. At the same time, it has moved to lock a future trade agreement, the Trans-Pacific Partnership (TPP), in place.

In Russia's western borderlands, the Obama administration has stoked the embers of regime change in Kiev into flames (fanned by local cheerleaders Poland and the Baltic nations) and into what clearly looked, to Vladimir Putin and Russia's leadership, like an existential threat to Moscow. Unlike the U.S., whose sphere of influence (and military bases) are global, Russia was not to retain any significant influence in its former near abroad, which, when it comes to Kiev, is not for most Russians, "abroad" at all.

For Moscow, it seemed as if Washington and its NATO allies were increasingly interested in imposing a new Iron Curtain on their country from the Baltic to the Black Sea, with Ukraine simply as the tip of the spear. In BMB terms, think of it as an attempt to isolate Russia and impose a new barrier to relations with Germany. The ultimate aim would be to split Eurasia, preventing future moves toward trade and commercial integration via a process not controlled through Washington.

From Beijing's point of view, the Ukraine crisis was a case of Washington crossing every imaginable red line to harass and isolate Russia. To its leaders, this looks like a concerted attempt to destabilize the region in ways favorable to American interests, supported by a full range of Washington's elite from neocons and Cold War "liberals" to humanitarian interventionists in the Susan Rice and Samantha Power mold. Of course, if you've been following the Ukraine crisis from Washington, such perspectives seem as alien as any those of any Martian. But the world looks different from the heart of Eurasia than it does from Washington—especially from a rising China with its newly minted "Chinese dream" (*Zhongguo meng*).

As laid out by President Xi Jinping, that dream would include a future network of Chinese-organized new Silk Roads that would create the equivalent of a Trans-Asian Express for Eurasian commerce. So if Beijing, for instance, feels pressure from Washington and Tokyo on the naval front, part of its response is a two-pronged, trade-based advance across the Eurasian landmass, one prong via Siberia and the other through the Central Asian "stans."

In this sense, though you wouldn't know it if you only followed the American media or "debates" in Washington, we're potentially entering a new world. Once upon a time not so long ago, Beijing's leadership was flirting with the idea of rewriting the geopolitical/economic game side by side with the U.S., while Putin's Moscow hinted at the possibility of someday joining NATO. No longer. Today, the part of the West that both countries are interested in is a possible future Germany no longer dominated by American power and Washington's wishes.

Moscow has, in fact, been involved in no less than half a century of strategic dialogue with Berlin that has included industrial cooperation and increasing energy interdependence. In many quarters of the Global South this has been noted and Germany is starting to be viewed as "the sixth BRICS" power (after Brazil, Russia, India, China, and South Africa).

In the midst of global crises ranging from Syria to Ukraine, Berlin's geostrategic interests seem to be slowly diverging from Washington's. German industrialists, in particular, appear eager to pursue unlimited commercial deals with Russia and China. These might set their country on a path to global power unlimited by the EU's borders and, in the long term, signal the end of the era in which Germany, however politely dealt with, was essentially an American satellite.

It will be a long and winding road. The Bundestag, Germany's parliament, is still addicted to a strong Atlanticist agenda and a preemptive obedience to Washington. There are still tens of thousands of American soldiers on German soil. Yet, for the first time, German chancellor Angela Merkel has been hesitating when it comes to imposing ever-heavier sanctions on Russia over the situation in Ukraine, because no fewer than 300,000 German jobs depend on relations with that country. Industrial leaders and the financial establishment have already sounded the alarm, fearing such sanctions would be totally counterproductive.

China's Silk Road Banquet

China's new geopolitical power play in Eurasia has few parallels in modern history. The days when the "Little Helmsman" Deng Xiaoping insisted that the country "keep a low profile" on the global stage are long gone. Of course, there are disagreements and conflicting strategies when it comes to managing the country's hot spots: Taiwan, Hong Kong, Tibet, Xinjiang, the South China Sea, competitors India and Japan, and problematic allies like North Korea and Pakistan. And popular unrest in some Beijing-dominated "peripheries" is growing to incendiary levels.

The country's number one priority remains domestic and focused on carrying out President Xi's economic reforms, while increasing "transparency" and fighting corruption within the ruling Communist Party. A distant second is the question of how to progressively hedge against the Pentagon's "pivot" plans in the region—via the build-up of a blue-water navy, nuclear submarines, and a technologically advanced air force—without getting so assertive as to freak out Washington's "China threat"-minded establishment.

Meanwhile, with the US Navy controlling global sea lanes for the foreseeable future, planning for those new Silk Roads across Eurasia is proceeding apace. The end result should prove a triumph of integrated infrastructure—roads, high-speed rail, pipelines, ports—that will connect China to Western Europe and the Mediterranean Sea, the old Roman imperial *Mare Nostrum*, in every imaginable way.

In a reverse Marco Polo-style journey, remixed for the Google world, one key Silk Road branch will go from the former imperial capital Xian to Urumqi in Xinjiang Province, then through Central Asia, Iran, Iraq, and Turkey's Anatolia, ending in Venice. Another will be a maritime Silk Road starting from Fujian province and going through the Malacca strait, the Indian Ocean, Nairobi in Kenya, and finally all the way to the Mediterranean via the Suez canal. Taken together, it's what Beijing refers to as the Silk Road Economic Belt.

China's strategy is to create a network of interconnections among no less than five key regions: Russia (the key bridge between Asia and Europe), the Central Asian "stans," Southwest Asia (with major roles for Iran, Iraq, Syria, Saudi Arabia, and Turkey), the Caucasus, and Eastern Europe (including Belarus, Moldova, and depending upon its stability, Ukraine). And don't forget Afghanistan, Pakistan, and India, which could be thought of as Silk Road plus.

Silk Road plus would involve connecting the Bangladesh-China-India-Myanmar economic corridor to the China-Pakistan economic corridor, and could offer Beijing privileged access to the Indian Ocean. Once again, a total package—roads, high-speed rail, pipelines, and fiber optic networks—would link the region to China.

Xi himself put the India-China connection in a neat package of images in an op-ed he published in the *Hindu* prior to his recent visit to New Delhi. "The combination of the 'world's factory' and the 'world's back office,'" he wrote, "will produce the most competitive production base and the most attractive consumer market."

The central node of China's elaborate planning for the Eurasian future is Urumqi, the capital of Xinjiang Province and the site of the largest commercial fair in Central Asia, the China-Eurasia Fair. Since 2000, one of Beijing's top priorities has been to urbanize that largely desert but oil-rich province and industrialize it, whatever it takes. And what it takes, as Beijing sees it, is the hardcore Sinicization of the region—with its corollary, the suppression of any possibility of ethnic Uighur dissent. People's Liberation Army General Li Yazhou has, in these terms, described Central Asia as "the most subtle slice of cake donated by the sky to modern China."

Most of China's vision of a new Eurasia tied to Beijing by every form of transport and communication was vividly detailed in "Marching

Westwards: The Rebalancing of China's Geostrategy," a landmark 2012 essay published by scholar Wang Jisi of the Center of International and Strategic Studies at Beijing University. As a response to such a future set of Eurasian connections, the best the Obama administration has come up with is a version of naval containment from the Indian Ocean to the South China Sea, while sharpening conflicts with and strategic alliances around China from Japan to India. (NATO is, of course, left with the task of containing Russia in Eastern Europe.)

An Iron Curtain vs. Silk Roads

The $400 billion "gas deal of the century," signed by Putin and the Chinese president last May, laid the groundwork for the building of the Power of Siberia pipeline, already under construction in Yakutsk. It will bring a flood of Russian natural gas onto the Chinese market. It clearly represents just the beginning of a turbocharged, energy-based strategic alliance between the two countries. Meanwhile, German businessmen and industrialists have been noting another emerging reality: as much as the final market for made-in-China products traveling on future new Silk Roads will be Europe, the reverse also applies. In one possible commercial future, China is slated to become Germany's top trading partner by 2018, surging ahead of both the US and France.

A potential barrier to such developments, welcomed in Washington, is Cold War 2.0, which is already tearing not NATO, but the EU apart. In the EU of this moment, the anti-Russian camp includes Great Britain, Sweden, Poland, Romania, and the Baltic nations. Italy and Hungary, on the other hand, can be counted in the pro-Russian camp, while a still unpredictable Germany is the key to whether the future will hold a new Iron Curtain or "Go East" mindset. For this, Ukraine remains the key. If it is successfully Finlandized (with significant autonomy for its regions), as

Moscow has been proposing—a suggestion that is anathema to Washington—the Go-East path will remain open. If not, a BMB future will be a dicier proposition.

It should be noted that another vision of the Eurasian economic future is also on the horizon. Washington is attempting to impose a Transatlantic Trade and Investment Partnership (TTIP) on Europe and a similar Trans-Pacific Partnership (TPP) on Asia. Both favor globalizing American corporations and their aim is visibly to impede the ascent of the BRICS economies and the rise of other emerging markets, while solidifying American global economic hegemony.

Two stark facts, carefully noted in Moscow, Beijing, and Berlin, suggest the hardcore geopolitics behind these two "commercial" pacts. The TPP excludes China and the TTIP excludes Russia. They represent, that is, the barely disguised sinews of a future trade/monetary war. On my own recent travels, I have had quality agricultural producers in Spain, Italy, and France repeatedly tell me that TTIP is nothing but an economic version of NATO, the military alliance that China's Xi Jinping calls, perhaps wishfully, an "obsolete structure."

There is significant resistance to the TTIP among many EU nations (especially in the Club Med countries of southern Europe), as there is against the TPP among Asian nations (especially Japan and Malaysia). It is this that gives the Chinese and the Russians hope for their new Silk Roads and a new style of trade across the Eurasian heartland backed by a Russian-supported Eurasian Union. To this, key figures in German business and industrial circles, for whom relations with Russia remain essential, are paying close attention.

After all, Berlin has not shown overwhelming concern for the rest of the crisis-ridden EU (three recessions in five years). Via a much-despised troika—the European Central Bank, the International Monetary Fund, and the European Commission—Berlin is, for all practical purposes, already at the helm of Europe, thriving, and looking east for more.

Three months ago, German chancellor Angela Merkel visited Beijing. Hardly featured in the news was the political acceleration of a potentially groundbreaking project: an uninterrupted high-speed rail connection between Beijing and Berlin. When finally built, it will prove a transportation and trade magnet for dozens of nations along its route from Asia to Europe. Passing through Moscow, it could become the ultimate Silk Road integrator for Europe and perhaps the ultimate nightmare for Washington.

"Losing" Russia

In a blaze of media attention, the recent NATO summit in Wales yielded only a modest "rapid reaction force" for deployment in any future Ukraine-like situations. Meanwhile, the expanding Shanghai Cooperation Organization (SCO), a possible Asian counterpart to NATO, met in Dushanbe, Tajikistan. In Washington and Western Europe essentially no one noticed. They should have. There, China, Russia, and four Central Asian "stans" agreed to add an impressive set of new members: India, Pakistan, and Iran. The implications could be far-reaching. After all, India under Prime Minister Narendra Modi is now on the brink of its own version of Silk Road mania. Behind it lies the possibility of a "Chindia" economic rapprochement, which could change the Eurasian geopolitical map. At the same time, Iran is also being woven into the "Chindia" fold.

So the SCO is slowly but surely shaping up as the most important international organization in Asia. It's already clear that one of its key long-term objectives will be to stop trading in US dollars, while advancing the use of the petroyuan and petroruble in the energy trade. The U.S., of course, will never be welcomed into the organization.

All of this lies in the future, however. In the present, the Kremlin keeps signaling that it once again wants to start talking with Washington, while Beijing has never wanted to stop. Yet the Obama administration remains myopically embedded in its own version of a zero-sum game, relying on its technological and military might to maintain an advantageous position in Eurasia. Beijing, however, has access to markets and loads of cash, while Moscow has loads of energy. Triangular cooperation between Washington, Beijing, and Moscow would undoubtedly be—as the Chinese would say—a win-win-win game, but don't hold your breath.

Instead, expect China and Russia to deepen their strategic partnership, while pulling in other Eurasian regional powers. Beijing has bet the farm that the U.S./NATO confrontation with Russia over Ukraine will leave Vladimir Putin turning east. At the same time, Moscow is carefully calibrating what its ongoing reorientation toward such an economic powerhouse will mean. Someday, it's possible that voices of sanity in Washington will be wondering aloud how the US "lost" Russia to China.

In the meantime, think of China as a magnet for a new world order in a future Eurasian century. The same integration process Russia is facing, for instance, seems increasingly to apply to India and other Eurasian nations, and possibly sooner or later to a neutral Germany as well. In the endgame of such a process, the US might find itself progressively squeezed out of Eurasia, with the BMB emerging as a game-changer. Place your bets soon. They'll be called in by 2025.

October 2014. Originally at TomDispatch.com

Pure War in Tehran

I've just spent a frantic week in Tehran. Before departure, I had made a conscious decision; only one book in the backpack. Maximum concentration. I ended up choosing *Pure War,* the 2008 reprint by Semiotext(e) in LA of the 1983 Paul Virilio classic I had picked up at the revamped Foyles in London a few days back.

For a roving correspondent, going to Iran is always extra-special. Getting a press visa approved usually takes ages. This was my sixth trip—and I had no visa. Just a number, tied to a visa at the airport. Until the last minute, I thought I'd be deported from Imam Khomeini International—back to Abu Dhabi, which is now pretending to bomb The Caliph. Then, a small miracle; a VIP room, a visa in 10 minutes and the next I know I'm zooming into an eerily deserted Tehran at sunrise on a Friday, past the psychedelic space station decked in green that is Imam Khomeini's shrine.

Why Virilio? Because he was the first to conceptualize that with the explosion of asymmetrical warfare, Total War had become local—on a global scale. I expanded on the theme in my 2007 book Globalistan and in my writings. Washington and Tel Aviv had been threatening to bomb Iran for years. Virilio was the first to assert that "peace" merely extends war by other means.

May 1968 as a theatre of the mind—a theatre of the imagination. When society could be an artwork, a performance, with the crowds in the street as the chorus. The last creative reaction against consumerism. "Power to the imagination".

A beautiful sunny morning in front of the Foreign Ministry compound. An exhibition/installation about the "imposed"—as it's widely known—Iran-Iraq war. A reconstructed minefield; a map of nations weaponizing Saddam; pictures of young fighters/martyrs who wouldn't have been older than 14. A theatre of painful remembrance. In late 1978, Tehran also had its crowds in the streets as chorus—against the shah. Khomeini was a reaction against consumerism; but was he "power to the imagination"? And then, all was engulfed in a theatre of cruelty—the tragedy of the "imposed" war.

War in the journalistic sense is national delinquency elevated to the scale of an extremely important conflict—It's the equivalent of the "tumults", as ancient societies called them. We can no longer even speak of wars, they are interstate delinquencies. It's State terrorism.

In Tehran, my immensely gracious hosts were the organizers of New Horizon: the International Conference of Independent Thinkers. After plenty of twists and turns, the Foreign Ministry ended up also being involved. The conference issued a important resolution condemning ISIS/ISIL/The Caliph; Zionism; Islamophobia; sectarianism; and Washington's blind support for anything Israel unleashes over Palestine: Israel's national delinquency, or State terrorism. The conference also called for cooperation and understanding between the West and Islam: that implies a struggle against interstate delinquencies.

The best defense is to attack; and to attack you must have some ideas; right now there aren't any ideas. Imagination today is in the image, and the image is in power. There's no imagination for anything but the image.

I have to leave a fabulous open-air traditional Persian dinner to go to Press TV studios for a debate with notorious neo-con Daniel Pipes about ISIS/ISIL/Daesh. We surprisingly agree more than I would normally expect. Well, not hard considering the Obama administration's non-strategy "strategy"; an image (bombs and Tomahawks) fighting an image (The Caliph's carefully edited beheading show).

Meanwhile, President Hassan Rouhani's speech at the United Nations kept making waves; "Extremists threaten our neighbors, resort to violence and shed blood." It's "the people in the region who can deliver" in the fight against The Caliph. Rouhani was not exactly referring to the made in USA jets allegedly deployed by the Gulf Cooperation Council coalition of the clueless/cowards; the House of Saud, UAE, Bahrain and associate member Jordan.

In all my conversations, a consensus emerges; the power vacuum of post-2013 Shock and Awe and occupation led to the rise of al-Qaeda in Iraq and eventually ISIS/ISIL/Daesh. But even as Tehran and Washington may have flirted about a joint move against The Caliph, Washington then denied it wanted help and Tehran rejected it outright.

Still, what Rouhani said in New York kept echoing day after day everywhere in Tehran; weaponizing the "new" Free Syrian Army in Saudi Arabia, of all places, amounts "to train another group of terrorists and send them to Syria to fight". And Washington's "strategy" is further enabling hardcore Sunni dictators who've made their careers demonizing Shi'ites.

And then that other "unofficial" Caliph, neo-Ottoman Recep Tayyip Erdogan, stepped in; there would be no use of Turkish "territory" or "military bases" by the "coalition" if "the objective does not also include ousting the Bashar al-Assad regime". Who needs Caliph Erdogan to fight Caliph Ibrahim? Major General Qassem Suleimani, head of the Iranian

Quds Force, can do it; his picture, side by side with Kurdish peshmergas, made a splash all over Iran when published by IRINN.

The cinema shows us what our consciousness is. Our consciousness is an effect of montage—It's a collage. There is only collage, cutting and splicing. This explains fairly well what Jean-Francois Lyotard calls the disappearance of the great narratives. Classless society, social justice—no one believes in them anymore. We're in the age of micro-narratives, the art of the fragment.

The joy of Laleh park—a Persian park crisscrossed by stray Persian cats as well as accomplished volleyball and badminton players and pram-pushing families. That's where Arash Darya-Bandari, medievalist extraordinaire with many years spent in the Bay Area, gives me a crash course on the finer points of one of the great surviving narratives; Shi'ism and Khomeini's concept of velayat-e-faqih. In Pure Non-War terms, this was always supposed to be about social justice. And that's why it's unintelligible to turbo-capitalism.

The park as Agora; a garden of intellectual delights. Nearly all my top conversations took place walking across or around Laleh park. And then one night, I went for a solitary walk, just to find a revolutionary movie/performance on a makeshift stage, complete with a trench and mortars. An audience of a few solitary men and some scattered families. The cinema keeping the consciousness of the Iran-Iraq war alive.

The end of deterrence corresponds to the beginning of the information war, a conflict where the superiority of information is more important than the capability to inflict damage.

The New Horizon conference could not but be about information war. The overall theme was the fight against the Zionist lobby. Everyone knows what the lobby means and how it operates, especially in the US.

And yet, in my short interventions, at the Foreign Ministry and at the conference, I preferred to focus on its global financial/economic reach. Follow the money. That's the only way to pierce the lobby's seemingly invincible armory.

Another face of information war. Everywhere I went, I had the pleasure to see how Gareth Porter's book—*Manufactured Crisis: The Untold Story of the Iranian Nuclear Scare*—was received as a blessing. The book was translated into Farsi by the Fars News Agency, in only two months, with meticulous care, and launched in a simple ceremony.

It's bound to become a best seller—as it conclusively proves, for instance, how the Iranian "plot" to equip missiles with nuclear warheads was entirely fabricated by the terrorist outfit Mujahedin-e Khalq (MEK) and then handed over to the International Atomic Energy Agency by the Mossad. Contrast the respect shown to Gareth in Tehran to the wall of silence of its US reception—just another reflection of the 35-year-old "wilderness of mirrors" opposing Washington to Tehran.

Predictably, the usual illiterate morons in the US dubbed the conference as an "anti-Semite hate fest". Gareth was described as "an anti-Israel journalist" and myself as "a Brazilian anti-Israel journalist". Obviously the moronic inferno is not familiar with the concept of "foreign policy".

Space is no longer in geography—it's in electronics. Unity is in the terminals. It's in the instantaneous time of command posts, multinational headquarters, control towers, etc. Politics is less in physical space than in the time systems administered by various technologies. ? There is a movement from geo- to chronopolitics: the distribution of territory becomes the distribution of time. The distribution of territory is outmoded, minimal.

Time to go to the bazaar—the ultimate urban distribution of territory. At the main entrance, a gaggle brandishing calculators and pieces of paper is involved in an incredible racket. With Roberto Quaglia—author of a wicked debunking of the 9/11 saga—we joke this looks like a slaves market. Not really. This is nothing less than a futures market on the course of the rial. With the national currency fluctuating so much because of the sanctions—it lost three quarters of its value in the past few years—the chance to make a bundle is irresistible.

We meet the beautiful Zahra—she sells handmade towels but is essentially a killer fashion photographer. And then the ritual I've loved since forever; haggling for the perfect tribal rug. In this case, a Zaghol from the 1930s, never to be reproduced because the local nomads are becoming sedentary and there are no new weavers. A case of distribution of territory becoming the distribution of (lost) time.

The Pharaohs, the Romans, the Greeks were surveyors. That was geopolitics. We're no longer there, we're in chronopolitics. Organization, prohibitions, interruptions, orders, powers, structurings, subjections are now in the realm of temporality. And that's also where resistance should be.

Which lead us, once again, to sanctions. Much had been made of what Rouhani told Austrian President Hans Fisher at the UN—about Iran being ready to deliver gas to the European Union. That's not happening tomorrow; the last figure I had, in Tehran, years ago, is that the country would need at least US$200 billion in investments to upgrade its energy infrastructure. Rouhani was forced to clarify it. And Tehran won't sell itself to the EU on the cheap.

The end of sanctions is all about chronopolitics.

We have entered an age of large-scale terrorism. Just as we speak of petty delinquency and major delinquency, I think the same should be said of petty and major terrorism. ... The military-industrial and scientific complexes continue to function on their own momentum. It's a crazy engine that won't stop.

Tehran thinks about the crazy engine all the time. I'm sort of "kidnapped" from a meeting and end up in a small think tank with a fabulous map on the wall detailing the US command centers. All the students are eager to know what the Empire is really up to with Iran.

A visit to the "nest of spies"—the former US embassy—is also inevitable. An apotheosis of 1970s technology—immaculately preserved like nowhere else in the world; radio equipment, proto-computers, telephones, telexes, rolodexes, a "forgery room" for fake passports. No wonder Washington could never recover from the loss of this sterling listening post of the whole Middle East. Will this building ever be a "normal" US embassy again? Someone should ask the hick Hamlet who almost turned into a mad bomber.

This is why the airport today has become the new city. ? People are no longer citizens, they're passengers in transit. No longer a nomad society, in the sense of the great nomadic drifts, but one concentrated on the vector of transportation. The new capital is ... a city at the intersection of practicabilities of time, in other words, of speed.

The last day had to contain an epiphany. I waited for it all day long—amid myriad interviews and a fabulous Indian lunch in North Tehran with Gareth and Dr Marandi of the Faculty of World Studies, University of Tehran; the ideal Platonic banquet of conviviality and intellect. Then, at night, a mad dash across town to the Rey shrine; working-class neighborhood, foundation stone of Tehran, one of the top pilgrimage sites in Iran alongside Qom and Mashhad.

Aesthetic illumination meets sensorial overload meets spiritual pull—with an extra kick because you're arguably the only Westerner in sight. Tens of thousands of pilgrims honor the death of Imam Ali's son-in-law. What's that thing about the death of grand narratives? Not in deep Iran.

And then it's all over, as in a Coleridge dream; did I dream this fleeting Persian interlude, or did Tehran dreamed a little dream of me? I'm back to my default mode—the essential passenger in transit; a nomad carpet, a backpack and a boarding pass. Next stop; a faceless city in an intersection of speed.

October 2014